A GENERATION

OF MATERIALISM

1871-1900

*the text of this book is printed
on 100% recycled paper*

THE RISE OF MODERN EUROPE

Edited by WILLIAM L. LANGER
Harvard University

* *In preparation*

A GENERATION
OF MATERIALISM

1871-1900

BY CARLTON J. H. HAYES

HARPER TORCHBOOKS
Harper & Row, Publishers
New York, Hagerstown, San Francisco, London

TABLE OF CONTENTS

TABLE OF CONTENTS

MAPS

LIST OF ILLUSTRATIONS

The illustrations, grouped in a separate section, will be found following page 178.

INTRODUCTION

Our age of specialization produces an almost incredible amount of monographic research in all fields of human knowledge. So great is the mass of this material that even the professional scholar cannot keep abreast of the contributions in anything but a restricted part of his general subject. In all branches of learning the need for intelligent synthesis is now more urgent than ever before, and this need is felt by the layman even more acutely than by the scholar. He cannot hope to read the products of microscopic research or to keep up with the changing interpretations of experts, unless new knowledge and new viewpoints are made accessible to him by those who make it their business to be informed and who are competent to speak with authority.

These volumes, published under the general title of THE RISE OF MODERN EUROPE, are designed primarily to give the general reader and student a reliable survey of European history written by experts in various branches of that vast subject. In consonance with the current broad conception of the scope of history, they attempt to go beyond a merely political-military narrative, and to lay stress upon social, economic, religious, scientific and artistic developments. The minutely detailed, chronological approach is to some extent sacrificed in the effort to emphasize the dominant factors and to set forth their interrelationships. At the same time the division of European history into national histories has been abandoned and wherever possible attention has been focussed upon larger forces common to the whole of European civilization. These are the broad lines on which this history as a whole has been laid out. The individual volumes are integral parts of the larger scheme, but they are intended also to stand as independent units, each the work of a scholar well qualified to treat the period covered by his book. Each volume contains about fifty illustrations selected from the mass of contemporary pictorial material. All noncontemporary illustrations have been excluded on principle. The bibliographical note appended to each volume is designed to facilitate further study of special aspects touched upon in the text. In general every effort has been made to give the reader a clear idea of the main movements in European history, to embody the monographic contributions of research workers, and to present the material in a forceful and vivid manner.

To a generation that has experienced two great World Wars, the closing quarter of the Nineteenth Century is bound, in retrospect, to appear in the light of a golden age. It was an era of peace in Europe, an age of great technological advance, a period of progress, of growing tolerance, of spreading liberalism. Or so at least it seemed at the time and so it appears to many even now. And yet, when viewed historically, when examined critically, the late nineteenth century emerges rather as an age of materialism, of smug self-confidence, of uncritical assurance. It was, as Professor Hayes sets forth, in many senses the seed-time of disaster, the prelude to an era of conflict and disillusionment. To essay a thorough revaluation is no easy task, for it requires a fine sensitivity, a keen insight and real critical honesty. Professor Hayes has gotten down to fundamentals. He has stripped away many of the easy misconceptions and has reexamined some of the basic assumptions and tenets of the modern world. If history is indeed but the prologue, no intelligent person can afford, amid the storm and stress of the contemporary world, to overlook this fascinating and stimulating reappraisal of the generation that bore our own.

WILLIAM L. LANGER

PREFACE

This volume, as it is, I could hardly have written before now. Born and prepared for college in the age which it attempts to recall, I saw those last three decades of the nineteenth century then—and for almost thirty years afterwards—as a stage, indeed a glorious stage, in the progress of Europe and our Western civilization toward ever greater liberty, democracy, social betterment, and scientific control of nature. I still see those decades thus, but I also now see them, even more clearly, as a fertile seedtime for the present and quite different harvest of personal dictatorship, social degradation, and mechanized destruction. It is, in my opinion, this dual character of the age—at once climax of enlightenment and source of disillusionment—which gives it peculiar interest and pregnant significance. It is this, certainly, which dominates the interpretations hereinafter set forth.

It has been a difficult volume to put together, not just because of the necessity of making new appraisal of the events of the age, but much more because of the multitude and complexity of the events themselves and of the all but universal practice hitherto of segregating them in national compartments—British, French, German, Russian, etc.—or else in such categories as "diplomatic," "political," "economic," "intellectual," etc. I have tried hard, though with what success or lack of success it is for others to say, to produce a history of Europe during the period, rather than a history of any particular country, and to make the history as many-sided and as richly variegated as was the period.

To add to the difficulties, the period is not an entity. It has two parts: first, the decade of the 1870's, which might more convincingly have been described in conjunction with the '60's; and second, the decades of the 1880's and 1890's, whose main currents flowed on uninterruptedly through the decade immediately antecedent to the World War of 1914. Perhaps, nevertheless, the joining of the two has advantage, in that it admits of connected treatment of the intermediate transition. For though it was then scarcely perceived, something of a revolution occurred at the end of the '70's and the beginning of the '80's.

I hope no one will question me too closely about my use of the word "materialism" in the following pages. I seldom use it in the strictly philosophical sense. Generally I use it in what I conceive to be the popular, common-sense way, as denoting a marked interest in, and devotion to, material concerns and material things. Nor let anyone be perplexed by my repeated reference to "dollars" as indicative of the value of commodities. They are all good prewar, gold-backed dollars, as reported in statistics of the time. I appreciate, of course, that there were fluctuations in money between 1871 and 1914, but they were slight relative to those we are now familiar with, and they do not seem sufficient to defeat the purposes of comparison for which "dollars" are cited.

My obligations are legion. As I think of the mountain of books and documents I have read, or at least looked at, and of the innumerable ideas and bits of information I have quarried from them, I know I should claim only the "synthesis" of this volume as mine and should publicly thank a myriad of persons for all the rest. Space forbids, however. I must content myself with a comprehensive bow, and with mentioning by name only those persons who have directly counseled me on what I should put in or leave out. It doubtless would be a better book if I could have followed all their wise counsels. But they sometimes disagreed among themselves, and anyway the final choice has had to be mine, not theirs.

Specifically, I gratefully acknowledge helpful advice on the whole manuscript by the patient Editor of the Series, Professor Wi' .m L. Langer of Harvard, and by two of my colleagues at Columbia, Professors Jacques Barzun and Charles W. Cole; on the chapter relating to liberalism, by Mrs. Shepard Morgan and Madame Charlotte Muret; and on particular sections, by graduate students of mine—Messrs. Thomas F. Power, William O. Shanahan, Daniel Thorner, and Richard W. Tims.

CARLTON J. H. HAYES

Jericho Farm,
Afton, New York
May 16, 1941

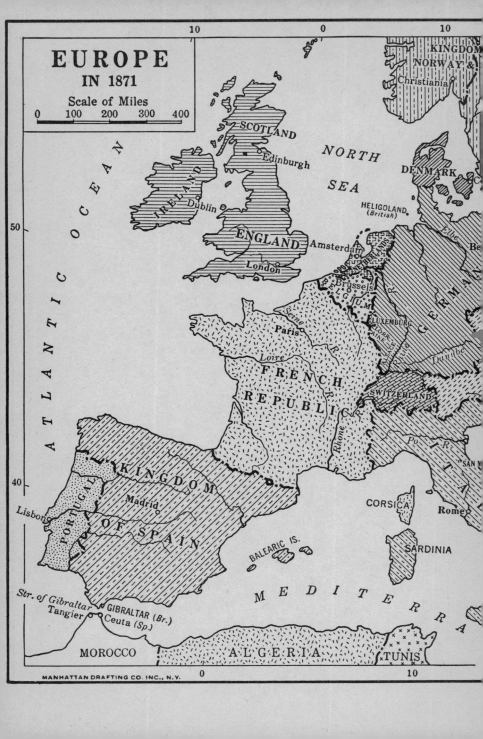

EUROPE
IN 1871

Scale of Miles

0   100   200   300   400

ATLANTIC OCEAN

NORTH SEA

KINGDOM NORWAY &

Christiania

SCOTLAND

Edinburgh

IRELAND

Dublin

ENGLAND

London

Amsterdam

DENMARK

HELIGOLAND
(British)

NETHERLANDS

Brussels

BELGIUM

LUXEMBURG

GERMANY

Elbe

Be

Seine

Paris

Loire

FRENCH REPUBLIC

SWITZERLAND

Danube

Rhone

Po R.

ITALY

SAN M

KINGDOM

Madrid

OF SPAIN

PORTUGAL

Lisbon

CORSICA

Rome

SARDINIA

BALEARIC IS.

MEDITERRA

Str. of Gibraltar
Tangier

GIBRALTAR (Br.)
Ceuta (Sp.)

MOROCCO

ALGERIA

TUNIS

MANHATTAN DRAFTING CO. INC., N.Y.

EUROPE
IN 1900

Scale of Miles

0   100   200   300   400

10   0   10

KINGDOM
NORWAY &
Christiania

SCOTLAND
Edinburgh

NORTH
SEA

DENMARK

IRELAND
Dublin

50

HELIGOLAND
(German)

Elbe

ENGLAND

Amsterdam

NETHERLANDS

London

BELGIUM
Brussels

GERMANY

Seine R.

LUXEMBNRG
LORRAINE

Paris

R.

ALSACE
Rhine

Rhone

Danube

Loire

R.

FRENCH
REPUBLIC

Bern
SWITZERLAND

KINGDOM

Rhone

40

KINGDOM
Madrid
PORTUGAL
OF
SPAIN

CORSICA

Rome

SAI

Lisbon

BALEARIC IS.

SARDINIA

ATLANTIC   OCEAN

Str. of Gibraltar
Tangier
GIBRALTAR (Br.)
Ceuta (Sp.)

MEDITERRAN

MOROCCO

ALGERIA

TUNIS

0

10

MANHATTAN DRAFTING CO., INC., N.Y.

Chapter One

POWER POLITICS IN THE WAKE OF NATIONAL WARS

I. AFTERMATH OF THE FRANCO-PRUSSIAN WAR

ON MAY 10, 1871, at the Swan Hotel in Frankfurt-on-the-Main, was signed the treaty which formally terminated the Franco-Prussian War. Less than five years previously. Prussia by force of arms had smashed the German Confederation. Its most cultured and renowned member, imperial Austria, she had contemptuously thrust aside. Some lesser members she had ruthlessly seized and made into Prussian provinces. The remaining ones she had compelled to become her confederates in what was subsequently known as the Second (Hohenzollern) German Empire. Now, with the aid of this more geographically limited though much more closely knit and powerfully armed Germany, she was victoriously concluding another staccato test of strength, this time with France. France, which had occupied the center of the European ring since the days of Louis XIV, and which under the First Napoleon had dominated the Continent, was at last brought low, singlehanded, by the new German Empire.

The signers of the treaty of Frankfurt were Jules Favre, for France, and Bismarck, for Germany. Favre had declared in the preceding September that France would cede "not an inch of her territory, not a stone of her fortresses." In May he set his hand to the definitive cession of the fortresses of Strasbourg and Metz, the entire province of Alsace (except the town of Belfort),[1] and about a third of Lorraine, and to the additional stipulations that France should pay an indemnity of five billion francs within three years, maintain a German army of occupation in the meantime, and accord to Germany "most-favored-nation" treatment in future commercial relations. Favre had no choice. France could offer no fur-

[1] Belfort had been excepted in the peace preliminaries at Versailles on February 26 on condition that the German army be permitted to parade in Paris.

ther resistance. Within six months, 139,000 French soldiers had been slain, 143,000 wounded, 339,000 hospitalized for various illnesses, almost three-quarters of a million taken prisoner, and over 90,000 interned in Switzerland. What remained of a French field army was fully engaged at the moment in the bloody task of subduing a madly rebellious Paris. Not until three weeks later was the Paris Commune finally suppressed and order restored in the midst of smoking ruins and heaped corpses in the French capital.

The peace of Frankfurt was therefore a dictated peace. In so far as there were any real negotiations, they were between the civilian and the military authorities of Germany. Bismarck confessed that "he had opposed the acquisition of Metz because of the disaffection of the inhabitants, and that he yielded only in consequence of the urgent demands of the General Staff." In the event, there was no pretense of consulting the wishes of the population of the ceded provinces, no plebiscite such as had attended most transfers of European territory during the preceding era. On the contrary, despite solemn and unanimous protest of the democratically elected deputies of Alsace-Lorraine addressed to both the French National Assembly and the German Reichstag, the provinces and their inhabitants were appropriated by Germany in a military way and primarily for military purposes. The Vosges Mountains would provide a stronger frontier than the River Rhine, and Lorraine's mineral wealth might profitably be utilized for German armaments. Behind the military front, of course, romantic German civilians shouted themselves hoarse over the triumph of German nationalism as now sealed by the "reannexation" of territories once German, but actually it was less a triumph of the nationalism prevalent from 1848 to 1870 than a harbinger of the ascendancy of material might during the ensuing years.

Nor was the formality at Frankfurt an isolated token of the passing of one era and the coming of another. On May 8, 1871, only two days before the signing of the treaty of Frankfurt, a treaty between Great Britain and the United States was concluded in faraway Washington, whereby the former expressed regret for unneutral acts during the latter's Civil War and agreed to arbitrate the resultant "Alabama Claims," and also to refer a long-standing dispute over the Oregon boundary to the adjudication of the German Emperor. This treaty, too, was an outcome of a triumph of might. Most Englishmen, like many other Europeans, had sympathized with the South and its heroic efforts to establish its independence. Yet after four years of hard fighting and frightful destruction of life and property, the North had proved itself superior in military and material resources. It had preserved and consolidated the American Union, and, as befitted a victor of the new era, it had dictated to the South the adoption of three amendments to the federal constitution, the last of which was ratified under duress in 1870. Great Britain had no stomach to hold out against a recreated nation of her own blood and of such exemplary prowess. And who was better qualified to pass upon a territorial dispute than the aged Prussian King, his title newly refurbished as German Emperor and his spirits rejuvenated by the conquest of Alsace-Lorraine?

Moreover, while the Franco-Prussian War was still in progress and shortly after the French disaster at Sedan, the Russian foreign minister, Prince Gorchakov, had notified the European powers that Russia would no longer be bound by the treaty which she had signed in 1856 following her defeat in the Crimean War, that specifically she would resume her "sovereign rights" in the Black Sea. In his circular note Gorchakov pointed out, perhaps a bit indelicately though quite realistically, "that it would be difficult to affirm that the written law founded on respect for treaties as the basis of public right and of rule for interstate relations has preserved the same moral sanction as in former times." Protests from Great Britain and Austria were purely verbal and led merely to a perfunctory international conference in London and a pious affirmation of "the sanctity of treaties." On January 7, 1871, just when the Germans were preparing for their final assault upon Paris, the London Conference formally endorsed the unilateral Russian action and erased the obnoxious clauses of the treaty of 1856. Obviously the Crimean War, in which France and Britain had sought to bolster up the Ottoman Empire and to set bounds to Russian expansion in the Near East, had been for naught. Russia was again preparing—only fifteen years after her setback—to resume an aggressive policy in respect to the Balkans and Constantinople.

There was still another portent. The French defeat at Sedan had occurred on September 1-2, 1870. On September 12 an army of the Italian government, without any declaration of war, invaded the independent Papal State, and on the twentieth, after breaching the walls of Porta Pia and brushing aside the ornamental papal troops, occupied Rome. Pope Pius IX promptly protested to the powers, but to no avail. In this instance there was not even the formality of convoking an international conference to perform the paradoxical function of proclaiming the sanctity of treaties and ratifying their violation. The Italian state had material resources which the Papal State lacked, and the violent seizure of Rome in 1870 was viewed as but a natural and fitting climax to the successive wars of 1859, 1860, and 1866 by which diminutive Piedmont had been forcibly expanded into the united kingdom of Italy. On January 26, 1871, two days before the capitulation of Paris to the Germans, the Italian parliament decreed the expropriation of Rome from the Pope and its designation as the national capital.

A new age was clearly at hand. The coming generation might pay lip service to older humanitarian ideals, but at heart it felt itself destined for a more realistic—and mightier—future. It began by witnessing, almost simultaneously, the disruption of the German Confederation, the extrusion of Austria from both German and Italian affairs, the *débâcle* and helplessness of France, the extinction of the States of the Church, and the hardly less surprising deference of Britain to a newly powerful America and to a newly aggressive Russia. The old dream of a European Commonwealth, with its temporal center at Vienna or perhaps Paris and its spiritual center at Rome, was finally dispelled. Likewise dispelled was the more recent dream of a pacific European federation of self-governing and mutually respectful nationalities. As the Austrian statesman Beust expressed it, "I no longer see Europe." What was seen by everybody was the shattering of Europe into national fragments, each an entity by itself and all resigned to

> the simple plan
> That they should take who have the power
> And they should keep who can.

This was hardly in line, to be sure, with any of the so-called idealistic philosophies of the past, whether Christian or Kantian or Romantic or even Liberal Nationalist. But the generation which opened with the military and political realities of 1870-1871 was enabled to justify them—and its own abiding belief in the continuous progress of the modern world—by identifying them with "realism" and accepting this as the pragmatically sound substitute for outworn and visionary idealism. So it happened that the series of national wars between 1848 and 1871 served not only to create new national states for Germans, Italians, Hungarians, and Rumanians, and thereby to forward the nationalizing process in Europe, but also to usher in a new era. There was henceforth less concentration on an idealistic goal for Europe as a whole—a federation of nations—and more on "realistic," that is, on material and forceful, means of assuring strictly national ends.

II. HERITAGE OF MATERIAL PROGRESS AND THE COMPETITIVE SPIRIT

The Franco-Prussian War occurred, we may recall, at the very time when scientific and technological developments were reaching revolutionary proportions throughout western Europe, when "progress" was being popularly associated with a rapid multiplication of material things—steam engines, iron works, cotton goods, railways, factories, machines—and with a phenomenal increase of wealth and power for individuals and for nations. The large-scale mechanizing of industry had begun in England, and in 1871 England was the foremost manufacturing and commercial nation of the world. As such she was the admiration and model of all ambitious Europeans.

Why was England great? She was still reputed in the latter part of the nineteenth century, as in the first part of the eighteenth, to be the palladium of political liberty and parliamentary institutions, but she now had a far more concrete claim to greatness. In 1870 she produced 110 million tons of coal out of a total world production of 213 million, and 6 million tons of pig iron out of a total of 11.9 million. She operated 37.7 million cotton spindles out of an estimated world total of 57.8 million. Her foreign trade, valued at 2.6 billion dollars, was almost a fourth of the whole world's com-

merce. Her national wealth was computed at the gargantuan figure
of thirty billion dollars. That such material progress redounded to
the advantage of a nation was vividly illustrated by the fact that,
whereas the population of agricultural (and therefore "backward")
Ireland had steadily dwindled since 1845, the population of industrial (and therefore "progressive") Britain had mounted from 10½
million in 1801 to 26 million in 1871.

Carlyle reminded his fellow Britishers in 1867, with the aid of
Teutonic capital letters, that "England (equally with any Judah
whatsoever) has a History that is Divine; an eternal Providence
presiding over every step of it, now in sunshine and soft tones, now
in thunder and storm, audible to millions of awe-struck valiant
hearts in the ages that are gone; guiding England forward to *its*
goal and work, which too has been highly considerable in the
world!" Carlyle fretted lest the British masses should be misled by
democratic idealism to ignore the realistic truth that might makes
right, but "incipiencies of this," he hastened to add, "I do expect
from the . . . heroes that will yet be born to us."[2] What Carlyle
here intimated with exuberant rhetoric, Walter Bagehot stated a
year later quite categorically: "Those nations which are strongest
tend to prevail over the others; and in certain marked peculiarities
the strongest tend to be the best."[3]

The issue of the Franco-Prussian War, and of the other national
conflicts of the time, was not determined by mere heroism of soul.
Individual valor was hardly as conspicuous in the armed forces of
Germany and Italy and the American North as among French
infantrymen, Austrian hussars, and the cavaliers of the American
South; even Papal Zouaves made a brave show. What proved
decisive was material might.

Shortly before the American Civil War a Southerner had
piquantly suggested the contrast between the material weakness
of his own region and the material strength of the North: "In
infancy we are swaddled in Northern muslin; in childhood we are
humored with Northern gewgaws; in youth we are instructed out

---

[2] Thomas Carlyle, *Shooting Niagara* (1867), in *Works*, XVI, 445. The italics are
Carlyle's.
[3] Walter Bagehot, "Physics and Politics," in *Fortnightly Review*, IX (April 1868),
453, 470.

of Northern books; . . . in old age we are drugged with Northern physic; and, finally, when we die our inanimate bodies, shrouded in Northern cambric, are stretched upon the bier, borne to the grave in a Northern carriage, entombed with a Northern spade, and memorized with a Northern slab!"[4] When the Civil War was ended, the backward agricultural South had gone down to defeat, overborne by the vastly greater resources of the industrial North in both man power and machine power.

In the pitting of Prussia and Italy against Austria in 1866, the former powers had a combined population of 51 million to the latter's 34½ million; and Prussia, with her newly industrialized districts of Westphalia, Silesia, and the Rhineland, possessed material backing which Austria lacked. Italy was much inferior to Prussia, but she was a giantess in comparison with the Papal State, and, as we know, her very material cannon effectually drowned out in 1870 the purely spiritual thunders of the Catholic Pontiff. In urging the seizure of Rome, an Italian professor—and typical Liberal—had explained that only when a nation is unified can the benefits accruing from large accumulations of capital and from big industrial enterprises be obtained.[5]

The Franco-Prussian War clinched the argument. In a polemic entitled *What We Demand of France*, which the German historian Treitschke dashed off in 1870, Germany's superiority to France was asserted in respect not only of "culture" and "religious life" but of "science" and "material progress"; the past subjection of Alsace to France was excoriated as "the vassalage of free men to half-educated barbarians"; and specific demand was made for the conquest of the rich province by Germany without any concession to the principle of self-determination, "which is the plausible solution of demagogues without a country."[6] The event was in keeping with Treitschke's counsels and convincing evidence of French decadence and German progress. France, it is true, had experienced some mechanical industrialization earlier than Germany, but just before the war Germany was forging ahead of France. In 1870 Germany mined 37½ million tons of coal to France's 16 million;

[4] Quoted by Clive Day, *A History of Commerce*, rev. ed. (1922), 545.
[5] Luigi Palma, *Del principio di nazionalità* (1867), 122.
[6] Heinrich von Treitschke, *Was von Frankreich fordern wir* (1870), 291, 328

she produced 2 million tons of pig iron to France's 1½ million; the value of her foreign trade was 1½ billion dollars, as compared with a French trade of 1¼ billion; and Germany's population exceeded that of France by two million. The war was won by the industrially stronger nation, and, in turn, the war materially strengthened the victor. By the conquest of Alsace, Germany increased the number of her cotton spindles by 50 per cent and took the lead over France in textile manufacture. By the conquest of Lorraine, Germany supplemented her already abundant mineral resources with great stores of iron and thus fortified her metallurgical hegemony on the Continent of Europe. By the acquisition of both provinces, Germany subtracted a population of one and a half million from France and added it to herself, thereby widening the gap between the two countries in man power.

The lesson was taken to heart by Frenchmen as well as by Germans. Ernest Renan acknowledged on the morrow of the French *débâcle* that "war is in a way one of the conditions of progress, the cut of the whip which prevents a country from going to sleep and which forces smug mediocrity to shake off its apathy."[7] On the other hand, Treitschke, after mature reflection, solemnly reaffirmed his "faith in the God who made Iron."[8]

Iron was indeed the symbol of the era beginning in 1871. It was the iron (and blood) of armies which Bismarck on a celebrated occasion had extolled. It was the iron of mechanized industry which all progressives now prized and hoped to profit by. But whether the symbol was heroically military or merely mercenary, it signified a heritage not only of material progress but also of competitive spirit. The industrialization which was already proceeding apace before 1871 had been guided from the outset, first in England and subsequently on the Continent, by individuals largely liberated from traditional restraints of state, church, and guild, and almost fanatically attached to the doctrine of the classical economists that the pursuit of "self-interest"—"rugged individualism"—was the indispensable condition of capitalistic enterprise and hence of material progress. In anxiety for mounting profits, individual owners

[7] Ernest Renan, *La réforme intellectuelle et morale* (1871), 111.
[8] Heinrich von Treitschke, *Deutsche Geschichte im neunzehnten Jahrhundert*, I (1879), 329.

of mines and factories and individual investors would strive with one another to increase production and to lower its costs. The result of such competition seemed axiomatic even if paradoxical. "Enlightened selfishness" would promote, in Bentham's phrase, "the greatest good of the greatest number." "He helps others who helps himself." The first thing to do, of course, was to help one's self, and one would do this consciously and zealously. The helping of others would follow so automatically that none need bother about it.

The competitive spirit, rife in European machine industry by the 1860's, was given a wider meaning and vogue by the international military occurrences in that decade. It was extended from individuals to nations, from economics to politics. The series of armed conflicts, culminating in the Franco-Prussian War, was cumulative evidence that the same praiseworthy kind of competition prevailed between nations as between individuals, that the materially strong must necessarily excel the materially weak, and that therefore each nation's chief aim should be the material strengthening of itself. National self-interest might eventually benefit all Europe. In the meantime it would surely benefit the individual nations. The heritage of material progress and its competitive spirit was combining with the heritage of national wars to atomize Europe.

III. HERITAGE OF DARWINISM AND "THE STRUGGLE FOR EXISTENCE"

If the *things* most esteemed in the new era represented a heritage of recent progress in the industrial arts, in technology, and in physical science, the most captivating *thought* of the era was the heritage of a still more recent development in biological science. Everybody was impressed by mechanical contrivances and the material things they produced in multiplying profusion. But the elite were especially enamored of a novel evolutionary conception of the universe, of which Darwinism was the main source and expression.

A general idea of "evolution" was, to be sure, no novelty. It had been a prominent feature, in the first half of the nineteenth century, of the thought of such various scholars as Laplace in astronomy, Lamarck in biology, Baer in embryology, Lyell in geology, Hegel in philosophy, Comte in sociology, and Marx in economics. The novelty about "Darwinian evolution" was its simplicity, its apparently universal applicability, and its timeliness.

Darwin had published his hypothesis, with a wealth of supporting data, in 1859, under the title *The Origin of Species by Means of Natural Selection, or the Preservation of Favored Races in the Struggle for Life*. The gist of it, in the author's own words, was that, "As many more individuals of each species are born than can possibly survive, and as, consequently, there is a frequently recurring struggle for existence, it follows that any being, if it vary however slightly in any manner profitable to itself, under the complex and sometimes varying conditions of life, will have a better chance of surviving, and thus be *naturally selected*. From the strong principle of inheritance, any selected variety will tend to propagate its new and modified form." This would apply, of course, to all organic phenomena—to plants and animals—and relate their existing heterogeneity, back through a long series of purely natural steps (and struggles), to an original simple form of life. It was a neat complement, on the biological side, to the already clearly formulated postulates of physics that all inorganic phenomena are ultimately referable to eternal matter and to a strictly constant amount of energy.

Darwin's evolutionary doctrine obtained prompt and influential backing from other distinguished naturalists of the day, including Sir Joseph Hooker, Sir Charles Lyell, Sir John Lubbock (Baron Avebury), Thomas Huxley, and John Tyndall, in England, Asa Gray in the United States, and Ernst Haeckel in Germany. None of these scientists overlooked the bearing of the doctrine upon man's nature and origin, and some of them wrote widely read books underscoring the essential oneness of the human race with other animals and with plants. In 1863 appeared Lyell's *Antiquity of Man* and Huxley's *Man's Place in Nature*; in 1870, Lubbock's *Origin of Civilization*; in 1871, Darwin's own *Descent of Man*; and in 1874, Haeckel's *Anthropogenie*.

Soon the doctrine began to affect and reinforce the predilections of a great variety of intellectuals. It figured in the economic classic of Karl Marx (1867), whose disciples grew ever fonder of likening the "evolutionary materialism" of "scientific socialism" to that of

Darwinism. It was assumed by Edward Tylor in his epochal text-book of anthropology (1871). It was utilized by the veteran religious critic, D. F. Strauss, to justify (1872) his complete abandonment of "spiritual philosophy" in favor of "the materialism of modern science." It was adopted by Wilhelm Wundt for his revolutionary physiological psychology (1874). It was invoked by the Polish-Jewish sociologist, Gumplowicz, to buttress his contention (1875) that the whole history of human civilization consists of an unending struggle between races, nations, and classes.

Most effectively the Darwinian doctrine was seized upon by Herbert Spencer and made the leitmotiv of the philosophy which he outlined as early as 1860 and filled in during the next thirty-six years. To Spencer belonged the credit of applying Darwinism most systematically if not always soundly to psychology, sociology, and ethics. In everything organic and inorganic, in the history of man-kind no less than of flora and fauna, he stressed "persistence of force," "indestructibility of matter and energy," and "natural evolution" through "struggle for existence" and "survival of the fittest" "from the homogeneous to the heterogeneous." Like nearly all of the first generation of Darwinians, Spencer was optimistic about the cosmic evolutionary process. He had as strong a faith in humanity's angelic future as in man's simian origin; and faith more than science led him—and other Darwinians—to identify evolution with progress, that is, to confuse the physically "fittest" with the morally "best." Good humanitarian as he was, Spencer shrank from glorifying modern warfare as a typical example of the perpetually improving struggle for existence; he was sure that man had already evolved beyond and above the need for that particular kind of struggle. Yet, "inconceivable as have been the horrors caused by the universal antagonism which, beginning with the chronic hostilities of small hordes tens of thousands of years ago, has ended in the occasional vast battles of immense nations, we must nevertheless admit that without it the world would still have been inhabited only by men of feeble types sheltering in caves and living on wild food."[9]

There were serious fallacies in the impulsive and manifold exploitation of Darwin's biological hypothesis of "natural selection."

9 Herbert Spencer, *Principles of Sociology*, II, 241.

Darwin might well have said to Spencer and many others what he wrote to Haeckel: "Your boldness sometimes makes me tremble."[10] Yet despite Darwin's own pleas for further painstaking observation and experiment, the bulk of his following accepted natural selection as all-sufficing. Thereby Darwinism, shortly after its begetting, ceased to be a tentative scientific theory and became a philosophy, almost a religion. As such it could be, and was applied to the whole gamut of contemporary intellectual interests, not least among which was the interest in international war.

Indeed, it would be difficult if not impossible to account for the immense vogue of sociological and philosophical Darwinism were it not for the spectacular series of national wars which from 1859 to 1871 accompanied its rise and eventually seemed to attest its truth. However apologetic Spencer might be about the "horrors" of modern warfare, many intellectuals in Germany, in Italy, and in the Northern States of the American Union could now be satisfied, "scientifically," that the latest wars had been necessary struggles for existence and had issued in the survival of the fittest—and the best. What truer test of a doctrine than the pragmatic?

This timeliness of Darwinism, let us emphasize, even more than its scientific basis, established it, in conjunction with industrial materialism, as the chief conditioning philosophy of Europe in the 1870's. Even among intellectuals who did not dogmatize about it and in countries which had not recently demonstrated their fighting fitness, brilliant literary men were influenced by contemporary events to reflect its spirit and to spread its vogue. In 1870 the Englishman Froude completed his stirring epic of the sixteenth-century triumph of Protestant England over Catholic Spain, and between 1872 and 1874 he produced three volumes in praise of English domination of eighteenth-century Ireland and in proof of the dictum that "the superior part has a natural right to govern; the inferior part has a right to be governed."[11] Simultaneously the Frenchman Taine, who was wont to attribute all culture to a trinity of physical forces—*"la race, le milieu, et le moment"* (or, as he fur-

---

[10] Letter of Nov. 19, 1868.

[11] James Anthony Froude, *History of England from the Fall of Wolsey to the Defeat of the Spanish Armada*, 12 vols. (1856-1870); *The English in Ireland in the Eighteenth Century*, 3 vols. (1872-1874).

ther defined them, "the internal mainspring, the external pressure, and the acquired momentum")—turned from literary and aesthetic criticism to social and political history in order to show that recent French defeat was a natural evolutionary outcome of the detestable French Revolution, which had been an "insurrection of mules and horses against men, under the conduct of apes possessing the throats of parrots."[12]

Simultaneously, too, appeared a significant volume by a Russian scientist, Danilevsky.[13] Although the author afterwards criticized Darwinism,[14] he betrayed in this volume of 1871 an indebtedness to current biological conceptions. His central theses were that there is no civilization of humankind or even of Europe as a whole but only of particular racial groups, and that the history of such groups is governed by "natural laws." Each people is an organism, passing through different stages of development. As plants are classifiable into separate species, so are nations. The Slavs are a distinct and superior species; and the Russians, being the largest and leading sub-species, have a natural obligation to act as the Prussians had acted for the Germans or as the Northerners in America had for the United States, that is, to federate all the Slavs in an imperial state with its capital at Constantinople. By means of this book Danilevsky was preparing the way intellectually, just when Gorchakov by repudiation of an international treaty was preparing the way diplomatically, for renewed Russian aggression.

That Russian aggression should be opposed not only by the Ottoman Empire but also by the British Empire was the burden of a sensational book which a famous English army officer and archaeologist, Sir Henry Rawlinson, brought out in 1875.[15] The supreme struggle for existence, it seemed, would be between Britain and Russia; and to ensure the survival of the fittest Britain should not hesitate to employ physical force.

[12] H. A. Taine, *Les origines de la France contemporaine*, 6 vols. (1878-1894). Cf. *Sa vie et sa correspondance*, III, 266, 325.
[13] Nicholas I. Danilevsky, *Rossiya i Evropa* (1st ed. 1871, 5th ed. 1895), trans. into German as *Russland und Europa* by K. Nötzel (1917). See P. N. Miliukov, *Le mouvement intellectuel russe* (1918), 377-439.
[14] See the two volumes of his uncompleted work on the subject (1885-1889).
[15] Sir Henry Rawlinson, *England and Russia in the East* (1875).

IV. THE EUROPEAN POWERS

It is historical fact as well as biological theory that the past—often the distant past—lives on in the present. The era from 1871 to 1900 exhibited circumstances of technological invention and examples of materialistic philosophy so peculiar and novel that one is apt to concentrate on them and thus obtain a myopic impression of the newness of the era as a whole. Actually, however, in the vast complexity and long continuum of human life, no brief era of thirty years could possibly be without more survivals than novelties. Conservation is always deeper and stronger, if less sensational, than change; and to this rule the era here under review offered no exception.

Among innumerable survivals from earlier times was the co-existence in Europe of a bewildering variety of ethnic groups and a congeries of independent sovereignties known as *powers*. Most Europeans spoke Aryan languages,[16] but only a little scholarly minority could perceive the common Aryan etymology of such apparently diverse speech as Romanic, Teutonic, Celtic, Slavic, English, and Greek. Each ethnic group was notoriously conservative in clinging to the language and habitat it had had in the Middle Ages and in resisting every effort at coalescence in a culturally unified Europe.

Nor had there ever been a politically united Europe. Attempts to create one by force of arms, whether by Roman emperors or by a Napoleon Bonaparte, had met with but partial and transient success; and the mid-nineteenth-century dream of a voluntary federation of European nations, analogous to the United States of America, had been dispelled by the Franco-Prussian War of 1870. What persisted was the old "system" of sovereign powers, theoretically equal in right and dignity and regularly maintaining formal diplomatic relations with one another as professed members of a "European family of nations." In reality, the European powers were very unequal and diverse. A select number, distinguished from the

---

[16] That is, the group of languages distantly related to the Aryan speech of India and also to Persian and Armenian. The only non-Aryan languages in Europe of any importance are Finnish, Estonian, Magyar (Hungarian), Turkish, and Basque. The first three of these belong to the so-called Turanian family of languages.

others by superior resources and armaments, were customarily styled *great powers*; and some of these pretended to a special importance by retaining or reviving the ancient title of *empire*.

The "system" remained, although within it occurrences of the nineteenth century, especially of the years from 1848 to 1871, effected changes of detail and shifts in what was described as "the balance of power." The rise of nationalism, with attendant striving of revolutionary Liberals to redraw the political map of Europe along lines of cultural nationality, was a direct challenge to those imperial powers which had long dominated disparate ethnic groups and held them together in a kind of Pax Romana. Once upon a time, for example, the Ottoman Empire had been the militant means of subjugating and controlling the many different peoples of southeastern Europe; it had been in fact if not in name the greatest of all great powers. Now, as its subject peoples caught the contagion of nationalism, the Ottoman Empire declined rapidly; its frontiers contracted, and it managed to survive at all only by exploiting the rival ambitions of more capable great powers. The Austrian Empire, too, was now fallen, though not so far, from the proud eminence it had once reached. Expelled from Italy in 1859 and from Germany in 1866, it continued to exercise imperial sway over the aggregation of Slavic (and other) nationalities in the central Danubian basin—and to stand as a great power—but only by recognizing the national rights of Hungary and sharing with it the governance of the empire.

Moreover, France was now worsted in war and bitterly humbled. She had proved unable to prevent the creation of a Prussian German Empire or its acquisition of Alsace-Lorraine; and as if to symbolize her debasement, she abandoned the pretentious title of *empire* in favor of the more plebeian *republic*. Nevertheless, with natural resources considerably greater than Austria-Hungary's, and with a population relatively homogeneous and intensely patriotic, France was still to be reckoned with as a great power.

The chief beneficiary of the setbacks to Austria and France was Prussia. Prussia, already accounted a great power, vested her magnified greatness in the German Empire, which she constructed and expanded. This empire, from its natal day on January 18, 1871,

when, ironically, it was proclaimed in the historic palace of Louis
XIV at Versailles amidst thunderous applause of victorious German
soldiers, assumed by might (and therefore by right) the primacy of
honor among the European great powers. Berlin was henceforth
the political center of the Continent, as Vienna or Paris had previously been.

Second only to the benefits accruing to the new Prussianized
Germany were those redounding to the new Piedmontese Italy.
Piedmont alone had never been a great power, but by championing
the cause of Italian nationalism and aligning herself successively
with France and Prussia she possessed herself of the other lesser
powers of the peninsula and thus established a united Italy which
gained grudging recognition as a great power.

The meteoric ascent of Italy and, even more spectacularly, of
the German Empire, accompanied as it was by the partial eclipse
of France and Austria, was disturbing to the whole European state
system, and in particular to the two great powers which on the side
lines of Europe had been mere bystanders during the stirring events
of the 1860's—Russia and Britain. Both had major reputations, the
one as the potentially richest, the other as the actually richest, of
all European countries; the one as the largest contiguous land
empire in the world, the other as the farthest-flung empire of land
and sea. Neither could be expected to remain indifferent to a tilting
of the European balance, and the shift that was obvious by 1871
aroused in both of them an anxiety not to be left behind in the
scramble for pre-eminence and an eagerness to secure compensatory
laurels—and territory. In Russia the lamp which had formerly cast
long rays in the direction of the Balkans and Constantinople but
which had been dimmed in the smoke of the Crimean War, was
retrimmed and refueled. In Britain resurged a wave of imperialism
which swept the "little-England" Liberals from office and raised
Queen Victoria to the new dignity of Empress of India.

Besides the six acknowledged great powers of Germany, Italy,
Britain, Russia, Austria-Hungary, and France, and the fast weaken-
ing Ottoman Empire, the European state system embraced in 1871
eleven "lesser powers": Spain, Sweden-Norway, Denmark, Portugal, the Dutch Netherlands, Switzerland, Belgium, Greece,

Rumania, Serbia, and Montenegro. All of these were small and weak in comparison with any of the great powers, and the majority of them were tied, like kite tails, to one or more of the great powers. Rumania, Serbia, and Montenegro, though accorded autonomy, were denied sovereignty; they still belonged, at least legally, to the Ottoman Empire. Greece was pledged to follow the advice of three "protecting powers"—Russia, Britain, and France. Belgium was bound by a treaty of neutrality imposed upon her in 1839 by Britain, France, Prussia, Austria, and Russia. Switzerland and the Dutch Netherlands were similarly bound by the Congress of Vienna of 1815. Portugal, by a still older pact, was virtually a protectorate of Britain. Only Spain, Sweden-Norway, and Denmark were fully "sovereign," and Denmark had recently had a taste of the misfortune in store for a lesser power which would exercise its sovereignty contrary to the will of a great power.

It should be observed that in 1871, despite preceding nationalist agitation and a series of nationalist insurrections and wars, the political boundaries of the eighteen European powers, "great" and "lesser," were still far from coinciding with the ethnic frontiers of the several European peoples. Most notably was this true in eastern Europe, where the Ottoman, Austrian, and Russian empires sprawled over a confusing assortment of nationalities. But it was true to some extent even in western Europe, where national states had long existed, and in central Europe where they had just been founded for Germans and Italians. Germany included Poles, Danes, and French-speaking Lorrainers, and excluded Germans in Austria and Switzerland. Italy lacked Italians of Istria, Trentino, and Switzerland. Sweden-Norway was a "personal union" of two different peoples. Belgium was half Flemish and half French. Switzerland was two-thirds German, one-sixth French, and a sixth Italian. Spain contained Catalans and Basques as well as Castilians. France embraced Bretons and Provençals, and in Britain Scots, Welsh, and especially Irish were much in evidence.

There was something impressive about the very word *powers*. It connoted might; and might took on added significance in an era of flourishing materialism, physical and intellectual. What things the powers had, they meant to keep. What things they wanted,

they meant to have. The means to the end would be pacific if possible—Europe was still haunted by humanitarianism—but if necessary they would be forceful. In backing the use of force the ethnic
groups, now inspired by nationalism, would be influential. But in
employing force the existent powers, particularly the great powers,
would be decisive.

V. THE ARMED PEACE

Of the hundred years which separated the battle of the Marne
from the battle of Waterloo, only a short middle span of seventeen
years (from 1854 to 1871) witnessed actual armed conflict between
European great powers. No such fighting occurred during the
period of thirty-nine years prior to 1854 and none during the even
longer period of forty-three years after 1871. A truce quite unprecedented in the annals of Europe!

Peace among the great powers may seem a stranger phenomenon in the last period than in the first. The generation after 1871
was not exhausted, as the generation after 1815 had been, by protracted warfare all over the Continent. On the contrary, the wars
with which it was ushered in had been brief and stimulating, somewhat in the nature of *apéritifs*. Intellectual fashions also had
changed. Mental dandies of the '70's were already a bit ashamed of
their grandparents' beruffled romanticism and crinoline pacifism;
they felt more up-to-date in a tailored realism and with a tight-
fitting faith in "war as an instrument of national policy."

That the great powers refrained from fighting one another for
four decades after 1871 is attributable less to a universal "will to
peace" than to the absorption of each in preparedness for war. For
the peace of the period was an uneasy peace and an armed peace.
Bismarck wittily described the situation to a Russian diplomatist
in 1879: "The great powers of our time are like travellers, unknown
to one another, whom chance has brought together in a carriage.
They watch each other, and when one of them puts his hand into
his pocket, his neighbor gets ready his own revolver in order to be
able to fire the first shot."[17]

What "will to peace" there was, was strongest in Germany and in

---

[17] Bismarck to Prince Orlov, *Krasnyi Arkhiv*, I (1922), 86-87.

her stout statesman, Prince Bismarck. Germany, in the latter's words, was a "saturated" and "satisfied" power. She had had her way with Austria; she had gotten what she wanted from France. She contemplated no further territorial conquests. She wished merely to preserve the fruits of her recent victories. The task before her, therefore, was to keep the peace herself and to deter other and less satisfied powers from resorting to any war which might impair or subvert the *status quo* of 1871 so advantageous to herself. This she would do by retaining the military superiority she had acquired during the '60's and by employing her enhanced prestige and the great diplomatic talents of Bismarck to draw as many powers as possible into the orbit of her influence.

Germany's military superiority was a legacy of Prussia's, and this had been pragmatically demonstrated in the wars of 1866 and 1870. Upon analysis it was generally conceded to derive from two peculiarities. One was the principle of universal compulsory army service (*Allgemeine Wehrpflicht*), the rule that all able-bodied young men were liable to military service and that as many of them as could financially be provided for should be put into the active army for a few years' continuous training and then passed to a reserve army (*Landwehr*) for occasional rehearsals. The other was a matter of organization, an emphasis on a fixed number of army corps, each regularly stationed in the territory where its regiments were recruited and from which they drew their reserves, and all co-ordinated and ultimately directed by an efficient general staff.

The development of these peculiarities in Prussia had been gradual but steady. The special type of army organization, begun by Scharnhorst during the Napoleonic era, was perfected by Count Moltke, chief of staff from 1858. Universal compulsory service in the army, though adopted in principle and more or less imperfectly applied during the Napoleonic Wars by several nations— France and Austria as well as by Prussia—had elsewhere been abandoned when those wars had ceased, in favor of the older army of professional soldiers, recruited voluntarily and hence fewer in number, but serving long terms and therefore more thoroughly trained. It was professional armies, supplemented by random conscription, which until 1866 had been generally employed. Prussia alone adhered to the principle of universal short-term service. To be sure, she no more than any other great power could carry it into full effect; necessary funds and *matériel* were lacking. Nevertheless, by paying her drafted amateur soldiers a mere pittance, instead of the higher wages required for professional soldiers, she was enabled for a given expenditure to keep at least three times as many men under arms as could be maintained under any voluntary system. What thereby she sacrificed in thoroughness of training, she compensated for in big reserves of partially trained men and in a relatively large officers' corps.

Until the early 1860's the Prussian active army had included annual levies of 40,000 men serving for two years. Then, under pressure from King William I and his war minister Roon, the term of service had been lengthened to three years and the annual levies increased to 63,000 men, so that the enlarged standing army comprised roughly one per cent of the total population at a per capita expenditure of two hundred and twenty-five dollars. This army justified itself in the ensuing war of 1866 with Austria, with the result that the German states which were forced into federation with Prussia adopted the Prussian army system at once, and Austria did likewise in 1868. Simultaneously France made a gesture at similar reform, though it was still essentially a professional army with which she met and went down to defeat before Prussia's better organized and better led conscript army.

The Prussian system was now fully justified. It had crushed all resistance to the creation of the Hohenzollern German Empire and its conquest of Alsace-Lorraine. It must be continued so as to preserve in peace what it had built in war. Accordingly, the system was immediately extended to all states within the empire, and in December 1871 the Reichstag voted funds to maintain until the end of 1874 one per cent of the whole German nation under arms.

The lesson was not lost on other great powers. In France a law of 1872 made every young Frenchman, with a few specified exemptions, liable to military service for five years and forbade substitutions, and another law of 1873 reorganized the French army after the German model, with territorial corps and a directing general staff. Although for financial and other reasons the standing army could absorb fewer than half of those liable to service, the reforms promised to expand it to a size comparable with Germany's. And meanwhile French military engineers were busily strengthening the line of fortifications from Verdun to Belfort, hard by the new Franco-German frontier. France was clearly determined to remain a great power, to suffer no repetition of her recent disasters, and to be ready, if opportunity arose, to regain Alsace-Lorraine.

Russia, too, soon imitated the German example. She had vaulting ambitions in the Balkans and a dangerously exposed flank between Germany and Austria. She must be prepared for war according to the latest and most approved principles. In 1874 she formally adopted the system of obligatory service, first for six years and then for five. Could she have fully applied it, she would have had an army as large as any two other armies combined. Indeed, her numbers (on paper) scared many a foreign publicist almost to death. Nevertheless, chronic shortage or mismanagement of public funds severely limited the number of conscripts that could be trained, and paucity of railways gravely handicapped the general staff.

Italy followed suit in 1875, reorganizing her army and basing it on the liability of every able-bodied young Italian to active service for from three to five years. Actually she trained only a small proportion of available recruits; she was too financially embarrassed to do otherwise. The new system was flattering to her, however, and helped her to keep up the appearance of being a great power.

Only Great Britain, of the six great powers, stuck to the professional long-service army. It seemed to comport better with her insular situation and with her special need of small but highly trained expeditionary forces for quick dispatch to distant possessions oversea. Yet Britain was not proof against the wave of military preparedness which swept over Europe in the wake of the Franco-Prussian War. Viscount Cardwell, war secretary at the time in Gladstone's cabinet, devoted himself vigorously to reforming the British army. Its organization was rendered more efficient by abolishing the purchase of officers' commissions and inaugurating a localization of units. Its rank and file were improved in quality and augmented in quantity by readjusting the wage schedule and authorizing supplementary kinds of voluntary enlistment, either for short service or in a reserve.

Even little Switzerland felt the military urgency. Wherever she looked out across her narrow borders, she saw preparations for war—in Germany, in Austria, in France, in Italy. In the circumstances, some military preparations on her own part might operate, more realistically than existing international treaties, to guarantee her neutrality. In 1874 Switzerland, by a new federal constitution, consecrated an interesting militia system, one that was widely imitated by "lesser" powers in later years. There would be no standing army in the strict sense of the term, but all Swiss men between the ages of twenty and forty-eight would receive periodical training in arms.

Of course, all this military preparedness could not be achieved overnight. It would take several years for France and Austria to remodel their armies after the German pattern and to raise them to maximum strength; and for Russia and Italy it would take still longer. In the meantime Germany's military preparedness was an accomplished and demonstrated fact. Her army had just won thumping successes, and it needed no respite to be ready for another test. No wonder, then, that while war ministers of other nations were studying and copying the German military system, sovereigns and foreign ministers were hastening to compliment the newly enthroned German Emperor and to curry favor with his astute chancellor.

The Austrian Emperor, Francis Joseph, was a stubborn man, a stickler for form and a firm believer in the God-given prerogatives of Austria and the Habsburgs. His foreign minister, Count Beust, had been notoriously anti-Prussian. Yet in the late summer of 1871 Francis Joseph and Beust consorted with the Emperor William and Bismarck at a variety of watering places; and in order to seal an Austro-Prussian entente, Francis Joseph obligingly parted with Beust and appointed in his place a pro-Prussian Hungarian nobleman, Count Julius Andrássy. Whereupon, in September 1872, William and Bismarck received at Berlin a state visit from Francis Joseph and Andrássy, and who should drop in upon the pleasant party but the Tsar Alexander II of Russia, accompanied by his foreign minister, old Prince Gorchakov (who imagined that Bismarck was a pupil of his), and the war minister Marshal Berg, who had won some renown by suppressing the Polish insurrection of 1863 and was to win more by championing a military alliance between Russia and Germany. William I was highly honored and Bismarck very happy.

In the following spring these amenities bore fruit in a definite Three Emperors' League. By a military convention signed at St. Petersburg in May, Germany and Russia pledged themselves that if either were attacked by another European power, the other would come to the aid of its ally with 200,000 men. Then, by a more general treaty signed at Vienna in June, Russia and Austria mutually promised, with the concurrence of Germany, to reach a preliminary agreement about any threatened aggression from another power and to consider what joint action they should take. Thus was revived, in new garb, the Holy Alliance of 1815. The same three great powers of eastern and central Europe were again formally committed to uphold monarchical institutions and the international *status quo*. Of the Three Emperors' League, however, not Russia or Austria, but Germany, was the leader, and the Russo-German part of it had military "teeth" instead of the merely pious mouthings which had characterized the old Holy Alliance.

The Emperors of Austria and Russia were not the only mothlike sovereigns attracted by the brilliantly illuminated countenances of the German Emperor and his chancellor. The King of Italy, hearty Victor Emmanuel II, who had been gratefully sympathetic with France in 1870, traveled hopefully to Berlin with his foreign minister, in September 1873, and, propelled on by Bismarck, they visited Vienna also! Italy was obviously associating herself with the Three Emperors' League. Great Britain was a trifle more aloof. Queen Victoria did not go in person to Berlin—she was still doggedly in widow's weeds for her Teutonic consort who had died a dozen years before—but she addressed innumerable encouraging epistles to the Emperor William, and her ambassador, Lord Odo Russell, reported from Berlin in February 1874 that "our relations with Germany were never better, more cordial, or more satisfactory than at present."

Bismarck had no illusions. He knew why all the great powers— except France—were temporarily gravitating toward Germany. He recognized that prolongation of his country's hegemony depended basically upon its own peaceful intent—and armed preponderance. In February 1874, therefore, he joined Moltke in begging the Reichstag to fix permanently the size of Germany's standing army at one per cent of her population, which for the moment would mean about 400,000 men. In the ensuing debates Moltke dwelt particularly upon the need of "defending for fifty years the fruits of the victories of '66 and '70," upon the useful role which the army performed at home as "the Prussian schoolmaster of the entire nation," and upon the rapidity with which foreign powers, especially France, were piling up armaments. Despite their best efforts, however, Moltke and Bismarck could not prevail upon the Reichstag to accept the military bill in perpetuity. They had to content themselves with its enactment for seven years, from the end of 1874 to the end of 1881. They were not too depressed. Subsequent septennates could and would be voted.

Following the German military enactment of 1874, France authorized in March 1875 some additions to her army. This was immediately seized upon by officials of the German foreign office as an alarmist text for a series of "inspired" newspaper articles, culminating in a famous article in the Berlin *Post* of April 8, "Is War in Sight?" At the same time German army officers talked openly about the desirability of a "preventive war"—a present attack by Germany upon France to forestall a future attack by France upon Germany.

It is almost certain that Bismarck himself had no mind to precipitate another war with France. Presumably he permitted the rattling of German sabers only in order to frighten France into halting her military preparations. Be that as it may, "the war scare" of 1875 caused him no slight discomfiture. The French foreign minister, the Duc de Decazes, appealed straightway to the other great powers to "save" his country from renewed invasion and partition by Germany. The other powers might respect Germany and seek alliance with her, but, as Moltke had recently said, none loved her and all feared her. Prince Gorchakov responded to the Duc de Decazes promptly and ardently: he assured the French ambassador at St. Petersburg that Russia would not allow Germany to make war on France; he secured similar assurance from Great Britain; and he journeyed to Berlin, with the Tsar in tow, to give personal notice to Bismarck of the joint Russo-British resolve. Bismarck was intensely irritated. In his memoirs he tells of having reproached Gorchakov: "It was not, I said, a friendly part to jump suddenly and unexpectedly upon the back of a trustful and unsuspecting friend, and to get up a circus performance at his cost; proceedings of this kind between us, the directing ministers, could only injure the two monarchies and the two states. If he was anxious to be applauded in Paris, he need not on that account injure our relations with Russia; I was quite ready to assist him and to have five-franc pieces struck at Berlin, with the inscription: *'Gorchakov protège la France.'* "

Bismarck's sarcasm scarcely disguised his anger and alarm. However unmerited, a rebuke had been administered to him. Germany, after all, regardless of peaceful intent, would not have a free hand with France. Russia was an undependable ally, and Britain a dubious neutral. Peace would have to be ever more heavily armed.

VI. THE RUSSO-TURKISH WAR AND THE CONGRESS OF BERLIN

The more or less imaginary crisis of 1875 in Franco-German relations was speedily overshadowed by a very real one within the Ottoman Empire. The "sick man of Europe" suffered in 1875 a recurrent attack of ague, and as usual his council of physicians, the great powers, disagreed about remedies.

The susceptibility of the Ottoman Empire to spasmodic chills and fever was a symptom of constitutional weakness. So long as the mass of its European subjects were primarily Christian and only incidentally nationalist, it had known how to manage them. So long, moreover, as its central government was backed by an army and a revenue comparable with other powers', it had been relatively efficient. In the nineteenth century, however, nationalism obsessed the Christian populations and incited in them an unwonted rebelliousness. Simultaneously, by falling behind the rest of Europe in material development, the empire was deprived of the means of maintaining an adequate army and a competent administration. Local tax officials gouged the peasantry and personally pocketed the greater part of the proceeds. Army officers made themselves quasi-independent of the central government and tyrannized over the districts they commanded. All of which contributed to the unrest of subject nationalities—and to international complications.

The bed of the "sick man" at Constantinople in 1875 was occupied by the Sultan Abdul-Aziz, who, like the proverbial man with the beer income and the champagne appetite, had squandered every penny he could get his hands upon[18] in palace-building and prodigal living. Fluttering about him, most solicitously, were a horde of banking and brokerage agents from Paris and London, together with a Russian general and a British admiral. The former of these, Count Nicholas Ignatiev, a scheming Pan-Slavist of the school of Danilevsky, intent upon supplanting the Ottoman Empire with a confederation of Slavic states, played the role of Russian ambassador at Constantinople. The latter, Augustus Hobart, a doughty adventurer who had done service for Great Britain as a naval captain in the Crimean War, for the Southern Confederacy as a blockade-runner in the American Civil War, and for the Ottoman Empire as an admiral in the suppression of a Cretan revolt in 1869, enjoyed the Turkish title of Pasha and saw his own advantage —and Great Britain's—in circumventing the Russian doctor and bolstering up the "sick man."

The sickness grew grave in 1875. In the spring the Austrian Emperor, prompted by his military entourage, who longed to regain in the Balkans some of the prestige they had lost in Italy and Germany, made a state tour along the Dalmatian coast, arousing the national spirit of his own Slavic subjects and also of their kinsmen in the Ottoman hinterland of Bosnia and Herzegovina. In July a revolt against Turkish rule broke out in Herzegovina, inviting further machinations not only of Austrian army officers

[18] He had utilized public loans floated in western Europe, and also monies paid him by the khedive of Egypt for the series of firmans from 1866 to 1872 which conferred upon the khedive hereditary rights and a practically independent status.

but also of Russian Pan-Slavists and of the autonomous governments of the adjacent Ottoman principalities of Serbia and Montenegro. In September, an abortive insurrection occurred in Macedonia among a people who were described as Bulgarians but about
whom Europe at large knew little—as yet. In October the Sultan
announced that he could pay only half of the interest due his
foreign creditors. In November Disraeli purchased from the Sultan's vassal, the khedive of Egypt, a controlling share of stock in
the Suez Canal. At the end of December, the Austrian foreign
minister Andrássy, fearful of the effects of a general Slavic upheaval upon his beloved Hungary, came forward with the familiar
prescription of "reforms" for the Ottoman Empire. The prescription was innocuous enough to be swallowed by the Sultan and to
produce no change in his condition. The rebels in Herzegovina
(and by this time in Bosnia too) would accept no homeopathic
"reforms"; they were out for liberty and loot.

In May 1876 the crisis reached an acute stage. To the Bosnian
rebellion, flaming fiercely, was added an uprising throughout the
Bulgarian provinces, accompanied by the murder of Ottoman
officials and impelling the Turks to fanatical frenzy and mad
retaliation. Turks massacred Bulgarians and demonstrated against
foreigners. At Salonica a mob killed the French and German con-
suls. At Constantinople another mob deposed the Sultan Abdul-
Aziz and put Murad V in his place.

Excitement over these events was quickly enhanced by sensational stories about Turkish "atrocities" in Bulgaria. According
to Eugene Schuyler, American minister at Constantinople, and to
Edwin Pears, correspondent of the London *Daily News*—both of
whom were strongly influenced by the propaganda of General
Ignatiev—dozens of Bulgarian villages had been wiped out and
tens of thousands of Bulgarian men, women, and children had been
slain, tortured, or sold into slavery. In England Gladstone, already
the Grand Old Man of the Liberal party, penned a pamphlet on
Bulgarian Horrors and the Question of the East, depicting the
atrocities in lurid colors and castigating the pro-Turkish policy of
the Conservative Disraeli. By the time the pamphlet issued from
the press, the Ottoman government had suspended all payments

on its foreign debt, which to numerous investors in England and France was another and more tangible "atrocity" of the "unspeakable" Turk.

At the end of June 1876 the principalities of Serbia and Montenegro went to war with their nominal suzerain, the Sultan, in behalf of the rebels in Bosnia and Herzegovina, and a Russian Pan-Slavist was made commander-in-chief of the Serbian army. Russia was only too ready to profit from the inflamed state of public opinion all over Europe against the Turks and to utilize the Serbian War as a preliminary to the complete dismemberment of the Ottoman Empire. With this general purpose Bismarck sympathized, and to achieve it he favored an early negotiated agreement among the great powers. He hoped that by settling the estate of the "sick man" in advance of his demise the danger of later litigation and conflict among prospective heirs would be lessened. He was particularly anxious to forestall conflict between Russia and Austria, Germany's associates in the Three Emperors' League.

Neither the Austrian nor the British government was eager to co-operate. Both were very suspicious of Russian designs in south-eastern Europe and inclined to believe that instead of encouraging them effort should be centered on prolonging artificially the life of Turkey. The official British view was pithily expressed by Queen Victoria: "It is not a question of upholding Turkey; it is a question of Russian or British supremacy in the world."[19] As for Austria, there was a good deal of wavering between the willingness of the army staff and the reluctance of the foreign minister to negotiate a limited partition, in which the Hapsburg as well as the Russian Empire would participate. Andrássy, however, was gradually swayed by pressure from the Emperor Francis Joseph and by anxiety not to alienate Bismarck. He responded amicably enough to overtures from St. Petersburg, and in July 1876 consented to a military convention with Russia, whereby, if Serbia and Montenegro were defeated, the territorial *status quo* would be maintained and Turkey obliged to execute the Andrássy "reforms"; if the principalities were victorious, they would share Bosnia and Herzegovina with Austria, and Russia would take Bessarabia; if Turkey

19 Monypenny and Buckle, VI, 132-133.

collapsed altogether, Bulgaria and Rumelia would be established as autonomous states (under Russian tutelage), Constantinople would become a free city, and Epirus, Thessaly, and Crete would be added to Greece. That Turkey would collapse was then generally believed. The very next month another "revolution" at the capital was reported as the death throe of the Ottoman Empire; the briefly reigning Murad V was deposed, and the reign of his brother and successor, Abdul-Hamid II, bade fair to be even briefer.

From the outset Abdul-Hamid II had a knack of belying the gloomy prognosis of his attending physicians and disconcerting them with signs of convalescence. He was shrewd and crafty, utterly without scruples about terrorizing his subjects into obedience and with a positive genius for sowing dissension among the great powers. Fortunately, too, he had an excellent and loyal general in Osman Pasha, as well as an able naval organizer and commander in Hobart Pasha.

Osman Pasha, at the head of a Turkish army, administered to the Serbians on September 1, 1876 a reverse so severe as to elicit from their prince, Milan, an appeal to the powers for intervention, and while Abdul-Hamid staved off compliance with the powers' request for an armistice, Osman at the end of October inflicted another and crushing defeat upon the Serbians. Whereupon, faced with a Russian ultimatum, the Sultan consented to the holding of an international conference at Constantinople to arrange terms of peace. The conference opened in December, and, thanks to German mediation between Russia and Austria, a nominal accord among the great powers was soon reached. Serbia, despite her defeats, was to be restored as she was before the war. Montenegro, which had held her own in the struggle, was to get a strip of Herzegovina. The remainder of Herzegovina was to be merged with Bosnia in a single autonomous province. Bulgaria was to be divided into two autonomous provinces—an eastern and a western.[20]

The British government, while sharing in the conference and formally endorsing its proposals, was encouraging the Sultan to defy it. In this curiously crooked course Disraeli had the earnestly

---

[20] The Bulgarian scheme was the work of the American minister, Eugene Schuyler, patronized and supported by the Russian minister, General Ignatiev.

moral backing of a large section of public opinion in England, which was enormously edified by Abdul-Hamid's dramatic promulgation, on the very day of the opening of the international conference, of a liberal Turkish constitution, with bill of rights, parliamentary government, and responsible ministry, all in the best English tradition. As the Sultan aptly asked, what was left for foreign powers to do since the Ottoman Empire could and would reform itself in the glorious light of modern freedom and progress? In January 1877 the Turkish government rejected the powers' proposals, and the international conference adjourned *sine die*.

Already, however, Russia was planning to accomplish by force of her own arms what the international peace conference failed to achieve. She could count upon the benevolent neutrality of both Germany and France; and by buying off Austria she might isolate Great Britain and deter her from intervening in a Russo-Turkish war. To this end Russia obtained from Austria in January 1877 promise of a free hand in Rumania and Bulgaria in return for a pledge that she would respect the *status quo* in Serbia and Montenegro and give Austria a free hand in Bosnia and Herzegovina. Accordingly, in March, through the good offices of Austria, peace was concluded between Serbia and the Ottoman Empire; and in April Russia prevailed upon Rumania to permit Russian troops to cross the principality for an attack upon Turkey.

Eight days later—on April 24, 1877—Russia abruptly declared war on the Ottoman Empire. The war itself was no brilliant performance. Prevented from utilizing the sea route from Odessa to Constantinople by Hobart Pasha's masterful handling of a superior Turkish war fleet, Russia had to content herself with a land campaign through Rumania and over the Balkan mountains. This she was barely able to conduct. Her troops were mobilized and supplied with difficulty, and the commander-in-chief, the Grand Duke Nicholas, was incompetent. Russia would have met with almost certain disaster if she had not had invaluable support from Rumanians, Bulgarians, and Serbs,[21] and if the Turkish defense had not been handicapped by bad generalship and much bungling.

[21] Rumania proclaimed her independence and as an ally of Russia went formally to war with the Ottoman Empire in May 1877. Serbia resumed hostilities against the empire in December 1877. Moreover, Montenegro had been continuously at war with

As it was, the Russians traversed Rumania and crossed the Danube without meeting serious opposition. In July they occupied Shipka Pass and were proceeding through the Balkan range when Osman Pasha, arriving from Serbia with his veteran army, entrenched himself at Plevna on the right flank of the Russian line of communications. Thrice the Russians vainly sought to dislodge him. In the three assaults they lost 30,000 men. They had to halt their advance and lay siege to Plevna. Eventually in December, Osman, threatened by starvation, attempted a sortie; he was severely wounded and forced to capitulate.

In January 1878 the Russians entered Sofia and overcame the last Turkish resistance at Philippopolis. They then swept on toward Constantinople. At the end of the month the Turks sued for an armistice, and on March 3 was signed the treaty of San Stefano, the terms of which were dictated by the Russian plenipotentiary, General Ignatiev. The Ottoman Empire was to cede to Russia the Asiatic towns of Ardahan, Kars, and Batum outright, and in Europe the Dobrudja (south of the Danube delta) for exchange with Rumania for the portion of Bessarabia lost by Russia in 1856; to raze all fortifications along the Danube; to pay a war indemnity; to recognize the independence of Rumania, Serbia, and Montenegro; to enlarge the latter two; to accord full autonomy to an extensive Bulgaria, including Rumelia and Macedonia; and to effect sweeping administrative reforms in Bosnia and likewise in the empire's remaining Greek and Armenian provinces.

There was immediate and widespread criticism of the treaty of San Stefano. Rumanians, and Serbs and Greeks also, felt that they were ill requited and grievously discriminated against in favor of the Bulgarians. Austria-Hungary was alarmed and angered by Russian dictation in the western as well as in the eastern Balkans. Great Britain perceived in the projected Bulgaria a Russian vassal state dangerously close to Constantinople, and in the extension of Russia's Transcaucasian territory a sinister menace to British imperial predominance in the East. Already in February 1878, before

the empire since June 1876, and by the beginning of 1878 Greece was preparing to join Russia. Many Bulgarian irregulars, as well as the regular Rumanian army, cooperated with the Russian forces.

the signing of the treaty, a British fleet sailed through the Dardanelles and anchored off Constantinople. It was an ostentatious reminder to Russia that Britain had interests in the Ottoman Empire and meant to safeguard them. Then, immediately afterward, Count Andrássy on behalf of Austria proposed that the treaty be submitted to a congress of the great powers for reconsideration and revision. In vain Russia objected to being haled before an international tribunal and presumably obliged to sacrifice fruits of her hard-earned victory. As the only alternative appeared to be another and far worse war, this time with Britain and Austria, Russia finally acquiesced in the proposed congress.

Berlin was the obvious place for holding the congress. Germany was the greatest and most disinterested of the great powers; and Bismarck, eager to keep peace among them, volunteered to serve as "honest broker." On the eve of the assembling of the congress, Great Britain took the precaution to arrange a working agreement with Austria, and to extort from Turkey a secret convention providing that if Russia extended her Transcaucasian frontier Britain might occupy and administer the island of Cyprus.

The congress met at Berlin in June 1878, a much be-ribboned array of statesmen and diplomatists. Bismarck presided with wit and energy. The British delegation was headed by the mercurial Disraeli, the Austrian by the picturesque Andrássy, the French and the Italian by their respective foreign ministers, the dignified Waddington and the decorous Corti. The doddering Gorchakov (whom Bismarck had not forgiven for the "Affair of 1875") was chief of the Russian representatives, and an Ottoman Greek, Karatheodory Pasha, of the Turkish. The habitual politeness of these distinguished gentlemen hardly masked their mutual suspicions and divergent strivings. Only Bismarck's personal prestige and driving force prevented a breakup of the congress and brought to conclusion, in a month's time, a general peace settlement.

The settlement arrived at in the hot days of July 1878, like many earlier and later settlements of the "Eastern Question," was proclaimed "final." The Ottoman Empire was once more "saved," and the "integrity" of its territories—what remained of them—was "guaranteed." Rumania, Serbia, and Montenegro were recognized as independent sovereign states. Rumania gained the Dobrudja; Serbia, the district of Nish; Montenegro, the Adriatic port of Antivari. Greece was promised an expansion northward.[22] Of the "big Bulgaria" of the treaty of San Stefano, only the northern third was erected into an autonomous principality; Rumelia was made an Ottoman province under a Christian governor, and Macedonia was returned unconditionally to Turkish rule. Russia was allowed to take Ardahan, Kars, and Batum from Turkey, and Bessarabia from Rumania. At the same time Austria was given a mandate to occupy and administer Bosnia, Herzegovina, and Novi-Bazar; and possible French opposition to Great Britain's appropriation of Cyprus was removed through assurances given to France that she might appropriate Tunis whenever she pleased.[23] Germany and Italy were the only great powers which got nothing for themselves from the Russo-Turkish War. But the Italian delegate, Count Corti, when he boasted that he returned from Berlin with "clean hands," was mobbed by his compatriots and thrown out of office.

Disregard of the principle of nationality has often been cited as the most serious flaw in the Vienna peace settlement of 1815, following the Napoleonic Wars. But it was even more egregious in the Berlin settlement of 1878. National aspirations of all the Balkan countries were flouted. Rumania, by being deprived of Bessarabia, contained fewer Rumanians after the settlement than before, and her pride was piqued by the stipulation that her numerous Jewish residents should possess all the rights of Rumanian citizens. Serbia, which already aspired to be the Piedmont of a united Yugoslavia, was confronted with a new and almost insuperable obstacle in Austria's enlarged dominion over Serbs. Greece was denied Epirus and Crete and had to sit idly by while Britain seized Cyprus. Worst of all fared the Bulgarians, whose national state was dismembered as soon as it was born. Nationalism in the Balkans, instead of being assuaged, was raised to fever pitch. If before 1878 the "Eastern Question" concerned one "sick man," after 1878 it involved a half-dozen maniacs. For the Congress of Berlin drove the Balkan peoples mad.

22 Through subsequent negotiations, Greece obtained Thessaly in 1881.
23 France pleased to occupy Tunis in 1881.

It is one of the ironies of the Berlin peace settlement that the powers most vocal in championing the territorial integrity of the Ottoman Empire should have despoiled it more than did Russia, the frank advocate of partition. To Russia the Turks lost only Bessarabia (which as a part of Rumania was already practically lost to them) and a few towns in the Caucasus. On the other hand, to their "protectors" the Turks lost Bosnia, Herzegovina, Novi-Bazar, Cyprus, and Tunis. If mutilated Bulgaria was a Russian gain (as was fallaciously assumed at the time), it was counterbalanced by what Britain and Austria secured from Turkey for their supposed protégés, Greece and Serbia.

Whatever satisfaction is afforded by the reflection that at any rate the Congress of Berlin preserved peace among the great powers in a time of severe crisis, must be qualified by the further reflection that the Ottoman Empire was made to pay—and to pay dearly— for the peace. Altogether, to maintain a "balance of power" between "hostile" Russia and "friendly" Austria and Britain, the empire was shorn of more than half of its European area and population and left in a desperate condition. In the circumstances it is not surprising, or out of keeping with the age, that Abdul-Hamid II promptly cast aside the liberal Turkish constitution of 1876 and sent for German military advisers to reorganize the Turkish army in the latest mode. Iron was to be the tonic for weakness, as well as the hall mark of material progress.

VII. ALLIANCES à Trois: PEACE BY MIGHT

As "honest broker," Bismarck perhaps overworked at the Congress of Berlin. At any rate he was haunted after it closed by terrifying nightmares. Russia, he knew, was profoundly chagrined and disposed to accuse him of favoritism to Austria and Britain and ingratitude to herself. Had not Russia stood aside while he plucked the fruits of victory from the Franco-Prussian War? Why should not he have behaved similarly in respect of the Russo-Turkish War? Instead, the Congress of Berlin had been, in the words of the Tsar, "a European coalition against Russia under the leadership of Prince Bismarck."[24]

[24] *Die Grosse Politik,* III (1922), 3.

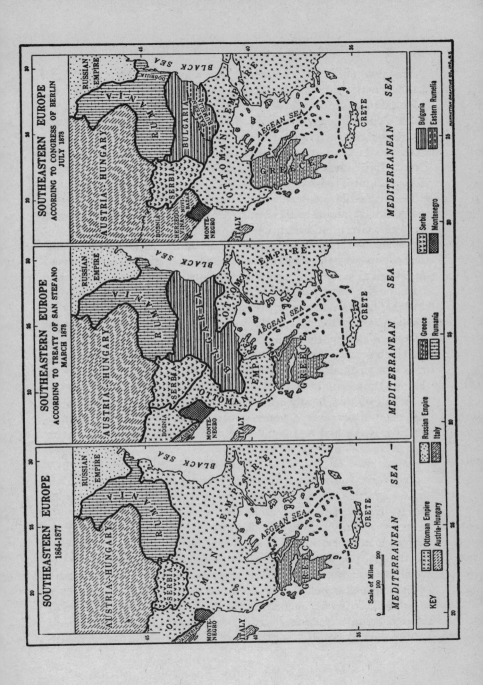

SOUTHEASTERN EUROPE
1864-1877

SOUTHEASTERN EUROPE
ACCORDING TO TREATY OF SAN STEFANO
MARCH 1878

SOUTHEASTERN EUROPE
ACCORDING TO CONGRESS OF BERLIN
JULY 1878

KEY

Ottoman Empire   Russian Empire   Greece   Serbia   Bulgaria

Austria-Hungary   Italy   Rumania   Montenegro   Eastern Rumelia

What would be the consequences to Germany? Here was food for Bismarck's nightmares. Russia, as another "unsatisfied" power, might well ally herself with France; and France, whom Bismarck did not fear so long as she was isolated, would become dangerous in combination with Russia. France, to be sure, he had just sought to divert from Continental undertakings to colonial enterprise in Tunis; but it was too much to expect that France would forget Alsace-Lorraine or scorn a Russian alliance. On the other hand, if he should now woo Russia and make public amends to her, he would almost certainly alienate both Austria and Britain and might push them into an even more imperiling union with France. In any event, the Three Emperors' League of the early 1870's seemed to be irreparably broken, and Germany must choose between her late allies.

Bismarck thought Austria the better bet. Her army was more efficient, if less numerically impressive, than Russia's; her largely German officialdom was more *sympathique*, in a period of quickening nationalism, than Russia's Slavic regime; and her Hungarian foreign minister, Andrássy, already pro-German, was now eager for German guarantees of Austria's newly privileged position in the Balkans. Andrássy welcomed advances from Bismarck, as Gorchakov could hardly have done; and at Vienna in September 1879 an alliance was negotiated between Germany and Austria. If either were attacked by Russia, the other would come to its assistance, and neither would conclude a separate peace. If either were attacked by any other power (that is, by France), its ally would observe at least a benevolent neutrality, though if Russia should join that power, both allies would fight. The alliance would run for five years and be kept secret.

In negotiating the Austro-German alliance, Bismarck had to overcome stubborn opposition of the Emperor William I, who was an uncle of the Tsar and eager to preserve the dynastic solidarity which had obtained between Prussia and Russia since the days of Frederick the Great and Catherine the Great. When, in October 1879, William finally consented to the signing and ratification of the treaty of alliance with Austria, he stipulated that its terms should be immediately communicated in secret to the Tsar, together with a letter stressing its purely defensive character. As an offset to this German gesture to Russia, Austria despatched a like communication to her "friend," Great Britain.

The Austrian alliance, Bismarck believed, would help to insure Germany, but a still bigger German army would help too. Accordingly, early in 1880—a whole year before the expiration of the septennate of 1874—he put through the Reichstag another military bill, providing for an increase of the standing German army from 401,000 to 427,000 men for the period from 1881 to 1888.

That Bismarck had suffered from nightmares was soon apparent. The Tsar, troubled by the spread of revolutionary agitation within Russia in the wake of the war of 1878, was quite averse from any special understanding with France, the traditional seat of revolution and now in process of reoccupation by republican radicals. On the other hand he feared lest, if Russia remained isolated, Austria would be enabled, with German backing, to forward her own Balkan projects and to frustrate Russia's. The situation, in his opinion, called for a Russo-German *rapprochement*.

Russia therefore made overtures to Germany for an alliance in 1880. They were cordially received by William I, and Bismarck's favorable response was expedited by the fact that Prince Gorchakov (whom he despised) was supplanted at the Russian foreign office, in fact if not yet in name, by Nicholas de Giers, a Protestant bureaucrat of German extraction and a consistent admirer of Hohenzollern Germany. Bismarck stipulated, of course, that any Russo-German alliance should be supplementary to, and compatible with, the existing Austro-German alliance, and Giers was so anxious to forge a bond between St. Petersburg and Berlin that he interposed no objection to the inclusion of Vienna. The Austrian government, however, was less willing. It was already protected against Russian hostility by alliance with Germany and friendly co-operation with Britain. If it should enter into an alliance with Russia, it would gain nothing and might lose not only British friendship but any chance of pursuing an aggressive policy in the Balkans.

A major factor in changing opinion at Vienna was a change of ministry in Great Britain in April 1880. Despite the "peace with honor" which he had brought his country from the Congress of Berlin, the Conservative Disraeli, pro-Turk and pro-Austrian, failed to command the necessary parliamentary majority and was succeeded by the Liberal Gladstone, notoriously anti-Turk and bombastically anti-Austrian. On the eve of his elevation to the British premiership, the latter publicly assailed Austria as "the unflinching foe of freedom of every country of Europe. . . . There is not an instance,—there is not a spot upon the whole map,—where you can lay your finger and say: 'There Austria did good.' "[25] Such words were calculated rather to confirm the prejudices of English Liberals than to express sound judgment or to inspire confidence at Vienna in a continuing Anglo-Austrian entente. So long as Britain was dominated by a "crazy professor"[26] who talked like that, Austria might well accept Bismarck's advice and join Germany and Russia in a triple alliance.

The treaty for this alliance was almost ready for signature when the Tsar Alexander II was assassinated in March 1881. For a moment there was doubt whether his son and successor would conclude the negotiations, for Alexander III was reputed to be very unfriendly to Germany and correspondingly inimical to Austria. Nevertheless the circumstances surrounding his accession filled him with a special horror of revolution and impelled him to favor a foreign policy which would emphasize the solidarity of the conservatively monarchical powers. The treaty of alliance was finally signed at Berlin on June 18, 1881. Each of the three powers promised to observe a benevolent neutrality if either of the others were engaged in war with a fourth power, except Turkey. If one of the three should engage in war with Turkey, it would consult the others in advance, and no modification of the territorial *status quo* in southeastern Europe would be made without agreement among the three. In an accompanying protocol, the three powers agreed that Austria, whenever she liked, might annex outright the Turkish provinces of Bosnia and Herzegovina which she already "occupied," and that similarly Russia might incorporate with her "vassal

25 Election speech at Edinburgh, March 17, 1880.
26 The expression was Bismarck's. The German chancellor grouped Gladstone with Gorchakov, Gambetta, and Garibaldi as "the revolutionary quartet on the G string." Conversations with Dr. Cohen, in Bismarck, *Gesammelte Werke*, VIII (1926), 379, 381.

state" of Bulgaria the Turkish province of Rumelia. The alliance, essentially a revival of the Three Emperors' League, and hence of the old Holy Alliance, was to be secret and in force for three years. In 1884 it was renewed for another three-year term. It thus endured until 1887 and served to keep peace between Austria and Russia and also to insure Germany against any joint disturbance of the peace by France and Russia.

Back of this triple alliance of 1881 was anxiety of each of the contracting powers to safeguard recent conquests: Alsace-Lorraine, by Germany; Bosnia-Herzegovina, by Austria; Bessarabia (and presumably Bulgaria), by Russia. But Italy felt the same sort of anxiety about safeguarding the Papal State which she had seized; and in the early '80's Italy's anxiety verged on panic. In the preceding decade France had been the only great power on really good terms with the Papacy and the only one minded to assist it in recovering its temporal rule, but although there had been tension in Franco-Italian relations, Italy had had no reason for alarm. France had been too weak to proceed alone, and both Germany and Austria had had internal conflicts with the Catholic Church which rendered them potential allies of Italy rather than of the Papacy. Now, conditions were changing. Although the French Republic was passing from clerical to anti-clerical control and hence becoming less favorable to interference in Italy, both Germany and Austria were quieting anti-Catholic agitation at home and displaying a new deference to the Pope. Might not these powers be susceptible to Catholic influence and Papal pleas? Might they not intervene in Italy? If they did so, Italian national unity would be disrupted and the royal government discredited and perhaps replaced by a revolutionary regime of wild Garibaldians. Italian statesmen, thoroughly frightened, strove frantically to extract pledges from Bismarck, who would give none without Austrian collaboration.

Austro-Italian collaboration was difficult to envisage. Memories of recent war still rankled. Austria still retained a sizable Italian population in Trentino and Istria which Italy coveted. Yet Bismarck was adamant in refusing an Italo-German alliance unless Austria were included.

Italy's reluctance to enter into an alliance with Austria was finally dissipated, curiously enough, by French action in Tunis. This African country, a nominal dependency of the Ottoman Empire, had for some time been alluring to Italy: it was directly across the narrowest part of the Mediterranean from Sicily; it was the site of ancient Carthage (what modern Italian patriot was ignorant of Punic implications?); and in it Italian settlers outnumbered all other Europeans. Yet while Italian imperialists dreamed about Tunis—and slept—Germany and Great Britain, for reasons of their own, were assuring France at the Congress of Berlin that she might take Tunis. There was no popular enthusiasm in France about the matter, but Tunis was adjacent to French Algeria, some Frenchmen had financial interests in Tunis, and the leading French statesman at the moment, Jules Ferry, was ardently imperialist. In the spring of 1881 Ferry despatched a French expeditionary force across the Algerian frontier into Tunis, allegedly to repress tribal disorders, and on May 12 the native bey capitulated and accepted a French protectorate. Italy appealed to Britain, to Germany, to Austria, to the Ottoman Empire, to rebuke such high-handed action of France and to dislodge her from Tunis. The appeals were in vain. Italy learned with dismay how utterly isolated she was. Even Bismarck was pro-French!

In October 1881 King Humbert, his prime minister Depretis, and his foreign minister Mancini journeyed as humble pilgrims and suppliants to Vienna. They would dutifully comply with Bismarck's requirement for Austria's inclusion in any Italo-German alliance. It could scarcely undo what had been done in Tunis but it might avert future floutings of Italy. The Emperor Francis Joseph and his new foreign minister, Count Kalnóky,[27] rose gallantly to the situation and concealed in the showy mantle of affability the contempt they must have felt. Negotiations continued during the next winter and spring, and at length on May 20, 1882, was signed at Vienna the treaty for the Triple Alliance of Italy, Germany, and Austria. It stipulated that if Italy were attacked by France, both Germany and Austria would assist Italy with all their

---

[27] Kalnóky, another Hungarian statesman, succeeded Andrássy as Austrian minister of foreign affairs in 1881.

forces; if Germany were attacked by France, Italy would aid Germany in like manner; if one or two of the allies were attacked by two or more powers, the others would join the defense; if any of the allies should make war, the others would observe a benevolent neutrality; all would take counsel together and all conclude peace together. The alliance was to be secret and to last for five years.

The Triple Alliance of Germany and Austria with Italy proved more enduring than the alliance of Germany and Austria with Russia. While this expired in 1887, the other survived, through repeated renewals, until Italy's entry into the World War in 1915. The relatively long life of the alliance with Italy was no reliable gauge, however, of its solidity and strength. From the start neither Bismarck nor Kalnóky had any illusions on this score. There might be a truce but hardly a definitive peace in Austro-Italian rivalry. And Bismarck thoroughly distrusted the Italians. "They have such a large appetite," he said, "and such poor teeth."[28]

Nonetheless, Bismarck was glad to hold to the Triple Alliance with Italy. It seemed a convenient corollary—a second line of defense—to the triple alliance with Russia. Just as the Russian alliance contributed to keep Russia apart from France and to lessen the chances of conflict between Russia and Austria, so the Italian alliance served to emphasize Italy's aloofness from France and to lessen the chances of conflict between Italy and Austria. To prevent war among the European great powers, whether in the Balkans or in the Adriatic and Mediterranean, was a cardinal purpose, we should bear in mind, of the German statesman, not because he sentimentally loved peace for its own sake, but because he had a very real fear that war between great powers could not be localized and might be utilized by France or Russia to weaken and perhaps to dismember Germany.

Into the Austrian and German orbit soon moved the two lesser powers of Serbia and Rumania. Both were notably anti-Russian after the War of 1877-1878. They felt that Russia had been basely ungrateful for the assistance they had given her and they were filled with jealousy and fear of the Bulgaria which Russia spon-

28 *Documents diplomatiques français*, II, Nos. 369, 440. W. L. Langer, "The European Powers and the French Occupation of Tunis," *American Historical Review*, Jan. 1926, p. 253.

sored and tried to extend at their expense. Resentment against
Russia affected them in the same way as Italy was affected by
resentment against France: it caused them to overlook past hostility toward Austria and to seek future security through alliances
with her. In the case of Serbia, Prince Milan had special need of
foreign subsidies to cover the cost of his personal carousals and
galanteries; and Viennese bankers were understanding and obliging.

On June 28, 1881, Prince Milan concluded with Baron Kalnóky
a Serbo-Austrian alliance. Both pledged friendly neutrality if
either was at war with a third power; Serbia promised not to
tolerate intrigues against the Habsburg Empire or against Austrian
occupation of Bosnia-Herzegovina, and not to make any political
treaty without Austrian consent; and for such abject dependence
Serbia was assured that her expansion southward into Macedonia
would not be opposed by Austria. The alliance would be secret
and for ten years. Its first fruit was Austrian approval of Prince
Milan's assumption, in 1882, of the title of King.

In the case of Rumania, the reigning Prince Charles, who took
the title of King in 1881,[29] was a Hohenzollern, devotedly attached
to his imperial cousin, the German Emperor. Under his leadership,
Rumania negotiated an alliance with both Austria and Germany,
which was finally signed on October 30, 1883. It provided that none
of the three should enter an alliance against either of the others;
that if Rumania were attacked, Austria would assist her; and that
if Austria were attacked by a power adjoining Rumania (that is,
by Russia or Bulgaria), Rumania would aid Austria. The alliance,
strictly secret, was originally made for five years. It constituted
a third triple alliance, elaborating the previous triple alliances of
Germany and Austria with Russia and with Italy; and, like the
second of these, it was renewed and continued (at least on paper)
for a third of a century.

As the decade of the 1880's advanced, a severe strain developed
in the complicated network of Bismarck's alliance system. It arose
chiefly from Russia's dissatisfaction with the working out of the
"Eastern Question." The Ottoman Empire was obviously growing

---

[29] He appropriately crowned himself with an iron crown made of cannon captured
from the Turks at Plevna in 1877.

weaker and its dismemberment was proceeding apace. But while France took Tunis in 1881 and Britain effected a military occupation of Egypt in 1882, Russia was estopped by the veto of her Austrian ally from supplementing the slight profit she herself had reaped in 1878. Moreover, Russia was not holding her own with Austria in the race between them for domination of the succession states in the Balkans. While Austria was securing allies and satellites in Serbia and Rumania and obtaining, besides, the warm friendship of Greece, and while, incidentally, Germany was gaining favor at Constantinople as the trainer of a reformed Turkish army, Russia was discovering that her lone protégé, Bulgaria, was a most unruly child.

The Bulgarians, inspired by a nationalism of their own, were not minded to take orders from Russia; and their Prince, Alexander of Battenberg, though a favorite nephew of the Tsar Alexander II and selected for his post with the latter's approval, speedily displayed a most disconcerting sympathy with his subjects rather than with his patron. The result was a bitter and protracted feud between the Russian government and Prince Alexander of Bulgaria, which reached a crisis in 1885. In September of that year an *opéra bouffe* revolution at Philippopolis, the capital of the Turkish Bulgarian province of Rumelia, led to Alexander's annexation of the province to his own autonomous principality, amidst vociferous rejoicing of all Bulgarians, impotent protests of the Ottoman Sultan, and obvious displeasure of Russia. Russia, of course, wished an eventual union of Rumelia with Bulgaria—such a union she had championed at the Congress of Berlin—but she thoroughly disapproved of the revolutionary methods by which it was attained and she strenuously objected to its realization under Prince Alexander.

To add to Russia's discomfiture, Serbia, in quest of "compensation," went to war with Bulgaria in November 1885 and was promptly and soundly trounced by Alexander's Bulgarian army. Only Austria's intervention in behalf of her ally saved Serbia from punishment and restored peace in the Balkans. In April 1886 Russia felt obliged to recognize the *fait accompli* and to reach an agreement with the Sultan whereby the Prince of Bulgaria would

be "governor" of Rumelia. Russia then avenged herself on Prince
Alexander by encouraging a group of disaffected Bulgarian army
officers to depose and banish him in August 1886. But worse was
yet to come. The Bulgarians would not permit Russia to choose
Alexander's successor; and the prince whom they finally chose
and installed, in July 1887, was Ferdinand of Saxe-Coburg, an
officer in the Austrian army and alleged to be pro-German and
anti-Russian!

For all these untoward events in Bulgaria, Russian public
opinion blamed Austria and Germany. There was a marked recru-
descence of Pan-Slavist propaganda in Russia, attended by many
diatribes against everything Teutonic. One of the most influential
Russian journalists of the time, the belligerently nationalistic
Katkov, called upon Russia to ally herself with France. His call
was splendid orchestration to French nationalists who at that very
moment were chanting the praises of General Boulanger—the
"man on horseback," the "apostle of revenge!"

Bismarck was gravely alarmed. The first, and to him most fundamental, of his triple alliances, the one including Russia, seemed
doomed. His bête noire of a Franco-Russian alliance loomed in
only too clear prospect. He must take extraordinary precautions.
In November 1886 he begged the Reichstag to adopt an amendment
to the septennate of 1881, increasing the German standing army
from 427,000 to 468,000 men. When the Reichstag refused, he
dissolved it and called for the election of a new one. So successfully
did he communicate his alarms to the German people that they
returned a Reichstag which in March 1887 accepted his proposals
and enlarged the army without serious debate.

Already in February 1887 Bismarck secured a renewal of the
Triple Alliance with Italy. This time Germany, rather than Italy,
was the suitor and willing therefore to make additional pledges.
Germany promised to aid Italy in an offensive war against France
if the latter should move in Tripoli or Morocco; and Austria was
induced to promise "compensation" to Italy if the *status quo* in
the Balkans were changed.

Bismarck did not stop here. In March 1887 he patronized a
"Mediterranean agreement" for "mutual support" among Italy,

Austria, and Great Britain[30] in every difference which might arise between one of them and a fourth power. Then, in May, Spain was prevailed upon to make similar engagements with Italy, Austria, and Germany.

Again fortune smiled on Bismarck. France dropped General Boulanger from office in May 1887, and on June 18 the Tsar Alexander III secretly agreed to a three-year "reinsurance" treaty between Russia and Germany, pledging each to maintain a benevolent neutrality if the other should be attacked by a third great power. Bismarck was so glad to be thus "reinsured" against a joint war with Russia and France that he paid for it, perhaps extravagantly, in a "very secret" protocol, promising particular German support of Russia in Bulgaria and also Germany's friendly neutrality in the event of Russia's seizure of the Straits and Constantinople. But, to deter Russia from acting on this last promise, Bismarck engineered in December 1887 still another triple agreement among Great Britain, Austria, and Italy for upholding the *status quo* in the Balkans and for concerting measures to be taken if it should be threatened by Russia. In other words, the German Chancellor took away from Russia with one hand what he extended to her with the other.

So peace was kept in Europe among the great powers throughout the chancellorship of the creator of the Hohenzollern German Empire. It was an achievement, only in part, of Bismarck's nimble ambidextrous diplomacy—his canny shuffling and reshuffling of three-card suits, with the aces always in his hands. The aces, after all, were armies, and the premier ace was the German military machine. This, by its might, had introduced the new era in 1871; fear of it was an abiding and basic feature of the entire era.

[30] Gladstone was out of office by this time and the more favorably disposed Conservatives were in.

Chapter Two

THE FRUITION OF LIBERALISM

I. LIBERALISM IN THE 1870's: ECUMENICAL AND SECTARIAN

THE "generation of materialism" began not only with war and heightening militarism. It began also with certain events which seemed to betoken the triumph of liberalism: the extinction of the pope's temporal power; the establishment of a "moderate" French Republic; Bismarck's acceptance of constitutional government; Gladstone's advent to the British premiership; the abolition of serfdom in Russia and of slavery in America; the heralded discovery, in Darwinism, of scientific proof of the liberating progress which would be universally assured by free competition. Such a multiplicity of omens could not fail to render old-fashioned the strenuous conflicts of previous decades between "liberals" and "conservatives" —between "revolutionaries" and "reactionaries." Liberalism, now so obviously a part of the evolutionary process, was no longer to be regarded as "revolutionary"; and most conservatives now felt constrained to disavow any sympathy with "reaction" and to concentrate on conserving those individual liberties which they held dearest. Thus, while liberals became a bit more conservative, conservatives were becoming a good deal more liberal. It was a tribute to contemporary pragmatism no less than to the comprehensiveness of liberal philosophy.

For liberalism by the 1870's was truly ecumenical. It had become all things to all men. The one constant in it, throughout its whole development, had been, of course, a basic regard for the individual and for safeguarding his liberty against despotic authority. But "liberty" and "authority" were relative terms, signifying a wide range of objectives; and an attack upon a particular kind of authority had tended to bring forward a special set of liberties, which usually made way for a different set when the attack shifted to another kind of authority.

46

If one passes over the Protestant Reformation as of questionably liberal character and effect, one finds that the first successful campaigns of modern liberalism were waged against political despotism and resulted, on the one hand, in "bills of rights," guaranteeing the individual against arbitrary taxation, arrest, and imprisonment, and promising him liberties of speech, press, and association, and, on the other hand, in "constitutional parliamentary government," putting an end to monarchical absolutism and vesting abridged powers of government in elective representatives of the nation. It was the political stage of liberalism which had been illumined by England's "Glorious Revolution" of 1689 and by the subsequent American and French Revolutions.

It appeared, however, that the French Revolution, at least in its Jacobin period, was a perversion of political liberalism; that it produced a mob tyranny as destructive of individual freedom as had been the previous tyranny of kings. Hence against the "excesses" of the French Revolution, many liberals reacted. These developed an almost pathological aversion to mobs.

The political stage of liberalism had further involved a reaction against the domination of one nation by another; and with the rise and diffusion of romanticism, it had become fashionable in liberal circles to favor the freeing of "oppressed" and "enslaved" peoples from alien and therefore "tyrannical" rule. In this way liberalism became an ally of nascent nationalism, without abandoning altogether its earlier attachment to the cosmopolitanism of the Enlightenment.

Presently the political stage of liberalism led into an economic stage. As industrialization took root in England and spread to the Continent, foreshadowing a material millennium in which Europe would no longer lack food and could have wealth and creature comforts in abundance, most liberals had become convinced that the one obstacle to the realization of such a pleasant prospect was the existing tyrannical regulation of trade and industry—fitting enough for medieval economy, but not at all compatible with the new need of large-scale capitalistic enterprise—and that steps should accordingly be taken to introduce freedom of trade and freedom of contract, freedom to buy and sell commodities and to employ and dismiss laborers with a minimum of restrictions by state, church, guilds, or trade-unions. This was the economic liberalism which stemmed doctrinally from the French Physiocrats, Adam Smith, and the Manchester School.

But certain liberals began to see a tyranny in capitalism itself and in the private ownership of the new industrial and commercial machinery; and, eager to free individual workingmen from "wage slavery," they furnished leaders to embryo socialism and anarchism. Thus the same fundamental concern with individual liberty which characterized economic liberalism entered into movements most critical of it.

Theoretically, all liberals were committed to religious toleration. But to some, the churches, and especially the Catholic Church, loomed as an "obscurantist" and peculiarly intransigent foe of individual liberty, and such liberals were impelled to move against the tyranny of "priestcraft" and "theocracy" as they had previously moved against divine-right monarchy, and at least to offer to the rising generation a secular schooling which would emancipate their minds. But it was also quite in the liberal spirit that still others should detect in anti-clerical legislation a threatening revival or extension of state despotism and should endeavor to protect individuals against it by invoking liberty of conscience and worship, and particularly liberty of religious education.

By the 1870's, therefore, there were many varieties of liberalism, affecting different persons in different ways. There was a political, an economic, an intellectual liberalism. There was a radical, an atheistic, a moderate, a conservative, a Christian liberalism. Wherefore such diverse groups as English Tories and French Radical Republicans, Italian followers of Mazzini or of Cavour, German admirers of Bismarck and German disciples of Karl Marx were all somewhere in the liberal tradition. They all adhered, in one way or another, to that "ecumenical liberalism" which had ever been actuated by a general and generous desire to free and dignify the individual and which drew support from every social class, from nobility and clergy, from bourgeoisie, peasantry, and proletariat.

Nevertheless, at the very time when such ecumenical liberalism was permeating all classes and parties and countries, something like a calamity befell it in the sudden upsurge of a special sect of liberals. These took to describing themselves as Liberals (with a capital letter) and anathematizing anyone who did not join their coterie and embrace their detailed and exacting creed. So seriously did they regard themselves that (following a not unusual human inclination) others accepted them at their own valuation and conceded to them the magical word "Liberal." In the long run, they were to discredit the name, and with it much of what was fine in the broad liberal tradition itself.

This fateful "sectarian liberalism" was grounded in peculiar developments of the 1860's and 1870's, particularly the speeding and spreading process of industrialization, the rising vogue of materialistic philosophy, and the stirring triumph, in international as well as in national affairs, of *Realpolitik*. Its main props were bourgeois promoters of big business: bankers, speculators, builders of railways and steamships, coal and iron magnates, proprietors of expanding foundries and factories. Supporting them, somewhat in the nature of a flying buttress, was an embellishing array of intellectuals: those scientists, engineers, physicians, lawyers, professors, and literary men who aspired to the utopia promised by Auguste Comte through the yoking of science with industry and who perceived the same axiomatic character in the "inexorable laws" of liberal political economy as in the physical law of gravitation. Both industrialists and their intellectual aides were urban people, and urban-mindedness was a conspicuous feature of the sectarians they mobilized and commanded among the petty bourgeoisie and the artisan class. Hence the newer Liberalism (with the capital letter) was much more narrowly urban and bourgeois than was the older and more general liberalism; and at least with its advocates among the *intelligentsia*, it was far more doctrinaire.

Its central stress was upon economic liberty, upon the paramount importance of encouraging individual initiative and private enterprise. Wherefore it demanded the lowering or entire removal of tariff barriers to trade, evinced hostility to labor associations in so far as they might interfere with freedom of contract, and vigorously opposed any governmental regulation of commerce or industry. As further means to its economic end, it appropriated and adapted much of historic political liberalism. The state, the Liberal doctrinaires explained, should be a "passive policeman" after the English model, with functions rigidly limited to the preservation of order, the protection of private property, the fostering of public education and necessary public works, and with a constitutional government in which the propertied classes would predominate and under which personal liberty would be large and public taxation small.

In international affairs the doctrinaires pursued what proved to be conflicting ideals. On the one hand, they realistically criticized war (in the abstract) as financially burdensome, as injurious to property and profitable trade, and as destructive of human life and liberty; and for the sake of thrift as well as of peace they sought to reduce expenditure for armaments. On the other hand, they were not averse individually to making profits from war loans and the munitions industry, and collectively they were quite patriotic and positively devoted to the belief that liberal nations must acquire and maintain leading positions in the world.

Finally, in the intellectual sphere, sectarian liberalism possessed a distinctive ethos. While in common with much of the older liberalism it postulated freedom of thought and liberty of press and speech, it placed novel emphasis upon the liberating blessings, ultimately, of technology, natural science, and "machine civilization," and immediately, of secularized popular education. Its horror of possible ecclesiastical dictation was prodigious. Religion it would concede to be a tolerable and probably temporary peccadillo of the individual's conscience, provided, of course, one's conscience was not too imperative.

II. THE VOGUE OF CONSTITUTIONAL PARLIAMENTARY GOVERNMENT

By 1871 liberalism had aroused all over the Continent a veritable passion for patterning political institutions and practices after those of traditionally liberal England and for enshrining them (as the English had never done) in a rigid written constitution. The passion was more pronounced—at least more fruitful—in southern and especially Latin Europe than in the North, and in the sophisticated and industrial West than in the "backward" East. But wherever it existed, it was shared by all sorts of liberals, even by some who preferred the title of Conservatives. It was certainly no monopoly of the narrowly sectarian Liberals of the 1870's: they merely accepted it and utilized it.

The English system of government—with its full complement of a bill of rights, a king who reigned but did not rule, a parliament which levied the taxes and made the laws, and a ruling ministry responsible to the parliament—all this had been formally embodied in written constitutions of Spain, Portugal, Belgium, Italy, Greece, Austria, and Hungary. In France, where there had been a plethora of written constitutions ever since the revolutionary days of 1791, the English system finally prevailed in the "constitutional laws" of 1875, except that the titular head was a president instead of a king. Written constitutions obtained in other countries, but while they provided for parliaments and ministries more or less in the English fashion, they usually left the ministry responsible to the monarch rather than to the parliament.

Only three states were without some sort of written and quasi-liberal constitution in 1871, and these were wholly in eastern Europe[1]—tiny Montenegro and the sprawling empires of the Ottoman Sultan and the Russian Tsar. In the case of the Ottoman Empire, the Sultan Abdul-Hamid II sought to curry favor with the West by ostentatiously promulgating a typically liberal constitution in 1876, but, failing thereby to ward off foreign intervention, he speedily annulled the document. In the case of the Russian Empire, the Tsar Alexander II, confronted with domestic unrest resulting from the Russo-Turkish War of 1877-1878, showed signs of a mild recurrence of his youthful indiscretions with liberalism. He appointed a reputed Liberal, General Loris-Melikov, to the chief ministry in 1880 and seemed ready to listen to constitutional proposals. But then in 1881 came the assassination of Alexander II, and in the ensuing excitement General Melikov was quickly discarded and the liberal Westernizers were discredited.

Preponderantly, however, the European state system, under broadly liberal influences, had become—or was becoming—"con-

[1] Exception should perhaps be made in respect of two states within the German Empire—Mecklenburg-Schwerin and Mecklenburg-Strelitz—which retained the medieval system of "estates" until 1918.

stitutional." At the same time it preserved almost everywhere at least the forms and trappings of monarchy. Republicans there were, of course, either from long-established habit, as in the democratic cantons of Switzerland and the oligarchic "free cities" of Germany (Hamburg, Bremen, and Lübeck), or from passionate adherence to principles exemplified in revolutionary France and America. Switzerland was and remained a republic, and so too, for their internal local affairs, did the German free cities. Only France modified the form of her government—for the third time—from monarchy to republic, and this she did hesitantly in the years from 1870 to 1875, and even then by reason less of the numerical strength of republicans than of divisions among monarchists. Spain, it is true, became a nominal republic after the abdication of King Amadeo in 1873, but at the end of 1874 the Bourbon monarchy was restored—with a constitution copied from England's. In England itself the protracted withdrawal of Queen Victoria from the public eye, following her loss of Prince Albert, cost her—and the monarchy—some popular favor, and a few Radicals, including the Birmingham manufacturer Joseph Chamberlain and the brilliant barrister Sir Charles Dilke, openly professed republicanism. Yet English republicans were curiosities, and liberal monarchy was presently raised to new heights of popularity in Britain by the resumption of the royal family's ceremonial round of laying cornerstones, unveiling monuments, holding levées, and reviewing soldiers and battleships.

Liberals could be royalist just as well as republican, if only monarchy was "limited"; and the fact that the English succeeded in reconciling the retention of a very showy royalty with the operation of an ideally liberal constitution encouraged emulative Continentals to be liberal royalists rather than liberal republicans. Republican political parties continued to flourish in France and to exist in Spain and likewise in Portugal, Italy, and Greece; and here and elsewhere on the Continent newly formed Socialist parties made light of monarchy. Yet the Republican parties, never large or compact, slowly declined in the 1870's (except in France, which in this respect was a pariah among the nations); and the Socialist groups, as they grew in size, tended to regard the overthrow of monarchy as of secondary importance compared to the destruction of capitalism.

Constitutional government with limited monarchy seemed solidly established in Europe. Wherever it existed, there was little serious effort to get rid of it or to abridge it, and in the few countries which still lacked it there was a good deal of agitation to establish it. That it would be the universal and enduring form of government for the future was ardently believed by all manner of liberals in the '70's and more or less reluctantly admitted by their critics and adversaries. Which witnessed to the past successes and continuing vitality of ecumenical liberalism, and which the sectarian Liberals of the day duly exploited.

The real questions concerning constitutional government had to do, during the era from 1871 to 1900, not so much with fundamentals as with details. (1) What should be the precise relations between king and parliament? (2) Who should participate in parliamentary elections? (3) How should parliamentary government function?

On the first question, the differences which prevailed in 1871 remained practically the same throughout the era. Wherever the titular head of the state was limited and parliament was paramount (as in Great Britain, France, Belgium, Switzerland, Italy, and Spain), Conservatives joined with Liberals in maintaining full parliamentary government. On the other hand, wherever the monarch dominated the ministry and possessed some share in legislation (as in Germany, the Netherlands, Denmark, and Sweden), the introduction of real parliamentary government was consistently championed only by doctrinaire Liberals, who were not strong enough to outweigh the support accorded the existing regime by Conservatives and acquiesced in by moderates. In Austria, where the constitution of 1867 had proclaimed the responsibility of ministers to the parliament, the Emperor could actually avail himself by the '80's of an emergency paragraph in the constitution and of nationalist conflicts within the parliament to direct legislation and to make the ministers responsible to himself. On the other hand, Norwegian Liberals, in combination with a patriotic peasantry, in 1884 wrested from their king (Oscar II of Sweden) a definitive recognition of full parliamentary government.

On the second question—the question of the parliamentary suffrage—there were wider differences and greater changes. It was not so much a question of liberalism as of democracy. So long as personal liberty was safeguarded by constitutional guarantees, it seemed of minor consequence whether the electorate was large or small, and originally at any rate the vast majority of liberals were not democratically inclined. Rather, they proceeded on the assumption that only men of wealth and higher education possessed the enlightened interest and the personal integrity and prestige requisite for choosing the makers of a nation's laws and the directors of its policies. This meant, of course, a very small electorate, and it was indeed just such an electorate which characterized most liberal states in the third quarter of the nineteenth century. For example, in England (until 1867), in Italy (until 1882), and in Belgium (until 1893), property and literacy tests restricted the suffrage to less than five per cent of the population.

The contrary proposition that everybody should participate in parliamentary elections was derived less from historic liberalism than from the egalitarianism posited by Rousseau and championed by French Jacobins (and Jeffersonian and Jacksonian Democrats in America). From the democratic standpoint, the great desideratum was the equality of all men in rights and privileges, and this could hardly be achieved by withholding from a majority the political rights which a minority enjoyed. Most democrats were undoubtedly liberal in aspiration and intent. They were fond of coupling the words liberty and equality and of affirming that individual liberties would be best assured by equal sharing of all individuals in political life. Yet, despite an increasing drift of liberals into the democratic movement, many held aloof from it if they did not actively oppose it, fearing lest it should lead, as the French Revolution had led, to "mob rule," to an inevitable sacrifice of liberty to equality, and thence to the worst tyranny and violence, ultimately perhaps (as Aristotle had foretold and Napoleon had exemplified) to military dictatorship.

Accordingly, efforts to enlarge the suffrage in a democratic direction had divisive effects among liberals. Those who favored democracy as a help to liberty were usually styled Radicals; those who frowned upon it as a hindrance or peril were known as Moderates or Conservatives. Prior to 1867 the only European countries in which the Radicals succeeded in instituting universal manhood suffrage were France and Switzerland (in 1848) and Greece (in 1864). To be sure, the French democratic franchise had been partially neutralized by various electoral devices which Napoleon III employed from 1852 to 1870; but it became a rallying cry of his opponents, who frightened him in the last year of his reign into guaranteeing it anew and who, after his downfall, wrote it finally and fully into the constitution of the Third French Republic. Though Radical Liberals claimed chief credit for this denouement, there can be no doubt that by 1871 the vast majority of Frenchmen were so bent on exercising universal manhood suffrage that neither Moderates nor Conservatives had any serious thought of opposing it.

The French (and also the contemporary American) example of a democratic franchise appealed powerfully to Radical Liberals everywhere. In most countries, however, the bulk of Moderate Liberals and liberal Conservatives were less impressed either by logic or by French example and more inclined to extend the suffrage, if at all, very gradually and in some relation to the extension of wealth and education. Between the two camps, the issue was joined, therefore, on a broad front. The Radicals were aided by the steady growth of political consciousness and ambition among the masses and likewise by party conflicts between Moderates and Conservatives. Occasionally, some Conservative statesman sought political advantage by fathering a far-reaching electoral reform. More often the Moderates, frightened by the specter of violent revolution, accepted a compromise with the Radicals.

The outcome varied in different countries. In Great Britain, a Conservative ministry, responding to pressure from Radical Liberals, so altered existing property qualifications in 1867 as to enfranchise most urban workingmen and thus to double the electorate. Carlyle called it "shooting Niagara," and the Conservative premier, Lord Derby, admitted it was "a leap in the dark." Then in 1872 a Liberal ministry under the leadership of the moderate Gladstone sponsored the introduction of the secret ballot for parliamentary as well as municipal elections. Next in 1884, again under Gladstone's auspices, the suffrage was extended to most rural workers. Finally, in 1885, under the guidance of a Conservative ministry of Lord

Salisbury, the whole country was redistricted so that members of the House of Commons would be chosen by approximately equal constituencies of about 50,000 people each. Thus it befell that between 1867 and 1885 Britain moved away from the oligarchical government which it had previously had and toward the political democracy which Radicals from Jeremy Bentham to John Bright had long demanded. Yet, though the direction was clear, the goal was not quite reached. Some slight property qualifications remained, and the privilege of plural voting was still enjoyed by half a million men.

In the case of Germany, Prussia had adopted the form of universal manhood suffrage as early as 1850 but had qualified it by a "three-class" indirect system of voting which enabled a small minority of well-to-do landlords and businessmen to outvote the mass of artisans and peasants. Then in 1867, when the Prussianized Germany began to take shape in the North German Confederation, the supposedly reactionary Bismarck astounded his liberal critics and flattered the masses by insisting that its Reichstag should be elected by straight universal manhood suffrage, without any class system at all; and, when the Confederation was transformed into the Empire of 1871, democratic election of the federal parliament was confirmed. This, however, did not signify a decisive triumph for democracy in Germany. The powers of the Reichstag were restricted, the princes of the several states retained important prerogatives (including the appointment of ministers), and the parliaments of Prussia and all the other federated states continued to be class affairs.

In Italy, where in 1871 only about two per cent of the population could vote, a Radical ministry sponsored in 1882 a suffrage reform, reducing property qualifications and enfranchising all men who had a primary school education, which allowed some seven per cent of the population to vote. In the Netherlands, extensions of the suffrage were made in 1887 and again in 1896, with the net result that the electorate was increased from two to fourteen per cent. In Austria, a four-class system, long limited to the propertied and professional classes, was supplemented in 1896, in response to Conservative demands, with a fifth class embracing the masses.

In a few countries, a narrowly restricted franchise was eventually replaced rather abruptly by universal manhood suffrage. Such was the case with Spain, which made the transition in 1890 under the guidance of the Liberal statesman Sagasta. Such, too, was the case with Belgium, which effected the change in 1893 under Conservative auspices—with a special provision, however, for plural voting by men with particular property or educational qualification. Such, finally, was the case with Norway which, under the leadership of a Radical ministry, introduced universal manhood suffrage in 1898.

In a number of countries, Moderate and Conservative influence was strong enough, in conjunction with that of downright "Reactionaries," to prevent, prior to 1900, any concessions to Radical demands for "electoral reform" and to maintain unimpaired the principle of mid-century liberalism that constitutional parliamentary government should be operated exclusively by an "enlightened" minority of brains and substance. This was true of most of the German states, of Sweden and Denmark, of Portugal and Serbia, and strikingly so of Hungary, where continuously from 1848 to 1918 suffrage qualifications based on age, property, taxation, profession, official position, and ancestral and national privileges kept all but five per cent of the population from any active share in political life. And, we may recall, there was no suffrage whatever in the Russian and Ottoman Empires, two states in Europe which remained without constitutional government.

Of the states which were most democratically inclined during the period from 1871 to 1900, it will be observed that universal *manhood* suffrage was the standard or goal of democratic achievement. The question of the enfranchisement of women—of really universal suffrage—was raised, at least by statesmen, seldom and not very seriously. John Stuart Mill, always as logical as he was chivalrous, did propose a woman-suffrage amendment to the British reform bill of 1867, but it was defeated in the House of Commons by a vote of 196 to 73. Though supporting it, the Radical John Bright confessed in 1871 that "I am never free from doubt as to whether my vote was a wise one. I do not think the bestowal of the suffrage on women will be of any advantage to *them*, and I fear at present, and perhaps always, it will strengthen the party

[Conservative] which hitherto has opposed every good measure [!]
I think it would add to the power of priestcraft in every part of
the Three Kingdoms."[2] There spoke the Radical Liberal, who when
partisanship and "priestcraft" were concerned was likely to be a bit
passionate. On the Continent sectarian Liberals were more in evidence than in England and still more passionate about imperiling
their anti-clerical policies by enfranchising "unenlightened" females.
So, despite agitation on the part of "advanced" women here and
there, and occasional parliamentary discussions of the subject,
woman suffrage was nowhere in Europe a reality, until the nineteenth century—and the heyday of liberalism—had passed.

If woman suffrage was a minor question, a major one was how
to make constitutional parliamentary government function on the
Continent as it functioned in England. The answer is, of course,
that it did not and could not. Parliamentary government in England
was traditional and the political customs and usages which had
grown up during its long evolution made the unwritten British
constitution. In England, moreover, most people, regardless of
whether they possessed the suffrage, were politically minded and
quite familiar and content with periodical alternations in office
between two political parties, which differed only about details,
which did not undo each other's constructive achievements, and
which agreed perfectly in extolling "English liberties" and the
"British constitution."

On the Continent, the situation was different. There, lacking any
indigenous precedents, liberals wrote constitutions imitative of what
they severally imagined the British constitution to be, and such
constitutions created the parliaments. Then, when the Continental
parliaments passed from blueprint specifications into actual houses
alive with human beings, it should occasion no surprise that they
seldom functioned with the experienced dignity, suavity, and
authority of the "mother of parliaments." Only in Belgium did
parliamentary practices and circumstances approximate those in
England: two major parties—both loyal to the constitutional regime
—alternating in power and providing fairly stable governments;
and a citizenry obviously growing in political-mindedness and

[2] G. M. Trevelyan, *Life of John Bright* (1913), 380.

refraining from extremes. Elsewhere parliamentary government was beset by various obstacles.

One was the multiplicity of perpetually shifting political parties or "groups," which militated against the stability of ministries and put a premium on adeptness at making or breaking combinations among "groups." Another was the presence, inside the parliaments as well as outside, of extremist factions, quite out of sympathy with the newfangled constitutional government or else with the "capitalists" who operated it, and much given to obstruction, denunciation, and even threats of revolution or counter-revolution. Besides, there existed, especially in Latin countries, a widespread popular indifference to, if not suspicion of "the government," and, on the part of those active in politics, a remarkably doctrinaire and uncompromising attitude. Nor was this last peculiar to Latin countries. In Germany, for example, many parliamentarians seemed more anxious to expound a *Weltanschauung* than to amend a government bill. In certain Continental states, moreover, dissident nationalities proved a grave handicap to the successful conduct of parliamentary government. They disturbed and eventually paralyzed it in Austria. They troubled it in Hungary and also in Germany. They impeded it in the Union of Sweden and Norway. They had something to do with the unwillingness of Tsar and Sultan to follow the vogue of constitutional parliamentary government then sweeping the rest of Europe.

III. SOCIAL CLASSES AND POLITICAL PARTIES

The operation of parliamentary government required and yielded political parties. If one were sufficiently dialectical and preferred theories to facts, one might suppose that the political groupings which were a distinguishing mark of the generation of materialism from 1871 to 1900 would correspond rather precisely to social classes. For at a time when the individual was presumably pursuing his own enlightened self-interest, especially his economic interest, he would naturally gravitate toward other individuals of the same class whose economic interests were similar, and with them he would logically co-operate in political action. And the free competition and conflict between political parties would thus mirror a class conflict, basic and needful for progress. Such reasoning was as cogent to "capitalistic" disciples of Ricardo as to "proletarian" apostles of Marxism; and by innumerable popularizers of the "eco, nomic interpretation of history" a trim formula was devised and circulated, equating "nobility" and "clergy" with "Reactionary" or "Conservative" parties, "bourgeoisie" with "Liberal" parties, and "proletariat" with "Socialist" parties.

But all this depended on individuals recognizing and following economic class interests. It ignored, moreover, the complexity of "classes" and certain permissible doubts as to whether any "class" really has coherent and characteristic "interests," and, if so, whether its individual members possess both the enlightenment and the will to follow those interests to the exclusion of others. At any rate, as soon as one examines in any detail the social classes of Europe from 1871 to 1900 and the various political parties, one fails to discover an intimate or universal correlation.

What were the social classes? There was everywhere in Europe, except in out-of-the-way areas like Switzerland, Norway, Greece, and the Balkan countries, a titled nobility. But about all it had in common as a class was some measure of pre-eminence in the world of fashion and sport, and some degree of historical or genealogical mindedness. Some of its members still possessed great landed estates and quasi-feudal privileges in particular countries, notably in Great Britain, Prussia, Austria-Hungary, Sweden, and Russia. In other countries, however, such estates and privileges were apt to be rarer and more restricted. In France and Belgium they were almost wholly reduced to the realm of memory. Besides, in most countries titled noblemen who still retained ancestral lands, newly identified themselves with industry and commerce, investing in stocks and bonds, becoming directors of business corporations, and treating their landed estates as secondary assets, perhaps merely as hunting preserves. It should be borne in mind, too, that a large percentage of the titles of nobility were of comparatively recent creation, not an inheritance from a medieval class of warrior land-lords but rather an essentially modern reward for striking success in banking or manufacturing or for special service, civil and political as well as military, to state or party. In Great Britain, for example, a nobleman might be a great agriculturist, but more often only a proprietor of distilleries, coal mines, steel works, or railways, or just a past politician.

All over Europe was a clergy, but by 1871 it was almost nowhere the richly privileged First Estate of the Middle Ages. Some of the higher clergy, notably prelates of the Protestant state churches in Britain, Prussia, and Scandinavia, and of the Catholic state church in Spain, Austria-Hungary, and Bavaria, might belong to "aristocratic" families and might derive princely revenues from ecclesiastical properties, but the rank and file of Protestant pastors and Catholic priests were drawn from all imaginable social classes and were notoriously impecunious. If these had been dominated by economic interests, they might well have aimed at becoming a top crust of the proletariat.

If "clergy" and "nobility" have little meaning as designations of homogeneous classes, the phrase "agrarian classes" possesses hardly greater significance. True, the phrase applies to all who have a major interest in agriculture, and as such it applied, from 1871 to 1900, to the majority of Europeans outside of England and Belgium and to an overwhelming majority in eastern Europe. Nevertheless, differences among them were as profound as differences between them and the "city classes." The agrarian classes included some titled nobles and country gentlemen, who held large estates but who in many instances were as much interested in urban enterprise as the wealthy bourgeoisie who married into their families and found recreation on rural properties purchased from them. The agrarians also included a mass of peasant proprietors, independent owners of small farms, and these, numerous in France, the Low Countries, Denmark, Norway, Westphalia, Rhenish Prussia, parts of Italy, and the Balkans and Greece, were as hostile to big landlords as to big businessmen and as eager as any petty bourgeois to save a little money for gainful investment in government bonds and corporation stocks.

Then, too, there were almost endless gradations of agricultural laborers, from well established and fairly prosperous "tenantry" (as in parts of England, Sweden, and Austria), through a much more precarious and penurious tenantry (as in Ireland and Spain), to a complex class of "share croppers," and on down to a great variety of groups whose only bonds of union were that they had no share in ownership of the lands they worked or the tools they used and that they were very poor: the regular and casual "hired men," the day laborers, the ex-serfs of Russia, many of whom alternated work on farms with work in factories and might as properly be included in the "proletariat" as in the "agrarian classes." Indeed, the popular migration from countryside to city which the spread of the Industrial Revolution enormously quickened—a phenomenon which we must later discuss at some length—served to blur the historic distinctions between peasantry and bourgeoisie just as a common infatuation with material progress was lessening the historic rivalry between landowning aristocracy and machine-owning bourgeosie.

The urban "middle class"—the "bourgeoisie"—was not a simple single class but a congeries of classes. There was a moneyed bourgeoisie, growing mightily in wealth and influence and spreading ever faster across Europe from west to east. It embraced well-to-do industrialists, commercial magnates, and bankers, but even it was not a unit. Between industrialists and commercial magnates developed conflicts of economic interest and political policy; and bankers who tried to resolve the conflicts found themselves frequently assailed from both sides. There was likewise a professional bourgeoisie, comprising lawyers, physicians, engineers, journalists, professors, trained civil servants, whose background was variously supplied by aristocratic, commercial, industrial, even peasant or "proletarian" families, and whose "interests" were correspondingly diverse. There was, most numerous of all, a petty bourgeoisie, made up of small manufacturers and traders, retailers and shopkeepers, handicraftsmen and clerks, and tailing off into an artisan class. These were very bourgeois in the sense that they had "city minds" as well as city habitations and were apt to be contemptuous of rural life and occupations, but on the whole they were paradoxically both envious and distrustful of the *haute bourgeoisie*.

Nor was there, save as an abstraction, a compact urban proletariat. The majority of urban dwellers in industrialized countries, it is true, owned little or no private property, and were dependent on wages. But between artisans and skilled mechanics, an "aristocracy of labor," on the one hand, and miners and factory operatives, on the other, a gulf existed which was hardly bridged by common disdain of unskilled, casual, or alien workers. Besides, we should remember that the chief part of the ever-growing migration of peasants into industrial and commercial towns went to swell the urban proletariat and thus to keep alive in it a considerable element of rural psychology and aspiration.

As with the so-called proletariat, so with the other conventionalized "classes" in the Europe of the age of materialism, there was a vast deal of fluidity. The doctrine of individualism, vitalized by widespread shifting from familiar agricultural to unfamiliar industrial pursuits, proved a solvent of the traditional European class system and an incentive to conflict within as well as between classes.

If now we turn from the somewhat chaotic social classes to the political parties of the '70's and '80's, we should not be surprised at the lack of any precise social pattern in the latter. Take, first, the "Reactionary" parties—those highly critical of constitutional, parliament government and bent upon restoring political and social institutions as they had been, in fact or fancy, at some date prior to the French Revolution. In England, where the Conservatives were merely moderate liberals, there were no Reactionaries at all. Yet in Germany, whose social alignment most closely resembled England's, there were numerous Reactionaries among the great landlords, the Lutheran clergy, and the military and civil services, all constituting an essentially reactionary Conservative party—the party, in popular parlance, of "the Junkers." Reactionary Conservative parties also flourished in Austria, Hungary, and Sweden, though here, as in Germany, not by any means all of the "Junkers" adhered to them. In Italy, there may have been Reactionaries, but if so they did not form a political party; the Conservative "Right" in the Italian chamber of deputies was as true to basic liberal principles as the Liberal "Left." And the same can be said of Greece and the Balkan states.

In France, however, there was a Reactionary party, the Legitimist, seeking in the 1870's to put the austere grandson of Charles X on a throne decorated with the lilies of the Bourbon family and the oriflamme of Jeanne d'Arc, and dedicated to close union with the altar. These French Legitimists were recruited mainly from noblemen who had little but titles and memories, from Vendean peasants and Catholic clergymen who were habitually anti-Revolutionary, from socially proper army officers, and from some members of the moneyed and professional bourgeoisie who tried to be fashionable and succeeded in being snobbish. Altogether they were a small minority of the "classes," to say nothing of the masses, and in advocating the cause of monarchy as against that of republic, they were outnumbered by Orleanists and Bonapartists, who were really liberal. In Spain the Carlists, and in Portugal the Miguelists, played a role similar to that of the Legitimists in France, and with similar ill-success. In vain the Spanish Carlists revolted against the liberal Republic of the early 1870's and the restored liberal monarchy of Alphonso XII in 1876-1877; they were repressed and obliged eventually to yield the sway of Spain to liberal royalists, whether of the Conservative "Right" or of the Liberal "Left." In Russia, of course, where Reactionaries enjoyed governmental backing and favor, they were exceptionally numerous, though, curiously enough for the student of social history, their strength was less among the nobility and wealthy bourgeoisie than among intellectuals, petty bourgeois, and civil servants (recruited from a wide variety of classes), who gave momentum to the Slavophil movement of the '70's and '80's.

Corresponding to Reactionaries on the extreme Right of political groupings, were Socialists and Anarchists on the extreme Left. These, nevertheless, were not so far removed from the liberal Left as Reactionaries were from the liberal Right. They represented extremes, perversions so to speak, rather than denials, of fundamental liberal principles. They surpassed ordinary liberals in devotion to materialist philosophy, and their peculiar tenets, which shocked and pained most liberals, they deduced from good liberal assumptions. The Anarchists thought that if man was better off with less government he would be best off with no government. The Marxian Socialists believed that if human welfare was first promoted by free competition between individuals it would be finally ensured by conflict between classes, with survival of the most numerous and the fittest—that abstract "proletariat." And when they condescended to leave the realm of dogma and enter that of practical politics, as occasionally they did, they were almost invariably to be found campaigning alongside of Radical Liberals in behalf of free trade, personal liberty, political democracy, and international peace, and in opposition to "clericalism," "landlordism," and all manner of real or alleged "reaction." The Anarchists were a fanatical sect, rather than a political party, and the Socialist parties were small and feeble until the decade of the '80's. The latter particularly boasted of being "proletarian," but their following comprised only a small portion of the urban workers, and their leaders were largely of the professional bourgeoisie with a few stray scions of aristocracy and plutocracy.

Defying every attempt to correlate political parties with social classes were the confessional, or "clerical," parties which arose and flourished in most parliamentary countries on the Continent. Such were the Liberal (Protestant) party in Switzerland, the Anti-Revolutionary (Protestant) party in the Netherlands, the Catholic parties in Belgium and Switzerland, the Center (Catholic) party in Germany, the Christian Socialist party in Austria, the later Liberal Action party in France. None was "reactionary" in the sense of opposing constitutional parliamentary government. Indeed, they all championed personal liberties, and some of them were downright "radical" in advocating extension of the franchise and social reform. What distinguished them, of course, was their zeal to conserve the historic religion of their several countries and certain ecclesiastical rights, especially in education. In this sense, they were "conservative." Yet each of them cut across all social classes, and included not only clergymen but some nobles, many peasants, every sort of bourgeois, and every kind of urban proletarian.

In nearly all the political parties of the era—among "conservatives," "clericals," and "socialists," as well as among "progressives" and "radicals"—there was a good deal of liberal sentiment and liberal conviction; and every party drew adherents from all social classes. Liberalism, at least of the historic ecumenical sort, was no monopoly of any social class or any political party. Even those parties which in the '60's and '70's arrogated to themselves the specific title of Liberal (with the capital letter) and developed a peculiarly liberal orthodoxy did not represent a single class or exactly homogeneous interests. The leaders and managers of these parties were drawn largely from the bourgeoisie, it is true, but it was a bourgeoisie of diverse elements and tendencies: the *haute bourgeoisie* of finance, industry, and commerce, who for various reasons stressed economic liberalism; and the professional bourgeoisie of lawyers, scholars, and journalists (themselves deriving from many different classes), who emphasized the intellectual aspects of liberalism. And the following of these expressly Liberal parties included some nobles, some clergymen, some peasants, many proletarians, and a preponderant portion of the numerous *petite bourgeoisie*.

Yet there can be little doubt that the sectarian liberal parties which emerged in the '70's were relatively more urban and bourgeois and much more exclusive than the older and more general liberalism, and their very vociferousness gave the impression that their particular liberalism was the complete and true liberalism and identifiable with urban-mindedness and capitalism. It must be acknowledged, moreover, that many members of these Liberal parties who were not capitalists themselves, were quite enamored of the human progress which they pictured as proceeding, under capitalistic auspices, from the advance of technology and the industrial arts, from the growth of cities and the increase of physical and material well-being.

IV. TEMPORARY PREDOMINANCE OF LIBERAL PARTIES

The heyday of the specifically Liberal parties was from 1867 to 1880. These parties, as we have said, were preponderantly bourgeois, and as such they usually comprised but a minority of a nation, though in countries where the suffrage was restricted by property qualifications they might constitute a majority of the electorate.

An interesting aspect of the newer type of Liberal parties was the prominence among them, not only of "free thinkers" of Christian antecedents, but also of Jews. Historic liberalism had fostered Jewish emancipation, and out of gratitude as well as for economic reasons Jewish financiers and Jewish intellectuals flocked to the urbanized Liberal parties. Wherever such Jews were fairly numerous, as in Germany and Austria, they exerted a far greater influence than their mere numbers might seem to warrant.

Another, if less obvious, aspect of these Liberal parties—at least on the Continent—was their association with Freemasonry. Particularly in the Latin countries almost all Radical Liberal politicians were Freemasons, as were many of the businessmen and intellectuals for whom and through whom they functioned. Freemasonry, while not precisely a religion, was a convenient substitute for one. It made its devotees aware that they belonged to an elite, that all were brothers, that they had a mission to perform for humanity and progress. It was faintly scientific and benevolent, and, above all, it was very solemn and secret. No wonder that its lodges were attractive to somewhat prosaic or pedantic Liberals and suitable for caucuses of party leaders.

In Great Britain the Liberal party of Gladstone was dominant from 1868 to 1874 and again from 1880 to 1885, and during the intervening years, when Disraeli and the Conservatives held office, it constituted a large and influential "opposition." It was doubtless less sectarian than the corresponding parties on the Continent. It still included some Whig landlords and commercial aristocrats, as well as more vulgar commoners and workingmen. It was not enmeshed in a political Freemasonry, and, though more sympathetic on the whole with religious non-conformity than with the established Church of England, it was not markedly anti-clerical, and its inveterate premier, Gladstone himself, was as pious in his Anglicanism as in his Liberalism. Altogether, despite personal distaste for it on the part of Queen Victoria, the British Liberal party was almost as socially respectable as its Conservative rival. Yet if one examines the roster of its cabinet officers from 1868 to 1885, one is struck by the predominance of the *haute bourgeoisie* in its councils. Gladstone himself came from a wealthy commercial family of Liverpool, and so too did his able war secretary, Edward Cardwell. George Goschen was a banker and William Harcourt a lawyer. From the ranks of eminently successful industrialists were drawn Bright and Chamberlain, Forster and Mundella, and

Campbell-Bannerman. Titled nobles there were, but most of them represented contemporary promotions from the middle class: Cardwell, who was made a viscount in 1874; Henry Bruce, a coal magnate, who became Baron Aberdare in 1873; and Robert Lowe, lawyer and economist, who was created Viscount Sherbrooke in 1880. Earl Granville, a second-generation peer, and the Earl of Rosebery, one of the fifth generation, were chiefly ornamental: the former was more admirable in the role of after-dinner speaker than in that of foreign secretary; and Rosebery was exquisitely gilded, especially after his marriage into the Jewish banking family of the Rothschilds.

In Germany, sectarian Liberals were distributed among three parties: the radical Progressives (or Freethinkers as later they frankly called themselves), who first appeared in the early '60's; the moderate National Liberals who seceded from the Progressives in 1867; and the Free Conservatives (or Imperialists), who separated, likewise in 1867, from the reactionary Conservatives. The National Liberal party topped all others in the Reichstag from 1868 to 1878, and in co-operation with the smaller Free Conservative and Progressive parties it shaped most of the legislation of the Hohenzollern Empire during its first decade. The leaders of both the National Liberals and the more stridently sectarian Progressives were almost entirely bourgeois, either of the "capitalist" or of the "intellectual" variety. Rudolf von Bennigsen, chief among the National Liberals, was a lawyer and civil servant, and his most zealous aides included the banker Ludwig Bamberger, the lawyer Eduard Lasker, and such academic personages as Gneist, Sybel, and Treitschke. The outstanding spokesmen for the Progressives—and, as Bismarck complained, they always spoke at length—were Eugen Richter a lawyer, Schulze-Delitzsch an economist, and Rudolf Virchow a physician and scientist. The Free Conservative leaders, on the other hand, were mainly landed aristocrats, though they enriched themselves not so much by cultivating ancestral estates as by promoting industrial and commercial enterprise. Their head was Wilhelm von Kardorff, owner of agricultural property in Silesia and also heavy investor in banks, railways, and coal companies, and founder (in 1875) of the Central Association of German Industrialists.

In Austria an intensely doctrinaire Liberal party—patriotically German and emphatically urban and bourgeois—exercised a controlling influence from 1867 to 1880. Its titular leader, to be sure, was the scion of an ultra-aristocratic family, Prince Adolf Auersperg, who was prime minister continuously from 1871 to 1879. But Auersperg was extraordinarily romantic in his devotion to "freedom" and "progress," and behind his imposing front was a solid array of professional men and businessmen, including the bulk of the Viennese Jewry. In the Dutch Netherlands, also, a similar urban constituency backed Liberal ministries from 1871 to 1879.

It was likewise with Belgium, though here, thanks to a somewhat earlier industrialization, a sectarian Liberal party had gotten control as early as 1857. In 1870 it encountered an electoral reverse at the hands of the rival Catholic party, less urban and more Flemish, but in 1878 it was back in power, under the guidance of a fanatically Liberal lawyer, Walther Frère-Orban, and so remained until 1884.

In Italy almost all the parliamentarians were aggressively Liberal in the tradition either of Cavour (the so-called "Right") or of Mazzini and Garibaldi (the so-called "Left"). The "Right" supplied the ministries of Domenico Lanza, a physician, and of Marco Minghetti, an engineer, from 1869 to 1876. Thenceforth until 1891 the ministries were formed from the "Left" by a succession of professional lawyers and politicians—Depretis, Cairoli, and Crispi.[3] In 1891 the "Right" returned to office under the Marquis di Rudini, one of the wealthiest landlords in Sicily, but he, unmindful of his landed interests, had been a supporter of Garibaldi and now pursued policies hardly distinguishable from those of the "Left." In Italy, at any rate, the predominance of sectarian Liberalism did not cease with the 1870's but continued into the twentieth century.

A similar sort of abstract Liberalism cropped up in Spain and Portugal, appealing to intellectuals in the learned professions and

[3] Cairoli had been a Garibaldian army officer during the *Risorgimento*, and both Depretis and Crispi had been disciples of Mazzini and Garibaldi.

also in the army. Army officers like General Prim and Marshal
Serrano, with a civil engineer like Sagasta, played decisive roles
in the Spanish revolution of 1868 and in the establishment of the
short-lived Liberal regime of Amadeo of Savoy from 1871 to 1873;
and the guiding spirit and practical dictator of the ensuing and
even briefer Spanish Republic was a very theoretical Liberal, Emilio
Castelar, lawyer and professor of history. With the restoration of
the Bourbon monarchy in January 1874, a more practical group
came to the fore, led by an army officer, Marshal Campos, and by
a lawyer and journalist, Canovas del Castillo. These, though styled
Conservatives, were sufficiently liberal to maintain constitutional
forms and to tolerate the return of Sagasta and even Castelar to
active politics. Indeed, from 1881 to 1897, Canovas and Sagasta
amicably rotated the honors and emoluments of public office between them; and much the same arrangement was worked out
in Portugal between a Canovas-like party of "Regenerators" and a
Sagasta-like party of "Progressives." In both Portugal and Spain,
the word Liberal had an irresistible attraction to professional politicians under the respective constitutional monarchies, but the thing
itself was less real to them than to the smaller groups of middle-
class intellectuals who made up the dissenting Republican parties.
Republicanism was the supreme Iberian expression of sectarian
Liberalism.

The narrowly restricted suffrage which obtained in Austria, the
Netherlands, Belgium, Italy, Spain, and Portugal was doubtless a
prime factor, along with industrial developments, in assuring the
supremacy of expressly Liberal parties in the parliaments of those
countries. In England and Germany, where the suffrage was wider,
a similar result was achieved by the relatively greater spell which
a prodigious access of industrialization cast over persons of moderate political opinion (representing diverse classes and "interests")
and which induced them, at least temporarily, to collaborate with
radical Liberals. The two most democratic countries of Europe—
France and Switzerland—presented further variations from the
norm.

In Switzerland the nominally Liberal party was really a confessional Protestant party analogous to the so-called Clerical party

among Swiss Catholics. Both were liberal in a general and historic sense, and both were committed to democracy and republicanism. But it was a third party, with the title of Radical, which most nearly resembled the specifically Liberal parties of Austria, Italy, and Belgium. It was largely urban and bourgeois, and markedly anticlerical; and ever since the civil war of the 1840's it had championed a centralizing policy in the Swiss Confederation. This policy was undoubtedly popular and helps to explain why the masses assured to the Radical party a majority in the federal parliament throughout the second half of the nineteenth century. After the 1870's, however, the ascendancy of the Swiss Radicals was more apparent than real, for the democratic electorate displayed a sobering tendency to utilize the peculiar institution of the referendum in order to block pet measures sponsored by Radical deputies.

France, much more permeated with abstract liberal principles than any other nation on the Continent, was unique in possessing no expressly Liberal party.[4] Indeed, France hardly had definitely organized political parties of any kind, but merely political groups clustering about particular politicians. And most of such groups, kaleidoscopic in external appearance, were in principle and profession quite faithful to the general liberal tradition. Only a minority of the royalists in the National Assembly from 1871 to 1875, the so-called Legitimists, were anti-liberal. The majority of royalists, the Orleanists, were devoted to the liberalism exemplified by the constitutional monarchy of 1830 and newly expounded by their leader, the Duc de Broglie; and all the republican groups vied with one another in paying at least lip service to liberal tenets. The Radicals among the latter played the role in France analogous to that of sectarian Liberal parties in Germany, Austria, Belgium, and Italy.

The emergent republican regime in France was one of professional politicians, closely associated with law and journalism and with capitalistic industry, usually too with Freemasonry, and overwhelmingly middle class. Of fifteen more or less typical republican leaders in France during the '70's and '80's, seven were lawyers

4 Except, very late, the small party of Catholic Republicans which followed the leadership of Count de Mun and Jacques Piou and took the name of *Action libérale* in 1899.

with some journalistic experience (Grévy, Gambetta, Dufaure, Ferry, Brisson, Spuller, and Floquet), three were wealthy industrialists (Waddington, Rouvier, and Casimir-Périer), two were engineers (Freycinet and Sadi-Carnot), two were teachers (Jules Simon and Dupuy), and one (Clemenceau) was physician and journalist. These differed greatly in degrees of radicalism, and on many matters of practical policy they quarreled and made up with fascinating suddenness and warmth. Some were known as Moderates, others as Extremists, but most of them nourished a sectarian liberalism of which the central feature was anti-clericalism. Jules Ferry, for example, though reputed a Moderate, was as radical in respect of the Church as his Extremist critics, Brisson or Clemenceau.

In eastern and far northern Europe, "Liberal" was much used as a party label, though seldom with the precise sectarian connotation which it possessed in central and western Europe. In Greece it was appropriated by personal followings of two rival lawyers, Tricoupis and Delyannis, whose recurrent premierships covered much of the period from 1874 to 1897. In Norway it designated a coalition which was formed in the '70's between a "lawyer's party" and a "peasant party" and which took charge of the government in 1884. In Denmark it represented a similar fusion (in 1872) of middle-class intellectuals with peasants, although in this case the majority which it gained in the lower house of parliament was flouted and successfully defied from 1875 to 1894 by a Conservative dictatorship. In Sweden, certain landed proprietors called themselves Liberals, but it was not until 1905 that a predominantly bourgeois and radical Liberal party was enabled to take office.

In Hungary, Liberalism was professed by groups of nobles and country gentlemen, with a sprinkling of middle-class intellectuals. Most sectarian, and at the same time most nationalistic, was the minority group that composed the Independence party of Kossuth. Scarcely less nationalistic, though more opportunist, was the larger Liberal party led by Count Koloman Tisza, great landlord and determined Calvinist, who held the premiership continuously from 1875 to 1890.

In the Balkan states, Liberalism was hardly more than a slogan.

In Rumania, Ion Bratianu, a man of considerable wealth who had been a student at Paris and an army officer, was instrumental, as a "Liberal," in deposing Prince Ion Cuza in 1866 and installing the Hohenzollern Charles I; and from 1876 to 1888 Bratianu was the latter's dictatorial prime minister. In Serbia, Jovan Ristić, who had been trained in law at Berlin and Paris, was the author of the constitutions of 1869 and 1889, and, as "Liberal" leader, directed the government almost continuously during the '70's and again from 1887 to 1893. In Bulgaria, Stephan Stambulov, who had been educated in Russia for the Orthodox priesthood but had abandoned it for the study of law, entered politics as a "Liberal" in 1879, and was president of parliament in 1884, regent in 1886, and virtual dictator from 1887 until 1894.

In the Ottoman and Russian Empires, the lack of parliamentary government involved, of course, the absence of formal Liberal parties. Yet in both areas, the "westernizing" movements which gathered headway in the '70's reflected the general liberalism of the West. An example of the Turkish Liberal of the time was Kiamil Pasha, a native of Cyprus and a graduate of the military school of Alexandria, who conceived an intense admiration for the parliamentary government and material prosperity of England; and as a member of the Sultan's ministry from 1878 to 1885 and Grand Vizier from 1885 to 1891 he advocated a gradual adaptation of Turkish political institutions and economic policies to the English Liberal norm. Kiamil failed to sway the Sultan Abdul-Hamid II or to overcome the entrenched forces of Turkish conservatism, but he inspired many younger men who eventually, in the twentieth century, would attempt a Liberal revolution.

Nor did the westernizing movement produce any immediate results in Russia, except some occasional halting deference to it on the part of the Tsar Alexander II and a multiplication of repressive measures against it by Alexander III. Yet, below the surface, it was much stronger and deeper in Russia than in Turkey; it involved more persons and groups and begot factions of more radical tendencies. A generation of idealistic young people representing all ranks and classes, from a Prince Kropotkin to common workingmen, undertook to "enlighten" the peasant masses and to bring Russia into step with Western "progress," and extremists among them espoused anarchism or socialism and resorted to terrorism. More respectable and probably more truly liberal were a goodly number of middle-class intellectuals—professors and journalists, engineers and retired army officers—and likewise numerous country gentlemen and lesser nobles in the local governmental bodies, the zemstvos, which Alexander II had established in 1864. The attitude of both these groups was indicated in the petition which a zemstvo despatched to the Tsar in 1879: "The Tsar in his care for the Bulgarians . . . has found it necessary to accord them self-government, inviolability of personal rights, independence of the judiciary, and freedom of press. The zemstvo of the province of Tver ventures to hope that the Russian people . . . will be granted the same benefits. . . ." A like attitude was manifest, moreover, among intellectuals of "oppressed" nationalities within the empire, notably Finns, Poles, and Jews, and it presently found favor among capitalistic beneficiaries of the industrialization which proceeded apace in Russia in the '80's and '90's. Nevertheless, fruition of the westernizing movement was belated in the Empire of the Tsars, as in that of the Sultans; and what it subsequently brought forth in the twentieth century was something quite different from the particular Liberalism in party and policies which flourished in the 1870's.

V. SECTARIAN LIBERALISM IN ACTION IN THE '70'S

In central and western Europe the decade of the '70's was blossomtime for sectarian liberalism, although the duration and luxuriance of its blooming varied somewhat from one country to another, depending upon local peculiarities of intellectual climate and material soil. In Britain the flowers, though crossed with others and rather pale of hue, had been almost perennial since 1846 and were at their prime from 1868 to 1874. In Germany and Austria they were comparatively short-lived but from 1867 to 1879 very gaudy. In Switzerland and the Netherlands they were less showy and longer-lived. In Belgium they bloomed anew in 1878 and then faded in 1884. In France they opened fully in 1879 and thenceforth remained in bloom. In Italy they were brilliant before the '70's and long afterward. In Spain and Portugal they blossomed spasmodically, and in the case of the former from 1868 to 1874 quite orchidaceously. In Hungary they peeped out in the '70's but their maturity was delayed until the '90's. In other countries they were mere exotic products of hothouse cultivation.

All this liberalism, wherever it flourished, had common characteristics: a solicitude for personal liberty, especially for freedom of the press; an almost religious devotion to science and secular schooling; a robust anti-clericalism; a curious kind of nationalism; and a sublime confidence in the rich blessings of material prosperity, to be attained through parliamentary government and the strict practice of economic liberalism.

Economic liberalism was indeed, along with constitutional government, the most obvious concern of the Liberal parties of the time, the most convincingly urged and the most widely fruitful. Everywhere it involved a positive and a negative program: positive, in support of legislation conducive to free trade and free industry and hence helpful to private capital; negative, in opposition to labor legislation. Under Liberal auspices the positive part of the program was extensively realized. Free trade became a European phenomenon in the 1870's. In Great Britain it had been sensationally inaugurated by the repeal of the old corn laws in 1846 and of the hoary navigation acts in 1849, carried forward by the sweeping reforms of Gladstone as chancellor of the exchequer in 1853 and 1860, and consummated by the removal of the tariff on timber in 1866 and on sugar in 1875. In Germany the tariff of the *Zollverein*, already reflecting the relatively liberal Prussian tariff of 1818, was further liberalized step by step in 1856, 1865, and 1867, so that when the Hohenzollern Empire was created it was largely a free-trade regime; and in 1873 it abolished remaining duties on iron.

In France the Cobden commercial treaty of 1860 with Britain and similar treaties of the next few years with Germany and other powers resulted in the annulment of all prohibitive tariffs and the scaling down of other duties by at least half; and this arrangement continued in force until 1882. In the Netherlands and Belgium, where tariffs had been high prior to 1850, they were gradually lowered until from 1860 to 1880 they were little more than nominal.

In Switzerland trade barriers between the cantons had been swept away in 1848 and the external tariff was slashed in the '60's. In Italy the free-trade policy which Cavour had derived from England and applied to Piedmont in the '50's was extended to other parts of Italy in the '60's and remained the national policy until near the end of the '70's. In Austria-Hungary a moderately protective tariff, introduced in 1848, was further moderated in 1860 and still more by a liberal trade treaty with Germany in 1868. Among the nations of western and central Europe only Spain and Portugal maintained high tariffs throughout the '70's, and they were "backward" countries and their Liberalism, hardly popular, was predominantly intellectual rather than material.

With free trade went a variety of other aids to commercial and industrial development. The political unifications of Germany and Italy and the compromise (*Ausgleich*) of 1867 between Austria and Hungary permitted and invited the establishment, for greatly enlarged areas, of uniform systems of coinage, weights and measures, credit and banking, public taxation and budgeting; and Liberals were quick to utilize all such opportunities. Everywhere, moreover, they sponsored legislation easing and expediting the formation of private corporations for manufacturing and trade. Likewise they were stout and practical champions of the right of free migration whether from country to city or from nation to nation; they would assure to expanding industry in their own lands a cheap labor supply and at the same time benevolently encourage the oversupply to seek its fortune in other lands, preferably overseas. The nuisance of passports fell into desuetude in the '70's, not to be revived until the illiberal reaction of a later date.

Improvement and extension of means of communication appealed strongly to Liberals. Under their constant patronage railway construction forged rapidly ahead from 1855 to 1880, not only in Britain, Germany, and France, but in Italy, Austria, and Hungary, while simultaneously national postal systems were perfected and uniform postage rates established. In general, Liberal governments subsidized from public funds the building of railways as needful "public works," but, convinced of the advantages of "private enterprise," they usually entrusted to chartered companies the ownership and operation of profitable railways. This was true in Britain, France, Italy, and most other countries, though in the case of Prussia the state, for military reasons, took over the railways as early as 1876.

Liberal regimes, while directly encouraging private enterprise and fostering the creation of commercial, banking, and industrial corporations for the enrichment of their several directors and investors, were indirectly serving the same ends by opposing large governmental expenditures, which would heighten the taxation of capital, and by rejecting proposals for labor legislation, which, it was argued, would hamper and burden business. "Retrenchment" was peculiarly sacred to Gladstone and his fellow English Liberals: it connoted that the state was not an eleemosynary institution, dispensing alms in an idealistic spirit, but a business affair to be managed by financiers expertly and with a keen eye on costs; and, allowing for greater human frailty on the Continent, Liberal statesmen there eloquently extolled "retrenchment" if they did not practice it quite so rigorously.

Of labor legislation there was almost none, either in England or on the Continent, during the Liberal ascendancy. A French law of 1874, limiting the employment of women and children and providing for factory inspection, was enacted by the monarchical and partially "reactionary" National Assembly, and it was almost nullified by exceptional decrees of subsequent liberal republican ministries. British statutes of 1874 and 1878, forbidding the labor of children under ten years of age and consolidating earlier factory legislation, were achievements of Disraeli's ministry rather than of Gladstone's, and they were scarcely epochal. By and large, Liberals in every country were hostile to state regulation of wages, hours of labor, or working conditions. They generally accepted the thesis that labor is a commodity like iron or cotton or cash and that it would be sufficiently regulated by the natural operation of the economic laws of demand and supply and by individual bargaining between employer and employee.

Liberals who upheld the right of employers to form partnerships and associations could not logically deny a similar right to employees. Actually, however, they were as suspicious of trade-unions as they were sanguine of industrial corporations and chambers of commerce. They perceived in the former a potential menace to the prosperity and progress promoted by the latter. Trade-unions were not "respectable." They were recruited from the lower classes. They were exposed to demagoguery. They stood for the heretical and very dangerous principle of collective bargaining, which, through sheer weight of proletarian numbers, would operate in practice to the disadvantage of employers and might lead, through strikes, terrorism, and socialistic exactions, to the utter ruin of capitalistic industry and hence of what was best and most promising in contemporary civilization. Yet workingmen pressed for the legalization of trade-unions, and certain Radical Liberals backed them, not because it was the logical thing to do, but because it seemed expedient.[5] Workingmen might thereby be aligned, out of gratitude, with the Liberal political parties, and given useful co-operative experience in self-help and thrift. If simultaneously the masses were educated (and public education, to most Liberals, was a panacea for all ills), they would become "enlightened" about the proper functions of trade-unionism and thoroughly alive to the necessity of making it an ally, rather than a foe, of capitalistic industry. With these considerations in mind, trade-unions were formally legalized in England in 1871, and in France, more hesitantly, in 1884. Likewise, legal favors were bestowed upon co-operative stores, savings banks, and "friendly societies" (fraternal insurance companies), as special aids to thrifty members of the lower middle and skilled laboring classes.

There can be no doubt that the economic policies of European Liberals in the '70's contributed potently to the swift progress of industrialization in the greater part of the Continent, most strikingly, perhaps, in Germany and Austria. Both free trade and improved means of communication stimulated commerce enormously, and this in turn spurred the large-scale mechanical production of goods.[6] Furthermore, free migration and the almost complete lack of any effective labor legislation permitted unprecedented profits

[5] Notably, John Bright in England, Schulze-Delitzsch in Germany, and Waldeck-Rousseau in France.
[6] For some details of the growth of commerce and industry during the whole era from 1871 to 1900, see below, pp. 88-102.

to accrue to investors in banks, railways, shipping, mines, and manufacturing plants. The '70's were indeed a gilded decade of capitalism
—and of wildcat speculation.

Sectarian Liberals put a premium on money-making, ultimately,
they all avowed, for the sake of those mystical entities described
as "civilization" and "humanity," but immediately, in concrete
instances, for themselves. Groups of intellectuals among them may
have retained an unspotted altruism and vestal innocence. But
some of the most influential elements in the Liberal parties were
not virginal; they evidenced no qualms of conscience about playing
the stock market, consorting with shady promoters and jobbers,
resorting to bribery of electors, legislators, and newspapers, and
using public office for private gain. Corruption was, of course, no
novelty of the 1870's. It was a chronic and hydra-headed manifestation of human nature. But now it was freer—more liberal.
It could be manifested on a wider front, by more persons, with
greater seeming justification, and with less restraint from religious
or other traditional sanctions. Not that those who practiced corruption called or even recognized it by that name. They called it,
in economics, "promoting progress," or, in politics, "assuring the
triumph of liberty."

The prospect of a material millennium and of individuals getting
rich quick, loomed large at the close of the Franco-Prussian War
in 1871. There was a sudden spurt of business, an infectious
enthusiasm for newly-formed companies, especially banks and
building societies, and a feverish activity on the stock exchanges.
Promoters and speculators had a merry day, and of the crumbs
which fell from the festal board Liberal parliamentarians and
officials partook.

There was a "morning after," however. A financial crisis was
presaged by soaring prices at Vienna in 1872, was checked temporarily by lavish spending for a world's fair at the Austrian
capital, and then eventuated in a terrifying panic there in May
1873. Stocks tumbled, banks closed, companies failed, trading halted,
factories shut down, thousands lost their savings and tens of thousands were thrown out of work, bread lines formed, and a major
economic depression was in full swing. A like panic, though of

less intensity, ensued in Italy in July. In September a frightful one seized New York and speedily affected the whole United States. In October Berlin was smitten, and by the end of 1873 every German city was in the grip of "hard times." Meanwhile, in November, London experienced a panic, and, with lesser and varying consequences, so did the commercial towns of the Netherlands, Belgium, and Scandinavia. France, strangely, was least touched by the epidemic; her turn came considerably later, following a succession of bank failures in 1882.

The panic of 1873 was succeeded by numerous civil and criminal trials at Vienna, Berlin, Rome, and elsewhere, in which a galaxy of Liberals—bankers, entrepreneurs, public officials, cabinet ministers—were charged with such unpleasant things as fraud, peculation, bribery, and conspiracy. There were relatively few convictions, but many unsavory or suspicious disclosures. In Austria, for example, the long trial of Ofenheim, a railway magnate, on the charge of fraud, though it resulted in his acquittal (February 1875), brought out damaging evidence against some of the most distinguished members of the governing Liberal party, including at least two members of the ministry. In Germany, a libel suit against Rudolf Meyer, while bringing about his conviction (in February 1877), showed that even Bismarck had been unduly influenced in financial matters by the Jewish banker, Gerson von Bleichröder. And apart from the washing of much dirty linen in the public law courts, there were implications of still more uncleanliness in the concurrent series of suicides in Austria and duels in Germany.[7]

The association of sectarian Liberalism with economic and political corruption was not isolated in time or place. It gradually assumed the aspect of a set and almost universal pattern. Only English Liberalism appeared incorruptible, and it was least sectarian. In Belgium the return of the Liberals to power in 1878 was celebrated by gargantuan frauds in the state bank. In Italy the financial dishonesty of Nicotera, minister of the interior in 1876, was so flagrant that he was excluded from the cabinet, but this did not deter his Liberal chief, Depretis, from continuing the practice

---

[7] See Max Wirth, *Geschichte der Handelskrisen* (Frankfurt, 1883), and the article by Albert Schäffle in *Zeitschrift für Staatswissenschaft* (Stuttgart, 1874).

of bribery on a princely scale; and despite charges of embezzlement (and proof of bigamy) Crispi held the premiership for many a year. In France a sterling Liberal, Jules Grévy, was shoved out of the presidency of the Republic (1887) because his son-in-law was caught selling decorations of the Legion of Honor, and subsequent exposure of the colossal Panama-Canal scandals involved such conspicuous Radical statesmen as Freycinet, Floquet, and Rouvier, along with the Jewish financial adventurers Cornelius Herz and Baron de Reinach. In Hungary political corruption became a fine art under Tisza; and in Rumania, under Bratianu.

Economy of public expenditure and hence of taxation was a maxim with Liberals, as we have said, but on the Continent they tended in time to honor it more in the breach than in the observance. Although there was stalwart niggardliness about expenditures which labor legislation might entail, there was little or none about outlays for public education, internal improvements, and national armaments, or for placement of "deserving" party members in governmental service. With accompanying reluctance to increase direct taxes or to impose customs duties, and with consequent heightening of interest charges on bank loans, Liberal regimes faced ever greater difficulty in balancing their budgets. In Germany the imperial budget showed an alarming deficit in 1877. In Belgium a deficit of six million francs in 1881 grew to twelve million in 1882 and to twenty-five million in 1883. In France the public debt, already large, mounted sharply in the '80's and the nation became accustomed to seeing the budget estimates exceeded by the actual expenditure. In Italy, despite frantic efforts of Liberals of the "Right" to balance the budget, and despite the continuation of extraordinarily burdensome taxation, the "Left" spent money riotously and brought the state to the verge of bankruptcy.

Most sectarian Liberals represented a curious compromise between the pacific cosmopolitanism which was part of the humanitarian tradition of the eighteenth century, and which free trade and free migration enhanced in the nineteenth century, and the belligerent nationalism which had recently been stimulated by the series of international wars from 1859 to 1871. As opposition to tariff protectionism was a reflection of their cosmopolitanism, so support of competitive military preparedness was a sign of their patriotism, and incidentally an important source of financial embarrassment to their governments. The Radicals of France, the Left Liberals of Italy, the doctrinaires of Austria were more hearty protagonists of the militaristic development of the late '60's and the '70's than any Conservative or "reactionary" group; and the German Liberals were less troubled by the military aspect of Bismarck's measures than by the constitutional.

Besides, all the Liberal statesmen of the time, while professing the broadest tolerance for minorities and an interest in the development of local self-government, pursued policies of administrative centralization and of nationalistic unification. In Austria the Liberals were popularly and properly called the Centralists; being drawn mainly from the German parts of the empire and convinced of the superiority of German culture, they opposed concessions, political or cultural, to provinces peopled by Czechs, Slovenes, Poles, Italians, or Rumanians. In Hungary Tisza pressed still more drastically a process of "Magyarization." In Germany the National Liberals and Free Conservatives were in the forefront of a campaign for strengthening the federal government at the expense of the states and for discriminatory legislation against Poles. In Belgium the Liberal government of Frère-Orban marked the ascendancy of French over Flemish inhabitants. In Italy the Liberals of the Left were stout upholders of centralization and zealous prompters of colonial ambition. In France the Radicals not only preserved but intensified the administrative centralization of Richelieu, Louis XIV, and Napoleon, and they proscribed more than their Jacobin forerunners the dissident languages of Breton, Basque, Provençal, and Corsican. In Spain Sagasta no less than Canovas was the advocate of Castilian supremacy and the opponent of autonomy for Catalans and Basques. Even in England Gladstone came to espouse Irish home rule late in life and chiefly as a political maneuver, and then could not carry with him such Radical Liberals as Chamberlain and Bright.

The great interest which Liberals had in popular education and the very real contributions which they made to its advancement were motivated by various considerations. Intellectuals among them were undoubtedly guided by the positivism of the era: by faith in "science" and in the human progress which would result from the wide diffusion of scientific knowledge. Those less purely intellectual and more richly endowed with material goods could afford to be benevolent, particularly in respect of an undertaking which, under Liberal auspices, would implant and spread sound economic principles among the masses and thus fortify them against revolutionary impulses and prepare them to take their appropriate places as cogs in the industrial machinery of a bright new age. Then, too, popular state education would be a most effective means of propagating national patriotism, of fitting individuals for intelligent participation in political democracy, in military service, and in their several trades and occupations, and also of undermining those forces, especially ecclesiastical, which still barred the way (or were supposed to bar the way) to salutary freedom of thought and behavior.

Elaborate systems of state-supported and state-directed elementary schools, whose teachers would be lay employees of the government and in which normally no religious instruction should be given, were inaugurated in Hungary in 1868, in Austria in 1869, in England in 1870, in Switzerland in 1874, in the Netherlands in 1876, in Italy in 1877, in Belgium in 1879, in France between 1881 and 1886; and in Germany, where state schools had long been the rule, they were largely secularized in the '70's. Schools under ecclesiastical control might be suffered to continue, but they were reduced to the status of private schools and in most instances, as a kind of protective tariff against them, they were deprived of public funds and subjected to other disabilities. Nor did the Liberals evince any squeamishness about invoking in behalf of popular education that very principle of compulsion which they were credited with abhorring. In one country after another the establishment of public schools was accompanied or soon followed by decrees for the compulsory attendance of every child. There was variation in the enforcement of such decrees. It was notoriously lax in Italy, for example, and remarkably strict in Germany and England. Nonetheless there succeeded everywhere a noteworthy increase of literacy, if not of intelligence, among the masses.

Formally, at any rate, the Liberal regimes were favorable to religious toleration, the right of every individual to adhere to any or no religion as he might choose. This was a legacy from the older and more ecumenical liberalism, and by the middle of the nineteenth century it was pretty well established in Great Britain, Belgium, France, Switzerland, the Netherlands, and Germany, although in most of these countries special privileges were still accorded to particular religious bodies: in Britain, to the Anglican Church; in Germany and the Netherlands, to both Protestant and Catholic Churches; in France and Belgium, to Judaism and Protestantism as well as to Catholic Christianity.[8] In overwhelmingly Protestant Scandinavia and in overwhelmingly Catholic Austria, Spain, and Portugal, religious toleration had been proclaimed a bit later; partially in Norway in 1845, in Denmark in 1849, in Sweden in 1860, in Portugal in 1864; and fully in Spain and Austria in 1868. In Italy it had attended the territorial expansion of Piedmont. In Britain, still greater gains for religious toleration (and equality) were hailed in the disestablishment and disendowment of the Anglican Church in Ireland (1869) and in the final recognition, as an outcome of the celebrated Bradlaugh case,[9] of the right of an avowed atheist, no less than of a Christian or a Jew, to be a member of Parliament (1886).

To the legacy of religious toleration, Liberals of the '70's added an emphasis upon secularization, upon the transference of many social functions and agencies from church to state. The most important of these were educational. Church schools, which had hitherto enjoyed almost a monopoly in the instruction of youth, were supplemented and largely supplanted, as we have already pointed out, by lay state schools. Not only elementary schools but institutions of higher learning were affected. In most Continental countries the universities were rapidly secularized and made centers of anti-clerical activity. In France, for instance, one of the first fruits of Radical ascendancy was a law of 1879 excluding clergymen from

---

8 In France and Belgium, for example, the state salaried not only Catholic bishops and priests but also Protestant pastors and Jewish rabbis and (in French Algeria) Moslem imams.

9 Charles Bradlaugh (1833-1891), a resolute "infidel" with real talents for popular oratory and journalism, was elected to Parliament as an advanced Liberal in 1880. For six years conflict raged over Parliament's refusal to let him take the deistic oath prescribed for admission. He was finally admitted by simple affirmation in 1886.

the Council of Higher Education and confining the name of university and the privilege of conferring degrees to state institutions. Indeed the series of steps actually taken in France to secularize and laicize education is illustrative of efforts put forth by Liberal regimes, with greater or less success, in all the countries which they dominated. A decree of 1880 closed Jesuit schools and those of other "unauthorized" orders. A law of 1881 forbade priests and members of any religious community to conduct schools without a state license, and a law of 1882 prohibited them from teaching in the public schools. Presently, in 1884, another series of enactments carried the campaign into other fields: religious emblems were to be removed from law courts, God was to be omitted from oaths, hospitals were to be laicized, divorce was to be freely granted by the state, and religious communities were to be denied the benefits conferred that very year on other associations.

Marriage, also, under most Liberal governments, was secularized. Persons might still be married in churches and by clergymen, but in France every marriage, to be legally valid, must be performed by a state official, and elsewhere civil marriage was accorded equal validity with religious marriage. Civil marriage was introduced in Austria in 1868, in Italy in 1873, in Switzerland in 1874, in the German Empire in 1875, in France in 1881, and it obtained in Spain from 1870 to 1876.

Suppression of religious orders, especially the Jesuits, and confiscation of their goods were even more characteristic of the period of constitutional Liberalism than of the era of "enlightened despotism." Following Cavour's suppression of 334 convents, housing 4,280 monks and 1,200 nuns, in the Kingdom of Piedmont in the 1850's, a law of 1866 expropriated the majority of monastic establishments (and many seminaries and benefices) throughout Italy, and in 1873 its provisions were applied to Rome. In Portugal and Spain attempts which had been made in the 1830's to outlaw religious communities were renewed in the '60's. Portugal dissolved certain congregations in 1861 and banned in 1862 all those which had been established since 1834. Spain in the revolutionary year of 1868 suppressed the Jesuits and all communities founded since 1837, and confiscated their property, although in this instance partial restitution followed the Bourbon restoration in 1875. Germany expelled the Jesuits in 1872, and in 1875 Prussia abolished all other orders except those engaged in nursing. Switzerland in 1874 banished the Jesuits and forbade the founding of new communities. Norway excluded Jesuits and monks by special legislation of 1878. In Austria the Liberals sponsored in 1876 a bill for the suppression of all monastic establishments, but it encountered serious popular opposition and eventually failed of passage. In France the Radicals accomplished by ministerial decree in 1880 what they could not achieve by parliamentary enactment, the expulsion of the Jesuits and the closure of their schools, the requirement of governmental licensing for all other orders, and the dissolution of 261 "unlicensed' convents.

The grandiose name of Kulturkampf—"battle for civilization"— was given by the eminent scientist Virchow (who was also an eminently partisan Progressive) to the anti-clerical and anti-Catholic campaign which German Liberals fought in the 1870's for the secularization of education, the limitation of ecclesiastical authority, and the suppression and confiscation of religious orders, and which necessitated a most illiberal utilization of police force and prison duress against recalcitrant clergymen. It was a curious kind of fighting for professed Liberals, as a leading Lutheran Conservative, Ludwig von Gerlach, was not slow to remark. In a parliamentary debate of 1873, after reminding the Liberals of their traditional tenets, he went on to say: "Now their watchword is the police—police to the right, police to the left, police in the rear, police in front—ministerial decrees and arbitrary courts without appeal. Are these the same Liberals who in 1848 hardly shrank from assailing the throne? Does the Left no longer know what it is to fight with the intellect? Does it know nothing but policemen, fines, and imprisonment in the realm of faith and the spirit?"

The answer to Gerlach's rhetorical questions was that the Liberalism of the '70's was essentially sectarian and that a distinguishing feature of its sectarianism was firm belief in the supreme menace of ecclesiastical authority, particularly that of the Catholic Church, to the material and intellectual and national progress of a new age, a conviction so compelling as to justify the taking of extreme and

exceptional measures. Nor was such a conviction or the action spring-
ing from it confined to Germany. Both were common to all Liberal
countries on the Continent. In fact the name of Kulturkampf might
appropriately be applied not only to the anti-clerical measures in
Germany in the '70's but to those simultaneously introduced in
Austria, the Netherlands, and Switzerland, and to those in Spain
from 1868 to 1874, in Belgium from 1878 to 1884, in France from
1879, and in Italy continuously from the '60's. Of this Kulturkampf
as a whole, of its manifold sources (in church as well as in state)
and its varying subsequent fortunes, more will be said in another
place. Here it has sufficed to connect a crucial stage of it with the
Liberalism of the 1870's.

Chapter Three

THE RAPID MECHANIZING OF WORK AND THOUGHT

I. PERFECTING OF MECHANICAL TRANSPORT

Two events of 1869—the opening of the Suez Canal and the completion of the first transcontinental railway across America—nicely presaged the perfecting and expansion of that steam-powered mechanical transport which had begun in England forty years previously. Western Europe was already familiar with glistening iron rails, screeching locomotives, and fast rolling trains of passengers and goods. By 1900 these phenomena were commonplace in eastern Europe (and throughout the world). In the interval, the growth of railway mileage in Europe from 66,000 to 172,000 was chiefly in Russia, Austria-Hungary, and the Balkans, while outside Europe new construction not only over American prairies, but across Siberian steppes and Argentinian pampas, up Indian rivers, down Japanese coasts, and into the interior of Australia, raised the total world mileage from 130,000 to nearly 600,000. Railway building was almost if not quite done by 1900. The capital invested in it was estimated at forty-five billion dollars, divided about evenly between Europe and the rest of the world.

Meanwhile, improvement in the efficiency and ease of steam-and-rail transport, though hardly sensational, was steady. Steel rails were gradually substituted for iron and made heavier. Roadbeds were better ballasted. Locomotives and rolling stock were improved. Mechanical safety appliances were installed. Sleeping cars (*wagons-lits* in Europe and Pullmans in America) were introduced in the '70's and dining cars in the early '80's. In the '90's came refrigeration cars.

It was similar with the steamboat, which had had a history before the opening of the Suez Canal in 1869. Thirty years later it was omnipresent on the high seas and in all the ports of the world, far

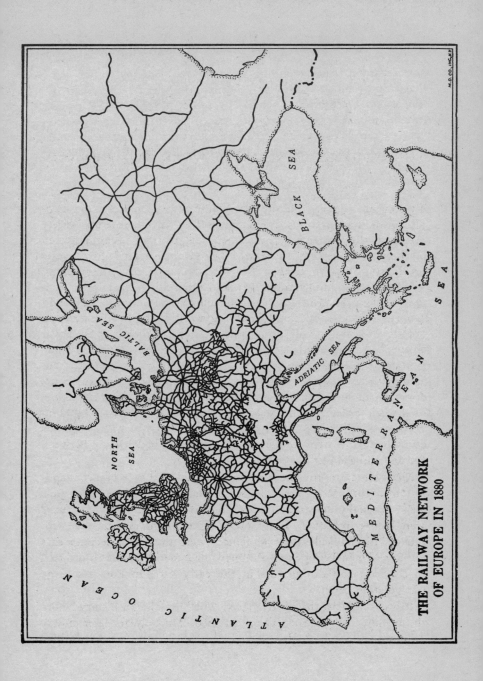

THE RAILWAY NETWORK
OF EUROPE IN 1880

more common than the sailing vessel. It, too, had undergone constant improvement. It was now normally of steel, rather than of iron or wood, and was operated by screw propellers. With new demands of trade and travel, it was employed for differentiated types of refrigeration ships, tankers, and the more elaborate and specialized passenger liners. Toward the close of the '90's came Parsons' marine turbine and Diesel's heavy-oil engine. The enormous growth of water as of land transport, during the era from 1871 to 1900, was accomplished by machines of steel and steam. Persons and goods might still be delivered at one's door by horse and wagon or carried by sailboat, but just as the extension of railways registered the universal popularity and utility of mechanical transport by land, so the enlarging of the Suez Canal in the '80's and the projecting of a Panama Canal in the '90's witnessed to the ubiquitous triumph of mechanical transport by water. For any considerable distance, inside and outside Europe, one traveled and dispatched one's wares, as a matter of course, by powered machinery.

Nor do steam locomotive and steamboat longer tell the whole story of mechanical transport. There were new auxiliaries. For example, the bicycle appeared, at first in the '70's as a sportive curiosity with its big front wheel and its ridiculous little rear wheel, but presently in "standard" form as a valued means of getting to work about town or out to play in the country. Ball bearings were introduced in 1877. Safety rear driving was generally adopted about 1885. Pneumatic rubber tires were added in 1889. In the '90's it became popular alike with classes and masses, and by 1900 its number was legion. There were five million bicycles in France, five million in Britain, four million in Germany, two million in Italy, and comparable numbers in other countries.

Then, too, in the late '60's rails had begun to be laid on city streets, and the tramcars drawn along them by horses were replaced in the '80's by electric tramcars. But hardly was electric traction established when it was challenged on streets and country roads—and on water too—by the internal combustion engine. In 1887 Gottlieb Daimler, a German inventor, put his "petrol engine" into a "four-wheeled, wood-built, light waggonette," and the gasoline-powered automobile was born. Its adolescence, however, was characterized by a bit more than normal trial and error, and its maturity was not reached, with revolutionary consequences, until the twentieth century. Henry Ford was to organize his motorcar company in 1902. In the meantime, the "petrol engine" was being experimented with for motor launches, for submarine boats (which stem from an American inventor, John Holland, in 1875), and also (*mirabile dictu*) for flying machines, about which the human race had dreamed even before it was conscious of any biological or atavistic relationship with birds.

Transport not only of persons and commodities but also of letters, messages, and news was immensely expedited and extended by mechanical devices. Railways and steamships carried ever larger quantities of mail, and on the several national post offices which consequently flourished was superimposed by international agreement in 1875 a Universal Postal Union with headquarters at Berne. Moreover, to the electric telegraph, which had paralleled railways since the 1840's, was successfully added in the late '60's, underneath steamship lanes, the submarine cable. Europe was thus put into direct telegraphic communication with the United States in 1866, with India and the Far East in 1870, and with South America in 1874. Then came the amazing work of Alexander Graham Bell, a Scotsman who had emigrated to America in 1870 and become professor of "vocal physiology" at Boston University. In 1876 he exhibited an apparatus embodying the results of his experiments with the transmission of sound by electricity. It was the telephone. It was immediately accepted in Europe and America, and before long the mileage of telephone wires surpassed that of telegraph wires.

But why any wires at all? Utilizing the theories of electromagnetism propounded by Maxwell in 1873 and proven by Hertz in the late '80's, Marconi patented in 1896 the practical machinery for wireless telegraphy and organized a company for its commercial exploitation. In 1898 wireless telegraphic communication was inaugurated over the English Channel. In 1900 it was tested in naval maneuvers. In 1901 a message—a single letter S—was sent by wireless across the Atlantic.

II. GROWTH OF MACHINE INDUSTRY AND THE CRISIS IN AGRICULTURE

In 1880 John Ruskin wrote of "the ferruginous temper" which in the preceding thirty years "has changed our Merry England into the Man with the Iron Mask."[1] While he wrote, the mask was visibly turning into steel and transforming not only England's aspect but the Continent's—and the world's. For machine industry, already preponderant in Britain (and Belgium) prior to 1871, acquired a like supremacy during the next thirty years in other countries—Germany and the United States, most strikingly; France, to a large extent; and, in lesser and varying degrees, Italy, Austria, Sweden, Spain, Russia. Its basis everywhere, of course, was in engines made of iron and stoked with coal, and its applications were to large-scale fabrication, as well as transport, of commodities. Indeed, the association of mechanical transport with mechanized industry was intimate. In Britain the industrial use of iron and coal led to railway and steamboat; on the Continent the building and operating of railways evoked "the ferruginous temper" and with it a general industrialization. After 1870 the inventors and promoters of industrial machinery were no longer limited to "Anglo-Saxons" and a few Frenchmen and Germans domiciled in England; they were as polyglot and cosmopolitan as the machinery itself.

Between 1871 and 1900, while the British production of pig iron increased by a third, the world output more than tripled. Of this a rapidly growing proportion went into the manufacture of steel. In 1871, when both the Bessemer "converter" and the Siemens "open hearth" were in their infancy, steel production amounted to scarcely a million tons, of which half was British. Then in 1878 came the "basic process" of Gilchrist and Thomas, permitting the utilization of phosphoric iron ores and hence the rich ones of Lorraine, with the result that by 1900 some thirty-three million tons of steel were being made, of which less than a sixth was British, while a fifth was German and a fourth was American. An age of steel was succeeding an age of wrought iron, and it was fittingly climaxed by

[1] *The Seven Lamps of Architecture* (1890 ed.), 70 *n*, quoted in J. H. Clapham, *An Economic History of Modern Britain*, II (1932), 47.

the new marvel of chromium-tungsten steel which the Bethlehem Steel Corporation of America (a curious title for a generation of materialism!) dramatically displayed at the Paris Exposition of 1900.

It was equally an age of coal. To fuel the railway locomotives and ocean liners, the smelters, and the spawning engines in factory and mill, to heat houses, to operate the swelling gas works which by the 1880's were giving light and cooking food in most urban centers and incidentally providing fertilizers for rural fields, and also to support the chemical industry newly and wondrously founded on coal-tar products, the mining of coal was vastly extended. Between 1870 and 1900 its output about doubled in England and Belgium, tripled in France, quite quadrupled in Germany, and increased eightfold in the United States. The world total waxed from 218 to 765 million metric tons.

If the latest material civilization rested on coal and iron (and steel), it was embellished by numerous other earthy extractions, such, for example, as copper and tin, aluminum and concrete. Quantities of copper, needed especially for novel electrical apparatus, were obtained from Rio Tinto in Spain and from the American states of Michigan and Montana. Tin, demanded particularly for the new canning industry, was supplied by bigger imports from the Malay peninsula, the East Indies, and Bolivia. For aluminum a multitude of uses led to its large-scale production by an electrolytic process patented in France and America in 1886. Concrete, made of "Portland cement," was notably improved in the '70's through a lessening of the water content and thenceforth was extensively employed. Many piers and docks were built of it, and in the '80's, "reënforced" by iron as "ferro-concrete," it entered into the construction of houses and factories.

Iron, coal, and auxiliary metals seemed the tangible sustaining buttresses of progressive life and work in Europe—and the Europeanized world—during the Generation of Materialism. But they had antedated and given rise to that generation. What that generation most distinctively originated had to do with electricity—something less tangible, something bordering on mystery, something which might perversely be described as a soul, rather than the body, of materialism. For while electricity remained, in theory, an incompletely explained phenomenon, its practical applications occupied after 1870 a central place in European interest and achievement. The only significant applications before 1870 had been to telegraphy, electroplating, and the arc light. Then in the '70's were devised the telephone, the incandescent filament lamp (by the American Edison), and, perhaps most important of all, the successful dynamo (by the German Siemens). Soon electric lighting was competing with (and later supplanting) gas lighting, and electric traction was supplementing steam traction. Parsons patented his high-speed turbine and an accompanying high-speed dynamo on the same day in 1884, and his first installations were for generating electricity on shipboard. In 1888 followed the induction motor by Tesla, a person who neatly symbolizes the cosmopolitan character of electrical progress: born in Croatia, the son of an Orthodox priest, educated at Vienna and Prague, employed as electrical engineer by the Austrian government, then emigrating to America and associated for a time with Edison, Tesla was one of the first to effect the successful transmission of electrical current from central power plants through lengthening systems of electric lighting and traction. To what diverse uses electricity would eventually be put was quaintly indicated by New York's enactment in 1888 that the death penalty for crime should no longer be inflicted by "hanging" but by a supposedly more scientific (and therefore humane) "electrocution."

Among novel industries, a close second to the electrical were the chemical. Of these, one of the most startling and epochal was the manufacture of synthetic dyestuffs, developing chiefly in Germany. Another was the chemical treatment of wood pulp or cellulose, for the making of paper much cheaper and far more plentiful (and fleeting) than that obtained from linen and rags, and also for the fabrication of artificial silk, or "rayon." Wood pulp paper appeared first in Britain in the '70's, and wood pulp "silk" was first patented by a Frenchman in the '80's. Still another great chemical (and physical) industry was photography. It had begun before 1870, but afterwards its advance was swift. In 1884 the roll film was invented. In 1888 was marketed the first "kodak." In 1891 color photography was introduced, and in 1895 the patenting of the "cinematograph" in France pointed to a coming craze of motion pictures.

For the chemical as for the electrical industries, and in fact for all the spreading and intensifying industrialization, machines became ever more numerous and complex. A pair of machines produced frequently and automatically, as it were, a litter of other machines, and the rabbitlike progeny furnished material evidence of the soundness of Herbert Spencer's philosophical dictum that "progress is from the homogeneous to the heterogeneous." Hand sewing was largely replaced in the '70's by the sewing machine, and an electric sewing machine was patented in 1889. Writing by hand was revolutionized and rendered easier and far more copious by the typewriting machine, invented in America in the early '70's and brought to Europe in quantities at the end of that decade. The first shift-key typewriter appeared in 1878, and the first "visible" writer in 1883. A tabulating machine was first employed for assembling the data of the United States census of 1890, and decimal tabulators were in use by 1898. In the meantime, the setting of type for printing was speeded up by the rotary typecasting machine introduced and improved by the London *Times* in the '70's, and still more by the linotype and monotype machines devised and perfected in the '80's and '90's.

The art of war, also, was progressively mechanized. The first machine gun, the Gatling, had been a by-product of the American Civil War of the '60's. Another, the mitrailleuse, was produced in France and utilized in the Franco-Prussian War. Then, in 1889, Sir Hiram Maxim, an American who acquired an English title, designed a truly automatic machine gun, which subsequently was widely adopted. Improved rifles, too, were poured out by the Vickers and the Armstrongs in Britain, the Krupps in Germany, the Creusot works in France; and amidst the deluge of guns and munitions were the dynamite and other high explosives contributed by the inventive and promoting genius of the Swede, Alfred Nobel, whose materialism was beguilingly decorated with the lavender of humanitarianism and the lace of pacifism.

Machines multiplied and whirred faster for the making of thread and cloth. The number of cotton spindles in Europe and America

almost doubled between 1870 and 1900, and much more than doubled in Germany, Italy, Bohemia, and Russia. Ring spinning, little
known in 1885, was a usual process fifteen years later, and power
looms were made so completely self-acting—so robotlike—that by
1900 they were commonly called just "automatics." Two or three
score of them could be tended by a single person. Machine-made
ready-to-wear clothes budded from factories in the '80's and blossomed in the '90's in the fashionable blouse and skirt, in the modish
suit and two pairs of pants. Laundering was done by machinery
from the '80's. By the later '90's machine-made boots were being
extensively sold in standardized sizes and half-sizes. Pottery entered
a new machine age when wheels became power-driven in the '70's,
and the grinding of grain when, in the '80's, steel rollers superseded
the traditional millstones.

If by the '90's one already ate machine-made food in machine-
made dishes, wore machine-made clothes and shoes, wrote and
calculated as well as sewed with machines, and shot off machine
guns, one as certainly traveled and dispatched all manner of
machine-made goods by steam engine or electric engine and was
beginning to use the petrol engine for speeding over highways and
soaring into the trackless heavens. Transportation was mechanized
along with all other major industries, not least among which was
agricultural industry.

Farm machinery evolved apace. The reaper and binder followed
the mere reaper from America to Europe, ever faster after 1878.
The cream separator was first exported from Sweden in 1879.
Wire fencing was introduced in the '70's and barbed wire in the
'80's. Glass "hothouses" became common. Chemical fertilizers were
in universal demand. In the '70's "canning" of fruits and vegetables
and "tinning" of meats grew into huge industries in America, in
Australia, in Argentina. Many of the cans and tins came thither
empty from European factories, and thence returned full to the
machine-operating populace of Europe. Presently the freezing
machine, which had been invented in England in 1867, was perfected, and mechanical refrigeration assured to Europe still bigger
imports of foodstuffs.

Until the 1870's the agricultural prosperity of a country had pretty uniformly attended its mechanizing of industry and the concomitant growth of its factory towns. Mounting demand for farm produce had been mainly supplied from fields within national frontiers and by relatively short haul of canal boat, railway train, or coasting steamer, and this had meant rising prices and profits for farmers in industrial countries. In Britain, for example, where industrialization was earliest and most thorough, even the removal of tariffs on foreign imports had not offset the advantage which native farmers possessed of proximity to their home market, with the result that an agricultural boom continued from 1840 to 1874.

From 1874, however, British farmers were staggered by an astounding spread of grain growing in the United States and in Argentina, Canada and Australia, Russia and Rumania, and by a still more astounding expansion of speedy long-haul shipping, whereby the plentiful cheap grain of those hitherto distant countries came flooding into British cities and underselling British-grown grain. In the circumstances the grain area of England and Wales shrank from eight and a quarter million acres in 1871 to five and three quarters million in 1901; and the financial profits from what remained tended to disappear. For a time the decrease of grain growing was partially compensated for by an increase of pasturage and animal husbandry. But by the '90's, through the perfecting of refrigeration for long-distance shipments, British cities were obtaining the major part of their meat, as well as their grain, from overseas. Not even British dairy products, or the woolen staple of Britain, were proof longer against foreign competition. Great Britain was at last clearly dependent on the outside world not only for the bulk of raw materials for her factories but also for most of the food for her congested industrial population. Her agriculture, despite mechanical and chemical aids, had ceased to be economically profitable.

A similar crisis in agriculture threatened every other country of western and central Europe in the '70's and '80's, and for similar reasons. With transport costs little heavier between continents than they had previously been between provinces, only the bulkiest and most perishable farm produce remained outside the range of international competition—hay, garden vegetables, fresh milk, butter, eggs, etc. That the issue in Europe as a whole was less disastrous than in Britain must be attributed in part to a specialization in dairying and truck gardening which strategically situated countries like Denmark and the Netherlands sedulously fostered, and in part to artificial tariff dikes which other countries, notably Germany, France, Italy, and Austria, reared against the natural inflow of cheap competitive farm produce from Russia and overseas. Thanks to this essentially illiberal device—this revival of a supposedly discredited mercantilism—Germany, for instance, well maintained her acreage of grain crops, vineyards, fruits, and hops, added to her potato acreage, built up a magnificent sugar-beet industry, and increased the quantity and bettered the quality of her livestock. While Germany approached Britain in industrialization, she thus contrived, like France and Italy, to keep a large measure of agricultural self-sufficiency and prosperity. But the story of the neo-mercantilism which made this possible concerns physical machines less than political action: it belongs to a later chapter.

III. GROWTH OF MATERIAL WEALTH AND CORPORATE BUSINESS

Certain fables of ancient Phrygia assumed strange verisimilitude in a modern Europe otherwise most critical of myths. French revolutionaries had donned Phrygian "liberty caps," and the whole European generation from 1871 bade fair to exercise the "golden touch" of Phrygia's King Midas and to exercise it without embarrassing consequences. For from the spreading and speeding-up of prosaic mechanical manufacture and transport were derived fabulous accumulations of material wealth. Not only were there more things to eat and wear and enjoy, but there was much more money both to spend on them and to put back into the business of producing still greater quantities. Beyond multiplying sums expended by persons and governments on immediate necessities and luxuries, capital investments in profitable enterprise at home and abroad rose with a rush. These at least doubled within Great Britain and France and tripled within Germany, while the amounts of British capital invested abroad increased from four to twelve billion dollars, of French from two and a half to six billion, and of German from none to four.

In fact, the flow of profits from the live springs of mechanized industry into banking and other credit reservoirs, and thence through the pumping stations of corporate "promotion" to the nourishment of ever bigger and newer industrial plants, seemed itself to go on with mechanical precision and efficiency. The mechanics of capitalism had, of course, been provided with "scientific" bases and given practical application during the century prior to 1870. Afterwards it merely underwent a perfecting (and extension) like the mechanics of locomotion or mass production.

The most significant novelty in financial organization was the trend toward combination and monopoly. Previously the family business firm or small common-law partnership, with unlimited liability for all partners and full freedom for masterful personalities, had wrought the major industrialization. It was such "private" firms or partnerships which had developed mining, metallurgy, shipping, the textile and a host of other mechanized industries, and which actually continued long after 1870 to own and operate all over Europe a vast number of petty establishments for the manufacture of *articles de luxe* and likewise of plebeian commodities like shoes and wagons and beer. In Latin Europe, especially, small personal businesses remained the rule rather than the exception. In Germany as late as 1907 a third of the industrial workers were attached to establishments employing not more than five persons. In Britain the Cunard steamship line was a family affair until 1878, the Stephenson locomotive works until 1880, the Guinness brewery until 1886.

Already in 1871 joint-stock manufacturing companies (*societés anonymes, Aktiengesellschaften*) existed, though they were still rare and generally unimportant except in the field of public utilities. Presently, however, they emerged into prominence in response to the growing need for big long-term investments in railways, gas and electric works, insurance companies, banks, and a wide range of perfecting and expanding machine industry. The process was expedited by contemporaneous legislation of Liberal parliamentarians. A British act of 1862 authorized any seven persons to constitute themselves a company with limited liability by simply subscribing a memorandum of association; and similar easing of corporate creation was effected in France and Germany by acts of 1867 and 1870 respectively. As the jester of Victorian England put it:

> Some seven men form an Association
> (If possible, all Peers and Baronets).
> They start off with a public declaration
> To what extent they mean to pay their debts.
> That's called their Capital.[2]

When individual manufacturers were slow to take the initiative, a new species of "promoters," perceiving a golden opportunity, appeared on the scene and through their persuasive powers (heightened by "promoting fees") succeeded in convincing the manufacturers that combination through limited-liability corporations would be to their advantage. Concurrently, moreover, the growing familiarity with stock exchanges, the increasing facilities for underwriting loans and selling stocks and bonds, the expansion of financial columns in the press, the accumulation of spare funds in the pockets of the middle class and in the tills of insurance companies and savings banks, the widespread formation of investing and speculating habits, all contributed to make the promoters' role pleasant and profitable and to endow the trend toward impersonal and large-scale business corporation with the appearance of a supreme and most beneficent law of nature.

The new type of business corporation dispersed nominal ownership and centralized actual control. It enabled a few directors and officials to enrich themselves on other peoples' money and to become irresponsible "captains of industry," tsars of paper-credit empires. At the same time it imparted to a mass of investors a blissful ignorance of sordid details and a heavenly manna of bond interest and stock dividends. It also promoted monopoly. For the corporation was big and rich compared with most individual and family enterprises, and the big fellow might buy up the little fellow, or, still more simply, might crush him in free and open competition.

By the 1880's industrial and financial combination was striding over the industrial world. It took somewhat different forms and names in various countries: in Britain, for example, the joint-stock merger, with "Ltd." written after it; in America, the "trust" or

2 W. S. Gilbert, "Utopia Limited," *Plays and Poems* (1935 ed.), 620.

"holding corporation"; in Germany, the "cartel," an arrangement among major companies for limiting competition. Everywhere the cartels or trusts or mergers were extending to banks,[3] department stores, oil and sugar refineries, whisky distilleries, steamship lines, electrical, chemical, and metallurgical industries. Nor was such combination confined within national frontiers. In 1883 a market-sharing agreement was arranged among the steel companies of Britain, Germany, and Belgium, and, though itself short-lived, it led to other and more successful experiments in treaty making by bankers and industrialists and in the rationing of producers. International shipping "rings" fixed freights and fares and rebates. Domestic manufacturers of firearms and war munitions, the Armstrongs, the Krupps, the Creusots, etc., shared foreign markets with skill and a fine disregard of the narrow chauvinism they sometimes exhibited at home. In 1886 the enlightened Nobel established the first international trust—the Dynamite Trust, Ltd.—with subsidiary monopolistic companies in Sweden, Germany, Britain, France, and the United States. In the '90's the sewing-cotton firm of J. & P. Coats, Ltd., by amalgamating rival British firms and then others on the Continent and in America, created a virtual world monopoly.

The Midas touch of big business was truly golden. Profits flowed from machinery (and monopoly) as never before, and the profits were now reckoned almost universally in gold currency. Until 1870 only Great Britain had based her currency exclusively and unswervingly on gold. In France and her associates of the Latin Monetary Union bimetallism had prevailed, and in central and eastern Europe silver alone. But thereafter, one country after another emulated Britain in adopting the single gold standard: the German Empire in 1871, Scandinavia in 1872, the Netherlands and the United States in 1873, Austria-Hungary and Russia soon after, France and the other Latin nations in 1878. Only very "backward" and out-of-the-way countries such as China, Mexico, and Ethiopia clung to silver.

Yet the actual supply of gold lagged seriously behind the rapidly increasing demand for it; and this shortage of the precious metal

[3] In Britain alone, there were over a hundred banking amalgamations in the decade of the '90's.

served, in conjunction with technological improvements in industry and agriculture, to lower the general price level of commodities. In fact, from the financial "panic" of 1873, the movement of prices was steadily downward. The nadir was reached in the early '90's. By this time the continuing universal demand for gold was far outstripping its supply, with the consequences that money was extraordinarily dear and that, while creditors and traders profited, the debtor and farming classes faced ruin. Hence ensued another peculiarly painful depression and, especially in Germany and the United States, a popular agitation for bimetallism and the cheap money which it would provide. Only the development of a new process for more productive utilization of gold ores[4] and the opening up of rich new gold fields in South Africa at the close of the '90's stilled the complaints of the farmer and the pleas of the bimetallist.

Nevertheless, with the exception of "hard times" in 1873-1876 and again in 1893-1896—which were explained by professional economists as natural cyclical disturbances—the materialist generation from 1870 to 1900 could view with optimistic satisfaction a steady access of wealth, of corporate business enterprise, of material well-being, and of that precious golden metal by which all things were measured and treasured.

IV. GROWTH OF URBAN POPULATION AND THE GREAT MIGRATIONS

Never had there been a century so prolific as the nineteenth, and the climax came in its last three decades. The population of Europe, which had grown by 11 per cent during the twenty years prior to 1870, increased during the next thirty years by almost 32 per cent. The birth rate, it is true, began to decline after reaching its recorded maximum in the '70's, but the death rate declined faster, and the mounting surplus was hailed as a normal and presumably constant accompaniment of material progress. In 1900 a quarter of the human race dwelt in Europe, the smallest of the five major continents, though the one most thoroughly industrialized. There were now ten Europeans for every four a century previously. Only Frenchmen failed to do their proper share of procreating (they

[4] The "cyanide process," patented in 1890 by MacArthur and Forrest.

added barely 600,000 a decade), but since the Franco-Prussian War their decadence was common knowledge. Between 1870 and 1900 the population of England rose from 22½ to 32½ million; of Austria, from 20 to 26; of Italy, from 26 to 32½; of Germany, from 40 to 56; of European Russia, from 74 to 105.

This remarkable increase of population throughout Europe redounded almost entirely to the growth of cities. While the birth rate remained as high in rural as in urban areas, a stationary or even dwindling number of people in the former sufficed, with the aid of agricultural machinery and foreign imports, to feed ever larger aggregations in the latter, and the excess of country-born persons naturally sought and usually found employment in manufacturing, commercial, or mining towns. Hence to the normal increment of cities was added an abnormally large migration from the countryside. Already in the '70's the major part of the British nation was street-bred; and London streets were England to nearly one Englishman in seven. On the Continent, where industrialization had been more belated, urban growth after 1871 was still more rapid. In Germany, for example, there were only eight cities of over 100,000 inhabitants in 1870, whereas in 1900 there were forty-one, of which eleven had over 250,000 inhabitants, and five had over half a million. Altogether the increase of Germany's urban population equaled the increase of her whole population during the era. Even in relatively backward European Russia, the number of cities with over 100,000 inhabitants grew from six in 1870 to seventeen in 1900, the population of Warsaw increasing by half a million, of St. Petersburg and Moscow by 400,000, of Odessa and Lodz by 300,000, of Riga by 200,000. Only France, of the major European countries, made no addition to the number of its large towns, although one of these, the capital city of Paris, registered a gain of over 800,000 inhabitants—almost half the increment of all France.

Not merely a better chance of gainful employment beckoned mass migration from country to city. The city was becoming peculiarly attractive as a habitation. By the middle of the '80's it was apt to be more healthful than the country and to afford greater opportunities for recreation. Its water was being made abundant and pure, and its scavenging, paving, lighting, and sewerage reasonably good. Slums and dingy tenement houses there still were, but there also were schools and libraries, parks and playgrounds, a variety of free amusements, and a profusion of cheap beer gardens, *brasseries,* or "pubs."

In vain professional uplifters among well-to-do and well-fed bourgeois urged on their poorer neighbors a "return to the land." No matter how poor these might be, they were held to the city as by a spell, and no migration from town to country offset that from country to town.

European migration, a prime and ubiquitous feature of the decades following 1870, was not confined within national frontiers or to Europe itself. Into England, chiefly into London, filtered a stream of Germans, Poles, and Jews, and a still bigger stream of Irish. Into Germany, especially into the industrial towns of Westphalia and the Lower Rhine, moved some 200,000 Poles. Into France came thousands of casual laborers from Italy, Spain, and Belgium. Every metropolis took on a more pronounced cosmopolitan character.

From almost every European nation, moreover, went forth across the seas to the ultimate frontiers of Europe, principally the American continents, a migration without parallel in the history of the globe. The early barbarian migrations into the Roman Empire were puny in comparison with this, and they had lasted for three centuries. Now, within three decades, at least twenty-five million Europeans—men, women, and children, with their lares and penates—took passage on ocean liners for new homes over 3,000 miles from natal soil. The large majority of these emigrants were peasants from rural regions of Europe, but most of them tended to settle in the cities, rather than on the farms, of the New World. Thus it befell that the migration of the era contributed to urban growth not only in Europe itself but still more notably in the Europeanized portions of the world outside—in the United States, in Argentina and Brazil, in Australasia.

Neither religious persecution nor political oppression was an important factor in stimulating this latest and climactic mass-migration. Outbreaks of anti-Semitism in Russia and Rumania doubtless speeded up Jewish emigration from those countries to England and Germany and more largely to the United States; and a desire to escape military conscription probably accounted for some of the emigration from Italy and Austria-Hungary. Yet the main motivation everywhere was economic. The depression of European agriculture, a common phenomenon of the period, served to unsettle multitudes of peasants in Ireland, Scandinavia, Spain, Italy, and Slavic lands; and the high-pressure salesmanship of steamship companies, together with reassuring news and remittances from relatives and friends who had previously emigrated, pointed such peasants—and likewise some of the floating population of European cities—toward New York or Boston, Rio or Buenos Aires, Montreal or Melbourne. Generally speaking, European emigration was greatest when economic conditions were relatively bad in Europe and good in America—in the early '70's, the middle '80's, and the end of the '90's. It fell off most sharply in the early '90's, when crises and depressions beset countries of both hemispheres.

During the era occurred a notable shift in the proportionate number of oversea emigrants from the several countries of Europe. Ireland continued to lead all the others in the percentage of emigrants, but Norway dropped from second place in 1871 to fifth place in 1901, Germany from fifth to twelfth, Spain from sixth to fifteenth, and England from eighth to sixteenth. On the other hand, Italy climbed from eleventh into second place, Poland from sixteenth into third, and Russia from thirteenth into seventh. In this respect, too, France was unique: she was the only European country where immigration constantly exceeded emigration.

If it is borne in mind that the 25 million who left Europe between 1871 and 1900 were additional to the almost 100 million by which population within Europe increased during the era, and further that the population of the European overseas "frontier" in the Americas and Australasia simultaneously rose by 60 million, the "expansion of Europe" ceases to be an idle phrase and becomes a basic literal fact—one of the most significant facts of the Generation of Materialism.

V. MEDICAL PROGRESS AND PUBLIC HEALTH

The stupendous growth of European population in the last third of the nineteenth century resulted less from an increase of the birth rate than from a decrease of the death rate, and this in turn was a consequence of fructifying progress in medical science combined with an extraordinary solicitude for public health. What centrally characterized medical progress during the period was the refinement and application of the discoveries which the chemist Louis Pasteur had made by microscopic research in the '60's as to the role of microbes in the twin processes of fermentation and putrefaction. Microbes, he had showed, were a prime cause of disease, indeed they were enemy number one of human health and happiness; and the clearly posed problem was how to fight and conquer them.

A method of destroying microbes, or overcoming their evil effects, in wounds and abscesses, and in surgical cases generally, by the use of carbolic acid, was announced by Joseph Lister in 1867.[5] It was subsequently improved, and antisepsis was replaced by asepsis, but Lister's work began a veritable revolution in surgery and led incidentally to a notable diminution of deaths in childbearing and to a widespread reform of hospitalization. A grateful British government honored Lister with a baronetcy in 1883 and a peerage in 1897.

The relationship of microbes to cellular pathology and their breeding in sewage and sewage-polluted water and milk were the particular concern of Rudolf Virchow, a scientist of great energy and many interests. Physician with a large practice, professor and popular lecturer in the University of Berlin, and withal a leading Liberal member of the Reichstag, he yet found time to provide the German capital with a scientific sewage system and a pure water supply. Virchow was thus a pioneer in a new sanitation, and his attack on microbes at their source, so to speak, was speedily extended by others throughout Europe (and America).

The tracing of particular diseases to particular microbes and the

[5] Lister's discovery of antisepsis had been anticipated by the Hungarian Ignaz Semmelweis, whose achievement, however, had been neglected by the rest of Europe much as Mendel's was.

preparation of specific vaccines and antitoxins for coping with them became the crowning lifework of Pasteur himself and of a younger German disciple of his, Robert Koch, professor of hygiene and bacteriology at Berlin. In 1876 Koch obtained a culture of the anthrax microbe (or bacillus). In 1882 he announced the discovery of the bacillus of tuberculosis, and in 1883 that of cholera. In 1885 Pasteur began the practice of inoculation for hydrophobia.

Bacteriology emerged as a full-fledged science, theoretical not only, but highly practical; and from a host of newly established research centers, including the Pasteur Institute at Paris, Lister's Institute of Preventive Medicine at London, Koch's Institute for Infectious Diseases and Virchow's Institute of Pathology at Berlin, came a rapid succession of brilliant discoveries. Germs were detected of leprosy, malaria, pneumonia, tetanus, erysipelas, typhoid, influenza, and bubonic plague; and against some of them means of immunizing were found. By the end of the century such scourges as cholera, plague, and typhoid were disappearing from the European world, and progress was being made in the control of diphtheria.

Knowledge of bacteriology, asepsis, and inoculation might have remained the *esoterica* of scientists, had its utility not been appreciated by a multitude of laymen and its application been enforced by governments. Under the newer industrialism, with its impetus to mass migration, mass working, and mass living, individual health was becoming a cardinal object of public concern. Epidemics were more serious in large than in small communities, among a mobile population than among a stationary one; and disease was a major economic burden to employer and employee alike and ultimately to the commonwealth. Hence the knowledge that many kinds of disease were caused by microbes and that these could be overcome by simple scientific procedures was acclaimed by the public and acted upon by state authorities. Even Liberal regimes did not cavil about violating the sacred precepts of *laissez faire* and invoking the most stringent police powers in the cause of public health.

Until 1900 the public-health movement had to do chiefly with environmental factors, with germs of disease and conditions which might favor their spread; and its mode of action was mainly through state and local health officials empowered by law to exercise drastic control of water supplies and waste disposal, of milk, meat, and markets, of sanitary conditions in schools, shops, and hospitals, and to vaccinate individuals against specific diseases. The next step in public health—the educating of the masses in positive health practices—was to come after 1900, and then there would be a sharp decline in death rates, especially in infant mortality. But the way for this was already paved. The death toll of infectious diseases was being lessened and the span of life lengthened.

VI. MECHANISTIC NATURAL SCIENCE

The cosmos, a popularizer of science concluded shortly after 1900, is "simply a machine, so orderly and compact, so simple in construction, that we may reckon its past and gauge something of its future with almost as much certitude as that of a dynamo or a water-wheel. In its motions there is no uncertainty, no mystery."[6] Such a conclusion seemed to be inescapably drawn from the then known facts of physics and chemistry and quite consonant with the best informed and most prevalent thought about them.

Since the days of Galileo and Newton, scientific knowledge had been piling up and pointing ever more clearly to the material nature and mechanical operation of the whole physical universe. Matter was conceived of, in a common-sense way, as something substantial and eternal, something that could be accurately weighed and measured, something too which functioned mechanically through an iron interplay of cause and effect. Toward confirming this conception and stimulating the search for still more facts in support of it, the mechanical industrialization of the nineteenth century contributed immensely.

By 1870 the steam engine had already given rise to the physical science of thermodynamics with its epochal twin laws of the conservation and the degradation of energy. By this date, moreover, the kinetic theory of gases was formulated, the wave theory of heat and light established, the atomic theory of the structure of matter capped by Mendeléyev's periodic law, and a new means found in

6 Carl Snyder, *The World Machine.*

spectrum analysis of identifying matter in the heavens with matter on earth.

Along all these lines much confirmatory progress was made during the next thirty years. By help of Mendeléyev's law, for example, new chemical elements were discovered: gallium in 1871, scandium in 1879, germanium in 1886. Helium, also, which by aid of the spectroscope Lockyer had detected in the sun in 1868, was found in 1895 by Ramsay in the earth in the mineral cleveite. Obviously the whole universe was constructed of the same material elements.

Furthermore, it was disclosed in the '80's by the Dutch physicist van't Hoff that the osmotic pressure of chemical solutions conforms with the principles of thermodynamics governing gas pressure, and by Arrhenius, a Swede, that it is likewise connected with the electrical properties of solutions. These disclosures were the cornerstone of a vast superstructure of physical chemistry, in which thermodynamics and electrical science were combined in ever-extending theoretical knowledge and practical industrial applications.

Probably the most novel scientific achievement of the last third of the nineteenth century, theoretical as well as practical, was in the domain of electrical phenomena, and certainly in generalizations about natural science the dynamo supplanted the steam engine as the favorite metaphor. In 1873 appeared Clerk Maxwell's great treatise on *Electricity and Magnetism*, a classic attempt to make the known facts of electricity fit the then generally accepted pattern of mechanics. It maintained the theory that electricity is matter moving in waves like those of light and radiant heat.

Toward the end of the century two new events of far-reaching importance occurred in electrical science. One was the promulgation of the electron theory. As far back as 1756 Benjamin Franklin had spoken casually of electrical "particles" and in the 1830's Faraday had based some interesting experiments on an atomic theory of electricity, but the significance of all this was long unperceived. Now, however, Joseph Thomson, working in his celebrated research laboratory at Cambridge on the conduction of electricity through gases, reached the certain conclusion that electricity is composed of particles (to which he gave the Newtonian name of "corpuscles") and demonstrated that these were constituent parts of atoms. Simultaneously Hendrik Lorentz, a Dutch physicist, pursuing a different line of research, arrived at much the same conclusion, except that, while Thomson explained electricity in terms of matter, Lorentz expressed matter in terms of electricity and named the particles "electrons"—a name which prevailed over Thomson's "corpuscles." At any rate the converging investigations of these two eminent physicists solved the problem—old as the Greeks—whether different kinds of matter have a common basis. The answer at last was an unqualified "yes."

The other event was the discovery of radio activity. It began with a German physicist, Wilhelm Röntgen, who accidentally stumbled upon X rays in 1895. The next year Henri Becquerel, professor at the Polytechnic in Paris, found radio-active properties in uranium, and at the turn of the century Pierre Curie and his equally gifted Polish wife managed to extract radium from pitchblende. Knowledge of X rays was immediately serviceable in experiments which confirmed the electron theory and also, most practically, in medicine and surgery.

The edifice of physical science as built up laboriously and continuously throughout three centuries appeared at the end of the nineteenth quite secure and well-nigh complete. In the future little would remain to be done, it was imagined, beyond measuring physical constants to the increased accuracy represented by another decimal place, investigating a bit more the mechanics of electrons, and resolving some recent doubts about the ether. The electron theory of Lorentz and Thomson assumed that the electrical particles moved within an atom in accordance with Newtonian dynamics and that the atom was like a solar system in miniature, with electrons revolving within it as planets swing around the sun. Further investigation, it was predicted, would prove this assumption—though the next generation of physicists learned with shock that it didn't.

The doubts about ether were already bothersome. Ether had been postulated as an intangible something filling all space, and it was very convenient to nineteenth-century physicists. It provided for a medium through which waves of heat, light, and electricity could undulate, like sea waves through water. It also validated the Newtonian conception of absolute motion, always and everywhere the same, for inasmuch as all stars were moving in the ether their motion could be considered as absolute by reference to it, just as a bird's motion can be referred to the air through which it flies. Unfortunately for the certitudes of physical science, a delicate experiment of two Americans, Michelson and Morley, in 1887 showed that motion through the "ether," and indeed the ether itself, could not be detected empirically. It thus discredited the whole ether hypothesis. Again and again the Michelson-Morley experiment was repeated in the hope that it might turn out differently. Only the generation of scientists after 1900 could bring themselves to do without "ether," and then Einstein would formulate his new doctrine of relativity.

VII. DETERMINISTIC BIOLOGICAL SCIENCE

To older and sustained interest in physics and chemistry, the latter part of the nineteenth century added a new and surpassing interest in biology. Just as physical science inspired confidence in its mechanistic and materialistic assumptions by reason of its practical contributions to technology, industry, and material wealth, so biological science, by its promise of promoting human health and happiness and raising up a superior race, obtained a most respectful hearing for its deterministic theories. In a period when, incredible as it may appear, health was even more eagerly sought after than wealth, the novelties of biology naturally attracted more attention than the somewhat staid and prosaic course of physics.

Biological investigation during the period followed two main lines which rarely converged. One was biochemical, physiological and microscopic, leading to a big access of precise knowledge about embryology, cellular structure of living organisms, pathology, and bacteriology. This was the province of such biologists as Pasteur, Virchow, and Koch, whose revolutionary achievements in medical science, particularly in the detection and prevention of germ diseases, have already been sketched.

This line of research carried into problems of heredity. In 1839

Theodore Schwann had formulated a "cellular" theory, that all living things originate and grow in very small structural units, or "cells"; and shortly afterwards other physiologists had recognized the existence within these cells of vital material to which was assigned the suggestive name of "protoplasm." Then in the 1870's August Weismann, professor at Freiburg, distinguished between ordinary bodily (or somatic) cells, which die with the individual, and reproductive (or germ) cells, which transmit a continuous stream of protoplasm from generation to generation and are potentially immortal. Weismann reasoned further in the '80's that inasmuch as hereditary characters can be transmitted only through germ cells, all acquired characters, which are variations occurring in somatic cells, cannot be inherited.

At the same time it was well known, at least to practical gardeners and farmers, that new varieties of plants and animals could originate in "sports" and be maintained by cross-fertilization and selection, and the article on "Horticulture" in the ninth edition of the *Encyclopædia Britannica* (1881) noted the fact: "An inferior variety of pear may suddenly produce a short bearing fruit of superior quality; a beech tree, without obvious cause, a shoot with finely divided foliage; or a camellia an unwontedly fine flower. When removed from the plant and treated as cuttings or grafts, such sports may be perpetuated. Many garden varieties of flowers and fruits have thus originated."

But none then knew outside a corner of Moravia that an Augustinian monk, Gregor Mendel, had discovered the hereditary principle by means of which "sports" could be bred scientifically. Already in the '60's Mendel had conducted in the garden of his cloister a series of ingenious experiments with the crossbreeding of peas and had reached the conclusion that in the germ cells are determinants of particular characters, which, when transmitted, become "dominant" or "recessive" according to fixed mathematical laws. But this pregnant conclusion, which confirmed and refined the deterministic cellular theory of Weismann and likewise explained the phenomena of variation and mutation, was buried away for thirty years in dust-gathering tomes of a local scientific society. Not until its resurrection by De Vries and Bateson at the beginning of the twentieth century did Mendelianism come into its own and make of heredity an exact experimental and industrial science.

In the meantime most biologists pursued another and quite different line of investigation, the one opened up by Darwin and leading to emphasis on environment. As we remarked in the first chapter, the distinctively Darwinian doctrine of natural selection attained a great vogue in the early '70's, partly because of its simplicity and seeming applicability to a wide range of human interests, and partly because of its concurrence with a high tide of industrial and military competition. The vogue remained throughout the era and gave continuing direction to a vast deal of inquiry, not only in biology but in psychology and the so-called social sciences. And the further the inquiry was carried, the more the results verified, or seemed to verify, the Darwinian thesis. Biologists themselves, with the help of anatomists and geologists, accumulated such a mass of confirmatory evidence as to leave no doubt in the mind of any well-informed person that all life was essentially one and that it had been differentiated into multitudinous species of plants, insects, reptiles, fishes, birds, and mammals by a perfectly natural evolutionary process.

Darwin himself did not regard natural selection as a complete explanation of the evolutionary process. He had buttressed it with Lamarck's hypothesis of the inheritance of acquired characters, and had still recognized its basic shortcoming. It explained why variations survived or failed to survive, but not how the variations actually occurred. Nevertheless his own early interest in a study of heredity which might meet this difficulty and his sympathetic attitude toward the first endeavors of Weismann were largely abandoned by his disciples. These (and Darwin too in his last years) engaged in most unedifying controversy with Weismann over the inheritance of acquired characters, and in total ignorance of Mendel and his work they went gaily on their way, brushing aside the specialists in heredity as though they were mosquitoes, and blithely assuming that natural selection was the proved and adequate cause of evolution and the origin of species.

Before long, of course, almost all biologists came to agree with Weismann in rejecting the inheritance of acquired characters, but not so a large number of evolutionary philosophers and sociologists. Herbert Spencer to the end of his days carried on bitter controversy with Weismann, and many others clung stubbornly to what they regarded as the chief prop of Darwinism and the surest pledge of human progress. And the Darwinian school that accepted the Weismann amendment only concentrated the harder on natural selection. By natural selection alone Haeckel in 1898 evolved the whole human race in twenty-six stages from chunks of carbon through simple structureless bits of protoplasm and on through the chimpanzee and the *pithecanthropus erectus*.[7] The physicist Helmholtz, under the spell of Darwinism, suggested that all life on earth might have evolved from a few germs brought hither from distant worlds in the interstices of meteoric stones. And Darwinian social scientists imagined even greater marvels.

An essential feature of Darwinism was its idea that external circumstances rigidly determine the nature of living creatures, including man himself; that environment is more significant than heredity; that neither human reason nor human will can act independently of its fateful past conditioning. Natural selection was a blind and brute process, operating under inexorable laws of its own and assuring existence and development only to such forms of life as were adapted to their physical milieu and enabled to survive the fierce and constant struggle waged against them from outside. Francis Galton, it is true, based his special science of eugenics on the supposition that intelligence or the lack of it is an hereditary quality, but his notion of heredity was more in keeping with the reasoning of his cousin Darwin than with the discoveries of Weismann and Mendel.

The vogue of Darwinism synchronized, we must recall, with the ascendancy of mechanical and material conceptions in physics and chemistry, and the one colored the other. To evolving life were applied the principles of the conservation of matter and energy, and this fed the belief that all the various activities of living organisms would presently be disclosed as mere modes of atomic motion and manifestations of mechanical or chemical energy. Already some

---

[7] This amusing family tree was presented quite seriously by Haeckel to the International Zoölogical Congress at Cambridge on August 26, 1898.

progress toward this end was being made in physiology. Physical activities of the body were traced to the chemical and thermal energy of the food taken into it. Phenomena of nervous action were found to be accompanied by electrical changes. The variety of idiocy known as cretinism was proved to be due to the failure of the thyroid gland.

Here and there a scientist or philosopher raised his voice in criticism of the prevalent trend, declaring that even if the problems of life were reduced to those of physics and chemistry the concepts of matter and force were but abstractions without ultimate explanation. Ultimates, it was said, could not be arrived at by methods of experimental science, whether physical or biological.[8] But voices of dissent were pretty effectually drowned in the wave of materialistic and deterministic certitude induced by the coalescence of Darwinian biology with physics, and the high-water mark was reached in 1899 with Haeckel's dogmatic book of revelations,[9] according to which life is but a form of matter and the highest faculties of the human mind but properties of brain cells evolved automatically from unicellular protozoa and thence spontaneously from inorganic compounds. Though direct evidence for this conclusion was unluckily lacking, it was widely accepted on faith, proving that even with scientists, or at any rate pseudo-scientists, faith may transcend knowledge. And as a hopeful addendum to Haeckel's faith, a publicist could prophesy that "in forty or fifty years" laboratory technicians might be manufacturing from inorganic materials "endless varieties [of life] as readily as they do new chemical varieties of sugar now."[10]

VIII. PHYSIOLOGICAL PSYCHOLOGY

The rise of "scientific" psychology with its laboratory methods was a conspicuous feature of the era of materialism, a whirling eddy

[8] Such *caveats* were expressed, for example, by the brothers du Bois-Reymond, Emil in *Über die Grenzen des Naturerkennens* (1872), and Paul in *Über die Grundlagen der Erkenntniss in den exacten Wissenschaften* (1890). Cf. Ernst Mach, *Die Mechanik in ihrer Entwickelung* (1883); R. H. Lotze, *Mikrokosmus,* 3rd. ed., 3 vols. (1876-1880); A. J. (Earl) Balfour, *A Defense of Philosophic Doubt* (1879); J. S. Haldane, *Essays in Philosophical Criticism* (1883); J. B. Stallo, *The Concepts and Theories of Modern Physics* (1888); F. A. Lange, *The History of Materialism,* 3 vols. (1873-1875).

[9] *Die Welträtsel,* Eng. trans. as *The Riddle of the Universe* (1900).

[10] Carl Snyder, *op. cit.,* p. 440.

in the merging streams of biology and physics. Its spirit, if one may so denote a very material thing, had been neatly prefigured by a German physician before 1871: "Just as a steam engine produces motion, so the intricate organic complex of force-bearing substances in an animal organism produces a total sum of certain effects which, when bound together in a unity, are called by us mind, soul, thought."[11] But its true foster father was another German physician, Wilhelm Wundt.

While professor at Heidelberg in 1863 Wundt had published some famous preliminary studies on the "human and animal soul." Then in 1874 appeared his *Foundations of Physiological Psychology*, the first monumental exposition of the physical bases of thought and behavior and of the affinity of human minds to those of the lower animals. Called the next year to the University of Leipzig, Wundt opened there his celebrated psychological laboratory, in which knowledge of human behavior was deduced from experiments on cats and dogs, rabbits and mice, and in which, too, a generation of younger men from all over Europe (and America) were inspired and equipped, when they returned home, to start similar laboratories and to conduct similar experiments.

Laboratory investigation of man's "animal mind" and of consciousness as a phase of physical activity yielded a considerable offspring, and the leading accoucheurs, appropriately enough, were medical men. Thus, an Italian physician, Cesare Lombroso, professor at Turin, won fame by his delivery of the "psychology of criminology." Criminals, it seemed, were born, not made. They were a special type of human animal whom evolutionary processes of degeneration and atavism had endowed with peculiar physical features[12] and necessarily therefore with peculiar behavior; they were not morally responsible for their acts. Subsequently, from quite a different slant, Sigmund Freud was to tackle the whole problem of psychological abnormality, and his fame would outstrip Lombroso's.

Meanwhile, in the early '90's, another physician, the Russian

---

[11] Ludwig Büchner, *Kraft und Stoff*, 10th ed. (1869), 147.

[12] You could recognize a criminal when you saw him by his "ape-like agility, projecting ears, thick head-hair and thin beard, square and protruding chin, large cheek bones, and frequent gesticulation."

Ivan Pavlov, following more closely in Wundt's footsteps, began a notable career by making detailed observation of animals and humans in terms of external physical stimuli and reactions and embodying the results in a system of "conditional reflexes." This, later described as behaviorism, fortified the notion that man's mind, no less than his body, consisted of matter and was governed machine-like by physical laws.

Also in the early '90's a French student of natural science and medicine, Alfred Binet, undertook in his psychological laboratory at the Sorbonne to construct simple tests for the gauging of intelligence and to correlate the mental differences thus disclosed with physical differences of head measurement and skin sensitivity. Although the search for such a correlation proved remarkably elusive and was eventually abandoned, Binet's work on intelligence tests prepared the ground, after the turn of the century, for a luxuriant crop of educational psychologists, including, as tares among the wheat, no small number of charlatans.

Still another and more "philosophical" product of the age was pragmatism. Its chief spokesman was an American trained in medicine in Germany, William James, who passed in 1875 from the chair of physiology at Harvard to that of psychology. James rebelled against the mechanical and fatalistic presuppositions of his contemporaries and yet distrusted reason and felt scant sympathy for earlier "idealism" or any system of absolutes. He viewed the world we live in as a world of change and chance, variety and variation, chaos and novelty. Every human trait, he held, operates as an instrument in the individual's struggle to live, and each is validated or invalidated by its effects upon the struggle. Such a pragmatic attitude fitted nicely into the mood of the age. It enabled one to scoff politely at logic and orthodox philosophy, and at the same time to entertain the hope that through trial and error and adaptation an irrational and purely material world could continue to progress. There was, of course, no absolute morality; but what "worked" was good and what didn't was bad. The proof of the pudding was in the eating. To a generation which began with Prussia's defeat of France and ended with Britain's triumph over the Boers and witnessed in the interval a steady advance of science and technology, the gospel of pragmatism was peculiarly attractive.

IX. POSITIVISM AND THE SOCIAL SCIENCES

Positivism was likewise attractive. Auguste Comte had died more than a decade before 1870, but his works lived after him. There were so many things in his positivist philosophy to appeal to the ensuing generation. It was like James's pragmatism in that it enshrined evolutionary conceptions, eschewed all ultimate explanations, whether "theological" or "metaphysical," and concentrated upon scientific fact-finding. Furthermore it exalted social science, that is, sociology, as queen of the sciences, just when industrialism was begetting mass movements and new social problems, and it ascribed to social science the same exact methods and the same fruitful principles as those characterizing physical science; in fact sociology was "social physics." Besides, Comte had imbued his scientific precepts with a rosy coloring of optimism and a faint aroma of benevolence which titillated a generation still distant from the World War. Humanity was to him and to his immediate disciples a mystical as well as a positivist phenomenon, not alone the subject of meticulous research but the object of religious worship, a substitute, as it were, for the Christian God. The highest service which could be rendered to humanity was the "good works" of collecting all possible facts about it and letting them speak for themselves, and this service its high priests, the research professors, would perform to the ever greater glory and progress of mankind.

Probably the number of persons who conned Comte's *Positive Philosophy* between 1870 and 1900 and fully absorbed it was but a fraction of the host of social scientists who emerged in those years. But consciously or unconsciously almost all of these—sociologists, economists, statisticians, political scientists, historians, anthropologists, archaeologists—were conditioned by the climate of positivism and adapted, as by a process of natural selection, to the pursuit of its method and its goal.

Sociological studies, multiplying after 1871, were of two main kinds. One was the synthesizing of data of history, economics, and politics with data of natural science and physiological psychology into generalized statements of the "laws" and "trends" presumably governing the behavior and evolution of human society. This was represented most elaborately by the three volumes of Spencer's *Principles of Sociology* (1877-1896), in which the opinionated author treated of society as an evolving organism, of religion as stemming from the worship of ancestral ghosts, and of the struggle for exist- ence as evidenced by a constant natural antagonism between nutri- tion and reproduction and between the productiveness of industry and the waste of militarism. The other kind was the analysis, through detailed "field" investigation, of the existing status of par- ticular social classes or groups. This was the aim of Le Play's notable studies, over a score of years, of family life in France and elsewhere throughout Europe, and likewise of numerous social surveys of urban centers, especially of their poorer population. The most monumental of these was the inquest into the "life and labor of the people in London," directed and financed by Charles Booth, a British capitalist and philanthropist, and reported *in extenso*, with maps and charts, by his staff of "experts," first in three volumes (1889-1891) and later in eighteen (1903).

Sociological viewpoints and methods were increasingly adopted by specialists in allied fields. Historians, for example, concerned themselves less with individual biography and political narrative, and more with social movements, with the evolution of social forces and social institutions. Political scientists, too, were moved to stress the practical rather than the theoretical aspects of govern- ment and to deal not so much with its structure as with its historic functioning in and on society at large. Economists also turned from *a priori* reasoning and the abstractions of the earlier classical school, either, as in Germany, to concrete study of the setting of economic problems in history and national society, or, as in Austria and Eng- land, to an appraisement of economic phenomena in terms of mathe- matical and physical science. Thus, while Gustav Schmoller and Adolf Wagner preached a kind of national socialism from their academic chairs at Berlin, Jevons, the leading English economist, demonstrated at least to his own satisfaction a correlation between commercial crises and sun spots.

A special importance attached after 1870 to statisticians, in part because of their indispensability to expanding business corporations and improving governmental censuses, in part because of their helpfulness to sociologists, mathematical economists, and social historians, and in part, also, because of the scientific airs they assumed. They claimed that the statistical method was the "exact" method of social science; nay more, that their method was science itself. As the foremost of them, Georg von Mayr, said: "Statistical science is the systematical statement and explanation of actual events, and of the laws of man's social life that may be deduced from these, on the basis of the quantitative observation of mathematical aggregates."

In emulation of physical and biological science and under the influence of positivism, vast masses of factual data were collected and published about man's present and past occupations and activities, about his social life, about his economic life, about his political life, about his cultural life. Never before had there been such an outpouring of doctoral dissertations, such a profusion of "scientific" monographs, such a proliferation of co-operative research and publication. Nor had there ever been such implicit faith in the social scientist's ability, by a mere marshaling of reported facts and figures, to discover the true inwardness as well as the whole outwardness of man and of human society.

The most original and reassuring contributions came from anthropologists and archaeologists about man's extraordinarily long history and his gradual ascent from savagery to civilization. A few specimens of what Boucher de Perthes called "ante-diluvian men" had been unearthed just prior to 1870. Afterwards many more were dug up, together with sufficient geological and archaeological evidence to indicate that they must have lived at a time long antedating Noah and his flood-riding ark. As excavating went feverishly on, the duration of man's "prehistoric" past rapidly lengthened. In the '80's it certainly reached to a "neolithic age," perhaps to a "palaeolithic age," anywhere from 20,000 to 100,000 years back. In the '90's the discovery of a few strange bones in faraway Java and the reconstruction from them of the singular *pithecanthropus erectus* pointed to the existence of evolving man half a million years ago and spurred on the search for still earlier creatures, half-human and half-apish, that must have climbed out of ancestral trees and laboriously learned to make fist hatchets.

Simultaneously archaeologists were re-examining the ancient classical foundations of European civilization. Schliemann, that German-American adventurer in high finance and deep digging, settled in Greece in 1868, and during the next score of years uncovered and identified the site of legendary Troy and unearthed at Mycenae and Tiryns ample proof of a civilization far antedating that of the historic Greeks. By the end of the century, thanks to the efforts of Schliemann and of many other and abler (if less self-advertised) archaeologists, it was possible to trace the history of the Aegean lands, Egypt, and Mesopotamia back several thousand years B.C.

Anthropologists, too, were exceedingly busy. Some, the "physical" group, were indefatigable in measuring skull shapes and other anatomical features of the quick and the dead and utilizing the results to classify the "races" of mankind. True, there were almost as many classifications as there were classifiers. But any such confusion failed to arrest the growing faith that there must be different races in different stages of evolution. By many physical anthropologists, notably by Francis Galton, the conclusion was drawn that an existing race could pull itself up to a higher plane, could transform its men into supermen, through obedience to "laws" of eugenics requiring the physically fit to breed and the physically unfit to practice birth control or be sterilized. In this respect, unfortunately, Galton's "fit" got mixed up about the dictates of "science"; it was they who proceeded to practice birth control.

Other anthropologists, the "cultural" sort, zealously gathered an immense miscellany of data about the speech, customs, crafts, and myths of primitive tribesmen all over the world, collated it with similar data concerning European peoples, and facilely hypothesized the evolutionary stages of man's cultural rise. Tylor published his standard textbook in 1871, and Frazer brought out the *Golden Bough* in 1890.

Comte had counseled social scientists to stick to "facts" and to refrain from metaphysical explanations. Though the generation after 1870 detested the word "metaphysical" with a horror and vehemence worthy of the master, they were too much under the spell of contemporary physics and biology, too much impressed by obvious progress in machine industry, and withal too human, not to perceive in the myriad facts they amassed a co-ordinating principle of mechanical evolution which was really metaphysical. Actually it was social scientists, more than natural scientists, who implanted this principle in the popular consciousness; and it was the postulates of social scientists, more than their facts, which inspired the most distinctive (and most varied) intellectual movements of the era: agnosticism in religion and realism in art, Marxism and integral nationalism, racialism and pacifism, enlightenment for the masses and quest of the superman.

Chapter Four

RELIGION AND THE ARTS DURING THE GENERATION OF MATERIALISM

THERE can be little doubt that the Christian religion, with its Jewish and Graeco-Roman background, had been the chief factor in creating and maintaining for centuries a sense of European solidarity, a sense of the essential oneness and distinctiveness of "European" or "Western" civilization. Without Christianity and its corollary of Christendom, "Europe" would have been an incidental geographical expression and "West" hardly distinguishable from "East." As it was, the rise and spread of Christianity during almost two millennia had provided Europe—and an extending European frontier overseas in America, South Africa, Australasia, and the Philippines—with a community of beliefs, ethics, customs, and loyalties.

In the latter part of the nineteenth century the large majority of Europeans still professed some form of Christianity, but its champions were confronted with a wave, or swift succession of waves, of criticism and attack more varied and with deeper swell than any which had previously threatened it. Hitherto, the most threatening waves had rolled in from the outside, from pagan barbarians and from Moslem Arabs and Turks, but they had ebbed or been stilled. Internal surges had, of course, been recurrent and sometimes tempestuous, but while breaking the framework of Christendom into Catholic, Orthodox, and Protestant parts, they had not seriously impaired its foundations. Throughout modern times, it is true, a secularizing process had been gradually transferring the control of one activity after another from church to state, but the states were all professedly Christian. Even the rationalism of the eighteenth century was directed less toward the subversion of Christianity than toward a simplification of theology, and it was more intimately associated with deism, pietism, and anti-clericalism than with atheism or agnosticism. Now, however, a great tidal wave swelled up within Europe, menacing the very bases of Christianity, and of all supernatural and revealed religion. Of the outcome the otherwise skeptical Huxley was certain: "That this Christianity is doomed to fall is, to my mind, beyond a doubt."[1]

To science both the critics and the apologists of Christianity usually ascribed the source of the tidal wave. This was easy to say but hard to prove without precision in the use of the word "science." When the man in the street talked about science he probably thought mainly of its practical applications to technology and public health—steam engine, dynamo, electric lighting, inoculation against disease, etc.—which, after all, had no direct bearing on religious faith. At most, applied science could only indirectly weaken faith by centering attention upon marvels of human achievement, by exalting engineers above preachers or priests, and by stimulating a greater ambition for creature comforts than for personal holiness. On the other hand, what the specialist in physics or chemistry, biology or medicine, meant by science was a particular method of observation, experimentation, and logical deduction, which was applicable only to phenomena that could be seen or handled. The "unseen world" and all "ultimates" were within the province of philosophical speculation, not of pure science; and in practice some of the most eminent scientists of the era, including Schwann, Pasteur, and Mendel, perceived no inconsistency between their laboratory findings and their profession of Christianity.

The trouble was, then, not with "pure" or "applied" science. Rather, it was with philosophical assumptions about science, and especially with the carrying over of these assumptions from natural science to so-called social science. To accept the working hypotheses of science as of equal validity with its established facts and to explain the origin and end of man, and his behavior as well as his body, in terms of mechanical physics and evolutionary biology, might be plausible, but scarcely scientific. It involved philosophy— and a philosophy which left no room for God's creation or man's soul and which repudiated therefore the fundamental postulates of Christianity.

Nor was the trouble rendered less acute by misguided and fanatical efforts of Christian apologists to avert it. Many of these failed to distinguish between the realm of scientific knowledge and that of religious faith, and in the latter between what was revealed dogma and what was merely conventional and demonstrably untenable belief. For example, they not only assailed naturalist speculation on well-authenticated facts about evolution but denied or made light of the facts themselves. Utterly forgetful of the argument of St. Augustine and other church fathers that it mattered little just how creation had occurred, they stubbornly clung to the idea of the separate creation of each species and dismissed all evidence to the contrary by heaping ridicule on anyone who would suppose that "men were descended from monkeys." Or again, many ardent Christians—especially many Protestants, who incidentally were in the habit of interpreting passages in the New Testament concerning the Lord's Supper and Peter's primacy in a figurative sense— insisted on a strict literalness in interpreting the first chapter of the Book of Genesis and accepted as equally "inspired" the biblical chronology which had been worked out by an Anglican archbishop in the seventeenth century and which precluded the existence of man prior to 4004 B.C. Scientific knowledge that man had existed long before that date was either ignored or met with some silly counter-claim such as that God had put misleading fossils into the rocks to test the faith of mankind![2]

In view of the intransigence or muddleheadedness of Christians who utilized what was imagined to be theology in order to combat what they regarded as the errors of science, it was but natural and probably inevitable that many scholars and more publicists should not only defend the substantial findings of pure science but carry a counter-offensive over into the questionable fields of philosophy and social science. Here, as we know, materialistic and deterministic assumptions were quite as impelling as the provocation of Christian

[2] Philip H. Gosse, *Omphalos, an Attempt to Untie the Geological Knot* (1857). Cf. Sir Edmund Gosse, *Father and Son* (1907), 108.

apologists, and here, then, was ample occasion for a queer sort of fight between "science" and "theology."

The fight began in earnest in the decade of the '60's over evolution and biblical criticism, and from 1871 to 1900 it raged on a wide front. The offensive passed early from "theology" to "science," whose heavy artillery was manned by such embattled Darwinians as Huxley, Tyndall, and Haeckel. Huxley neglected scientific research of his own from the '70's onward, so busy was he in the role of "Darwin's bulldog" barking and biting at theologians.[3] He rejected Christianity totally, pronouncing it "a varying compound of some of the best and some of the worst elements of paganism and Judaism, molded in practice by the innate character of certain peoples of the western world," and adding, for full measure, that "the actions we call sinful are part and parcel of the struggle for existence." Tyndall, Huxley's chief lieutenant in Britain, contended in a famous public address at Belfast in 1874 that "matter" was "the promise and potency of all terrestrial life," and pretty constantly kept up a fire against religious dogma and authority. Simultaneously another notable Briton, George Romanes, interspersed amateurish biological studies with cannon shots at basic religious beliefs; he published *A Candid Examination of Theism* in 1878, and in 1890 founded a celebrated lectureship at Cambridge to carry on the good work after his death.[4] In Germany the outstanding artilleryman was Haeckel. He was no mere agnostic. He was as sure of scientific atheism as any theologian was of Christianity, and he was neither tongue-tied nor pen-bound in proclaiming his faith.

While the big guns boomed, line after line of infantry—"higher critics," anthropologists, sociologists, psychologists—advanced unwaveringly with brand-new weapons against the old citadels of Christianity. After the initial assaults of Strauss and of the Tübingen school on the divinity and historicity of Jesus had come Renan's naturalistic explanation of Him, and then followed quickly a series of detailed destructive critiques of the Bible, the Jewish religion, and the origins of Christianity. There were Colenso's critiques in England, Kuenen's in Holland, Wellhausen's in Germany, Robertson

---

[3] *Collected Essays*, 9 vols. (1898).
[4] Romanes's last book, *Thoughts on Religion* (1895), verged strangely toward orthodoxy.

Smith's in Scotland. The last-named author, who gave wide currency to "higher criticism" in the article on the Bible which he wrote for the ninth edition of the *Encyclopædia Britannica*, finally decided that while religion has some social utility it is indistinguishable from magic. A much more temperate though still essentially critical view was taken by the era's foremost authority on Christian origins, Adolf von Harnack, whose monumental *History of Dogma* (1885-1890) stressed the influence of Greek thought on evolving Christian organization, liturgy, creed, and morals. The upshot of all such study was a spreading conviction that neither Judaism nor Christianity was unique or "revealed," that both were transient stages in the evolution of religion and superstition, and that the Bible was no truer or more "inspired" than Homer's *Iliad*.

A typical popular reaction was expressed fairly early by Matthew Arnold in his *Literature and Dogma* (1873). "What is called theology is in fact an immense misunderstanding of the Bible due to the junction of a talent for abstract reasoning combined with much literary inexperience." The Bible, he thought, should be prized as good literature, like the *Iliad*; and although one would have to dismiss as mythical its recorded prophecies and miracles, and in particular the dogmatics of its Gospel according to St. John, one might still admire the "righteousness" running through it like a theme song. Arnold's reaction was carried further by his niece, Mrs. Humphry Ward, in her enormously popular novel of *Robert Elsmere* (1888), the tale of a young clergyman who, compelled by the evidences of higher criticism to throw over Christian theology and leave the Christian Church, was moved by the spirit of righteousness to go in for social uplift and set up a creedless church for workingmen.

"Higher criticism" of Bible and Christian origins was reinforced by the work of anthropologists on comparative religion. These, too, started with evolutionary assumptions, and the data which they amassed about curious cults and ceremonies of ancient peoples and primitive tribes they presented with a view to showing the original derivation and gradual development of all modern religions from remote animism and nature worship. Major contributions to this new "social science" were made, as we have elsewhere re marked, by the Englishmen Tylor and Frazer, but the climax was reached, at least quantitatively, by a French Jew, Salomon Reinach. Reinach, who did comparatively little investigating on his own account, was indefatigable in reporting and interpreting the discoveries of a host of field workers in archaeology and cultural anthropology; he published a hundred books and five thousand articles! With literary felicity as well as facility he read signs of totemism and taboo into all the cultures of antiquity, set forth the subsequently discredited "law" of "unilinear religious evolution," and pontifically defined religion as "a sum of scruples which interfere with the free exercise of our faculties."[5]

These anti-Christian interpretations of comparative religion were incorporated, along with the materialistic and evolutionary aspects of physics, biology, and physiological psychology, into most of the sociological and philosophical systems of the period. Eugen Dühring, the crotchety German author of the "philosophy of reality," as well as of a program of national socialism, was passionate in denunciation of everything which like mysticism might veil reality, and he was almost Lucretian in his anger against religion. The only explanation of conscious and physical states, he said, was reality, that is, matter. The sociology of Herbert Spencer was as dogmatically anti-religious as it was evolutionary; and both Gumplowicz and Ratzenhofer attributed all human advance to a most un-Christian struggle between nations and races. The leading American sociologist of the time, Lester Ward, edited a violently anti-religious journal, *The Iconoclast,* and his masterpiece, the two-volume *Dynamic Sociology* (1883), contained a sweeping arraignment of religion as the chief impediment to science and progress. Marxism also, it is hardly necessary to add, was in flat contradiction with basic religious postulates, and its principal theorists, notably Engels and Kautsky, carried on, as a major operation in the class war, a strenuous campaign against traditional religion.

Social scientists are probably more inclined than physicists or biologists to step over the line separating them from mere publicists. They find it harder to subject their peculiar kind of speci-

[5] See, for summary, his *Cultes, mythes et religions,* 5 vols. (1905-1923), with an abridged English translation by Elizabeth Frost in 1 volume (1912), and his *Orphéus, histoire générale des religions* (1909).

mens—human beings—to severe laboratory tests, and easier and more tempting to lecture the specimens. At any rate, in the warfare between science and theology, it was sociologists and historians crossing back and forth between science and propaganda who most zealously urged popular enlistment against theology. Some were Marxists, seeking recruits from among a somewhat hypothetical proletariat. Many more were stalwart Positivists, with a much broader appeal. For example, John Draper, native of Liverpool and college president in New York, brought out in 1874 a stirring *History of the Conflict between Religion and Science.* Likewise, Andrew D. White, product of wealthy American parents and of study in France and Germany, and first president of Cornell University, expanded a popular lecture into a widely read booklet and eventually (in 1896) into a two-volume "best seller," *History of the Warfare of Science with Theology in Christendom.*[6] And while Bradlaugh preached atheism to the masses in England, Robert G. Ingersoll orated for thirty years in America on the "scientific" grounds for disbelief in God, in eternal punishment, and in the inspiration of the Bible. A like-minded publicist, writing shortly after the close of the period, thought the victory won by science. Once upon a time, he said, "the conception of a creative Being was simple—perhaps, in the mists of primitive ignorance, imaginable. This is true no longer. Our modern knowledge has pushed back immeasurably the limits of the world; it has disclosed the immeasurable duration of time. It has given us a rational account of the planet on which we live, the system of which we form a part. It has indicated a probable origin and a probable end."

On one important subject, that of practical ethics, there was surprisingly little conflict during the era between "scientists" and "theologians." In everyday life traditional Christian virtues were still generally held to be the highest virtues. Herbert Spencer reprobated egotism and lauded altruism and self-sacrifice with the fervor of a Franciscan friar. Karl Marx was as good a family man as any Christian bourgeois, and his apostles, who adhered to a fatalistic creed analogous to Calvinism, approached to a moral

---

[6] Cf. also W. E. H. Lecky, *History of the Rise and Influence of the Spirit of Rationalism in Europe,* 2 vols. (London, 1866), new ed. (London, 1890).

puritanism reminiscent of Calvin's Geneva. Almost all the evolutionary philosophers imagined that progress was upward and on toward complete fulfillment of the "good life" already foreshadowed in the Christian myth. Almost everybody who shared Haeckel's conclusion that man must be an insignificant cog in the cosmic machine of matter, persisted in treating him practically as if he were endowed with the high dignity of personality and entitled to the justice and mercy explicit in the Sermon on the Mount.

This curious divorce of morals from beliefs, this paradoxical retention of the one and rejection of the other, represented what later sociologists have described as a time lag. Shift in moral attitudes did not keep pace with shift in religious beliefs. It was apparently easier to change one's ideas about the universe than to alter one's pattern of personal and social behavior.

It was not that ethical speculation was lacking or traditional morality spared from attack. Nietzsche, for instance, did not hesitate to follow up the assault on Christian theology with a polemic against Christian morality. This, he declared, was a slave morality, useless and outgrown. Its ideals of sacrifice, generosity, and gentleness had no foundation in nature; its extolling of "the good, the true, and the beautiful" was purely illusory. The appropriate morality for the future race of supermen, he prophesied, would be built on man's instinctive will to power and would require a ruthless trampling of the strong upon the weak. Nietzsche's gospel, however, made no big conquests immediately. Its converts were mainly confined, during the era, to a coterie of youthful writers who were enamored by the form of *Thus Spake Zarathustra* as much as by its philosophic content.

Most ethical speculation showed less concern with devising a new morality than with seeking a new and non-religious justification for the old morality. Spencer sought it in a naturalistic "moral sense" which had been evolved like any other feature of man. Henry Sidgwick, professor at Cambridge and easily the most influential moralist of the generation, sought it in a combination of Mill's utilitarianism with Kant's notion of conscience as an innate "categorical imperative."[7] The search in either direction was not

7 *The Methods of Ethics* (1874), 7th ed. (1907).

very rewarding, and at the end of the era James Ward, Sidgwick's successor at Cambridge, who had studied physiological psychology under Wundt at Leipzig, confessed that the only solid and sane base he could find for ethics was an idealistic and theistic interpretation of the universe.[8]

Here, at the end, was disquieting revolt, on moral grounds, against that philosophy of materialism which had been ascendant for thirty years and more. The revolt refortified the idealistic castles of Thomas Hill Green in England and of Rudolf Eucken in Germany, and in turn it received fresh impetus from Henri Bergson's vitalism in France and Benedetto Croce's neo-Hegelianism in Italy. Though affording slight comfort to orthodox religion, it served, along with impending revolution in physical science, to arrest and to "date" the epochal "warfare of science and theology."

II. THE DRIFT AWAY FROM TRADITIONAL RELIGION AND THE RISE OF MODERNISM

Most front-line fighters under the banner of "science," flushed with initial successes, expected an utter rout of traditional religion, though Huxley cautioned that it would be "neither sudden nor speedy." Actually, no rout occurred; and to attribute the retreat which did take place solely to the campaign of science against theology is a gross exaggeration. The active campaigners were relatively few; they constituted a small professional force, not a conscript army, and although they partially compensated in quality for what they lacked in quantity, they had no monopoly of brains or prowess. They included many eminent scientists and literary men, but also a disproportionate share of pseudo-intellectuals whose self-esteem exceeded their competence and whose tendency to gallop gaily into untenable positions was the despair of soberer and more calculating comrades.[9]

---

8 *Naturalism and Agnosticism* (1899).

9 This despair must have possessed Huxley when he wrote in his last years: "It is the secret of the superiority of the best theological teachers to the majority of their opponents that they substantially recognize the realities of things, however strange the forms in which they clothe their conceptions. The doctrines of predestination, of original sin, of the innate depravity of man and the evil fate of the greater part of the race, of the primacy of Satan in this world, of the essential vileness of matter, of a malevolent Demiurgus subordinate to a benevolent Almighty, who has only lately revealed himself, faulty as they are, appear to me to be vastly nearer the truth than

The real significance of the campaign lay in the fact that it capped and gave timely direction to hostile or indifferent attitudes which had been engendered by quite other developments. It was a weather vane for a variety of winds which the circumambient *Zeitgeist* exhaled.

A secularizing development had long been manifest, a gradual transference of social functions from church to state, from clergymen to laymen. It had made big strides during the Reformation in Protestant countries, and since the French Revolution in Catholic countries. By the 1870's, throughout western and central Europe, it was reaching the goal of state-directed lay education and charity and was affecting organized religion in two deleterious ways. On the one hand it accustomed the masses to look to the secular state as the ultimate source of light and sustenance and to regard the church as a superfluity or luxury, like the theater, which one attended or stayed away from according to one's habit or whim. In other words it made for indifference toward religion. On the other hand, in branding as "clericals" those who attempted to arrest or reverse the secularizing trend and condemning them to a losing battle, it extended and invigorated "anti-clericalism."

Anti-clericalism, in some degree, had always been a natural reaction to historic Christianity's segregation of clergy from laity. Laymen who were taught to respect clergymen as divinely called to administer the sacraments, preach the Gospel, and govern the Church, who were not allowed to participate in their selection or counsel, and who at the same time observed their human frailties or differed with them about political and temporal affairs, such laymen were at least potential anti-clericals. They might be good practicing Christians, quite orthodox in theology, and yet be critical of priests and bishops and anxious to confine their activities within narrowly religious limits. And when, in modern times, many high-placed clergymen defended an unpopular political or social system

---

the 'liberal' popular illusions that babies are all born good, and that the example of a corrupt society is responsible for their failure to remain so; that it is given to everybody to reach the ethical ideal if he will only try; that all partial evil is universal good, and other optimistic figments, such as that which represents 'Providence' under the guise of a paternal philanthropist, and bids us believe that everything will come right (according to our notions) at last."—"An Apologetic Eirenicon," in *Fortnightly Review*, n.s., LII (1892), 569.

and opposed popularly supported legislation, anti-clericalism grew and took on new significance as a cause or a slogan which could be utilized by irreligious politicians to rally an increasing number of "born" Christians who seldom if ever went to church. Anti-clericalism, of course, by reason of the difference between Catholic and Protestant conceptions of the clergy, was more usual and disturbing in Catholic than in Protestant countries, although the attitude of non-conforming sectarians toward established Protestant churches, as in England and Prussia, surely savored of anti-clericalism.

With or without express anti-clericalism, there was a strong tendency in the nineteenth century to associate the fortunes of Christianity with those of outmoded political and social institutions. Whether in Catholic or in Protestant countries, the higher clergy were apt to come from aristocratic or plutocratic families and to direct a wistful thinking of their subordinates and of the faithful generally toward the "good old days" of the "union of throne and altar," and of the static agricultural society in which the masses had obediently followed the dictates of their superiors. Such "reactionary" tendency had been strengthened by the stand which all the major Christian bodies perforce took against "excesses" of the French Revolution and still more by the romantic religious revival of the early decades of the nineteenth century, which served to disinfect the nobility and a large part of the upper middle class of previous rationalist errors and to win them back to Christian faith and practice. By the 1870's organized Christianity seemed in clear and definite alliance with ultra-conservative against radical elements, with aristocracy and *haute bourgeoisie* against petty bourgeoisie and urban masses. The great majority of peasants still adhered to it from habit, but the alienation of industrial proletariat and lower middle class made rapid headway after 1871 in France, Austria, Italy, Spain, Russia, Britain, Scandinavia, and northern Germany.

Both the sectarian liberalism of the '60's and '70's and the socialism of Karl Marx proved powerful magnets in drawing urban dwellers away from traditional religion. In a sense they were substitute religions. Liberalism of the older ecumenical sort had at least some of its roots in the Christian tradition, but the newer sectarian liberalism on the Continent was not merely anti-clerical but rampantly anti-Christian. Its philosophy was utilitarian and positivist, and its adepts warmly sympathetic to the evolutionary and materialistic aspects of natural and social science. Entrenched in radical political parties, in Continental Freemasonry, and in propagandist societies like the French *League of the Rights of Man*, it actuated much of that legislation looking toward the complete laicizing of the state and popular education and the minimizing of any ecclesiastical influence which we have outlined in a previous chapter.

However much Marxian socialists might assail the economic tenets of liberalism—its devotion to capitalism and its sanctification of the freedom of contract—and however much they might denounce its practical incitement to self-seeking and profiteering, they were blood brothers to the sectarian liberals in basic philosophy and trench comrades with them in warfare against "religious superstition." The only difference was that Marxians were a bit more valorous; they made frontal attacks, while Liberals were engaged in flanking movements. Marxian socialism was dogmatically materialist and determinist. Its goal was a strictly earthy paradise, and its declared method of reaching the goal was through class conflict and the abolition of private property. And its tactics involved counter missionary enterprise against religion as "opiate of the people" and against the churches as "tools of capitalism."

Both socialism and liberalism drew inspiration and weight from the development of machine industry and the attendant magnifying of urban centers. Indeed, this development, so thoroughly characteristic of the decades after 1870, was itself of prime importance in promoting indifference, if not hostility, to the claims of traditional religion. It made the marvels of technology seem greater and more useful than those of religion. It promised to assure human comfort and happiness without recourse to prayer or creed. It produced new forms of popular entertainment and diversion more alluring than the old round of church feasts and fasts. By stimulating extensive migration from field to factory, from country-side to city, it uprooted a large fraction of Europe's population and broke it loose from ancestral traditions and usages, especially those of religion. Relatively few priests or pastors accompanied the emigrants from rural communities, and city churches were too few or too cold and strange to attract the host of new arrivals.

Finally, among major developments of the era was nationalism. It might conceivably have been compatible with historic Christianity, for the Protestant and Eastern Orthodox churches had always been markedly national and the Catholic Church had recognized the principle of nationality and made frequent concessions to it. Nevertheless, in its emergent totalitarian form, nationalism was subversive of Christian teaching and tradition. Like Marxian socialism, it was a rival religion. Its concern was not with Christendom but with the nation, not with Christian ideals of the brotherhood of man under the fatherhood of God, but with the superiority and forceful expansion of a particular national "race." It was inordinately jealous of any international or supranational religion which might divide the allegiance of citizens and dampen their patriotic ardor, and hence it reinforced the anti-clericalism of Marxists and Liberals. Of course, wherever a long-established form of Christianity had taken on a national complexion, prominent nationalists were likely to entertain a sentimental regard for it and to encourage the masses to do likewise, but in such situations the appeal, for example of Barrès in France or D'Annunzio in Italy, was not to any absolute truth in Christianity but rather to its charm and value as a national asset.

Each of the developments here indicated—"science," secularization, industrialization, liberalism, Marxism, and nationalism—had originated before 1871, some of them several generations before; and it was only because they were pretty fully matured and producing joint effects that the generation of materialism from 1871 to 1900 stands out as marking a grave religious crisis, or rather the first stage in a crisis which has continued to the present day and which poses the fundamental question whether European or Western civilization can endure if cut off from its historic Christian roots. The net results of the whittling away at these roots during the generation from 1871 to 1900 were the outright repudiation of Christianity by a sizable minority of Europeans, the drift of a much larger number away from any but the most perfunctory Christian observance, and the rise of conflict among the defenders of Christianity as to how much or little of it was reconcilable with the newer "modernist" developments.

The outright seceders from Christianity comprised, in the main, three groups: a comparatively large percentage of the "intellectual class," especially of professional literary men and of university scholars in the fields of natural and social science; a sprinkling of more or less influential persons among the learned professions of medicine, law, journalism, and education and among the petty bourgeoisie of booksellers and other shopkeepers; and a rapidly increasing quota of urban workingmen. Most of the last and a few in the other groups were converts to Marxian socialism. The rest sought refuge in a positivist "religion of humanity" or "religion of nationalism," in a creedless "ethical culture," in a vague pantheism, or, most commonly perhaps, in mere agnosticism. They gave substance as well as tone to Radical political parties throughout western and central Europe and swelled the forces of opposition to the Tsarist regime in Russia.

Outright secessionists, it must be borne in mind, constituted a minority of the total population of Europe, as did likewise the active defenders of dogmatic Christianity. The majority went their wonted way, evincing more and more interest in scientific achievement, in nationalism, in liberalism or socialism, but still adhering formally to the religion of their fathers. With many, such adherence grew lukewarm and tenuous. This was more noticeable among men than among women, in urban centers than in the countryside, and in France (even in rural districts of France), in Scandinavia, and in certain parts of Austria and Italy than in Russia, Ireland, Spain, or the Rhenish countries. Wherever it was in evidence, it involved a waning support of church activities, an access of anti-clerical sentiment, and a progressive abstention from ecclesiastical services except highly personal and ceremonial ones like christening, first communion, confirmation, marriages and funerals.

Among the active proponents of Christianity—those who busied themselves with warding off the attacks of seceders and overcoming the indifference of drifters—and consequently among the portion of European population that still maintained a strong religious loyalty, differences appeared of tactics and of apologetic trend. Where a church was closely linked with a state and that state dominated by an ultra-conservative regime, as in the Russian Empire, the authority of the civil government was employed to safeguard religious orthodoxy and to penalize agnostics and dissenters. There, force or the threat of force obviated any argument.

In central and western Europe, however, where statesmen were more inclined to public neutrality, where the irreligious and antireligious campaign was more vocal and vital, and where therefore churchmen had to rely pretty exclusively on argument and moral persuasion, the basic lines of Christian defense were thrown out in three directions. One was toward what for lack of a better title may be described by the later American term of "fundamentalism," a rigidly uncompromising position in support of conventional Christian beliefs, particularly an insistence on the absolute literal truth of the Bible and on the inherent falsity of Darwinian evolution and every other "scientific" theory at variance with it. This line was manned principally and most vociferously by members of evangelical Protestant sects, and with a kind of foolhardiness by some individual Lutherans, Calvinists, low-church Anglicans, and even Catholics whose zeal outstripped their knowledge.[10] Its ranks perceptibly thinned with the lapse of time.

The second—and more enduring—line aimed also at preserving historic dogmatic Christianity, whether Catholic or Protestant, but simultaneously at showing that it was not in conflict with actual findings of science and scholarship. The gist of the argument here was that current discoveries about the material universe and the antiquity of man did not disprove the existence of God and the spiritual universe; that Darwin's evolutionary hypothesis, if true, could explain only certain physical aspects of creation, not ultimate causes or the creation and functioning of man's soul; that contemporary higher criticism of the Bible and the church was destruc-

[10] An odd extension of this line was the Christian Science movement, which originated in America in the '70's and later secured some slight following in western Europe. Though "scientific" in name and "modern" in its practical solicitude for physical health, it was radically anti-materialist and in theology essentially fundamentalist. The Salvation Army, founded in England in 1880, in so far as it had a theology, was also fundamentalist.

tive and biased, but that, if pursued constructively in truly scholarly fashion, it would only confirm the uniqueness and validity of Christian teaching; and that the Bible, anyway, was not a textbook in science and that parts of it, as early church fathers had fully recognized, were susceptible of allegorical as well as literal interpretation. This was the line taken officially for the Catholic Church by the remarkable pope of the period—of whom we shall say more in the next section. It was likewise taken, with various deviations here and there, by thoughtful conservative theologians and sizeable groups of "orthodox" laymen in the major Protestant churches.

The third line was far more sensational. It looked toward a radical reorientation of Christianity in the light of modern science, a bringing of religion "up to date." This modernism, as it was called, would frankly accept Darwinism and the implications of current higher criticism. Accordingly, it would discard miracles, including the primary ones of Christ's incarnation and resurrection. It would stress the beauty rather than the truth of the Bible and the Christian religion, prizing the former as fine literature and the Founder of the latter as a poetical idealist or social reformer. It would do without dogmas and would derive Christian morals not from revelation but from experience.

Modernism eventually affected some Catholic priests and publicists to such an extent that shortly after the turn of the century the papacy felt obliged to anathematize it and to take drastic measures to repress it. But while it thus produced a brief and passing spasm within the Catholic Church, it found comfortable perduring lodgment and wrought a veritable revolution within Protestantism. To appreciate the nature and significance of this revolution, we may recall here certain peculiarities of Protestant Christianity, leaving those of Catholic Christianity for treatment in the next section.

Protestantism was more favorable than Catholicism to the rise of modernism, for in general it was more adaptable to the whole complex of intellectual and industrial developments during the era of materialism. Industrialism, which had begun in overwhelmingly Protestant England, permeated most thoroughly the predominantly Protestant countries of Germany and America, and Protestant apologists delighted to identify the ideal of material progress and capitalistic prosperity with the rugged individualism and sober thrift of traditional Protestant ethics. Moreover, the individualism of Protestantism, especially of its more radical forms, seemed peculiarly harmonious with the individualism of economic liberalism and political democracy. Then, too, the major Protestant churches had always been national churches, subservient to secular government and responsive to patriotic emotion; they could foster and profit from the newer nationalism. But still greater incentives to adaptation were supplied by a curious paradox of Protestantism in the latest age. On one side, it was extraordinarily embarrassed and upset by the devastating higher criticism of the Bible, inasmuch as in rejecting the papacy and ecclesiastical authority it had exalted the Bible as the sole rule of individual faith and conduct. On the other side, it was enabled and driven to find ways out of the embarrassment by invoking the distinctively Protestant "right of private judgment," that is, by allowing each Protestant to put his own interpretation on the Bible as well as on "science."

It followed therefore that while many Protestants took the extreme "fundamentalist" position and many others the moderate conservative attitude, a gradually growing number became radically modernist. These remained Protestant Christians in name and actual church membership but they adapted church creeds and the Bible itself to the latest fashions in scientific speculation and higher criticism. They had their snuggest home in an intellectual sect like the Unitarian, but they gradually made fruitful gardens for themselves in leading theological seminaries, whether Lutheran, Anglican, Calvinist, or evangelical. And as there was no central authority in any of the Protestant churches capable of effectual opposition to modernism, it was fairly rapidly communicated from Protestant seminaries to the rising generation of Protestant clergymen and thence, ever more widely and deeply, to Protestant laymen. By the end of the nineteenth century, a modernist change was occurring in Protestantism far more revolutionary than that religious upheaval of the sixteenth century in which Protestantism had originated.

Innumerable, of course, were the gradations of modernism within

Protestant churches. What distinguished it as a whole was its evolutionary attitude toward religion in general and Christianity in
particular. It perceived in history a steady, ever higher evolution
of man's religious experience, from primitive myths to early Christianity and from "superstitious" Catholicism to "enlightened"
Protestantism. Such an attitude was as antithetical to orthodox
Protestant as to Catholic tradition. It involved a sharp reversal of
the Protestant habit of seeking pure religion in an old volume
and identifying ecclesiastical reform with a return to primitive
Christianity.

It likewise involved a quaint shift of emphasis from "faith" to
"good works." Protestants had previously been as dogmatic and
theological as any Catholic about the central articles of Christian
faith and extremely fond of Luther's "justification by faith," but
now, to modernist Protestants, faith became nebulous and the
words "dogma" and "theology" almost as repulsive as the word
"superstition." Yet these same Protestants evinced extraordinary
concern with justification by "good works," not the old theological
ones, to be sure, but those of modern humanitarianism: social
uplift, popular education, public health, and crusades against alcoholism, against juvenile delinquency, against cruelty to animals.
And as dogmatic theology receded, moral theology retreated.
"Good works" were to be judged less by any absolute standard
proclaimed once for all from Sinai than by the relative standard
of experimental utility.

Protestantism remained, with probably as many communicants
in 1900 as in 1871, but almost all its numerous churches and sects
were confronted with a rising tide of outside criticism and with a
marked inside drift away from traditional beliefs and practices.
It was becoming at the end of the nineteenth century a different
thing from what it had been in the sixteenth and seventeenth centuries. Its one tight link with the past was the right of private
judgment. By clinging to this a new modernist Protestantism could
go on "protesting" against the Roman Church and do some novel
"protesting" against fundamentalism and other survivals of historic
Protestantism.

Developments of the era had analogous and equally disturbing effects upon Judaism. Historically, Judaism was a tribal religion, based not only on the ancient Hebrew Bible but also on the progressive elaboration of an essentially tribal way of life—social, ceremonial, and dietary. Now it was confronted with two distinct yet related problems: how to preserve its tribal character and separate community life in the face of spreading liberalism and mounting nationalism; and how to preserve its religious faith against the flood of materialist philosophy, biblical criticism, and modernism. On these problems Jews divided into three camps. One consisted of those who, while still thinking of themselves as Jews in "race," drifted away from the Jewish religion, severed any connection with the synagogue, and, like the outright seceders from Christianity, became frankly agnostic or devotedly Marxian. The second camp, including the bulk of Jews in eastern Europe, remained severely orthodox, resisting higher criticism and holding to all the traditional Jewish laws and observances; they were comparable with the fundamentalists among Christians. The third, waxing strong in central and western Europe (and in America) became "reformed," which was another name for modernist; in various ways they rationalized and universalized their religion, abbreviating its ritual, softening or neglecting its special laws, and approximating it to the contemporary Unitarian and Ethical Culture movements in Protestantism.

It will be noted that religion was least disturbed in eastern Europe. Here, Eastern Orthodox Christianity and Judaism, and also Islam, held to their respective creeds and rites and retained the allegiance of their customary followers. In central and western Europe, on the other hand, the disturbance was acute and profound. It induced a surge of agnosticism and skepticism. It gave rise to modernistic Protestantism and Judaism. It immensely troubled the largest of Europe's religious communions, the Catholic Church.

III. PONTIFICATE OF LEO XIII

When Pius IX died on February 7, 1878, after the longest and one of the stormiest pontificates in Christian history, the Catholic Church seemed to be at losing feud with the whole modern world, intellectually, politically, and morally. Its influence on the life and thought of the fashioners of public opinion—leading men of letters, journalists, educators, and scholars—was fast disappearing, and its hold was gone on a large fraction of the bourgeoisie and on the bulk of the urban proletariat. It appeared impotent to dike anywhere the flood tide of "science," liberalism, Marxism, anti-clericalism, and secularization. Its foes had mastered Italy and despoiled the church of its age-old capital city and of a vast deal of popular prestige. They were dominant in Austria and Switzerland, and were waging in Germany a bitter Kulturkampf against it. They had recently assailed it with revolutionary ardor in Spain, and in Belgium they were just returning to power and battle. Likewise in France, "the eldest daughter of the church," foes of Catholicism in the guise of Radical Republicans were besting its friends, the Monarchists. And in England, the "second spring" which the Oxford movement once promised had proved disappointingly backward. The definition of papal infallibility at the Vatican Council in 1870 seemed a Pyrrhic victory for the papacy; if it closed the Catholic ranks, it also depleted them and aggravated enemy attacks.

With fear and trembling sixty-four elderly cardinals entered the conclave in the Vatican to choose Pius's successor. To forestall possible external interference, they acted quickly; and on the third scrutiny, on February 20, they chose Cardinal Pecci, the scion of an impoverished noble family,[11] who took the title of Leo XIII. He was already close to sixty-eight years of age and had been archbishop of Perugia for thirty-two years. He was almost unknown outside Italy, except by the few who recalled him as papal nuncio to Belgium back in the 1840's. His election was a makeshift. He was frail and not expected to live long.

Yet Leo XIII lived on a quarter century to the age of ninety-three, acquiring fame comparable with any medieval pope's. This unexpected outcome was a product of his personal qualities and of changing circumstances of his pontificate. Leo might be frail of physique, but within his emaciated body resided a brilliant mind and an iron will. He was, too, a humanist, at once artist and scholar, and cultured man of the world. A facile writer of Latin verse and

---

[11] His father had been a colonel in the Italian army of Napoleon Bonaparte, and his mother was descended from the medieval revolutionary, Cola di Rienzi!

Ciceronian prose, he also had sympathetic understanding of the intellectual problems of the modern age and a singular practicality in dealing with them. He was as determined as any of his predecessors to combat materialism, agnosticism, and indifferentism, but he was not content simply to repeat the anathemas of Pius IX. He must constructively expound Christian alternatives.

In almost the first of his long series of encyclicals—the *Æterni Patris* of 1879—Leo pointed to the medieval scholastic philosophy of St. Thomas Aquinas, with its reconciling of faith and reason, of theology and "science," as the fundamental corrective of the vagaries of modern philosophy, and urged its revival and extension. To this end he founded and endowed at Rome an academy bearing the great schoolman's name, directed the preparation and publication of a new edition of the *Summa*, and patronized centers for neo-Thomistic study at Louvain, Paris, Fribourg, and Salzburg, and also at the Catholic University of America which he personally chartered in 1889. Similarly, he encouraged the study of church history, opening the Vatican archives and library to historical research in 1883, and honoring such scholars as Newman and Hergenröther (whom he made cardinals in 1879), Denifle, Grisar, Pastor, Gasquet, Mancini, Ulysse Chevalier, Luchaire, Duchesne, and Baudrillart. He also fostered Christian archaeology and biblical studies; and to demonstrate his respect for natural science he procured an eminent staff of physicists and the most up-to-date instruments for the astronomical observatory at the Vatican.

Of the political principles of Pius IX, Leo XIII professed not to change an iota. He insisted that the Catholic Church is a perfect society in itself, whose authority in its own spiritual realm is, by divine institution, independent of and superior to the authority of any temporal state or sovereignty, and hence that it should occupy a privileged position in the state. Yet he was never a "reactionary" in the earlier sense. He contended, especially in the encyclicals *Immortale Dei* (1885) and *Libertas* (1888), that democracy is as compatible with Catholic philosophy and tradition as any other modes of civil government, and that real personal liberty, as distinct from sectarian liberalism, has its firmest base and surest prop in Catholic Christianity. He would Christianize democracy and liberty.

Church support of the current trend toward democracy, Leo perceived, might be serviceable to the church. It would show the masses that they could expect the fulfillment of their political aspirations under Catholic as well as non-Catholic auspices, and it might thus bring them back to the faithful practice of their religion. A like policy, looking toward the same end, Leo pursued in respect of popular demands for social reform. He would Christianize modern industrial society; and for such a Catholic social movement his most famous encyclical, *Rerum novarum* (1891), supplied chart and inspiration. Against Marxian socialism this document defended private property as a natural right, emphasized the key importance of the family, protested against the exalting of the state, condemned the doctrines of economic materialism and determinism, and declared that "class is not naturally hostile to class." On the other hand, against economic liberalism, it held that "labor is not a commodity," that "it is shameful to treat men like chattels to make money by," that the state has both right and duty to prevent the exploitation of labor, to encourage collective bargaining, and to enact social legislation. Specifically the encyclical urged a wider distribution of private property, a fostering of industrial trade-unions and agricultural co-operative undertakings, a restriction of the hours of employment, especially of women and children, and the assurance of a "living family wage." It stressed the dignity of labor and stated that "everyone has the right to procure what is required to live." It dwelt upon the part which religion in general and Christianity in particular should perform in bringing about a better social order, and it besought the co-operation of Catholics everywhere.

The response to this as to other pleas of Leo XIII was not altogether gratifying. Many Catholic employers paid little attention to it and it did not stop the spread of Marxian socialism among workingmen, just as the Pope's democratic counsels went unheeded by numerous Catholic aristocrats and snobs, or just as, in the general intellectual life of Europe, there was no marked abatement of materialism and positivism. Yet the response was considerable. In

Germany, Belgium, Austria-Hungary, Switzerland, and Holland, well-knit Catholic parties subscribed to Leo's platform of Christian democracy and Christian liberty, and gained large popular followings. In these countries, moreover, and also in France and elsewhere, the Leonine social movement gradually developed, with attendant Catholic trade-unions and Catholic propaganda among urban and rural workers. Thereby, new energy was infused into Catholic ranks, and the drift away from the church was checked among the masses as among the classes. "We must not have any illusions on this score," said a prominent French Marxist in 1898; "the only redoubtable adversary which confronts revolutionary socialism is organized Catholicism, which now has a social conscience and is a party of concessions."[12]

The organizing of Catholics on the religious, intellectual, social, and political *terrains* was an outstanding achievement of the pontificate of Leo XIII. Its climax was the series of Eucharistic Congresses, inaugurated in 1881, which, by bringing together in one city after another throughout Christendom ever vaster multitudes of worshipers, periodically testified in most impressive manner to the hold which their religion had upon them.

Certain circumstances in the Europe of the '80's and '90's aided Catholic activity. There was widespread reaction against economic liberalism and against the doctrinaire liberal parties which championed it and which had been the spearhead of anti-clericalism. There was a new concern with overseas imperialism and with the Christian missions which fortified it; as Gambetta pithily said, "anti-clericalism is not a proper export commodity." Besides, there was almost a panic among statesmen and propertied citizens over the advance of Marxian socialism and a consequent anxiety to oppose it with a coalition of conservative forces, including those of religion and especially those of well-organized Catholicism. All such circumstances made it easier for Leo XIII than it had been for Pius IX to come to terms with secular governments, and Leo was not slow to utilize for this purpose his notable diplomatic talents as well as his personal prestige.

In Italy alone no improvement was effected in the relations of

[12] Hubert Lagardelle, *Le Devenir social* (1898), 81.

church and state. Leo resolutely stuck to his predecessor's policy of denouncing the "usurpation" of Rome by the Italian government, immuring himself as a "prisoner of the Vatican," prohibiting the participation of Italian Catholics in Italian politics, and inviting foreign intervention. Such abiding intransigence was not without advantage abroad. It prevented the papacy from being subordinated to Italian national interests, and it stimulated ubiquitous sympathy for the pope as a "martyr" and attracted to him a stream of foreign visitors and funds. In Italy, however, it had serious disadvantages. It left the state entirely in the hands of radical anti-clericals, and although these did not quite venture to violate the Catholic conscience at home and abroad by carrying their hostility to its logical conclusion, they perpetually pinpricked the papacy and helped to alienate large numbers of the Italian people from all but the most casual observance of their religion.

There might have been—and eventually there was—equally serious trouble for the Catholic Church in France. Here its historic alliance with the royalist cause cost it much popular favor, and when republicans got control at the end of the '70's they proceeded forthwith to secularize education, to suppress religious congregations, and to enact other "laic laws." They would probably have gone still farther had it not been for the consistently conciliatory attitude of Leo XIII. He was pro-French in personal sentiment and eager not to embitter relations with a country most likely to back him in his quarrel with Italy. If his earnest entreaty of 1892 to French Catholics to support the Republic had been loyally obeyed by all of them instead of by a mere fraction—the so-called Ralliés —it is extremely doubtful whether the tide of French anti-clericalism would have risen to the height it did after his death.

The only other worsening of affairs for the church was in Hungary, where in the '90's a belatedly Liberal prime minister, Dr. Alexander Wekerle, against the expostulations of the pope and the strenuous opposition of the local Catholic party, put through some drastic anti-clerical measures; and in Austria, where a Pan-German "Los von Rom" movement made progress among German nationalists in certain localities highly critical of the court-controlled hierarchy. In Austria, nevertheless, the losses were more than counterbalanced by the rise of the Christian Socialist party and its success, under the inspiriting leadership of Karl Lueger, in enrolling large sections of the Viennese masses as well as of the peasantry and thus becoming the most numerous political party.

In Germany the ably led and well-disciplined Catholic Center party succeeded, through adroit combinations with other groups, in putting a stop to the Kulturkampf in 1880 and constraining Bismarck himself to "go to Canossa." He resumed full diplomatic relations with the Vatican in 1881, and consented in 1886 to the repeal of the most oppressive of the earlier anti-Catholic laws. In Belgium, the sectarian liberal regime was supplanted, following decisive elections of 1884, by a Catholic government, which reestablished diplomatic relations with the papacy in 1885, and which only strengthened its continuing dominance by the democratic franchise it introduced in 1893. In Spain the restored Bourbon monarchy abrogated most of the anti-Catholic measures of the previous revolutionary period, and neither there nor in Portugal did any serious new crisis arise between church and state during Leo's pontificate.

Under Leo XIII, Catholics notably increased their numbers in Switzerland, in the Dutch Netherlands, and, most strikingly, in English-speaking countries. A Scottish hierarchy was re-established in 1878 after the lapse of three hundred years. In England the trickle of converts, particularly from Anglicanism, was steady; and, what was more curious, the rapid development of an Anglo-Catholic movement within the Church of England served not only to offset in part the drift of other Anglicans toward modernism but also to accustom Englishmen in general to Catholic practices and attitudes. And the continuously heavy migration from militantly Catholic Ireland laid foundations for a greatly enlarged and extended Catholic Church in the United States and throughout the British Empire.

Leo XIII hoped and labored for an ending of the schisms and divisions which had long existed in Christianity and which gravely handicapped it in the crucial conflict with irreligion. He appealed to Protestants in letters of 1893 on the Bible and of 1894 on Christian reunion. He addressed special pleas to the Eastern Orthodox

Church in 1894 and to Anglicans in 1895.[13] It was all unavailing. He neither would nor could contemplate any reunion which did not involve agreement with the dogmas of the Roman Church and acceptance of papal supremacy—and this the dissident churches quite as stubbornly refused. Christian disunion had had too long and too sore a history to be suddenly ended.

IV. CHRISTIAN MISSIONARY ENTERPRISE

If Christianity was on the defensive in Europe, it certainly conducted a vigorous offensive, during the generation of materialism, outside Europe. It had always been a zealously proselytizing religion; and in the last three decades of the nineteenth century it flung its outposts farther afield and won more converts than in any earlier period of like duration.

Paradoxically enough, contemporary materialism had an important share in this latest spiritual adventure. The very industrialization which nourished materialistic philosophy furnished unexampled means and opportunities for Christian missions. It made possible a wider and more effective organization of missionary societies within Europe (and America). It enabled these, by the cheap mechanical printing and transport which it proliferated, to flood the Christian population with propaganda favorable to foreign missions; and it provided them, from the wealth which it accumulated, with greatly increased financial support. Moreover, as industrialization led to a big expansion of European trade with, and capital-investment in, the other and more "backward" continents, and hence on to a climactic stage of European imperialism, it followed that Christian missionaries had special incentive and exceptional opportunity to establish themselves in those continents. Even the most materialistic statesmen and citizens, who were quite unsympathetic with Christianity or any supernatural religion and who directed or backed anti-clerical policies at home, were likely to abet Christian missions abroad as steppingstones or bulwarks

---

13 There was much talk in the '90's, on the part of leading Anglo-Catholics and of some Continental Catholics, about "corporate reunion" of the Church of England with Rome. It was stilled by Leo XIII's pronouncement, in 1896, that Anglican orders, unlike those of the Eastern Orthodox Church, were invalid. The Russian nationalist and Orthodox Christian Vladimir Soloviev (1853-1900) advocated cooperation with Roman Catholicism.

to the imperialism of their respective nations. Perhaps, also, many ardent Christians found in distant missionary activities a welcome relief from the materialism and indifferentism they met with in Europe. At any rate it is not without interest that France, supposedly the most de-Christianized of all the European nations, supplied more Catholic missionaries and larger funds for them than all other countries combined, or that the vast majority of Protestant missionaries came from the most highly industrialized and presumably the most materialistic nations, England and the United States.

In 1868 Lavigerie, the most famous Catholic missionary since Francis Xavier, began his labors in North Africa; and the order of White Fathers, which he founded shortly afterwards for the conversion of the Dark Continent, soon became a major auxiliary to the much older Société des Missions Étrangères and a prime stimulus to the multiplication of Catholic missions all over the world by other religious orders—Franciscans, Dominicans, Jesuits, etc.— and also by the German Society of the Divine Word and the Belgian Society of Scheat. In December 1872 the Church of England inaugurated an annual "day of intercession for missions," and less than five months later the much-publicized death of David Livingstone on the faraway shore of Lake Tanganyika aroused all Protestantism to new missionary endeavors. In 1880 and again in 1884 Pope Leo XIII eloquently urged upon Catholics the "primary duty" of spreading the gospel. In 1885 Cambridge University, reputed the hub of materialistic science and philosophy, rolled a famous band of young Protestant graduates out to an "inland mission" in China; and in 1886 arose in America the "Student Volunteer Movement," which, with its watchword "the evangelization of the world in this generation," spread presently to England and by 1900 enlisted from various colleges and universities some three thousand members, half of whom became active foreign missionaries. For Protestants an ecumenical missionary congress was held at New York in 1900, and for Catholics the concurrent celebration of a jubilee year was attended by an impressive missionary exhibition in the venerable offices of the Propaganda at Rome.

By 1900 the army of Christian missionaries in Africa, Asia, and Oceania was comparable in size and morale with the expeditionary forces of any great power. The Catholic contingent numbered about 41,000, comprising 8,000 European priests, 6,000 native priests, and 27,000 sisters and lay brothers. Protestants counted some 18,000, consisting of 5,700 European (and American) clergymen, 5,000 native clergymen, 2,800 laymen, and 4,500 unmarried women. The Orthodox added 2,000 priests and religious. The grand total of 61,000 was unprecedented in the long history of Christian missions, as was also the large proportion of medically trained missionaries who sought in heathen lands the cure of bodies as well as souls, and the still larger proportion of women. Feminism has usually been deemed a product of modern industrialism and "radical" philosophy, but the latter factor loses much of its cogency in minds that recall the tens of thousands of Catholic nuns and Protestant women workers who after 1870 made their way, unattended by mere males, on mission fields far distant from family and friends.

From large-scale planting, a considerable crop was harvested. The Catholic Church registered its growing gains by the establishment of full-fledged hierarchies for China in 1875, for northern Africa in 1884 (with Lavigerie as Cardinal Archbishop of "Carthage"), for India in 1886, and for Japan in 1891. When the century closed, Catholics numbered two and a quarter million in India, a million in China, sixty thousand in Japan and two and a half million in Africa; Protestants of one kind or another totaled one and a half million in India, a quarter of a million in China, eighty thousand in Japan, and two and a half million in Africa; while the Russian Orthodox Church had a hundred thousand followers in Japan and as many more in China. Altogether, Christianity in 1900 was professed outside Europe and America—outside the traditional "West"—by some forty-one million persons, of whom the majority were the fruit of missionary activity during the last three decades.

But this activity had other and more incalculable fruits. For, while actual Christian converts constituted a very small proportion of the populations of India, China, Japan, and even Africa, Christian missionaries proved effective instruments (along with traders and financiers) for spreading at least the externals of "Western" civilization among a large part of those populations and thus contributing to the "Europeanization" of the whole world. Particularly through the numerous schools and hospitals which missionaries founded, many natives who did not become Christian acquired at any rate a taste for the education, the science, the machinery, the clothing, and the pastimes of contemporary Europe.

Nor was the impact of Christianity and "Western" civilization on the "East" without influence on Hinduism and Buddhism. Some of the priests of these great indigenous religions sought to invest them with ethical principles borrowed more or less consciously from Christianity, while among intellectuals who traditionally professed them there was a rise of a kind of modernism or of outright agnosticism comparable with that in the Christian West. If Christian missionaries were helping to transform a European into a world civilization, it was becoming more dubious whether this world civilization would be based, as Europe's had been, on a common religious faith and experience, or whether it would be purely material.

V. SOCIOLOGICAL REALISM IN ART

That traditional religion seemed to be declining in Europe faster and more catastrophically than it actually was, may be attributed to the contemptuous if not hostile attitude toward it on the part of almost every first-rate literary man and almost every outstanding artist of the generation from 1871 to 1900. Immediately before, there had been Christian novelists like Dickens and Dostoevski and Christian painters like Millet and the pre-Raphaelites, and just afterwards there would be Undset and Chesterton, Meštrović and Eric Gill; but in the meantime there was an obvious dearth of Christian pens, brushes, and chisels. The irreligion or anti-religion of the generation of materialism, while affecting many natural scientists and most social scientists, possessed practically all artists, and these, having extraordinary gifts of expression, were far more influential than the others in fashioning the thought and mood of the intellectual and would-be intellectual classes.

The early nineteenth-century conflict between classicism and romanticism had already been superseded by one between idealism and realism; and the realism that gradually emerged victorious in the '50's and '60's was represented most characteristically by discursive novels, which either, like Thackeray's or Balzac's, portrayed the weakness of individuals and the shams of society, or, like Hugo's *Les Misérables*, Stowe's *Uncle Tom's Cabin*, and the novels of Disraeli, Turgeniev, and Tolstoy, dealt in a spirit of humanitarian uplift with practical problems of poverty, slavery, crime, and war. After 1870 the discursive realistic novel was supplemented by the realistic drama, and both were given a powerful fillip—and a somewhat different slant—by the new generation's engrossment in evolutionary sociology and psychology and in positivistic factualness. To the literary lights of the period, social problems loomed very large and humanity's need of grappling with them appeared especially exigent. Yet it seemed worse than idle, in view of the "facts of modern science," to be romantic about contemporary problems or, on the other hand, to expect any help for them from pure reason or classical precedent. One must recognize facts and record them in photographic detail and exactness. One must not touch them up, as a Dickens or a Hugo had been wont to do, with a background of moral earnestness or with any transcendental trimmings. Rather, one must grasp the halting gradualness of man's ascent from the savage animal origins and the atavistic, pathological, and irrational features of his present existence; and one must let the facts speak for themselves.

Most of the dominant realistic literature of the era can be broadly classified as either sociological or psychological, and analogous categories are applicable to much of its pictorial and plastic art. We shall here indicate the nature and cite examples, first of the sociological and then (in the next section) of the psychological realism, though it should be borne in mind that the two sorts were synchronous and complementary and that only in combination did they express the ethos of the period.

In literature, sociological realism was concerned primarily with problems of family or class, nation or society at large—eugenics, feminism, democracy, labor, alcoholism, racial decadence, backward peoples, the White Man's burden. Of these it usually treated in interminable quasi-journalistic prose, with a wealth of sordid and presumably scientific detail, with an underlying philosophy of naturalism and determinism and yet with an oddly sure and buoyant optimism that somehow through evolutionary processes everything must eventually turn out right.

Zola set the pace during the three decades after 1871 by relentlessly pursuing, through no fewer than twenty beefy tomes, the pathological case history of several generations of a sorry and degenerating French family, and by dashing off, in spells of perverted recreation, a somber novel on supposed Malthusian laws of population, a lugubrious one on labor conditions, and a very melodramatic one on hereditary drunkenness. Thomas Hardy devoted his much greater literary talents to exposition of the barnyard aspects of human life and particularly of the fateful workings of the struggle for existence in peasant and village life in the English countryside of Wessex. In Norway Björnson followed up his romantic sagas of a peasant nation with Zola-like didactic novels on heredity and environment. Even Tolstoy, who retained a hankering for Christianity and grew more illogically mystical, revealed in the communistic preachments of his later novels, *The Kreutzer Sonata* and *Resurrection*, a similar concern with sociological data.

The sociological drama was ushered in by Ibsen's grim diagnoses of hypocrisy and other woeful ills; and *A Doll's House* (1879) and *Ghosts* (1881) exerted profound influence on Hauptmann's murky *Before Sunrise*, on Sudermann's *Honor* (which should have been entitled *Dishonor*), on Chekhov's whimpering *Seagull* and *Cherry Orchard*, on the sex triangles of Pinero and the medico-salacity of Brieux and Schnitzler. Above all, Ibsen, in conjunction with Samuel Butler's mockery of religion and traditional morals,[14] swerved Bernard Shaw from art criticism and socialist pamphleteering to a career as the most shocking European dramatist at the turn of the century. Shaw was then the author of *Unpleasant Plays* and *Plays for Puritans* about prostitution, militarism, the Nietzschean superman, etc.

It is doubtful whether any of these dramas and novels had wide

---

[14] Butler's masterpiece, *The Way of All Flesh*, was written between 1872 and 1884 but was not given to the general public until 1903, the year after his death.

popular appeal. It was *de rigueur*, of course, for the sophisticated and the fashionable to give ear or eye to them and to buzz approval, but even in such rarefied ranks the buzzing may have concealed some of the boredom which elicited unabashed yawns from those whom social scientists dubbed the underprivileged classes. At any rate the cleavage between what intellectuals deemed great literature and what most people preferred to read was sharpened. Sociological realism was plentiful, but its spiciest and most smelly kind was caviar to the general public.

The taste of the more discriminating among the masses was served, half realistically, half romantically, by adventure stories of a Robert Louis Stevenson, by a Barrie's whimsical novels and plays, by a Daudet's quixotic *Tartarin*, by a Lewis Carroll's continuing excursions with a perplexed *Alice*; and that of a still wider public, by a profusion of exciting narratives concerning strange peoples and strange things which current science, geographical, archæological, and physical, was bringing to European consciousness. From the French naval officer who wrote under the pseudonym of Pierre Loti flowed a series of autobiographical romances about exotic Turks, Tahitians, and Senegalese. From Bret Harte, sojourning in Europe after 1878, emanated two score of blood-and-thunder stories about the American wild West which he had known in his youth. From Maxim Gorki came lurid tales of Russian tramps and outcasts; and from Rudyard Kipling, who spent his early years in India and some later ones in America, came *Plain Tales from the Hills, Jungle Books,* and that stirring yarn of deep-sea fishery, *Captains Courageous.* Like Kipling's denizens of the jungle, the storied birds and insects of John Burroughs and the "br'er rabbit" of Joel Chandler Harris appealed to a generation which was tempted to believe that humans are but compatriots with birds and beasts in a democratic animal kingdom.

The appeal was likewise enormous of the "archæological romance"—the fantastic accounts of the life and love, intrigue and doom, of ancient Egypt, for example, by George Ebers, or of ancient Mexico by General Lew Wallace, or of aboriginal (and amazingly rich and resourceful) Africa by Rider Haggard, or of Christian origins in Wallace's *Ben-Hur* and Sienkiewicz's *Quo*

Vadis. Quite as popular was the type of novel which looked into the future and gave to the wildest guesses concerning the further progress of technology and natural science an appearance of plausibility and an air of realism. This type, originally exemplified in the '60's and '70's by Jules Verne's thrilling travels down to the center of the earth, up to the moon, under the seas, and around the world, reached most perfect fruition in the '90's with H. G. Wells's "scientific" romances of *The Time Machine, The Stolen Bacillus, The War of the Worlds.* Presently and naturally Wells would soar from scientific to sociological (and messianic) futurism, and take myriads of readers along with him.

The age was prosy, if not prosaic. Sociology did not lend itself to verse, except to very free verse. Poetry languished or withdrew into waste spaces or second-class cafés. Walt Whitman, it is true, kept producing new and enlarged editions of his *Leaves of Grass* as sustaining fodder for manly democratic comrades, and William Morris composed rousing *Chants for Socialists,* but there was lingering doubt whether the *Leaves* and *Chants* were genuine poetry or hortatory prose that merely looked like poetry. Outside of the symbolists, who appeared late and were immune to social science, it was left to Swinburne, almost alone, to wear the laurels of a master poet. These he won by fitting pieces of classicism, humanitarianism, and romantic liberalism with patches of Darwinian and Nietzschean philosophy into a colorful quilt of alliterative rhetoric, peculiarly beguiling to youth. Not until the end of the century did Swinburne go out of fashion and Kipling the poet come in. Only then did melody pass from soprano to bass, from plaintive arias about "the pale Galilæan" to stentorian odes about "lesser breeds."

The art of caricature, which flourished throughout the nineteenth century as never before, broadened its appeal during the century's final era, in part because of the greater number and wider circulation of comic journals, and in part because of the continuing technical excellence of its practitioners and their utilization of a large range of timely subjects. Tenniel remained the premier caricaturist of *Punch* and marked with genial satire every major political event of the era. In succession to Daumier—the Balzac of French caricature—arose the incomparable Forain, whose merciless picturing of the corruption of republican politicians and bourgeois capitalists added no little fuel to the Boulangist and Dreyfus fires.

The painting of the era was less distinguished and much less "sociological." Its total quantity greatly increased in response to growing demands for the adornment of public buildings, for the filling of museums, and for the cultural ostentation of wealthy industrialists (and their wives). But a good deal of it was second-rate, and among the superior was a bewildering variety of "schools." One, including Leighton and Alma-Tadema, stuck to tiresome imitation of classical models—gods and goddesses, fauns and nymphs, and all the rest. Another echoed the romanticism of a Delacroix or a Meissonier and employed it for some of the best (as well as the worst) of the nationalistic painting, with which the era abounded. The "schools" that came nearest to being original in technic and subject matter were the impressionist and post-impressionist; the latter was too introspective to be concerned with social problems; and only a humorless *savant* could perceive social significance in the pictures of chorus girls, prizefighters, workwomen, and jockeys which such impressionists as Degas and Lautrec loved to depict. What sociological realism there was in painting, comparable with that in literature, was most clearly represented by the horribly gruesome war pictures of Vereshchagin, himself a participant in the Russo-Turkish war of 1877 and a victim of the Russo-Japanese war of 1904. It should be added, however, that Puvis de Chavannes was moved by the social science of the time to make his murals in the Boston Public Library a pictorial tale of human evolution.

The sculpture of the period was prolific and much of it carried unmistakable social message, either nationalist or laborite. Meunier, with consummate craftsmanship, preached in stone the new gospel of the exceeding worth of industrial and agricultural workers, and Meunier inspired innumerable disciples. On the other hand, the gospel of nationalism was carved afresh, widely and with popular appeal, in the baroque outbursts of Begas at Berlin, in the florid sensuousness of Dalou, Falguière, and Bartholomé at Paris, and in the "realist" statues of Saint-Gaudens in America. It is noteworthy that Dalou, always radically minded, turned in his later days from celebrating the triumph of Republican France to projecting an apotheosis of Marxism.

Of musical art the prevailing mood remained romantically nationalist. Such operatic geniuses of the preceding era as Gounod, Verdi, and Wagner survived well into, or even through, the new era, the last named with ever-increasing devotion to German mythology;[15] and the tradition of "national schools" thus established was preserved by Saint-Saëns and Massenet, Richard Strauss, and Puccini. Besides, there was a veritable epidemic of "folk music." Brahms followed up his *Song of Triumph* in honor of German military victories of 1870 with lively *Hungarian Dances*. Tschaikovsky based his *Eugen Onegin* on a folk story by Pushkin and composed his most famous overture in commemoration of Napoleon's repulse in 1812. Toward a distinctively Russian opera, Moussorgsky contributed the fateful *Boris Godunov*, and Rimski-Korsakov, *Sadko* and *Coq d'Or* with their modernist enshrinement of folk tunes. Smetana and Dvořák elaborated folk music for the Czechs, Grieg for the Norwegians. And the operettas of Sullivan, with Gilbert's indispensable librettos, were as British and as cleverly satirical as the drawings of Tenniel.

Architecture, the most enduring of the arts, was least affected by the intellectual fashions of the generation. Classical styles continued their predominance with eclectic variations, and even the romantic Gothic, which lost some favor, was still widely employed for church construction and was newly embodied in parliamentary buildings at Budapest and Ottawa. Yet there was the beginning of the revolutionary movement known as functionalism, which derived from Darwinian philosophy its cardinal principle that form must be rigorously adapted to environment and functions. Its first major fruits were the Eiffel Tower at Paris, the Bishopsgate Institute at London, the stations of the urban railway at Vienna, the Wertheim department store at Berlin. Its big crop would ripen in the twentieth century.

VI. PSYCHOLOGICAL REALISM

Next to social problems, the realism of the age was most concerned with psychological analyses of individuals, particularly with

15 "Wagnerism," like "Marxism," was chiefly post-1880.

their "fated" response to domestic milieu and to traditional conventions and institutions. Unlike sociological realism, the psychological was likely to be pessimistic, or at least ironical, and to be meticulously expressed. Its prototype, in literature, was Flaubert's *Madame Bovary*, which had been regarded as smutty when it first appeared in 1857 but which in the '80's was acclaimed as sound psychology and the finest art. By this time Maupassant's sardonic pornography was giving peculiar meaning to the "French" *conte d'amour* and making Flaubert seem tame.

In England flourished Meredith, whose *Egoist* and *Diana* were greeted in the '80's with kid-gloved applause for their keen dissection of feminine character and for their epigrams and brilliant dialogue. Followed Henry James, with a style still more involved and with plots and characters more shadowy; his business was to track members of the leisured class, like ghosts, into the cupboards of their minds.

A rather different and less baffling kind of mental study was supplied from the '80's by Anatole France, who had all of Voltaire's lucidity and wit and all his religious and moral skepticism, and in addition a disillusioning pessimism and a total lack, at least until 1900, of any reforming zeal. The novel of the French naturalist species was transplanted to British gardens in the '90's by the *Esther Waters* of that painter of moods, George Moore—Irishman by birth and Frenchman by choice.

Curiously enough, to a generation which doubted or denied the existence of souls in the theological sense, the existence of national and other group "souls" seemed more or less axiomatic, and as a special branch of psychological realism, these "souls" were duly and deftly portrayed. Historians and critics of literature, Taine and Matthew Arnold for example, laid bare the "souls" of Saxon, Norman, Celtic, and many another ethnic group. The Russian "soul" usually turned out to be melancholy, the German *gemütlich*, the Spanish passionate.

Collective psychoanalyzing was practiced by certain novelists and poets like Bourget and Verhaeren, who, not having cut themselves loose from Christianity, and feeling a nostalgia for rural communities where it was still rooted (and where there were no factories or industrialists), discoursed in a minor key about the "soul" of countryside and its hapless fate in the "soulless city." But the main practitioners of the art were writers like Barrès and D'Annunzio, who began as frank disciples of Nietzsche and then, under the influence of Taine's alchemy, transmuted their base personal egotism into a precious soul-endowed national egotism. Barrès's first trilogy, *The Cult of Myself,* was published at the end of the '80's, and his second, *The Romance of National Energy,* at the end of the '90's. In view of the subsequent role of the psychological nationalism which he espoused, perhaps Barrès is less "dated" than contemporaries like Henry James and Anatole France.

The masses, it must be confessed, could not appreciate and would not read James or Meredith or even Flaubert, and Anatole France left them cold. But they did read and immensely enjoy a good detective story, to the production of which the general psychological interests of the era were especially conducive. Between criminal and detective was waged a battle of minds, with material wealth and success the stakes, and with new scientific weapons at hand. Wilkie Collins petered out in the '70's, but a greater than he, the matchless Conan Doyle, introduced Sherlock Holmes in the '80's. Already, in every European language, Nick Carter and countless other pennydreadfuls were selling like hot cakes.

All the arts were tinged with psychological realism. It showed in impressionist painting, in symbolist poetry, in the music of Debussy. It especially characterized the allegorical painting of Arnold Böcklin, the portraiture of Sargent and Lavery, and that outgrowth of impressionism which went under the name of post-impressionism. Cézanne, the stepfather of the last, belonged originally to the "school" of Manet and Pissarro, but, wishing to emphasize the "realistic" aspects of his art and to produce more striking psychological effects, he took to employing thick layers of paint for pictures at once simple, vivid, slightly distorted, and highly individualistic. His most distinctive work was done in the '90's, almost simultaneously with the egotistical and soulful painting of those insane geniuses, Vincent van Gogh, who died by his own hand, and Paul Gauguin, who went "savage" on South Sea islands. None of these post-impressionists enjoyed any immediate vogue, but they were products of their era and eventual fashioners of the "modern art" of a later and more weary generation. Theirs was the psychology of Nietzschean willfulness. As one of Gauguin's disciples explained, "He freed us from all restraints which the idea of copying placed on our painter's instinct. . . . We aspired to express our own personality, our own soul. . . . If at any moment a tree looked reddish to us, we might paint it in vermilion; if a girl's shoulder struck us just right, we might stress its curve to the point of deformation."

The sculpture of Rodin, however, was the most perfect mirror of the era's intellectual trends. He was alive to them all, and knew how in stone to make them romantically and vividly pictorial. His celebrated *Thinker* is more eloquent of physiological psychology and of man's evolution from the beasts than all the learned volumes of Wundt and Darwin. His *Gate of Hell* is the ultimate enduring monument to the era's discontents and doubts.

VII. IMPRESSIONISM AND ECLECTICISM

The majority of artists of the materialistic generation faced its "facts" and acquired from them a strongly sociological or psychological bent. But a minority, including some of the most remarkable painters and poets, ran away from the facts, so to speak, in an erratic quest of "art for art's sake." Why this should have happened, is not altogether clear. Perhaps it was an emotional reaction against the certitudes of natural and social science. Perhaps, on the other hand, it was a reasonable conviction, born of the acceptance of those certitudes, that man, being only a chemical flutter, had nothing much to do except to seek sensations and to play at art.

In painting, this runaway aesthetic movement was tagged "impressionism" in 1874, although it had begun a decade earlier with Manet, and "luminism" would have been a more descriptive title. All the painters who participated in it—Manet himself, Pissarro, Degas, Fantin-latour, Monet, Renoir, Zorn, Whistler, Sorolla—fairly worshiped light and the sense organ of vision. Anything which light revealed to the eye of the artist as beautiful he should paint, as if he were inspired, without reference to anyone else's opinion. Nothing could be learned from "academic" painters, and not much from any of the historic schools, except as the canvases of El Greco, Rembrandt, and Velásquez revealed the secret of peculiar luminosity and queer distortion. New and ingenious expedients the impressionists would contrive for, capturing in paint the coruscation of the noonday sun, the subtler mystery of moonlight, the complexities of artificial illumination.

Here, then, was the movement's central current. But accompanying it, as side eddies, were a dreamy poetical mood emanating from romantic sources (notably Corot) and a special appreciation of the decorum and decorousness of recently discovered Japanese art. With the exception of Pissarro the impressionists were notoriously faulty draftsmen, and their intense subjectivity and aesthetic posturing at first rendered them ridiculous to critics and bewildering to the general public. Yet by the '90's they were becoming fashionable. In 1877 Manet had proposed to aid Monet by buying ten pictures at a hundred francs each. In 1896 Monet was heading a national subscription to buy Manet's *Olympia* for the Louvre. And without impressionism, there could have been no post-impressionism and no "modern" painting.

Analogous to impressionism in painting was symbolism in literature. This involved a careful choice of just such words and phrases as would convey an appropriate "atmosphere"—usually a quasi-mystical atmosphere—with the implication at least that form is more than content and sound is more than sense. "Not sharp colors but pastel shades, not a literal exactness but a suggestive use of words," was one definition. Symbolism, in some degree, was apparent in the studied striving for atmosphere and effect which characterized such prose writers as Meredith, Maupassant, Bourget, Anatole France, and Chekhov. But it was principally the poets of a preponderantly prosaic age who stampeded from materialism and found refuge in conscious and acknowledged symbolism.

The formal founder of symbolist theory, and its premier poet, was Stéphane Mallarmé, a mild-mannered French professor of English literature, who taught that beauty can best be sensed through words mysteriously suggestive of color, sound, taste, and touch. He was enamored of Poe's poetry, which he translated into French, and he held that the most perfect phrase in all literature was Poe's line about "the viol, the violet, and the vine." His own poetry, beginning in 1876 with the celebrated *Après-midi d'un faune,* he clothed with a richly jeweled magnificence and a vaguely haunting impressionism. As he aged, he grew more obscure and finally abandoned punctuation.

For years Mallarmé presided every Tuesday evening over a salon at which he held forth on aesthetic feeling to a flock of literary neophytes. And the influence which he thus exerted at Paris was paralleled at Oxford by that of Walter Pater, whose *Marius the Epicurean* (1885) encased a similar gospel in subtly poetical prose. By the late '80's and throughout the '90's the devotees of symbolism and literary aestheticism were numerous and notorious. They included, for example, the French "decadents," Verlaine and Rimbaud, the Belgian Verhaeren, the Anglo-Irishman Wilde, as well as a swarm of minor poets—the period specialized in minor poets— who reveled in Japanese prints and renaissance brocades, in lilies and sunflowers, in absinthe and hashish and the strangest amours. There were those also who, like the young pioneers of the Celtic revival in Ireland, evoked in symbolic form (frequently with unintelligible footnotes) a dim and legendary national past. Likewise, there was Maeterlinck. The reputation he made with *Pelléas and Melisande* in 1892 he sustained with a succession of symbolic plays suggesting the "souls" of orphan princesses, blind beggars, and pale Arthurian knights, who, in shadowy bodies beyond time and space, mysteriously stir about and vaguely sigh according to the dictates of some inscrutable but perpetually thwarting fate. Under a Maeterlinckian spell, even Ibsen, in his declining years, forsook sociological realism and took to penning dramas in which no comprehensible content but only an esoteric "art" remained.

Symbolism in literature was no more popular than impressionism in painting. It, too, was an easy butt of ridicule, and for one person who really liked Wilde's *Salome* there were scores who heartily encored Gilbert and Sullivan's *Patience.* Yet if symbolism, like impressionism, belongs only chronologically to the generation of materialism, it was ahead of its time, not behind.

This was strikingly true of the impressionistic music which issued from Debussy's experimentation in the '80's with unusual scales and mystical dissonances calculated to appeal to sophisticated imagination rather than to simpler emotions, and which received novel expression in his settings of Mallarmé's *Après-midi* and Maeterlinck's *Pelléas*. Before the end of the '90's Debussy's innovations were carried further, in the direction of literary symbolism, by the young Russian Scriabin, whose peculiar system of harmony, he claimed, was consonant with a natural color scheme; and still further by the youthful Austrian Schönberg, who, like the impressionist painters, threw over the whole cargo of rules and models and relied upon "natural inspiration." "Modern music" was in the making.

Over against all such novelties in music, painting, and literature, must be set the stolid classical conservatism of architecture. What novelty there was in the most monumental and enduring of the arts was the functionalism which has already been mentioned, and it represented no running away from the realities of the age, no lapse into mysticism or preciousness; rather, it was Darwinian in inspiration and almost brutally utilitarian in object. On the other hand, the all-prevailing architectural mode was not at all novel. It was an adaptive or eclectic classicism—a decorative baroque classicism, varying from one country to another in accordance with historic and national circumstance, and not disdaining to make use of up-to-date materials, such as iron and concrete, or of alien embellishments borrowed from Egypt or the Orient. It seemed singularly appropriate to Europe's latest stage of evolution, for while it conserved the inveterate classical (and pagan) tradition, it reflected, in its very grandeur and ornateness, the magnitude and éclat of the modern nation's machine industry, material wealth, and imperial ambition.

Nations vied with one another as to which could rear the heaviest and most grandiose pile of eclectic classicism. Belgium led off with the gigantic palace of justice at Brussels (1866-1883). Austria doubled with the imposing museums of art and natural history and other imperial structures on the rebuilt Ringstrasse at Vienna (1870-1889). Germany outbid both with the Reichstag building (1882-1894) and Protestant cathedral (1888-1895) at Berlin and the Supreme Court edifice (1884-1895) at Leipzig. But the honors, at least for size and extravagance, went to Italy for the Victor Emmanuel monument at Rome (1884-1911). France had to content herself with the bizarre Trocadero (1878) and with the lighter and more graceful form of eclecticism which she exported to the Chicago World's Fair of 1893 and perfected in the Little Palace at the Paris Fair of 1900.

Two eclectic variants appeared during the period. One was the revival of a Byzantine style, illustrated by the church of the Sacred Heart, the erection of which in Paris atop Montmartre was voted by the royalist majority in the French parliament in 1874 as "an act of national expiation for the crimes of revolution," and by the Catholic cathedral of Westminster, in London, which was begun in the '90's. The other was a special kind of domestic architecture, aiming at picturesqueness in appearance and livableness in interior appointments. It represented an adaptation, on the Continent, of the Swiss châlet, and in England (and the United States), of the house of Queen Anne's time. It was congruously suburban and bourgeois. "Modern" architecture for tenements and workshops of the urban proletariat awaited a great new event in European history—the full emergence of the masses.

Chapter Five

EMERGENCE OF THE MASSES

I. TRADE-UNIONISM

IT IS one of Clio's curious paradoxes that in the closing era of the nineteenth century, when individual men were being reduced to the status of automatons in a mechanized universe and to family relationship with lower animals and chunks of carbon, the masses of mankind attained to a self-consciousness and a social importance without previous parallel, unless it were in those medieval times which good moderns were taught to contemn. In the Middle Ages, at least locally, the masses had made their voice heard and their influence felt in craft guild or manorial court, in communal government or peasant insurrection, and there had then been a degree of actual if unnamed "feminism." But from the sixteenth to the early nineteenth century the ordinary populace of town and country had been generally submerged under the weight of centralizing despotism of princes, extending privileges of landed nobility, and rising ambition and achievement of middle class. Guilds fell into decay, *jacqueries* all but ceased, the condition of women was worsened, and in certain regions the large percentage of popular illiteracy grew still larger.

The industrialization of the nineteenth century changed all this. By prompting mass migration to cities and factories for the mass production of goods, it broke multitudes loose from local economy and customary dependence on nobleman or country gentleman and herded them in big metropolitan centers peculiarly favorable to mass suggestion and mass action. Here they learned to pit against the self-interest and industrial combinations of employers a self-interest of their own and the institution of trade-unionism. Here, too, they had incentive and opportunity to agitate for democratic government, for popular education, for social reform. Here, finally,

they provided abundant fertile soil for the propagation of nationalism or Marxism. In the resulting emergence—or re-emergence—of the
masses on a national and international scale, women conspicuously
shared from the outset, and so also in time did rural folk by virtue
of the progressive industrialization of agriculture and the special
services of rail, post, and wire.

The trade-union movement was a kind of working-class ther-
mometer of industrialization. It developed originally, as one might
expect, in England in the early part of the century, and presently
spread, with machine manufacture, to Belgium, France, Germany,
and other Continental countries. In 1868 was held the first British
trade-union congress, representing a membership of 250,000, and
in the same year the first trade-union of the British type was established in Germany. British trade-unions, barely tolerated by parliamentary acts of 1824-1825, were finally sanctioned in 1871 and
1876. France legalized trade-unions partially in 1864 and fully in
1884. Austria authorized them in 1870.

The prevailing trade-unionism of the '70's and early '80's was a
craft unionism, confined mainly to skilled workmen in particular
trades, notably building, engineering, coal mining, cotton manufacture, printing, hatmaking, etc. It spasmodically sponsored strikes
for higher wages, shorter hours, and better working conditions, but
its chief and constant function was mutual insurance against sickness, accident, and death. It was utilitarian and opportunist, and
what philosophy it had was untinged by ideas of class conflict. It
postulated the desirability and practicality of democratic co-operation between capital and labor and accepted, perhaps a bit naïvely,
the current liberalism of middle-class "radicals." In Britain its
pretension to political neutrality hardly concealed its sympathy
with the John Bright wing of the Liberal party, and on the Continent it was an open ally of the sectarian Liberals. In Germany
its earliest and most "respectable" form was fashioned by two eminent Progressives—Hirsch and Duncker—and faithfully served
their partisan purposes.

Another form took shape fairly early. Almost simultaneously
with the establishment of Hirsch-Duncker unions (*Gewerkvereine*),
a disciple of Lassalle inaugurated in Germany a few Socialist unions

(*Gewerkschaften*); and these, like some of the labor organizations in France, were soon permeated with Marxian principles. Until the late '80's, however, Socialist unions were not very important. In France they suffered setbacks from the suppression of the Paris Commune in 1871, from the ensuing popular reaction, and from internal controversy. In Germany they were seriously handicapped by governmental hostility and by the anti-Socialist legislation of 1878. In Britain they were simply nonexistent.

The progress of trade-unionism was most pronounced during the years of comparative economic prosperity from 1871 to 1873, 1879 to 1882, 1886 to 1892, and 1896 onward. In the intervening times of crisis and depression, it was stagnant if not in retreat.

It was during the spell of relative general prosperity from 1886 to 1892 that a "new unionism" arose and made unexpected gains. This, unlike the old, was articulated or at least impregnated with Marxian socialism; it sought working-class organization by industries rather than by crafts; it enlisted unskilled laborers as well as skilled artisans; it was distinctly militant. It was ushered in by a bitter and bloody strike of Belgian miners and glass workers at Charleroi in Belgium in 1886. In the same year, a national federation of French labor unions was effected under Socialist auspices, and very shortly afterwards Marxists gained control of budding trade-union movements in Austria, Italy, the Scandinavian countries, Holland, and Spain. In Germany, where the Liberal Hirsch-Duncker unions barely held their own, the Socialist unions forged rapidly ahead, especially after the lapse of discriminatory legislation in 1890. In Britain the "new unionism" was greatly forwarded by the London dock strike of 1889, and though in this instance it remained largely impervious to the specific gospel of Karl Marx, it tended to favor and eventually to identify itself with the separate and quasi-socialistic Labor party which a Welsh miner, Keir Hardie, founded in 1893. Incidentally it was during the same period that the American Federation of Labor was formed (1886), and that under Catholic sponsorship and in keeping with the counsels of Leo XIII a "Christian" trade-unionism was initiated in France, Italy, Germany, Austria, and Belgium.

Between 1886 and 1900 trade-union membership rose in Britain from one and a quarter million to two million; in Germany, from 300,000 to 850,000; in France, from 50,000 to 250,000. At the highest these figures represented only a relatively small minority of the urban proletariat and practically no agricultural workers. Trade unionism was a movement among, not of, the masses. Its constituency continued to be an "aristocracy of labor."

Nor was the movement revolutionary. In England, even after the rise of the new unionism with its fighting creed and its many notable strikes, the portion of union funds expended on strike pay was less than a fifth; four fifths still went for insurance benefits and administrative expenses. In Germany the Socialist trade-unions constituted an increasingly conservative element in the Socialist party, while the Christian and Hirsch-Duncker unions were eminently staid. Only at the end of the '90's and only in Latin countries where trade-unions were comparatively weak did any appreciable number of them avow the aims or adopt the tactics of "revolutionary syndicalism."

Yet the significance of trade-unionism must not be underestimated. It was undoubtedly a major factor in shifting the trend of public interest and opinion from the individualism and competition of the first two thirds of the nineteenth century to the socialism and co-operation of the last third, and it was truly a mass movement in that its leaders no less than its followers came from factory and mine and were quite unknown to either academic or polite society. To be sure, it was as yet but a leaven among the European masses as a whole, but it was an expanding and continually more effective leaven. After the turn of the century it would become a major force in politics and economics. Already it was a prime stimulus to the co-operative movement, to political democracy, to popular education, indeed to all developments favoring the emergence of the masses.

II. THE CO-OPERATIVE MOVEMENT

Related historically and logically to trade-unionism was a much broader co-operative movement, which spread among the masses in the wake of the Utopian agitation of the 1830's and 1840's. It assumed many forms. One was the co-operative retail store of the type first successfully exemplified in England by the Rochdale Pioneers (1844). This gradually gained the support of a host of urban dwellers, workingmen and lower middle class; and, thanks to the tireless endeavors of Vansittart Neale, a Christian Socialist *à la* Kingsley, and of Thomas Hughes, author of *Tom Brown* and apostle of "muscular Christianity," it received full public sanction and protection by parliamentary enactment of 1876. Thanks also to the lifelong labors of George J. Holyoake, it was popularized throughout the United Kingdom and abroad. By 1900 there were in Britain more than 1,400 stores modeled after the Rochdale plan, with nearly two and a quarter million members, and a large number of similar stores in France, Germany, Switzerland, Italy and elsewhere. Primarily these stores were distributing organizations, but nearly four fifths of them engaged in some production, notably baking or bootmaking.

Another form of co-operation was the fraternal insurance society —the "friendly society," as it was called in England where it had originated in the 1840's. It included frankly commercial "mutual" societies like the "Royal Liver" of Liverpool, numerous local burial or building associations, certain nation-wide "orders" like Odd Fellows, Foresters, Rechabites, and Shepherds which catered to human fondness for mystery and ritual as well as to working-class need for insurance benefits, and organizations such as the Royal Antediluvian Order of Buffaloes which was solemnly reported to the government in 1871 as being "wholly convivial." After parliamentary legislation of 1875 in their behalf, the growth of all such friendly societies was phenomenal. By 1885 nearly seven million— and twenty-five years later nearly fourteen million—adults, mostly wage earners, were active members and thus enabled to make some provision for themselves and their children by way of insurance. By the '80's, furthermore, the fraternal orders had overflowed in torrential proportions into the European and American continents. A foreign visitor who studied England of that decade against Friedrich Engels's background of the England of the '40's, wrote of "the complete revolution . . . in the lives of a large number of English workmen" and of "an improvement . . . beyond the boldest hopes of even those who, a generation ago, devoted all their energies to the work."[1]

As England was the home of co-operative stores and insurance companies and trade-unions, so Germany was the source of still another form of co-operation, that of credit banking. Here, co-operative loan banks for peasants which Raiffeisen had started in 1849 were counted after 1880 by the thousands, as were also the corresponding banks for urban craftsmen which Schulze-Delitzsch patronized in the '50's and '60's. By 1900 Europe at large had 30,000 co-operative credit societies, exclusive of building associations, and while they were still strongest and most numerous in Germany, they were widespread and important in the Scandinavian countries, Italy, Austria, France, etc.

Co-operative credit furnished impetus from the '80's to co-operative agriculture. Farmers united to manufacture or to market their products, or more often to buy and operate expensive machinery and to insure against risks. The most remarkable and thorough development was in Denmark, where a single co-operative dairy in 1882 multiplied to a thousand in 1892, at which date four fifths of all Danish milk, butter, eggs, fruit, and bacon were produced and marketed co-operatively. Following the lead of Denmark, similar co-operative agriculture struck firm root in Germany, France, Italy, Belgium, Holland, Finland, and Ireland. The first Irish co-operative dairy was established through the efforts of Sir Horace Plunkett in 1889. The French *syndicats agricoles*, starting in 1893, soon ran into thousands and their membership into hundreds of thousands.

Special forms of the co-operative movement flourished in particular countries. In Belgium a specifically Catholic form arose in rural districts, and Socialist *maisons du peuple* in industrial centers. In Italy a far-flung *Società di Lavoro* embraced co-operative labor gangs of navvies, stevedores, masons, ditchdiggers, agricultural workers, etc. Even in the huge and supposedly backward Russian Empire was a network of *artels*, consisting of groups of ten to fifty migratory workmen, frequently ex-serfs, who hailed from a particu-

[1] J. M. Baernreither, *English Associations of Working Men*, Eng. trans. (1889), 5.

lar locality and while industrially employed roomed together, kept a common table, and paid each his part of the common expense.

Whatever form the co-operative movement assumed—*artel, maison du peuple,* farming, banking, insurance, retail selling—it was essentially a working-class movement, both urban and rural, without great intellectual personalities. It was of and for the masses.

III. POPULAR EDUCATION

A most impressive—and perhaps in the long run the most fateful—phenomenon of the last third of the nineteenth century was the progress of literacy among the European (and American) masses and their consequent entry into the *Buch-und-Lesen* culture of modern times. Prior to the late 1860's the only countries where almost everybody could read and write were Prussia and adjacent German and Scandinavian states; and in these the impulse to popular education had come not from the masses themselves but from princes and Protestant clergymen who wanted disciplined soldiers and obedient and pious subjects. Elsewhere, despite educational projects put forth by eighteenth-century *philosophes* and despite some fostering of common schools by French revolutionaries and Napoleon, by Guizot and Cavour, by the English parliament from the 1830's and the Belgian from the 1840's, the vast majority of Europeans were still illiterate in the early '60's. Almost a third of the male and nearly half of the female population in Great Britain could neither read nor write; over half of the entire population in France and Belgium; three quarters in Italy and Spain; nine tenths in Russia and the Balkans. And these statistics minimize the extent of illiteracy among the masses, inasmuch as the middle and upper classes in all countries were generally literate. Schooling was still, in the '60's, usually a class and not a mass affair.

Many factors contributed to the movement for mass education from the late '60's onward. Fundamental was current industrialization, which provided necessary funds and mechanical means for the establishment and maintenance of great national systems of elementary schooling. Moreover, the urbanization which attended industrialization was helpful; mass education could be carried on more expeditiously and economically in congested cities than in sparsely inhabited rural districts. Then, too, the intellectual liberalism of the period, whether ecumenical or sectarian, predisposed the middle classes and many persons in the upper classes to champion mass education. Liberals were heirs of the eighteenth-century Enlightenment, which, in their somewhat immodest opinion, had made them the benevolent and progressive beings they were; if it was spread among the masses it might render them similarly decent and intelligent and liberal. From schools ordinary people could learn sound principles of economics and politics, and receive training in self-discipline and self-help. Also, at a time when multitudes were being uprooted from traditional habitat and habits and exposed to the peculiar vices of city life, popular schooling might exercise a most salutary moral influence in accordance with Guizot's epigram, "the opening of every schoolhouse closes a jail."

Besides, it was argued, the same elementary schooling for everybody would emphasize that "equality of opportunity" which philanthropic liberals talked so much about and otherwise did so little to realize; and surely it would be a basic means of adapting whole nations to the political, economic, and intellectual trends of an advanced age. Literacy and proper indoctrination would prepare the masses to participate intelligently in democratic government. Literacy and some technical training would improve their industrial efficiency and enable them to avoid unemployment and penury. Literacy together with patriotic and physical education would increase their national loyalty and their effectiveness in the new conscript national armies. A right sort of popular education, depending upon which party to the contemporary "warfare between science and theology" directed it, might either rescue the masses from "superstition" and "clericalism" or save them for "Christian civilization."

To the liberal and enlightened classes the cause of popular education quickly became a sacred cause, an object of humanitarian crusading zeal. But it appeared no less attractive to articulate sections of the populace—to trade-unions and friendly societies, and to popular political parties including, in the forefront, Marxian socialists. It promised emancipation for the masses, their approximation to the classes, their full emergence into the light and life of modern society. It was a cause, therefore, in behalf of which the urban proletariat was ready and eager to unite with the intellectual and industrial bourgeoisie. However dilatory the latter might be in conferring the political franchise on the former, once a democratic regime was set up almost its first act was to create or consolidate a state system of popular elementary education. Presently with both masses and classes backing public schools, it became a race between nations to reach the highest degree of literacy; those left behind were deemed as backward as if they had lost a war or lacked industrial machinery.

In 1868, one year after the Austro-Hungarian *Ausgleich* and the establishment of parliamentary government in both parts of the Dual Monarchy, Hungary provided by law that every locality should maintain an elementary school and that every child between the ages of six and twelve should attend; and the next year Austria adopted similar legislation. In 1870, three years after enfranchising urban wage earners, Great Britain enacted an education bill sponsored by Gladstone's Liberal ministry, increasing state subsidies for denominational schools[2] and newly erecting a supplementary nationwide system of secular schools. In 1872, one year after the proclamation of the German Empire and five years after the introduction of democratic suffrage into the federal constitution, the existing Prussian school system was consolidated,[3] nationalized, and in large part secularized. In 1874 Switzerland embodied in a new constitution a provision for compulsory attendance of all children at cantonal schools. In 1877 Italy undertook to oblige children between the ages of six and nine to go to school. In 1878 Holland and in 1879 Belgium extended and secularized public education. Between 1878 and 1881 Republican France, following the behests of Gambetta and Ferry, elaborated a state system of primary and normal schools. School attendance was made compulsory for British children in 1880 and for French children in 1882. Remaining tuition fees were abolished in France in 1886, in Germany in 1888, in Britain in 1891.

Few persons in any of these countries ventured to question the

2 Such subsidies had started in 1833 with the modest amount of £20,000; they rose gradually to £894,000 in 1870, and then sharply to £1,600,000 in 1876.
3 The direct financial contribution of the Prussian state to elementary education rose from 4,500,000 marks in 1871 to 146,000,000 in 1901.

desirability of popular education or the propriety of achieving it by a state-directed and state-financed system of elementary schools. Nor was any hue and cry raised, even by the most individualistic and doctrinaire Liberals, against the enactment or enforcement of state laws compelling school attendance in Germany, Scandinavia, Switzerland, France, and Great Britain. Only in Austria-Hungary and Italy, where industrialization was relatively backward, was compulsion tempered by popular inertia and administrative negligence.

The single question which excited continuous and acrimonious debate about all this popular education was whether it should include religious instruction or be exclusively secular and lay. At first, during the '70's and early '80's, the protagonists of secular education were usually successful. In Switzerland, in Holland and Belgium, in France (finally in 1886), and largely in Austria-Hungary, they banished religious instruction from state schools and confined it to strictly private and barely tolerated church schools. Only in Great Britain did the government continue financial contributions to church schools. Gradually, however, as sectarian liberalism passed into decline and something of a conservative and clerical reaction set in, the protagonists of religious instruction gained the upper hand. In addition to the Scandinavian countries, where such instruction had always been given in the public schools, it was extended in Germany and restored in Austria-Hungary in the '80's. Belgium provided for it partially in 1884 and fully in 1895. Holland began the subsidizing of denominational schools in 1889, and in Great Britain governmental support of them was greatly fortified by the Education Act of 1902. Only France and Switzerland adhered rigorously to an exclusively secular system of public schools.

The movement for mass education was strongest, it will be noticed, in western and northern Europe; it was much weaker in south-central Europe, and almost nonexistent in eastern Europe. It clearly correlated with the intensity of mechanical industry. In corresponding degree, too, it made the masses literate. Between 1870 and 1900 the percentage of literacy among the entire adult population of Great Britain rose from 66 to 95, of France from

60 to 95, of Belgium from 55 to 86. By the latter date the vast majority of these nations, like that of Germany, Holland, Switzerland, and Scandinavia, could read and write. In other countries, progress was slower or quite lacking. In 1900 almost a third of the Austrian population was still illiterate; a half of the Italian and the Hungarian, two thirds of the Spanish and Portuguese, and four fifths of the Russian and Balkan.

The movement was still mainly limited, even in the West, to elementary schooling of children under fourteen years of age. Only a beginning had as yet been made with continuation or trade schools or with university extension; and any big development of public education at the secondary-school level awaited the twentieth century. Nevertheless, to conscript all children of the masses as of the classes for a general war on illiteracy, to regiment them in state schools, to arm them with primers and writing pads and multiplication tables, was an undertaking novel and herculean enough for one generation.

It probably gave the masses more in the way of great expectations than any immediate or tangible benefit. Ambition was not necessarily fed by formal schooling, and the leaders whom the masses furnished to trade-unionism or co-operative enterprise, and likewise the individuals who ascended from their ranks into the middle class, were as likely to be self-taught as school-taught. To be sure, great expectations were not to be despised; they stimulated what in eras less materialistic have been called the virtues of faith and hope and what at the end of the nineteenth century was described as self-confidence.

One tangible result of popular education which is apt to be overlooked was the mustering of a very numerous staff of teachers, a kind of officers' corps, for the vast armies of mobilized children. Many of the teachers came, like their pupils, from the masses; and through the special training which they received at government expense and the common work which they did, they developed a strong corporate *esprit* and applied it to forwarding their own vested interests and to strengthening the attachment of the masses to their respective national governments.

Another result was long unperceived and is still debatable, the increase of gullibility as well as of enlightenment among the masses. Schools taught everybody to read and to pay attention to what the teacher said. If one read something with one's own eye, one was inclined to believe it; and if a licensed teacher vouched for it, it must be true. The school, in other words, was a marvelous propagandist instrument, the full potentiality of which could be appreciated only when popular education was reinforced by popular journalism, cinema, and radio. The advent of cinema and radio was delayed, but popular journalism dogged the steps of popular education.

IV. POPULAR JOURNALISM

According to careful contemporary estimates, the number of newspapers in Europe stood at about 6,000 from 1866 to 1882, and then jumped to 12,000 in 1900.[4] But this doubling of journals within two decades, significant as it is, tells but a small part of the story.

Most of the 6,000 newspapers of the '60's and '70's were slight affairs of few pages, owned and managed by individual proprietors, conducted as journals of personal or political opinion, and limited in circulation to a local clientele among the middle and upper classes who could afford to pay the relatively high subscription price. Even the more substantial newspapers which enjoyed national and international repute, such as the London *Times* or *Post*, the Paris *Temps* or *Journal des Débats*, the Berlin *Vossische Zeitung* or *Kreuzzeitung*, the recently established *Neue Freie Presse* of Vienna, *Tribuna* of Rome, *Secolo* of Milan, had no mass circulation. They cost too much. They were too literary or sophisticated, or else too prosaic and dull. One had to read them leisurely over coffee or tea served by valet or butler, or in upholstered chairs of office, drawing room, or club.

Three main developments conspired to introduce in the '80's a truly popular journalism. One was mechanical, enabling publishers to speed up production, to expedite news gathering, and to lower the price. From about 1871 began the series of inventions by Kasten-

---

4 These figures are derived from Eugène Hatin, *Bibliographie historique et critique de la presse périodique française* (1866); Henry Hubbard, *Newspaper and Bank Directory of the World* (1882); *Encyclopædia Britannica*, 10th ed. (1902-1903). Europe had had about 2,200 newspapers in 1828 according to the *Revue encyclopédique* of that year, i, 593-603.

bein, Mergenthaler, and Lanston which eventuated in the automatic typesetting machines of the next decade. Simultaneously another series of inventions by Tilghman and Eskman led to the large-scale manufacture of cheap wood-pulp paper and its substitution in newsprint for the more expensive (and durable) rag paper. Besides, the telephone of 1877 proved especially serviceable to reporters and editors, and the perfecting of photography to the attractive yet inexpensive illustration of newspapers. Moreover, rapidly improving means of communication invited the dispatch of "special correspondents" to distant and unusual places in search of interesting "eye-witness" stories, and at the same time it permitted a wider and speedier distribution of the finished product. And the Walter press which the London *Times* installed in 1869 and the Hoe press which the same pioneering journal adopted in 1895, were noteworthy landmarks in the progress of quick and quantitative mechanical printing.

A second development favorable to journalistic enterprise was the vogue of liberalism and its political issue in governmental guarantees of the freedom of the press. This particular freedom had been a constant and central article in the liberal *credo*; and in England, the native land of ecumenical if not sectarian liberalism, it was as firmly established two generations before 1870, and as inviolable, as the Englishman's proverbial castle. Then, as liberals gained ascendancy on the Continent, they almost invariably prefaced the written constitutions which they sponsored with pledges of freedom of the press. This was true, for example, of the Italian and Dutch constitutions of 1848, the Austrian of 1867, the Swiss of 1874, the Spanish of 1876. The climax came with legislation during the heyday of liberalism in the '70's and early '80's. Great Britain abolished the last special tax on newspapers in 1870 and required of them, by act of 1881, merely that they register with the government. The French Republic disclaimed from 1871 any censorship of the press, and guaranteed its full liberty by a model law of 1881. The German Empire enacted a liberal press law in 1874.

With liberty finally assured to journalism everywhere in western and central Europe and with new mechanical means of quickening and cheapening the publication and distribution of newspapers, it was natural that the number and circulation of these greatly increased and that many of them became important business enterprises, shifting in character from "journals of opinion" to "journals of information" and relying for their profits less on subscriptions than on the advertising which the advance of industrialization rendered ever more impelling and lucrative. The greater the circulation of a paper, the more advertising it could secure; and the more advertising it carried, the better it could afford to reduce its subscription price in order to obtain wider circulation. One of the first and most influential examples of the newer kind of journalism was the London *Daily Telegraph*, which early cut its price to a penny and in the '70's blossomed forth, with a wealth of advertising, as the foremost organ of the English middle classes, high and low, supplying them with copious and colorless information, and in its editorial policy not so much forming as following public opinion. It was Liberal at first, then critical of Gladstone's foreign policy, and ultimately nationalist and imperialist; and it netted a fortune for its proprietors, Joseph Moses Levy and his son, who took the name of Lawson and gained the title of Baron Burnham.

Comparable with the *Daily Telegraph* were such famous journals as the London *Daily News*, which became a penny paper in 1868; the New York *Herald*, whose founder, the Scottish James Gordon Bennett, died in 1872, and the *New York Times* after its acquisition in the '90's by Adolph Ochs; the Paris *Matin*, which was launched in 1884; the Berlin *Neueste Nachrichten* and the Rome *Messaggiero*. Yet it was mainly from the enlarging middle classes that all such newspapers derived their increased circulation and their financial success. A really popular journalism could arise only when the twin developments of cheapening production by improved mechanical processes and of freeing it from governmental interference were supplemented by a third development—the spread of literacy among the masses and their consequent emergence as prospective readers of newspapers.

A conspicuous inaugural monument in the actual rise of popular journalism was the work of an American of Jewish extraction, Joseph Pulitzer. In 1883 he purchased the *New York World*, a moribund paper which had started twenty years earlier as a highly

Sixty-two Illustrations
Drawn from Unusual Sources
and Specially Chosen by
the Author

for

A GENERATION
OF MATERIALISM

1 8 7 1 – 1 9 0 0

by

CARLTON J. H. HAYES

1. Emperor William I's Triumphal Entry into Berlin, 1871
From a contemporary lithograph

2. Queen Victoria shortly after her Diamond Jubilee, 1897

3. Parliament Building Erected at Berlin "to the German Folk"
in the style of eclectic classicism

4. Making Steel by the Bessemer Process
From an engraving of 1875

5. Making Machine Tools in the 1870's
From a contemporary Lithograph

The Bettmann Archive

6. Supplying Power for First Electric Street Railway in Europe, Frankfort

The Bettmann Archive

7. Tramcars on First Electric Street Railway in Europe, Frankfort

8. H. L. F. von Helmholtz (1821-1894)

9. Werner von Siemens (1816-1892)

10. Sir Charles Parsons (1854-)

The Bettmann Archive

11. Wilhelm von Rontgen (1845-1923)

FOUR INVENTORS OF THE ERA

12. Prophecy of Mechanized War
From a Lithograph by Robida, 1882

13. Building the Trans-Siberian Railway
From a Russian drawing of 1893

14. Pasteur in his Laboratory
From a contemporary drawing

The Bettmann Archive

15. Administering Anaesthesia in a Paris Hospital
From "L'Illustration," 1880

16. Popular Scientific Lecturing by John Tyndall in the 1870's.

17. Thomas Henry Huxley (1825-1895)

18. Ernst Haeckel (1834-1919)

19. August Weismann (1834-1914)

20. Wilhelm Wundt (1832-1920)

FOUR EVOLUTIONISTS

21. Pithecanthropus Erectus,
the "Ape Man"
From the hypothetical reconstruction
of J. H. McGregor

22. "The Thinker"
From the statue by Auguste Rodin
in Metropolitan Museum, New York

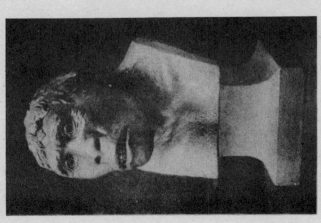

23. Herbert Spencer (1820-1903)

24. Missionary "White Fathers" of Cardinal Lavigerie in North Africa

25. Friedrich Nietzsche
From a portrait by H. Olde

26. Richard Strauss (1864-   )   27. Giacomo Puccini (1858-1924)

28. Peter Tschaikovsky (1840-1893)   29. Claude Debussy (1862-1918)

FOUR MUSICAL COMPOSERS

30. Émile Zola (1840-1902)

31. Leo Tolstoy (1828-1910)

32. Anatole France (1844-1924)

33. Henrik Ibsen (1828-1906)

FOUR LITERARY MEN

34. Miners. From the Sculpture by Constantin Meunier

35. Self-Portrait by Manet in the Impressionist Style

36. Self-Portrait by Cézanne in the Post-Impressionist Style

Courtesy Museum of Modern Art

37. Night Café in Arles

From the painting by Vincent van Gogh, 1888

38. Three Tahitians
From the painting by Paul Gauguin, 1891

39. Side Show
From the painting by G.-P. Seurat, 1889

40. At the Moulin Rouge

41. London Society in the '90's
From a woodcut by George DuMaurier

42. Preparations for a Strike

From a painting by the Hungarian artist, Michael Munkaczy

43. August Bebel (1840-1913)

44. Jules Guesde (1845-1922)

45. Prince Peter Kropotkin (1842-1921)

The Bettmann Archive

46. Bismarck's Anti Socialist Law
From a cartoon in "Punch," 1878

47. Suffrage Demonstration at Brussels, May Day, 1886

48. Departure of Peasant Emigrants from German Village
From a painting by C. L. Bokelmann

49. Women Clerks in Paris Telegraph Office
From a lithograph of the early 1880's

50. Cecil Rhodes, British Empire-Builder

51. Carl Peters, German Empire-Builder

52. Kitchener, Victor of the Sudanese and
Boer Wars

53. Leopold II, Builder of the Congo Free
State

54. Kipling and the "Lesser Breeds"
From the etching by William Strang

55. A German View of British Imperialism
From a cartoon in "Simplizissimus"

56. Pope Leo XIII

57. Emperor Francis Joseph

58. Tsar Alexander III

59. Joseph Chamberlain

60. An English View of William II as the Bad Boy among European Sovereigns.
From "Punch," 1890

61. William II Sees the European Powers Confronting the "Yellow Peril."
From his own design, 1895

62. Bismarck in Retirement

moral and religious sheet; and he soon transformed it into the most widely read journal in the United States. This he did by appealing directly to the masses through sensational headlines, a simple and staccato style of writing, a screaming patriotism, an enthusiastic if somewhat vague reforming spirit, a marked attention to "human-interest" stories of adventure, love, and crime, and a profusion of "special features"—cartoons and "funnies," sporting pages, a page for women, another for children, vari-colored "editions" for almost every hour of the day and night. But Pulitzer's *World* merely blazed trails which a decade later were expanded by others into broad and well-paved thoroughfares of "yellow journalism." By 1900 the recently founded Hearst papers were selling like hot cakes in New York, Chicago, and San Francisco, while at European capitals similar papers were meeting with similar success.

At Paris the daily sales of *Le Petit Journal* exceeded 2 million and a quarter, and of *Le Petit Parisien*, a million. At Berlin, under the guidance of August Scherl, who had had his training in America, the *Lokal-Anzeiger* surpassed the million mark. At London appeared in the late '90's those rival masters of popular journalism, the Harmsworth brothers and Arthur Pearson, whose respective half-penny *Daily Mail* and *Daily Express* promptly entered the "over-a-million" class[5] and won such popular favor that their proprietors were eventually raised by a dazzled and unconsciously humorous government to the British peerage—the Harmsworths as Lord Northcliffe and Lord Rothermere, Pearson as Viscount Cowdray.

Mass literacy, in conjunction with cheapness and freedom of the press, prompted a vast deal of popular propagandist journalism. Socialist publications multiplied, and edified myriads of working-class readers; the Berlin *Vorwärts* vied in circulation in the '90's with other Berlin dailies and stimulated emulation by Marxian journalists in every industrialized nation. Likewise, religious publications flourished as never before; the French Catholic *Croix*, beginning in 1880, had by 1895 a hundred weekly supplements for pro-

[5] If one contrasts the daily sales, running into the millions, of this class of papers in 1900 with the sales of the staid *Times* back in 1860 when they exceeded those of all other London newspapers put together and still amounted to but 51,600, one appreciates what is meant by the rise of popular journalism during the intervening forty years.

vincial towns and countryside. There were also popular anti-
Semitic journals like the *Libre Parole* of Paris or the *Deutsches
Volksblatt* of Vienna, and a host of other propagandist sheets
preaching colonialism or navalism or some kind of social reform.
Nor should one overlook the sporting papers, comic weeklies, and
story magazines which from the '80's onward circulated widely
among the masses.

That popular journalism followed popular education and that
both attended industrialization receives confirmation from an
analysis of the estimated number of newspapers in 1866 and again
in 1900. For all Europe, as has been said, the number doubled. But
there was hardly any increase in Russia and the Balkan countries,
and a very slight one in Austria-Hungary, Italy, and Spain. On
the other hand, the number almost doubled in France and Switzerland, slightly more than doubled in Great Britain and Scandinavia,
and tripled in Germany. And it is a reasonable inference that corresponding discrepancies characterized the vastly greater increase
of journal circulation.

In general, the masses did not conduct the new journalism or
express themselves in it. They made it possible, however; and their
likes and dislikes, their prepossessions and desires—at any rate what
these were imagined to be—conditioned its orientation and much
of its content. "What the people want," was its slogan, and if one
found fault with the sensationalism, the cheapness, or the puerility
of the popular press, one was told to look at the circulation figures
for unanswerable proof that "the people were getting what they
wanted." At least in the minds of managers and proprietors of
great newspapers the emergence of the masses was a fact.

V. MARXIAN SOCIALISM

The heaps of Marxian literature which have piled up since 1871
have persuaded many scholars as well as large sections of the
"general public" that Marxian socialism has been the mass movement, *par excellence,* of modern times; that it sprang from the
masses, that it reflected their needs and desires, that at least from
the 1880's it was the most potent force among them and the prime
factor in their emancipation. There can be no doubt that the rise

and spread of this socialism did constitute a distinguishing and significant development of the era from 1871 to 1900. But if one avoids the propaganda and sticks to the hard cold facts of the era one is likely to arrive at a rather modest appraisal of Marxism as a mass movement during those years.

It did not spring from the masses, as did trade-unionism or the co-operative movement. It sprang from the brains of two bourgeois intellectuals, Karl Marx and Friedrich Engels, and by them and other middle-class intellectuals it was preached, like any philosophy or religion, to the masses—for some time without much effect. From the obscure publication of the *Communist Manifesto* in 1848 to the dissolution of the paltry "First International" in 1876, the gospel of Karl Marx was less a concern of workingmen (to say nothing of society at large) than of police officials. The former largely ignored it. The latter were unduly alarmed by it.[6]

The alarm of police and secret service, if undue, was natural. They did not understand that Marx always claimed a bigger following and wider influence than he really had, or that his loud praise of the revolutionary and bloody Paris Commune was for propagandist purposes and not because any appreciable number of his disciples were actual participants in it; and they were pardonably confused by his hobnobbing now with a rabid nationalist like Mazzini and anon with a wild anarchist like Bakunin. The latter of these "men of violence" formed in 1868 a "Social Democratic Alliance," with secret statutes and with a program calling for "universal revolution," immediate destruction of all governments and churches, and eventual common ownership of land and the implements of labor. It was a loose and sparse organization, comprising only some clockmakers in the otherwise obscure Swiss canton of Neufchâtel and scattered "sections" of crack-brained persons in Latin countries. Yet the affiliation of the "Alliance" with Marx's "International" in 1869 more than doubled the latter's size; and the highhanded expulsion of the Alliance, three years later when Marx finally broke with Bakunin, brought on the dissolution of the International. This held

[6] In Russia, amusingly enough, the authorities permitted the publication of *Das Kapital* on the ground that while it had "socialist" tendencies, "it is not written in a popular style . . . and is unlikely to find many readers among the general public." Cf. Isaiah Berlin, *Karl Marx* (London, 1939), 237.

its last real "congress" at Geneva in 1873; funeral rites for it were celebrated in 1876 by a corporal's guard at the remote and unconcerned World's Fair in Philadelphia.

As for Bakunin's "Alliance," its annual congresses steadily dwindled, until a little remnant, meeting for the last time at London in 1881, sorrowfully confessed that "the masses take no part in the movement"; it recommended special "study of chemistry, which has already rendered great service to the revolutionary cause." Although anarchism, from its very nature, could hardly beget any strong or stable organization, it continued after the demise of the Alliance and the death of Bakunin to inspire a number of intellectuals, including the Russian Kropotkin, the Frenchman Reclus, and the Austrians Most and Peukert, and through them to influence stray groups among the lower middle and laboring classes, especially in the Latin countries, in Austria, and in Russia. But that it was at any time a popular movement is belied by the mass hysteria and the mass applause of repressive legislation which invariably attended the application by anarchists of their "study of chemistry" to the assassination of political potentates: the Tsar Alexander II in 1881, the French President Carnot in 1894, the Austrian Empress Elizabeth in 1898, King Humbert of Italy in 1900, President McKinley in 1901.

In the meantime, whatever appeal Marxian socialism made to intellectuals and to the populace at large must be attributed less to its character as a mass movement than to the "timeliness" of its philosophy. Its philosophy (and prophecies), which had had few disciples and practically no influence during the rise and heyday of liberalism from 1848 to the late '70's, first assumed importance at about the date of Karl Marx's death, in the early '80's, when a general reaction set in against liberalism and individualism and in favor of socialization and what the French call *étatisme*. Of this it was a reflection rather than a cause; it profited from it more than it contributed to it. Moreover, the claims advanced in behalf of Marxism that it was the "scientific" kind of socialism, that it was evolutionary and materialistic, fitted nicely into the intellectual mood of a generation fully convinced of the postulates of Newtonian physics and Comtean sociology and newly enamored of Darwinian evolution and Haeckelian materialism.

Furthermore, Marxism enshrined just enough of the radical liberal tradition of the Enlightenment to attract nostalgic ex-liberals: a loudly professed humanitarianism and internationalism, a devotion to free trade, free press, and free schools (unless these taught "superstition" or were run by "clericals"), a predilection for political democracy (if the "right people" were likely to benefit), and a contemptuous attitude toward any specific reform not dictated by conscious self-interest. Self-interest, this was the very essence of liberalism and of Marxism too, although by the latter it was applied to classes rather than to individuals. If the proletarians wanted reform—and they should—let them accomplish it themselves; it was no one else's business. A function remained, of course, for Marxian intellectuals: they might stimulate the class consciousness of the masses, and they might expound the "scientific" principles involved and the sound "tactics" to be pursued. All of which, in the last two decades of the nineteenth century, was very opportune.

It was middle-class converts, of radical liberal background, who brought Marxian socialism out of obscurity and won for it some standing in working-class quarters. For example, the effective originator of the movement in Germany was Wilhelm Liebknecht, who came of a distinguished family of scholars and state officials proudly claiming descent from Martin Luther, and who received appropriate university training at Giessen and Berlin. He participated as a youthful liberal and democrat in the abortive German revolution of 1848, and then, taking refuge in London, met Karl Marx and became his ardent disciple. Back in Germany in 1865, he won to his new views an exceptionally able and broadly self-educated young Saxon mechanic, August Bebel; and four years later the two organized their small following as the "Social Democratic Workers' party." This they enlarged in 1875 by drawing into it, against the protests of Marx, the older and more moderate Lassallean socialists.

In France the "fathers" were Paul Lafargue and Jules Guesde. Lafargue was a native of Cuba and a resident of Paris, in turn a republican and a Proudhonian anarchist until, on a visit to London to complete his medical studies, he encountered Marx, married his daughter, and accepted his gospel. Guesde, the son of a boarding-school teacher and by profession a journalist, was a radical republican prior to his five-year exile for having taken part in the Paris Commune. Returning to France as confirmed Marxists, Guesde and Lafargue, between them, so manipulated the handful of delegates to the congress of the embryonic federation of French trade-unions at Marseilles in 1879 as to commit a majority of them to the Marxian principle of collectivism. Then, failing to prevent a reversal of this action by the next year's congress at Havre, the two leaders, backed by Marx and obedient to his instructions, entered the political arena in 1882 with a "French Labor party."

The English leader, if a man with almost no following can be called such, was Henry Hyndman, wealthy Cambridge graduate, traveler and sportsman, glib talker, and for a time war correspondent with Garibaldi's redshirts. In 1880 he chanced to read a French translation of the first volume of *Das Kapital*, and with characteristic impulsiveness he paid an instant visit of homage to the somewhat startled and skeptical Marx. The next year Hyndman, in conjunction with the poet and mystic William Morris, launched a "Social Democratic Federation," but it enrolled few members, and Morris, who had the haziest notions of Marx's doctrine,[7] soon withdrew.

Everywhere the same sort of bourgeois intellectual conducted the propaganda and furnished the leadership for Marxian socialism: the scholarly Anseele and Vandervelde in Belgium, the opulent physician Adler in Austria, the well-to-do journalist Turati in Italy. Of its chief apostles, only the Spaniard Iglesias and the German Bebel could be classed as "proletarians": the former was an ex-printer and the latter an ex-wood turner; both were would-be intellectuals and both made their living as propagandists and organizers. In Germany Bebel shared leadership of the movement with Liebknecht and a galaxy of other middle-class persons, including Kautsky the philosopher and Vollmar the social scientist.

---

[7] Said Morris, "I do not know what Marx's theory of value is, and I'm damned if I want to know," but he did know that "the rich are rich because they rob the poor," which was political economy enough for him. Philip, Viscount Snowden, *An Autobiography* (1934), 62.

Until the end of the '80's the spread of Marxism among the masses was painfully slow. In Great Britain, where industrialization was most thorough, and where, *ex hypothesi,* conditions were most favorable for mass acceptance of Marxian socialism, a negligible number of workingmen rallied to it. The bulk of them neither read Marx nor listened to his missionaries; they seemed quite content to stick to their indigenous kinds of trade-union, co-operative store, and friendly society. True, a socialistic Fabian Society appeared in 1883 and enlisted some young literary men—Shaw, Wells, Sidney Webb—but its principles were eclectic rather than orthodox Marxian and its essays were caviar to the popular taste.

In Germany, on the other hand, where industrial conditions were also favorable (though theoretically less so than in Britain), the Social Democratic party captured a large fraction of trade-unionists as well as a relatively large contingent of intellectuals. It polled half a million votes in 1877 and almost as many during the next decade when socialist agitation was checked by special laws. Yet this seemingly large number constituted barely ten per cent of the total electorate. Obviously in Germany, the supposed stronghold of Marxian socialism, the great majority of the masses, urban as well as rural, were enlisted in hostile camps.

In France the Labor party of Guesde and Lafargue, by the utmost effort, polled 30,000 votes in 1885 and 120,000 in 1889, and nonetheless failed in either year to elect a single one of the six hundred Deputies. In Belgium, proportionately much more industrialized than France, it was not until 1885 that Anseele succeeded in forming a Labor party and not until 1894 that it adopted a frankly Marxian platform or won any parliamentary representation. In agricultural Denmark a Social Democratic party, organized in 1878, elected in 1884 two members of parliament; and a similar party in Alpine Switzerland returned the same number in 1890. Marxian parties were also started in Austria in 1888 and in Sweden and Norway in 1889, though for several years thereafter they were extra-parliamentary and comparatively insignificant. Prior to 1890 there were no organized parties, only little knots, of Marxians in Italy, Holland, Spain, Hungary, and eastern Europe. In general, the European masses were still unmoved.

It befitted the liberal and Jacobin tradition of the leaders of Marxian socialism that they inaugurated the so-called "Second International" with a congress at Paris on July 14, 1889, the centenary of the destruction of the Bastille and the beginning of what in polemical writings they were wont to describe as "the middle-class revolution." The congress was attended by 395 delegates, of whom 221 were French. The large majority were professional propagandists, of good bourgeois background, and very doctrinaire. They squabbled with a rival congress of anarchists and other dissidents and ended by profession of Marxian orthodoxy and adoption of mild resolutions in behalf of equal pay for women and international observance of May Day.

Subsequent congresses were held at Brussels in 1891, at Zurich in 1893, at London in 1896, at Paris again in 1900. At all of them the same leaders—Liebknecht, Bebel, Kautsky, Guesde, Lafargue, Anseele, Vandervelde, Adler, Turati—figured prominently and exercised decisive influence; and by all of them the faith was refined, and anathemas worthy of early church councils were hurled at heretics and schismatics, particularly at the anarchists. The Zurich Congress, by declaring for "the collective ownership of the soil," practically removed the large peasant population of Europe from participation in Marxian parties; and it hemmed about its formal condemnation of international war with a refusal to sanction the use of general strikes to halt war. The London Congress, reflecting, chameleon-like, its surroundings, put forth demands that were generically democratic and liberal rather than specifically socialist: universal suffrage and the referendum, emancipation of women, abolition of customs duties, limitation of armaments and of colonial expansion. The Paris Congress of 1900 finally fashioned a definite international organization of Marxists. A permanent central office was established at Brussels, and membership in it and in future congresses was opened to any national party or association adhering to "the essential principles of socialism," which were defined as "socialization of the means of production and exchange, international union and action of the workers, conquest of public powers by the proletariat organized as a class party."

The decade of these congresses witnessed the first big advance of Marxian socialism among the electorates of western and central Europe. In Germany the popular vote of the Social Democratic party went up to a million and a half in 1890 and thence to three million in 1898, and the number of its Reichstag members from 35 to 56 (out of a total of 397). In France the Labor party elected Guesde to the Chamber of Deputies in 1893; and by collaborating with dissident Socialist groups and securing the invaluable co-operation of such new middle-class converts as Jaurès, Millerand, and Briand, it raised the total Marxian vote in 1898 to 700,000. In Belgium it rose in 1894 to 350,000—roughly a quarter of the whole. In Italy, through Turati's tireless efforts, a distinctively Marxian party took form in 1891; with 35,000 suffrages in 1895 it elected 12 members of parliament, and with 200,000 in 1900 it won 33 seats (out of a total of 508). And despite franchise restrictions, Austria in 1900 had fourteen Socialist Deputies, and Sweden one.

Great Britain still baffled Marxian propagandists. Her proletarians were far more numerous than any other country's, and long before 1900 almost all of them could read and vote. Yet Hyndman's Social Democratic Federation made no progress among them; the Fabian Society hardly touched them; and the Independent Labor party which the miner Hardie founded in 1893, and which was less Marxian than Evangelical Christian, polled fewer than 45,000 and returned not a single member of parliament. Presently, the British trade-unions would federate with these little socialist groups in a comprehensive Labor party, but that would be for the defense of trade-unions and not for the preaching of Marxism. In Britain the Socialist tail would not wag the trade-union dog.

Even on the Continent, after thirty years' endeavor, Marxian socialism was scarcely the substantial and supreme mass movement which it claimed to be. Almost without exception its formulators and carriers were urban-born and urban-minded, having scant association or sympathy with peasants and agricultural laborers; naturally enough, it made no appeal to the rural masses. Nor did it make any successful appeal to the numerous lower middle classes of the towns. Except for individual radicals and intellectuals who might hail from any class, it was only that segment of the masses referred to in Socialist parlance as the "proletariat" which yielded an appreciable number of converts to the Marxian cause. But the "proletariat" was really not a simple entity; it was a congeries of classes, some of which took to Marxism more readily than others.

Indeed, the biggest conquests for Marxian socialism were made in those countries where a relatively late though fairly thorough industrialization generated an especially numerous and ambitious "aristocracy of labor" with well-organized trade-unions, and where, at the same time, the political regime remained sufficiently un-democratic or reactionary to alienate trade-unionists (and other "progressive" citizens) and to impel them toward the political party of most vociferous protest. This was certainly exemplified by that prize exhibit of Marxian socialism in the '90's, the German Social Democratic party. But to enlist "proletarian" trade-unionists under its banner, the German party catered to them more than to other elements of the "proletariat"; and to attract all possible "pro-test" voters it pursued tactics which pointed less to proletarian social revolution than to a general democratic reform. The larger the party grew, the more moderate it became—in fact if not in theory.

From the first, Marxian socialism, particularly its German ver-sion, had had a disproportionately large number of professional theorists or (to use their own appalling word) "theoreticians." Which was another indication that the movement was no ordinary mass movement, but that it was intellectual, esoteric, theological. Like other theologians, Marxian "theoreticians" were addicted to interminable debate about what constituted the original deposit of faith and revelation and what were the proper and orthodox meth-ods (or "tactics") for realizing its promises in the future. They did not always reach the same conclusions, and sometimes, in the best theological manner, they anathematized one another, thus giving rise to most regrettable schisms. Among French Socialists, who were ultra-logical and ultra-quarrelsome, as many as five denomi-nations appeared![8] In most countries, nevertheless—and eventually in France—the desire to present a common front for electoral and other "tactical" purposes usually overcame the scruples of the

---

[8] In addition to the Guesdists, there were the Blanquists, the Broussists, the Alle-manists, the Malonists!

masters of orthodoxy and set them to devising formulas for harboring different schools of thought within a single organization still calling itself Marxian. To them, as to contemporary Christian modernists, the church loomed more important than the creed, and the church must be "broad."

In the late '90's an extremely difficult problem of tactics was posed by the rise of "higher criticism" of the gospel of Marx and the doubt it cast upon the accuracy of the master's prophecies. He had foretold that, through an inevitable evolution of capitalism, the bulk of the middle class would fall into the category of proletarians and that the class-conscious proletariat, thus becoming a numerical majority, would be enabled by sheer weight of numbers to possess political power, to abolish private property, and to erect the collectivist state and society. But it was now pointed out, with array of statistics, that while the management of capital was being concentrated in fewer hands, its ownership was being extended, that synchronizing with the descent of middle-class persons into the proletariat was a disconcerting ascent of proletarians into the middle class, and that there was no immediate prospect of a class-conscious proletariat's having the numerical strength of itself to capture by democratic means any existing government. If the "higher critics" were right—and what quantities of polemical literature issued from the Socialist press on this point!—then some revision of Marxian tactics was required. But in what direction? More polemical literature poured forth.

Eduard Bernstein, a prominent intellectual of the German party and one of the most trenchant of the "higher critics," argued that Socialists should move toward the "right." They should stress evolution and co-operation rather than revolution and class conflict. Instead of employing tactics which isolated them from all other parties, they should collaborate with any party or group that was democratically minded and willing to advance the socialization of industry. This revisionism or reformism of Bernstein was bitterly assailed by Kautsky, the premier expounder of orthodoxy, and seriously questioned by most of the other recognized "theoreticians," but it found favor with a considerable number of political leaders, notably Jaurès in France and Vollmar in Germany, and, more pregnantly, with the rank and file of trade-unionists and "protest" voters. The upshot was a practical compromise, for which the adroit Bebel was largely responsible within the German party and also in the International Congress at Amsterdam in 1904. To keep the record straight, reformism was condemned; and to prevent the loss of voters, reformists were suffered to remain and to go on "boring from within."

On the other hand, Georges Sorel, a French engineer who styled himself a neo-Marxist, began arguing in the late '90's that in view of the disclosures of "higher criticism," Socialists should move toward the "left." Lacking a numerical majority, they should abandon the democratic dogma, intensify the class struggle, precipitate a violent revolution, and set up a dictatorship of the proletariat. Against any such leftward trend, Kautsky and all the orthodox were as adamant as Bernstein and the heterodox "right"; and prior to the World War, at any rate, it made little headway in the organized Marxian parties, save only the Russian, which was newest and infinitesimal and "a party in exile." Sorel's counsels appealed, however, to heirs of the anarchism of Bakunin, to extremists in an absolutist and industrially backward country like Russia, and to sizable groups of unskilled workers in southern Europe who had a deep-seated distaste for parliamentary government. In the syndicalist or "direct-action" movement which arose at the turn of the century, Sorel perceived a practical demonstration of how the masses might dominate industry and the state without wasting time or frittering away energy on the sham battles of parliamentary democracy.

At best but a fraction of the vast masses of the European peoples adhered to Marxian socialism in any or all of its forms—orthodox, reformist, syndicalist. Though the fraction would temporarily grow much larger during the early years of the twentieth century, it would still be a fraction and would suffer almost cataclysmic shrinkage and disruption from events of the World War and its aftermath. Marxian influences would remain, and the most populous and backward of European countries would be subjected to a professedly Marxian regime. Yet the Russian "proletarian" dictatorship of the future would hardly be what even a Sorel had anticipated, and it certainly would not be what organized Marxian socialism had worked for and tended toward from 1871 to 1914. In truth, real Marxian socialism, just beginning its public career in 1871, was passing maturity and nearing death in 1914. It proved to be a flutter of the Generation of Materialism.

One should not underestimate the significance of that flutter. Although not a mass movement in inception or control, Marxian socialism was directed at the masses and served to implant in a large section of them, especially in urban workingmen, a sympathy for materialistic philosophy and other intellectual currents of the age, a feeling of self-importance, and a habit of corporate militancy. By these gifts it enormously contributed to the emergence of the masses, and incidentally to their training for a stellar role in the subsequent world drama entitled "The Rise of Demagogic Dictatorship."

VI. BEGINNINGS OF FEMINISM

Prior to 1870, fully half of all the European masses—and classes too—had been pretty well submerged for the simple reason that they happened to belong to the female sex. Back in the Middle Ages there had been a degree of women's rights and a kind of feminism, as evidenced in the careers of a Countess Matilda, a Catherine of Siena, a Blanche of Castile, and a large assortment of regnant queens and imperious abbesses. But by the sixteenth century the "regiment of women" appeared "monstrous" to many men other than John Knox; and the "enlightened" Europe of the seventeenth and eighteenth centuries was distinctly a man's Europe. The *Vindication of the Rights of Women*, which Mary Wollstonecraft published in 1792, with its demand for equal rights and equal opportunities for all human beings, irrespective of sex, found no substantial support then or for half a century afterwards. Humanitarians of those years were too busy emancipating men and talking about the emancipation of Negroes to give thought to the emancipation of women. The theoretical democrats of the French Revolution definitely excluded women not only from the franchise but even from public meetings and political agitation. Practically no opportunities existed anywhere for the education of girls beyond the most elementary stage. In the eyes of the law, whether the common law of England or the Code of Napoléon, the daughter was a household serf, the wife a chattel.

Reform of the legal status of women and their emergence as an important self-conscious force in cultural, economic, and political life came in the latter part of the nineteenth century. Several factors contributed to the process. The basic one, no doubt, was the gradual disintegration of traditional family life, consequent upon mass migration from country to town and large-scale employment of wives and daughters in factory, office, and shop. This tended in a highly practical way to give cogency and application to the tenet of doctrinaire liberalism that the unit of the social order was not the family group but the individual human being; and from the appearance of John Stuart Mill's epochal *Subjection of Women* in 1869, few intellectuals of radical proclivity had reason to doubt that females were individuals quite as much as males and deserving of equal consideration.

That women, even of the upper classes, were in need of emancipation had already been sensationally demonstrated by the *cause célèbre* which Ferdinand Lassalle pressed in Germany for ten years and before thirty-six tribunals in behalf of the Countess Hatzfeld; and afterwards a galaxy of internationally famous literary men, such as Ibsen and Shaw, Zola and Meredith, gave powerful impetus to the movement,[9] as did a number of influential social scientists. Lewis H. Morgan, for example, dwelt in his *Ancient Society* (1877) on the importance of women in primitive tribal life and in the evolution of civilization, and Lester F. Ward put forth in his *Dynamic Sociology* (1883) a "gynæcocentric theory" of the natural priority and superiority of the female sex. The last provided a rationale for full-fledged feminism.

August Bebel, too, turned feminist and brought out in 1893 *Die Frau und der Sozialismus.* This was not a scholarly work but cleverly written propaganda to draw women into Marxian socialism. It borrowed from Morgan for its idealization of woman's role in primitive, pre-capitalistic society, and in the part devoted to modern

---

[9] On the other hand, a classic attack on feminism was made by the Swedish writer, August Strindberg, in *Giftas*, the collection of stories which he published in 1884-1886.

times it connected the submergence of women with the rise of capitalism. Bebel's book attracted a large reading public in Germany—it reached a fiftieth edition in 1910—and was translated into most other European languages. Not every Socialist "theoretician" agreed with Bebel. Belfort Bax, for instance, published a counterblast in 1896 under the suggestive title of *The Legal Subjection of Men*, and followed it up with a diatribe which he frankly called *The Fraud of Feminism*. But Bax was a bit heterodox and belated. In the meantime Engels and Kautsky and Liebknecht and most other pillars of Marxian orthodoxy, together with English Fabians and French Reformists, endorsed and amplified the thesis of Bebel. Let Socialists espouse the emancipation of woman, and women will be foes of capitalism and devotees of socialism. And the ensuing numerous enrollment of women in the several Marxian parties proved the soundness of the new tactic.

Even the Christian churches were not unsympathetic with the milder forms of the feminist movement. They kept more of a hold on women than on men, and they did so, in part at least, because they patronized and fostered a remarkable multiplication of auxiliary women's organizations—missionary circles, aid societies, devotional leagues and guilds, working-girl clubs. Some "liberal" churches of England (and America) took the revolutionary step of ordaining women preachers,[10] and among the larger and more conservative churches, whether Catholic or Anglican or Lutheran, most of the increased teaching and nursing services and much of the expanding foreign-missionary enterprise were entrusted to religious women. "Deaconesses" and sisterhoods were new phenomena in the Anglican Church, and in the Catholic Church the growth of religious communities for women was remarkable.

But whether their underlying philosophy was Christian or Marxian, conservative or radical, women in general displayed after 1870 an unusual self-assertiveness. From themselves emanated demands for something like equality in schooling, in opportunities for business and professional careers, in property rights, in political life. Gradually, also, through sheer press of numbers, guided by effective

[10] The Salvation Army counted 5,000 women officers in 1890. As the *Pall Mall Gazette* declared in a leading editorial on April 18, 1889: "The Hallelujah Lass and the Primrose Dame march in the van of the Women's Movement of the World."

propaganda and aided by liberal and susceptible males, European (and American) women secured the ends they sought. Naturally enough the speed and thoroughness of the process depended upon the degree of a country's industrialization and its attachment to liberal principles. It was fastest and most comprehensive in England, slowest and least obvious in eastern Europe.

New careers opened up for women. In England, by 1900, there were some forty thousand nurses and forty-five thousand women schoolteachers. A still greater opening occurred for women stenographers and secretaries. There must have been none of these before 1870, or else Dickens, who died that year, would have introduced us to one. According to census returns, however, England had 7,000 in 1881; 22,200 in 1891; 90,000 in 1901. The Bank of England began employing women as clerks in 1893. The new telephone service, almost from the start, was a female monopoly. Besides, despite a large amount of restrictive labor legislation, the number of women employed as operatives in factories (especially textile mills) and as sales girls in department stores and other retail shops steadily increased, while the number in old-time domestic service remained fairly constant and that of governesses and tutors rose.

The new national systems of popular elementary schooling which took shape in the '70's and '80's were for girls equally with boys, and they spread literacy with a fine impartiality as between the sexes. In opening higher education to women, the University of Zurich led the way in 1867, and Paris followed shortly afterwards. The universities of Sweden and Finland admitted women to their lectures and degrees in 1870; those of Denmark in 1875; those of Italy in 1876, and of Russia in the early 1880's. The University of London conceded degrees to women in 1878, and Dublin in 1879. The universities of Russia and Norway followed in the early 1880's; those of Spain and Rumania in 1888; those of Belgium and Greece in 1890; those of Scotland in 1892. Meanwhile, to offset the still adamantine opposition of "reactionary" Oxford and Cambridge to "women's rights," separate women's colleges were founded in England—Girton in 1872, Newnham in 1875, Somerville and Lady Margaret in 1879; while newly established provincial universities in England, like contemporary Western ones in America, were militantly coeducational.

The old honored professions of medicine and law were gradually opened to women. By 1870 Holland and various American states were admitting women to the practice of medicine. England followed in 1876; Belgium and Russia in 1890. Admission of women to the bar was generally slower, France not sanctioning it till 1900 and Great Britain not till 1903.

The right of women to their own property and their own earnings was recognized in Great Britain by parliamentary acts of 1870 and 1882; and most other European countries eventually arrived in various ways at approximately the same position. Moreover, a kind of local franchise was conceded to English women fairly early for vestries and boards of health, in 1869 for town council elections, in 1870 for school boards, and in 1888 for county councils.

From 1867, when John Stuart Mill had proposed to extend the parliamentary franchise to women on the same terms as to men, a general women's suffrage movement definitely crystallized. Much fun was made of it, and some of its leaders and protagonists undoubtedly merited the popular appraisal of them as "short-haired women and long-haired men." But during the decade of the '70's the petitions which these presented annually to Parliament averaged 200,000 signatures; and in 1888 was organized an "International Woman Suffrage Alliance" whose membership mounted rapidly and whose conventions were attended by delegates from an ever-increasing number of countries.

It was on distant and oversea frontiers of Europe that the first tangible fruits of the suffrage movement were reaped—Wyoming in 1869, Colorado and New Zealand in 1893, South Australia in 1894, Utah and Idaho in 1896. Not until the first decade of the twentieth century would Finland and Sweden become pioneers within Europe of the political enfranchisement of women, and not until then would the alarming violence of the Pankhurst women, Emmeline and Christabel, bring the British movement close to fruition. But then would come the climax of materialism (and much else) in the World War, which at least incidentally showed that the female as well as the male masses had emerged fully out of the preceding generation with electoral rights—and belligerent duties.

Chapter Six

RESURGENCE OF ECONOMIC NATIONALISM AND NATIONAL IMPERIALISM

I. REACTION AGAINST DOCTRINAIRE LIBERALISM IN THE 1880's

THE decade of the 1880's witnessed a sharp reaction against that sectarian liberalism which had characterized the previous decade.[1] It was not a reaction against constitutional government or guarantees of freedom of religion, press, association, etc. Such constitutionalism had been inspired by an earlier and more ecumenical liberalism, and, though it was extolled and exploited by political parties of Liberals (with the capital letter) during their ascendancy in the 1870's, it long outlived their eclipse. The reaction was rather against the urban-mindedness of those political parties and against the particular materialist conception which underlay their economic policies. They were too logically Lucretian. Enamored of mechanical industry and the material profits to be derived from it, they assumed that it operated naturally and most successfully through a simple concourse of competing and clashing atoms. All that any government should do in the premises was to equalize opportunity for atoms. In practice this meant free trade, free business enterprise, free contract, free competition, private ownership of machines, private operation of public utilities, a minimum of governmental interference with industry, a minimum of legislation in aid of agriculture or labor.

For the reaction which set in during the 1880's the Liberals themselves were partly responsible. In a sense they dug their own graves. Industrialization, which they so lavishly patronized, soon passed beyond their mental range from personal to corporate control, and the rights which they bestowed upon associations of employers they could hardly withhold from unions of employees. Moreover, as devotees of the latest materialistic science they could not

---

[1] See Chapter Two, above, especially pp. 66-87.

stop short with Lucretian physics; they had to embrace Darwinian biology, with its stepchild of Spencerian sociology, and before long they were painfully aware of "organismic" theories of the state superimposed by "sound political science" on their atomic notions. Besides, there was nationalism, whose growth they had fed as an aid to personal freedom and an antidote to otherworldly superstition, but whose full stature, reached after the Franco-Prussian and Russo-Turkish Wars, cast over individual interests and individual competition the shadow of national interests and national competition.

Incidentally, the Liberal parties were accused of attracting to their banners a disproportionate share of Jews and also of tolerating an inordinate amount of financial peculation and political corruption. Jews had been emancipated too recently and were still too much despised by the generality of Europeans to occupy conspicuous places in any political party seeking popular favor; they were too easy targets for counter-attack. Also, there was enough abiding respect for traditional morality throughout the generation of materialism to evoke widespread disgust with "crooked" politicians and to give volume to the cry of "turn the rascals out."

But what clinched the fate of the Liberal parties was the emergence of the masses, and to this the Liberals themselves contributed by espousing political democracy, by legalizing trade-unions and co-operative societies, and, most momentously, by fostering that secular national education which by the '80's was rendering almost everybody in central and western Europe literate and peculiarly amenable to journalistic propaganda. Eventually it proved to be not so much the propaganda of the Liberal parties with which the emerging masses found themselves in sympathy, as that of rival parties, which were thus enabled to gain ground and to give a novel orientation to national policy. In the main, it was away from *laisser faire* and toward economic nationalism—and national imperialism. Not the individual, but society, especially national society, was to be the goal.

The sudden appearance of Marxian Socialist parties in the '80's was one obvious sign of change and a notable stimulus to it. To be sure, these parties were more akin to sectarian liberalism than any of its other rivals. They, too, were materialist. They, too, were urban-minded. They, too, aspired to a this-worldly utopia of machinery and personal health and happiness. They, too, took the side of science in the current "warfare" with theology; and their persistent championship of free trade, no less than their resonant anti-clericalism, should have endeared them to the Liberals. Yet Liberals and Marxists quarreled and fought as only blood relations can. The latter claimed the former's property, threatened to employ state power and even revolutionary violence to get it, and pledged it, when gotten, to the "toiling masses." And short of an ultimate holocaust of private property, the Marxists preached, we all know, the anti-Liberal gospel of the class conflict, of the supremacy of class interests over individual interests, and insisted that the state has the immediate right and duty to enact drastic social legislation in behalf of the "proletariat" and to put the burden of taxation squarely upon the "bourgeoisie." Small wonder that dyed-in-the-wool Liberals were shocked or that crowds of urban workmen turned Socialist.

Another kind of opposition to the Liberal parties was supplied by marshaling of traditionally religious forces either into pre-existing Conservative parties or into newly formed confessional parties. Generally speaking, the rural masses and even a sizable segment of the urban masses and middle classes were still responsive to Christian ideology and antipathetic to the materialistic and atheistic tendencies of doctrinaire liberalism and to its lack of "social conscience." When, in the '70's, the Liberal parties made frontal attacks upon church schools and other ecclesiastical institutions and privileges, religious people rallied in defense. By the '80's the defense passed to an offensive. Particularly was this true of Catholics, who, in reacting against the Kulturkampf, built up a strong Center party in Germany, an important Christian Socialist party in Austria, influential Clerical parties in Belgium, the Netherlands, and Switzerland, and later the "Liberal Action" in France and the "Popular Action" in Italy. All these parties made democratic appeal, all of them cut through social classes, and all produced programs of social reform.

These programs were evolved, chiefly in the '80's, by a noteworthy group of Catholic intellectuals: Moufang and Hitze in Germany, Vogelsang and Rudolf Meyer in Austria, de Mun and La Tour du Pin in France, Decurtins and Bishop Mermillod in Switzerland, Périn in Belgium, Cardinal Manning in England; and in 1891 appeared Pope Leo XIII's confirmatory encyclical, *Rerum Novarum*. Thus took shape a Catholic social movement which combated economic liberalism no less than Marxian socialism. On a wide front it helped to crystallize demands for tariff protectionism and labor legislation, and, though less precise and more opportunist than the Marxian movement, it was almost equally effective in weaning the masses away from Liberalism.

The reaction of Protestant Christians was less systematic. With the exception of the Calvinist party in the Netherlands, they founded no distinctively confessional party. But in Germany militant Lutherans gave renewed vigor to the Conservative party, and in Switzerland Protestants appropriated the so-called Liberal party (the sectarian Liberals constituting there the Radical party), while in Great Britain the rank and file of professing Anglicans were devotedly Conservative.

Nor should we overlook the anti-Semitic movement in the early '80's. It was not yet wholly a "racial" movement, but rather a capitalizing of popular prejudice against Jews in order to discredit both the Liberal and the Marxian parties, in which so many of them were enrolled. Over against those parties, it urged defense of Christianity and a species of national socialism. It was influential in building up the Christian Socialist party in Austria and in temporarily reviving clerical royalism in France, and it enabled a demagogic Lutheran clergyman, Adolf Stöcker, to add to the nationalist Conservative forces in Germany a small but fanatical band of shock troops.

Undoubtedly the most significant development of the '80's was a new lease of life by Conservative parties. They were predominantly agricultural in outlook and interest, suspicious of urban-mindedness, and devoted to such traditional European institutions and customs as church, army, nobility, patronage, and *noblesse oblige*. They had never looked with favor upon doctrinaire liberalism, and they felt a natural scorn for its talkative votaries. So long as Conservative leaders enjoyed a profitable return from landed property, with a surplus for investment in mechanized industry, they could endure, though bewail, Liberal ascendancy. But when, in the late '70's, a pronounced agricultural depression set in and presently promised to become permanent, the same leaders bestirred themselves mightily. They would enlist the rural masses—peasant proprietors, farm tenants, even agricultural laborers—in a crusade to throw the Liberals out of office and to restore, by state action, a proper balance between agriculture and industry, between labor and capital. And by advertising their own solid attachment to national traditions and national honor and decrying the Liberals' white-livered pacifism, they might expect, in an era of quickening nationalism, a still broader popular recruitment.

Invaluable aid was afforded the Conservative cause by the "national historical school" of political economists. Its teaching was a characteristically German product, woven out of the Prussian cameralism of the eighteenth century and already patterned in the 1840's by Friedrich List and Wilhelm Roscher, though not becoming a staple and one for export until after the stirring nationalist events of 1866-1871. Then to its elaboration rallied the elite of professorial economists in the German universities, including Adolf Wagner at Berlin, Gustav Schmoller at Strasbourg, Georg Hanssen at Göttingen, Bruno Hildebrand at Jena, Karl Kines at Heidelberg, Georg Knapp at Leipsic, Lujo Brentano at Breslau. Wagner was typical of the "school." Publicist as much as scholar, he was at once a political Conservative, a pious Lutheran, and a flamboyant German patriot. He had discharged diatribes, as fiery as Treitschke's, against France in 1870, and in the '80's he was to be Stöcker's first lieutenant in anti-Semitic agitation. In 1872 he joined with Hildebrand, Schmoller, and others in issuing the "Eisenach Manifesto," which declared war on economic liberalism, lauded the recently established German Empire as "the great moral institution for the education of humanity," and demanded legislation that would enable "an increasing number of people to participate in the highest benefits of German *Kultur*." The national state, according to Wagner and his associates, should no longer be a Liberal puppet— a mere "passive policeman." It should be an active guide and disciplinarian. It should regulate and plan the whole national economy —agriculture, industry, trade, labor.

From Germany the anti-Liberal, anti-Manchester gospel of the "national historical school" was exported, though in somewhat adulterated forms, to France, Italy, and Britain. In the last-named country, for example, it found ready consumers—and able propagandists—in Archdeacon Cunningham, Arnold Toynbee, and William J. Ashley. Wherever it penetrated, it both reflected and heightened a trend toward economic nationalism and political Conservatism.

The Conservative parties, utilizing the platform and arguments of their professorial allies, and likewise their own ultra-patriotic sentiments, carried to the masses the fight with doctrinaire Liberalism. In Germany they patronized the energetic popular propaganda of the "Union for Social Politics," which issued from the Eisenach Manifesto of 1872, and later, in the '90's, the still more strident agitation of the "Agrarian League," the "Pan-German League," and a swarm of military, naval, and colonial societies. In Britain the group of Tory Democrats led by Lord Randolph Churchill, launched in 1883 the Primrose League, which, through honorific titles and decorations, ceremonial observances and floods of pamphlet literature, appealed alike to aristocrat and plebeian, man and woman, age and youth. Children were enrolled as "Primrose Buds," and Primrose Dames (no less than Salvation Army lassies) contributed to the contemporary feminist movement. The League's adult membership (Knights, Dames, and Associates) mounted steadily from 950 in 1884 to 910,000 in 1890, and on to 1,550,000 in 1900. Each of these had to declare, "on my honor and faith that I will devote my best ability to the maintenance of religion, of the estates of the realm, and of the imperial ascendancy of the British Empire." It was a neat Conservative pledge, and in electoral campaigns of the period the League performed signal service for the Conservative party.

Under the impact of propaganda from social Conservatives, social Christians, and Marxian Socialists, and of changing economic conditions which favored popular acceptance of such propaganda, schisms appeared in the individualistic Liberal parties. In Germany the National Liberal party moved farther and farther toward the Right, away from their dwindling Radical brethren and into gradual alignment with the Conservatives. In France many erstwhile Radicals deserted to the protectionist and imperialist Moderates, while others, induced by conviction or political expediency to evince a social conscience, gravitated toward what was subsequently dubbed the Radical Socialist party. In Britain a sort of social Liberalism was fostered by land-reform agitation of John Stuart Mill, Alfred Russel Wallace, and Henry George, and by urban-reform activity of Joseph Chamberlain; and when the last-named, a good imperialist withal, fell foul of Gladstone over the latter's Irish Home Rule Bill of 1886, he carried a large fraction of the more socially and imperially minded Liberals with him into a new organization, the Liberal Unionist party, which before long was swallowed by the Conservatives. The socializing of the remaining English Liberals had to await Gladstone's demise—and the Boer War—at the end of the century. In Italy, no like doctrinal squeamishness stayed the left-wing Liberal leaders, Depretis and Crispi. They were valiantly imperialist and heretically "social" throughout the decade of the '80's.

The ubiquitous reaction against the old-line Liberal parties was registered by parliamentary election returns. In Great Britain the era of Liberal supremacy, which had endured almost continuously since 1846, was rudely interrupted in 1874 by Disraeli's accession to the premiership with a Conservative majority of fifty in the House of Commons. Thenceforth, with the exception of a stormy interlude from 1880 to 1885, the Liberals were in a minority, and during the brief ministries which Gladstone headed in 1886 and again in 1892 he leaned for support upon the shaky reed of Irish nationalism. Altogether, the years from 1874 to 1906 were an era of Conservative supremacy. The Conservatives (with their Liberal Unionist allies) won majorities of 110 in 1886, 152 in 1895, and 134 in 1900.

In Germany the democratic Reichstag elections of 1878 indicated the trend of the ensuing decades. The Liberal factions lost their majority—the National Liberal seats being reduced from 141 to 109 and those of the Progressives (or Radicals) from 40 to 30. On the other hand the Conservative groups increased their representation from 78 to 116, and the Catholic Centrists (with associated Poles, Guelphs, and Alsatians) from 126 to 133. Of popular votes the Liberals lost 130,000 and the Opposition gained 550,000.

In Austria the Liberal regime was supplanted in 1879 by a ministry under Count Taaffe, who speedily came to an understanding with the feudal and federal elements victorious in the parliamentary election of that year; and he remained in power, with Clerical, Polish, and Czech help, for the next fourteen years. By that time the Christian Socialists were the largest single party in Austria, with the Marxian Social Democrats in second place. In Hungary the intensely nationalist (and agrarian) Count Koloman Tisza dominated the political scene from 1875 to 1890. In the Dutch Netherlands, the Calvinist "anti-revolutionary" party took office in 1879, and in 1888 began collaboration with the Catholic party, while in Sweden the premiership passed in 1880 into conservative Agrarian hands.

In Belgium the elections of 1884 ended Liberal rule and inaugurated a long period of Catholic supremacy. By 1893, when universal manhood suffrage was established, the Belgian Chamber consisted of 105 Catholics, 29 Socialists, and only 18 Liberals. In France the elections of 1885 reduced the Republican majority by half, and during the ensuing fourteen years the ministries were manned by Moderate, rather than Radical, Liberals, and by Moderates who were spurred on to nationalist and imperialist policies by the Boulangist and anti-Semitic movements and to some measure of social legislation by the growing pressure of Marxian Socialists and Social Catholics.

Simultaneously, it may be noted, the huge Russian Empire was committed more unambiguously than ever to conservative reaction. The assassination of the reputedly liberal Alexander II in 1881 brought to the throne the Tsar Alexander III, who surrounded himself with ultra-reactionary agents. The all-important ministry of the interior, with its police power and censorship control, was entrusted to an arch-Conservative, Count Dmitri Tolstoy, until his death in 1889, and then to a rigid bureaucrat, Durnovo. The regulation of church and education was committed to Constantine

Pobêdonostsev, an implacable foe of liberalism in all its aspects; and the ministry of foreign affairs, to Baron de Giers, essentially a German Junker. The only surviving quasi-Liberal in the entourage was Bunge, the finance minister until 1887—and he was an economic nationalist. The '80's were a golden age in Russia for Slavophiles and Pan-Slavists.

Practical effects of the general European reaction against doctrinaire liberalism were soon manifest in the protective tariffs, socializing legislation, and national imperialism which are outlined in the following sections of this chapter, and likewise in the intense nationalism whose rise is sketched in the next chapter.

II. RETURN TO TARIFF PROTECTION

"Every nation ought to endeavour to possess within itself all the essentials of national supply." So Alexander Hamilton had said just after the War of American Independence,[2] and his words, echoed in Europe in the 1840's by Friedrich List, bore special significance for the generation that issued from the nationalist wars of 1870-1871 and 1877-1878 and that maintained the ensuing "armed peace." To a statesman like Bismarck it appeared axiomatic that a nation, to be truly prepared for military assaults from without, must possess adequate means from within for supplying food, munitions, and money. Bismarck surely knew!

But by the latter part of the 1870's it was becoming very doubtful whether, under the existing regime of international free trade —or approximation to it—any nation on the Continent of Europe could attain to economic self-sufficiency. Continental industry was still "infant industry" in comparison with Great Britain's, and the depression which hit it in the middle '70's was aggravated by the dumping of British manufactures. Furthermore, the agricultural production of central and western Europe was gravely menaced by new competition, a result of improving land and water transportation, from Russia, Rumania, and especially America. Already by 1876 rapid extension of the area of cultivation in the United States, combined with the use of farm machinery as well as of steam-powered ocean liners, was raising the value of American

[2] In his famous "Report on Manufactures" (1791).

agricultural exports to half a billion dollars. And how without fully developed domestic agriculture and mechanical industry could a modern nation be prosperous? And how without prosperity could it yield the taxes requisite for up-to-date war preparedness?

Protective tariffs were the answer. They would protect infant industries, it was urged. They would protect domestic agriculture. They would assure increasing national wealth and corresponding governmental revenue. They would render the nation self-sufficing, and to that extent invulnerable to foreign attack. Incidentally they would ameliorate the condition of the working class in factory and field, for without protective tariffs foreign competition would cause either a reduction of wages or an access of unemployment. It was even argued by some protectionists still haunted by cosmopolitan ghosts that high tariffs would benefit mankind at large, inasmuch as they would enable nations to escape exploitation by each other and to reach the same happy goal of material well-being.

The European procession away from free trade was led, paradoxically perhaps, by industrially backward countries. Russia, whose trade had never been very free, raised her tariff rates about 50 per cent in 1876 by prescribing their payment in gold instead of in depreciated paper money. The next year, Spain under the leadership of the Conservative Canovas, established two sets of duties, one for countries according her most-favored-nation treatment, and the second, at higher levels, for other countries; and in 1878 Italy, responding to the importunities of Piedmontese industrialists, adopted an "autonomous," though still moderate, tariff.

The procession was then joined, and henceforth headed, by Germany. In 1879, with the help of the new Conservative and Centrist majority, Bismarck piloted through the Reichstag a protective tariff. The duties, which were largely specific rather than *ad valorem*, applied chiefly to grains, meat, and textiles. The duty on iron was restored, and numerous other manufactures received moderate protection. Industrial raw materials, with few exceptions, were admitted free of duty, but timber and tallow, produced plentifully in Germany, were subject to duties. Luxury goods were taxed lightly, primarily for revenue.

The German tariff of 1879 fed protectionist agitation and provided a model for imitation elsewhere. France took advantage of the approaching expiration of the Cobden trade treaty with Great Britain, and of a Republican majority in the Chambers peculiarly anxious to conciliate both industrialists and merchants, to raise tariff rates in 1881 on many manufactured imports, especially woolens, and at the same time to promote shipping and shipbuilding by means of bounties. Russia effected a series of tariff increases during the '80's at the behest of her able finance minister Bunge, and in 1891 she adopted a revised and comprehensive tariff measure, imposing practically prohibitive duties on coal, steel, and machinery, and very high duties on other manufactures. Austria, between 1881 and 1887, under the Conservative ministry of Count Taaffe, repeatedly hoisted duties upon foreign manufactures and also upon grain imports from Rumania and Russia.

If the first steps on the path of tariff protection were taken in the interest of "infant industries," the following long strides were prompted by agrarians. These insisted that their needs were quite as imperative as the manufacturers', and that their importance, as the nation's real backbone, was greater; and in most countries of the Continent they were sufficiently numerous and by 1885 sufficiently well organized (in co-operative societies and political leagues) to exert decisive influence on governments. Germany jacked up imposts on foreign foodstuffs in 1885 and again in 1887. Simultaneously France undertook tariff protection of sugar beets, rye, barley, oats, wheat, and flour. Italy followed suit in 1887 and Sweden in 1888. In 1891 Switzerland departed from its long-standing free-trade policy and enacted a protective tariff. The next year was France's turn again, this time mainly as a result of peasant demands and their championship by the Moderate leader, Jules Méline. While adding to the protection of machinery and most of the textiles, the new French tariff raised agricultural duties approximately 25 per cent and granted bounties for silk, hemp, and flax.

Indeed the only nations which did not conform to the protectionist trend in the '80's and '90's were Great Britain, Belgium, and Holland. Commercial outweighed agricultural interests in all three, and in the first two industrialization had so clearly passed the infant stage that anyone who then proposed tariff protection for it was likely to be laughed at or thought mad. That erratic genius Lord Randolph Churchill did sponsor in 1881 a "Fair Trade League" in behalf of a moderate tariff for Britain and preferential treatment of British imports in the colonies, and the leader of the League, a Conservative M.P.,[3] translated and published, for the first time in English, Friedrich List's *National System of Political Economy* (1885). But not until Joseph Chamberlain took up cudgels for "tariff reform" after the turn of the century did protectionism become a live issue in Great Britain, and not until after the World War did it reach fruition. In the meantime, the Conservative party threw sops to British agriculture. A Board of Agriculture was re-created in 1889, and its president was admitted to cabinet rank in 1895. In 1892 the importation of foreign live stock was prohibited on grounds of disease, and in 1896 occupiers of farm land were relieved of half the local taxes.

Wherever protectionism was the rule—and that meant most of the Continent from the 1880's onward—it undoubtedly stimulated industrialization and at the same time helped to preserve some balance in national economy between manufacturing and agriculture, a balance which Great Britain, through adherence to free trade, lacked. Its effects on the lower middle and working classes, on wages and the cost of living, were more debatable. William H. Dawson pronounced them bad, but perhaps he infused his scholarship with a pretty strong tincture of classical economics and English Liberalism. Equally eminent German writers, such as Sombart and Max Weber, have witnessed to great blessings conferred upon the masses by tariff protection. The debate has naturally soared from the ground of economic fact into the empyrean of patriotic faith. Which, after all, was the prime purpose of tariff protection, at least in the minds of statesmen, and its most obvious and certain result. For it subordinated the concept of individual enterprise to that of national enterprise, and sublimated competition between individuals into competition between nations.

This competition involved an obvious paradox. On the one hand, each protectionist nation wanted to protect its home market from foreign products. On the other hand, it was unwilling to have its

[3] Sampson Lloyd.

products excluded from foreign markets. In efforts to resolve the paradox, tariff protection led to international tariff bargaining, not infrequently to international tariff wars, and usually to a compromise which, in view of strenuous domestic opposition from interests adversely affected, was apt to be brief. Germany, for example, after piling up barriers from 1879 to 1887 against foreign grain, felt obliged in 1891 to adopt a policy of reciprocity, that is, consenting to lower duties on agricultural imports from such countries as would lower their duties on her industrial exports. Consequent bargaining eventuated fairly soon in reciprocity treaties between Germany and most of her neighbors. With Russia, however, agreement was reached only after a three years' tariff war and then to the dismay of German agrarians, who did not cease their lamentations and organized protests until they persuaded the government, by a new tariff of 1902, to annul the reciprocity treaties and raise the grain duties to towering heights. Meanwhile, Germany waged other tariff wars, notably with Spain from 1894 to 1899, and with Canada from 1897.

France, by her tariff act of 1892, provided for a somewhat different basis of bargaining. She adopted two sets of duties, a maximum and a minimum. The latter she might concede to nations which favored her. The former was applied to others. The scheme was similar to the Spanish of 1877, and was later imitated by Norway. In the case of France, it aggravated a tariff war with Italy, which began in 1888 and lasted until 1899, and it brought on an acute tariff conflict with Switzerland from 1893 to 1895.

Altogether the protective tariffs of the '80's and '90's represented a reversal of the laissez-faire commercial policy which had featured the period of Liberal ascendancy in the '60's and '70's. They marked a return to previous mercantilist policy. But whereas the export taxes and the trade prohibitions of that earlier policy were not revived, its rates of import duties were now considerably exceeded, and for the new mercantilism there was popular and nationalist support in much greater degree than there had been for the old. Moreover, by reason of intensified international competition in the economic domain, tariff rates were ever advancing, never retreating. Germany's reciprocity treaties and France's minimum schedules of the '90's carried higher average rates than any previous tariffs of those countries.[4]

Nor were import duties the only instruments of the new protectionism. Embargoes were laid, in the guise of sanitary regulations, on foreign importation of vegetable or animal products. Export bounties were provided, and so too were shipping subsidies, and preferential railway rates for domestic commodities. It is more than mere coincidence that in the very year 1879, when Germany embarked upon tariff protection, the Prussian government declared flatly and finally for state ownership and operation of railways. This was achieved in Germany within the next five years, and before long, at least in central Europe, telegraphs and telephones, as well as railways, were nationalized and pressed into the service of national economy.

III. SOCIALIZING LEGISLATION

In his *Merrie England*, an immensely popular book of the early '90's, Robert Blatchford pointed to municipal gas works, free public schooling, factory legislation, building acts, national ownership of telegraphs, as evidence "that socialism has begun, so that the question of where to begin is quite superfluous."[5] Blatchford was right. Tariff protection was but one indication of a tidal change in Europe during the '80's: the ebbing of *laisser faire*, of economic liberalism, and the incoming rush of state socialization, of economic nationalism. The change was equally evidenced by a wide range of directly socializing enactments.

In at least three fields—education, health, and charity—the most doctrinaire Liberals had already contributed with singular enthusi-

---

4 The United States had built up by the '80's, it should be remembered, a tariff wall much higher than any in Europe, and it was successively heightened by the McKinley tariff of 1890 (with its reciprocity arrangements) and the Dingley tariff of 1897. Likewise Canada and other British Dominions reared tariff walls to dizzy heights.

5 As Wingfield-Stratford says (*History of British Civilization*, p. 1226), while William Morris, the Webbs, G. B. Shaw, and H. G. Wells were addressing socialistic appeals to the middle classes, "Robert Blatchford, of the true spiritual lineage of Cobbett, spoke straight to the heart of the masses, pleading in good muscular English the cause of Britain for the British, and contrasting the Dismal England of capitalism with the Merry England she had been and might yet be made." After selling 20,000 copies of *Merrie England* at a shilling, Blatchford reduced the price in 1894 to a penny. It preached a nationalistic socialism, and was vastly more influential in England than any Marxian propaganda.

asm to a veritably revolutionary extension of the functions of government and to an even more startling exercise of compulsion on individuals for achieving a social end. It was Liberals, more pertinaciously than anyone else, who constructed and fortified whole systems of state-maintained and state-directed schools, who substituted compulsory for voluntary attendance at school, and who, in the interest of public schools, erected essentially protective tariffs against private ones. It was Liberals, likewise, who most zealously championed the cause of public health, and for its sake implemented the "police power" of the state over individual conduct, even over individual property rights. It was also Liberals who, despite their penchant for economy, voted multiplying appropriations for public hospitals and homes, as well as for prisons and reformatories. Your Liberal of the '70's would oppose tariff protection as an outrageous violation of his principles and a dangerous interference with "economic law" and personal liberty, but he felt differently about measures of public charity, public health, and public education. These expressions of humanitarianism were his proud, if somewhat illogical, heritage.

Factory legislation the doctrinaire Liberal was less sure of. It clearly impaired the freedom of business enterprise and perhaps the more subtle "freedom of contract." Yet gradually, thanks to spasmodic efforts of Conservatives and crusading humanitarians, the principle of factory legislation had been asserted and actually applied throughout the industrialized areas of Europe prior to the Liberal ascendancy of the '60's and '70's; and when this came, your Liberal compromised his principles and let existing factory legislation stand. Indeed, he found he could justify a moderate amount of it on the grounds that it involved matters of public health and that it might stave off the far worse evils of revolutionary agitation and industrial socialism.

Nevertheless, the subsequent elaboration and stiffening of factory legislation, though lukewarmly acquiesced in by Liberals, was part and parcel of the general reaction against Liberalism, and was promoted chiefly by Socialists, Conservatives, and Clericals. A royalist and clerical majority in the French National Assembly enacted the important Act of 1874, with its provisions for state inspection of industrial establishments; and the later and more comprehensive Act of 1892 was an achievement of Conservative Republicans. Similar statutes were enacted, under clerical auspices, by Belgium in 1889 and Austria in 1883, and, under either Socialist or Nationalist influence, by Italy in 1886 and Spain in 1900. In Great Britain, Conservative governments carried through parliament the successive "Consolidating Acts" of 1878, 1891, and 1901. In Germany, a coalition of Centrists and Conservatives, with pressure from Socialists, insured in 1891 the radical recasting and strengthening of the earlier Labor Code.

All such measures were intricate, and were frequently amended to cover new industries, new techniques, and new business procedure. They usually regulated, in detail, mines and foundries and retail shops, as well as factories in the strict sense. Progressively the work hours were limited, the working age for children and young persons raised, and higher standards prescribed for ventilation, lighting, sanitation, and other arrangements for the efficiency, health, and comfort of employees. Special attention was given to safeguarding workers in dangerous trades, and to means of enforcing the factory laws more adequately. Although the legislation frequently dealt with such matters as fines and other deductions from wages, and payment in truck in place of money, it did not yet aim at fixing wage rates. A bill to this effect, covering "sweated" labor, was introduced into the British House of Commons by Sir Charles Dilke in 1898, but it failed of passage; and minimum wage acts had to await a still more socialistically minded generation.

Meanwhile, "municipal socialism" developed. A pioneer in this movement was Joseph Chamberlain, wealthy manufacturer and provocative Radical, who subsequently deserted the Gladstonian Liberals for more congenial association with nationalistic and imperialistic Conservatives. As mayor of his native city of Birmingham from 1873 to 1876, he socialized the municipal water supply and gas works, improving the quality of both and lessening their cost to the public, and he executed, with notable success, the first municipal project of slum clearance, dispossessing private owners, replacing their rookeries with city-owned model tenements, and devoting some of the expropriated acres to public parks and recreation centers. A like work, on a larger scale, was performed by Karl Lueger, the chief of the Christian Socialist party in Austria. As mayor of Vienna from the '90's onward, he municipalized its gas, water, and streetcar systems, surrounded it with a zone of forest and meadow closed to building speculation, and, in fine, made Vienna the most "socialized" and best administered city of the time. The movement of which Chamberlain and Lueger were conspicuous exponents, spread with great rapidity in the '80's and '90's to most of the capitals and industrial centers in Europe. Especially in Germany, though to a considerable degree in Italy and elsewhere, municipally owned and operated public utilities were the rule by 1900—gas works, electric lights, tramways, markets, laundries, even slaughter houses and labor exchanges[6]—and in charge of them were "city managers" with an extending array of expert advisers, bureaucrats, and police.

Another, and more striking, departure from Liberal norms was the compulsory insurance of workingmen which Germany inaugurated on a national scale in the '80's. Bismarck's main motive in proposing it seems to have been a desire to discredit the Marxian Socialists by stealing some of their thunder. In 1878 he persuaded the Conservatives and National Liberals in the Reichstag to outlaw Marxian agitation and propaganda, and the very next year—the year of Germany's adoption of tariff protectionism—he had his venerable Emperor bespeak the co-operation of the nation's deputies in seeking legislative remedy for social ills, "for a remedy cannot be sought merely in repression of Socialist excesses—there must be simultaneously a positive advancement of the welfare of the working classes." Then, after two years' preparation by a special commission, including representatives of labor, a bill was laid before the Reichstag for the compulsory insurance of workingmen against industrial accidents. It was viewed by Radical Liberals (the Progressives) as a heinous offense against personal liberty, and by most National Liberals as an insuperable handicap to German industry; but in broad outlines it was sympathetically received by Conservatives and Catholic Centrists, and these, between them,

6 Free municipal labor exchanges, or employment agencies, were established at Berlin in 1883 and at Düsseldorf in 1890; by 1900 some eighty-three other German cities maintained them.

had a parliamentary majority. The Centrists, it is true, refused to vote for the bill unless it were so amended as to render its proposed administration less bureaucratic and to put the whole financial burden on employers.

For some time Bismarck hesitated about accepting such amendments. But he had to have the support of the Centrists for any program of social reform, and at length, after another general election had strengthened them still more, he arranged a compromise. The result was a law of May 1882, compulsorily insuring workingmen against sickness for a maximum term of thirteen weeks in any year, and a second law of July 1884, insuring them against accidents. Contributions to the funds for the latter were to be made entirely by employers, and for the former jointly by employers and employees in the proportion of one-third to two-thirds. The administration of both was entrusted to existing agencies so far as possible—co-operative and mutual-benefit societies, local and regional associations, etc.—all under general state supervision.

A third project of workers' insurance—against old age and invalidity—was realized by a law of 1889. By this time the National Liberals, the party of big business, had come to perceive that their earlier fears were unjustified, that national insurance was a help rather than a hindrance to German industry, and so they supported the old-age insurance and, in conjunction with Conservatives, brought its administration more directly into line with the bureaucratic state socialism which Bismarck had originally advocated. Its funds were to be obtained equally from employers and employees, with a per capita subsidy from the national exchequer.

Here, then, was a vast and impressive defense reared by a first-class industrial nation against the chief hazards of working-class well-being—accidents, sickness, old age and invalidity. In the next few years, many detailed additions were made. Benefits were increased and opened to agricultural laborers and to certain other groups previously excluded. Free medical attendance and hospital care were extended. According to an official report, some fifty million Germans (sick and injured, incapacitated and dependent) received between 1885 and 1900 social insurance benefits totaling over 750 million dollars and exceeding workmen's contributions by 250 million. And a much greater development of the system was to come later, including insurance against unemployment.

German example stimulated imitation in other countries. Austria adopted accident insurance in 1887 and sickness insurance in 1888. Denmark copied all three of the German insurance schemes between 1891 and 1898, and Belgium between 1894 and 1903. Italy accepted accident and old-age insurance in 1898. Switzerland, by constitutional amendment of 1890, empowered the federal government to organize a system of national insurance. Certain other countries, while not following the German program, obliged employers to compensate their workmen for accidents. Thus Great Britain in 1897 enacted a Workmen's Compensation Act sponsored by Joseph Chamberlain and affecting half of the nation's wage earners; France enacted a similar law in 1898; Norway, Spain, and Holland, in the same decade.

Still another type of social legislation which appeared during the era was in aid of tenant farmers. In Rumania, an interruption of nominally Liberal rule enabled the "Young Conservatives" to control parliament from 1888 to 1895, and their prime minister, Carp, took in 1889 the first steps toward breaking up large landed estates and distributing them among peasant proprietors. A better known example of the same trend was the series of Irish Land Purchase Acts which the British Conservatives, anxious to offset Gladstone's Home Rule efforts, sponsored, beginning with the Ashbourne measure of 1885, and continuing through those of 1891 and 1896 to the Wyndham Act of 1903. The last was the most prodigal of all, but even before its enactment the British government had already advanced over 100 million dollars toward the transformation of Ireland from a country of large estates into one of peasant proprietorships.

Of course, all this varied social legislation necessitated for the several European states greatly increased expenditure and hence greatly increased revenue.[7] Heightened tariffs produced some of the additional revenue for countries blessed with the new protec-

---

[7] In Great Britain, aside from a growing national debt, much of which had been incurred for army and navy and imperial undertakings, the total local debt increased, principally for social services, from 460 million dollars in 1874-75 to 960 million in 1887-88, and on to 1,375 million in 1898-9.

tionism. But statesmen of socializing proclivities, in free-trade Britain as well as on the Continent, presently bethought themselves of direct taxes which would overcome threatening deficits and at the same time serve social ends by weighing more heavily on large fortunes than on small. In other words, taxation began to be conceived of as a means to social reform and state regulation of wealth. The particular forms which rather suddenly and widely seemed appropriate for the dual purpose were the income tax and the inheritance tax. Great Britain had long known both, but mainly in emergencies and at modest rates, and always hitherto for revenue only. The Grand Old Man of English Liberalism, Gladstone himself, had used an income tax for his beautifully balanced budgets, but he abhorred it, and in 1887 pontifically anathematized it as "the most demoralizing of all imposts," a "tangled network of man traps for conscience," and "an engine of public extravagance."[8] Seven years later, however, Gladstone was finally out of office, and another Whiggish Liberal, Sir William Harcourt, in the responsible post of chancellor of the exchequer, was putting through parliament definitely graduated income taxes and death duties. They were a funeral wreath for the old Liberalism and a portent of the awful things in store for twentieth-century taxpayers when Lloyd George should head the exchequer and affiance a resurrected Liberalism to state socialism.

In Germany the several states which made up the empire took to levying income taxes, Prussia steeply graduating hers in 1891 and Bavaria having the temerity in 1900 to distinguish between "earned" and "unearned" income. Austria introduced progressive income taxes in 1898, and so, too, in the same decade, did Norway and Spain. Simultaneously Italy, which had long taxed everything that was taxable, raised the rates of income tax; and France resorted to progressive inheritance taxes in 1901.

A final sign of the socializing trend in Europe deserves mention. It was the restoration in 1900 by the Conservative majority in the British parliament of that prohibition of usury which Liberals back in 1854 had removed, they fancied forever, from the statute books. It was a minor sign but one which, in the words of Professor Clap-

8 *Nineteenth Century,* June 1887.

ham, "gauged perhaps better than any other the strength of the current which had set in against *laisser faire* and old-style utilitarianism."[9] National governments would regulate money lending, as well as income and inheritance of individuals, conditions of labor, foreign and domestic trade, education and health, the balance between industry and agriculture. From the 1880's economic nationalism was ascendant.

IV. BASES OF A NEW NATIONAL IMPERIALISM

Synchronizing with the revival of protective tariffs and the extension of socializing legislation toward the close of the 1870's, was a tremendous outburst of imperialistic interest and activity. The outburst was common to all great powers of Europe (except Austria-Hungary); and it was so potent that during the next three decades greater progress was made toward subjecting the world to European domination than had been made during three centuries previous.

This may seem odd in view of the fact that the immediately preceding era of Liberal ascendancy, say from the 1840's into the 1870's, had witnessed a marked decline of European imperialism. There had been, to be sure, some spasmodic additions to British India, some scattered efforts of Napoleon III to resuscitate a colonial empire for France, some continuing Russian expansion in central and northeastern Asia. Although China and Japan had been forcefully opened to European (and American) trade, the opening had been for practically everybody on free and equal terms and had been unattended by any considerable expropriation of territory. The surviving farflung British Empire had ceased to be an exclusive preserve for British merchants since the 1840's, and in 1861 France had freely admitted to her colonies the commerce of all nations. In 1870-1871 European colonialism appeared to be approaching its nadir. Gladstone was prime minister of Great Britain, and he was notoriously a "Little Englander."[10] The provisional French government so slightly esteemed the colonies it had inherited that it

---

9 J. H. Clapham, *Economic History of Modern Britain*, III (Cambridge, Eng., 1938), 445.

10 See R. L. Schuyler, "The Climax of Anti-Imperialism in England," *Political Science Quarterly*, XXXVI (Dec. 1921),537-61, and C. A. Bodelsen, *Studies in Mid-Victorian Imperialism* (New York, 1925). But cf. Paul Knaplund, *Gladstone and Britain's Imperial Policy* (New York, 1927).

offered them all to Bismarck at the end of the Franco-Prussian War if only he would spare Alsace-Lorraine. Bismarck spurned the offer, as he had recently refused Portugal's offer to sell him Mozambique. A colonial policy for Germany, he said, "would be just like the silken sables of Polish noble families who have no shirts."[11]

A favorite explanation of why European imperialism turned abruptly within a decade from nadir to apogee, has been the economic. It was advanced originally by publicists and statesmen to win the support of business interests for imperialistic policies, and it received classical treatment, at the time of the Boer War, by John A. Hobson.[12] Latterly it has been taken up by Marxian writers and integrated with their dogma of materialistic determinism, so that the argument now runs in this wise: Imperialism is an inevitable phase in the evolution of capitalism, a phase in which surplus capital, accumulated by the exploitation of domestic labor, is obliged by diminishing returns at home to find new outlets for investment abroad. Hence it seeks non-industrialized areas ever farther afield where it may dispose of surplus manufactures, obtain needed raw materials, invest surplus capital, and exploit cheap native labor. The resulting "new imperialism," unlike the old, is not primarily a colonizing or a simply commercial imperialism, but rather an investing one in regions ill-adapted to European settlement. Conditions are alleged to have been ripe for it about 1880, when tariff protection restricted customary markets of European capitalists and impelled them to seek new ones.[13]

Doubtless large-scale mechanized industry, with accompanying improvement of transportation facilities, did immensely stimulate an ever-widening quest for markets where surplus manufactures might be disposed of, necessary raw materials procured, and lucrative investments made. Nor can there be any doubt that by the

[11] M. Busch, *Tagebuchblätter* (Leipzig, 1899), II, 157.

[12] In his *Imperialism, a Study* (London, 1902). See also J. M. Robertson, *Patriotism and Empire* (London, 1899).

[13] Chief among Marxian studies are: Karl Kautsky, *Nationalstaat, Imperialistischer Staat, und Staatenbund* (Nürnberg, 1915); Rosa Luxemburg, *Die Akkumulation des Kapitals* (Berlin, 1913); N. Lenin, *Imperialism, the Last Stage of Capitalism*, Eng. trans. (New York, 1927); M. Pavlovitch, *The Foundations of Imperialist Policy* (London, 1922); F. Sternberg, *Der Imperialismus* (Berlin, 1926); Henryk Grossmann, *Das Akkumulations- und Zusammenbruchsgesetz des kapitalistischen Systems* (Leipzig, 1929).

1870's, when industrialization on the Continent was beginning seriously to vie with England's, the quest was being as eagerly pursued by commercial and banking houses of Hamburg and Bremen, Marseilles and Paris, as by those of London and Liverpool. In Germany, for example, at the very time when Bismarck was disdaining the French proffer of colonies, his banking friends, Bleichröder and Hansemann, were helping to finance distant trade ventures of various Hanseatic firms—O'Swald's in East Africa, Woermann's in West Africa, Godeffroy's in Samoa and other South Sea islands. In 1880 some 335,000 marks' worth of German goods were shipped to West Africa alone, while 6,735,000 marks' worth of African products entered the port of Hamburg.

Yet the only novel feature of all this was a relatively greater importation of tropical and sub-tropical products and hence a special concern with Africa, southern Asia, the Indies, and Oceania. Surplus manufactures from industrialized countries of Europe, even after the imposition of protective tariffs, still found export markets principally within that Continent or in temperate zones outside, notably in America, Australasia, northern India, and the Far East. What actually started the economic push into the "Dark Continent" and the sun-baked islands of the Pacific was not so much an overproduction of factory goods in Europe as an undersupply of raw materials. Cotton grew finer in Egypt than in the United States, and with the partial cutting off of the latter's copious supply by the American Civil War it was but natural that dealers in raw cotton should enter the Egyptian field and raise its yield ninefold during the next twenty years. Rubber was now needed also, and it could be got from the Congo and from Malaysia more cheaply and plentifully than from Brazil. Copra, with its useful oil, was to be had in the South Sea islands, and the Godeffroy firm at Hamburg made a specialty of going for it. Tin was essential for the new canning industry, and gold, for measuring the new industrial wealth; rich supplies of the former were obtainable in the East Indies, and of the latter in Guinea and the Transvaal. Sugar cane and coffee, cocoa and tea, bananas and dates, if not directly serviceable to industrial machinery, were very palatable to the enlarging European multitude that tended it.

But commercial expansion into the tropics was a novelty of degree rather than of kind and hardly suffices to explain the political imperialism of the '70's and '80's. This was inaugurated prior to any general resort to tariff protectionism in Europe, and prior also to any universal export of capital. Neither Russia nor Italy had surplus manufactures to dispose of or surplus wealth to invest; yet both engaged in the scramble for imperial dominion, the one with striking success and the other not. Germany exported little capital until after she had acquired an extensive colonial empire, and France secured a far more extensive one while her industrial development lagged behind Germany's. Great Britain had long had all the supposed economic motives for imperialism—export of manufactured goods, demand for raw materials, supply of surplus capital—and yet these did not move her in the '60's as much as they did in the '70's.[14] On the other hand, Norway, whose ocean-borne commerce was exceeded only by Great Britain's and Germany's, remained consistently aloof from overseas imperialism.

Apparently the flag of a European nation did not have to follow its trade—or its financial investments. But once flag raising became common and competitive in Africa and on the Pacific, economic considerations undoubtedly spurred most of the European participants to greater efforts and keener competition in those regions. Then the tariff protectionism of Continental nations was applied, in one form or another, to their respective colonies, and the more colonies each one had the greater were its opportunities for favorable trade and investment and the closer it approached to the ideal of all-around self-sufficiency. And to prevent too much of the world from being thus monopolized by France, Germany, Italy, or any other protectionist power, Great Britain moved mightily to gather the lion's share into her own free-trade empire. In other words, neo-mercantilism, once established, had very important imperialistic consequences.

14 It should be remarked, however, that the depression which began in 1873, by limiting opportunities for profitable investment in countries already largely industrialized, probably stimulated investment in "backward" regions and may thus have contributed to a revival of imperialistic interests and ambitions. Nevertheless, this was truer of Great Britain than of any nation on the Continent, and it scarcely suffices to explain why with almost all the great powers (and only with them) political imperialism preceded any substantial financial investment in particular regions appropriated.

The fact remains, nevertheless, that the founding of new colonial empires and the fortifying of old ones antedated the establishment of neo-mercantilism, and that the economic arguments adduced in support of imperialism seem to have been a rationalization *ex post facto*. In the main, it was not Liberal parties, with their super-abundance of industrialists and bankers, who sponsored the outward imperialistic thrusts of the '70's and early '80's. Instead, it was Conservative parties, with a preponderantly agricultural clientele notoriously suspicious of moneylenders and big business, and, above all, it was patriotic professors and publicists regardless of political affiliation and unmindful of personal economic interest. These put forth the economic arguments which eventually drew bankers and traders and industrialists into the imperialist camp.

Basically the new imperialism was a nationalistic phenomenon. It followed hard upon the national wars which created an all-powerful Germany and a united Italy, which carried Russia within sight of Constantinople, and which left England fearful and France eclipsed. It expressed a resulting psychological reaction, an ardent desire to maintain or recover national prestige. France sought com-pensation for European loss in oversea gain. England would offset her European isolation by enlarging and glorifying the British Empire. Russia, halted in the Balkans, would turn anew to Asia, and before long Germany and Italy would show the world that the prestige they had won by might inside Europe they were entitled to enhance by imperial exploits outside. The lesser powers, with no great prestige at stake, managed to get on without any new imperi-alism, though Portugal and Holland displayed a revived pride in the empires they already possessed and the latter's was administered with renewed vigor.[15]

Public agitation for extending overseas the political dominion of European national states certainly began with patriotic intellec-tuals. As early as 1867 Lothar Bucher, one of Bismarck's associates in the Prussian foreign office, published in the influential *Nord-*

---

[15] For fuller treatment of national prestige as the basic factor in imperialism, and incidentally for devastating criticism of the Marxian interpretation, see Arthur Salz, *Das Wesen des Imperialismus* (Leipzig, 1931), and Walter Sulzbach, *Nationales Gemeinschaftsgefühl und wirtschaftliches Interesse* (Leipzig, 1929). A kindred "atavis-tic" theory has been propounded by Professor Joseph Schumpeter in *Archiv für Sozial-wissenschaft und Sozialpolitik*, XLVI (1918-9), 1-39, 275-310.

deutsche Allgemeine Zeitung a series of articles endorsing and advertising the hitherto neglected counsels of Friedrich List: "Companies should be founded in the German seaports to buy lands in foreign countries and settle them with German colonies; also companies for commerce and navigation whose object would be to open new markets abroad for German manufacturers and to establish steamship lines. . . . Colonies are the best means of developing manufactures, export and import trade, and finally a respectable navy."[16]

The next year Otto Kersten, traveler and explorer, founded at Berlin a "Central Society for Commercial Geography and German Interests Abroad," with an official journal, *Der Export*. Simultaneously the "Royal Colonial Institute" was founded at London; and a brilliant young English gentleman, Sir Charles Dilke, returning from a trip around the world, published his patriotic and immensely popular *Greater Britain*.[17] Two years later, in the midst of the Franco-Prussian War, the redoubtable Froude scored his fellow Englishmen in the pages of *Fraser's Magazine* for their blindness to imperial glories. In 1872 Disraeli practically committed the Conservative party in Britain to a program of imperialism, and in 1874 Paul Leroy-Beaulieu, dean of political economists in France and implacable foe of tariff protection, plumped for French imperialism in a "scientific" treatise, *De la Colonisation chez les peuples modernes*.

These were foretastes. Heartier fare was served immediately after the Russo-Turkish War and the Congress of Berlin. In 1879 Friedrich Fabri, a pious promoter of Christian foreign missions, asked rhetorically "Does Germany need Colonies?" and answered with a resounding "Yes!" Germany's surplus population, he argued, should have places where it could go and still buy German goods and share in the other blessings of German *Kultur*. Fabri was eloquently seconded in 1881 by Hübbe-Schleiden, a lawyer and sometime explorer in equatorial Africa, who now insisted that through imperialistic endeavors "a country exhibits before the world

[16] Friedrich List, *National System of Political Economy*, Eng. trans. by Lloyd (London, 1916), 347.

[17] Dilke anticipated what was to come by emphasizing the economic and military value of "uncivilized" colonies in the tropics, while disparaging the alleged worth of such "white" colonies as Canada. His book reached an eighth edition in 1885.

its strength or weakness as a nation."[18] In like vein the historian Treitschke edified his student audiences at the University of Berlin with the moral that "every virile people has established colonial power."

In 1882 a frankly propagandist "Colonial Society" was formed in Germany through the joint efforts of a naturalist, a geographer, and a politician,[19] while in France Professor Leroy-Beaulieu brought out a new edition of his classic with the dogmatic addendum that "colonization is for France a question of life and death: either France will become a great African power, or in a century or two she will be no more than a secondary European power; she will count for about as much in the world as Greece and Rumania in Europe." The following year Professor John Seeley published his celebrated Cambridge lectures on the *Expansion of England*. The book took the British public by storm. It sold 80,000 copies within a brief time and won for its author the warm discipleship of Lord Rosebery and a knighthood.

In 1883 the stridently imperialistic "Primrose League" was launched by Tory Democrats, and soon afterwards the more sedate "Imperial Federation League" by nationalistic Liberals. In 1883, also, was founded a "Society for German Colonization." And capping the academic contributions to the imperialist cause, Froude published *Oceana* in 1885, while Alfred Rambaud, historian of Russia and first occupant of the chair in contemporary history at the Sorbonne, edited in 1886 a co-operative work on *La France coloniale*.

Already, statesmen were following the professors and proclaiming that commerce and investments should follow the flag. If Gladstone hesitated, Disraeli and Salisbury did not; nor did such "new" Liberals as Rosebery, Chamberlain, and Grey. Jules Ferry surely did not hesitate. Replying to parliamentary critics of his aggressive policy in Tunis and Tonkin, he marshaled in speeches from 1881 to 1885 all the professorial arguments: that superior races have a civilizing mission to inferior races; that an industrial nation needs

18 Friedrich Fabri, *Bedarf Deutschland der Kolonien?* (Gotha, 1879); Wilhelm Hübbe-Schleiden, *Deutsche Kolonisation* (Hamburg, 1881).
19 Freiherr von Maltzan, Herr von der Brüggen, and Prince Hohenlohe-Langenburg. Cf. See, *Die deutsche Kolonialgesellschaft, 1882-1907* (Berlin, 1908).

colonial markets; that coaling stations are requisite for navy and mercantile marine; and that if France refrained from imperialism, she would "descend from the first rank to the third or fourth."[20] Bismarck seemed to hesitate more than he actually did.[21] He privately expressed sympathy with imperialist ambitions in 1876 and publicly backed them, at least in the case of Samoa, in 1879. By 1884-85 he was persuading the Reichstag that colonies were vital to national economy. "Colonies would mean the winning of new markets for German industries, the expansion of trade, and a new field for German activity, civilization, and capital."[22]

Most simply, the sequence of imperialism after 1870 appears to have been, first, pleas for colonies on the ground of national prestige; second, getting them; third, disarming critics by economic argument; and fourth, carrying this into effect and relating the results to the neo-mercantilism of tariff protection and social legislation at home.

There were, of course, complexities in the imperialistic movement. In so far as it was economic, it did not affect the "capitalist class" as a whole, but only particular business interests: exporters and manufacturers of certain commodities such as calico and cheap alcoholic beverages; importers of rubber, raw cotton, coffee, copra, etc.; shipping magnates; some bankers, though a very small percentage of all; and those "parasites of imperialism," the makers of arms and uniforms, the producers of telegraph and railway material, etc. But these last did not "cause" imperialism; they merely throve on it.

Christian missions provided an important adjunct to imperialism. They spread and multiplied in the second half of the nineteenth century as never before, in part as a reaction, we have suggested elsewhere, to the prevalent materialism in Europe, and in larger part because of the immensely improved means of travel and communication throughout the world. A missionary might have gone

---

20 The economic arguments of Ferry were clearly *ex post facto*. They were stressed in his preface to Leon Sentahéry's *Le Tonkin et la Mère Patrie* (Paris, 1890).

21 See M. E. Townsend, *The Rise and Fall of the German Colonial Empire* (New York, 1932), and, for a somewhat different view, H. R. Rudin, *Germans in the Cameroons, 1884-1914* (New Haven, 1938).

22 *Verhandlungen des deutschen Reichstages,* March 16, 1885, p. 1864; Jan. 10, 1885, p. 524; June 26, 1884, p. 1073.

his way, like a merchant, the one conveying spiritual and the other material goods to heathen peoples, without any thought of raising a national flag over them or subjecting them to European rule. Actually, however, missionaries like merchants lived in a nationalistic age, and many of them were quite willing, on occasion, to invoke the naval or military protection of their respective national states. Not a few of Europe's footholds in other Continents were obtained as penalties for the persecution of Christian missionaries. Even where missionaries did not directly prompt the extension of European dominion, they frequently paved the way for adventurers who did; and stories published back home by them or about them stimulated popular interest in, and support of, imperial undertakings. About David Livingstone, for example, something like a cult grew up in England, so that when he died in the wilds of Africa on May Day, 1873, his body was borne with hierophantic solemnity all the way to Zanzibar and thence under naval escort to England, where finally it was deposited amid Britain's national heroes in Westminster Abbey on April 18, 1874. The year was that of Disraeli's accession to the premiership, and for the popular favor accorded his subsequent imperial activities, he should have thanked the dead Livingstone more than any live merchant or banker.

It was a time, too, when evolutionary biology was beginning to occupy a central place in European thought, when hundreds of naturalists, emulating Darwin, engaged in scientific expeditions to strange distant regions and furnished millions of ordinary stay-at-homes with fascinating descriptions of the extraordinary flora and fauna they had observed. Already in 1861 the Franco-American Du Chaillu had reported from Gabun in equatorial Africa his amazing discovery of the gorilla, which was readily imagined to be the "missing link" between ape and man. In 1867 he published an account of a race of pygmies he had found, and for years afterwards his pen poured out popular tales of African adventure. Meanwhile, in the early '70's, Faidherbe was exploring upper Egypt, Nachtigal was visiting Khartum, De Brazza was following Du Chaillu into the hinterland of Gabun, Skobelev with notebook in hand was investigating the borders of Turkestan, Evelyn Baring (the later Lord Cromer) was describing the natural wonders of

India, and Henry Morton Stanley was "finding" Livingstone for the New York *Herald* and an avid public, and then heading an Anglo-American scientific expedition into the vast Congo basin. Presently George Goldie was exploring the Niger country, Joseph Thomson was leading an expedition into east-central Africa, Harry Johnston was traversing Angola and meeting Stanley on the Congo, and Frederick Lugard, a young veteran of the Afghan War, was penetrating Nyasaland and Uganda.

Of these explorers, the majority had military training. Faidherbe was a French general, former governor of Senegal, and Skobelev a Russian general who was to win laurels in the Russo-Turkish War. Nachtigal was a German army surgeon, De Brazza a French naval officer. Cromer and Goldie and Lugard had all been British soldiers. As a group they were intensely patriotic, and they nicely combined with scientific interests a zeal to serve the political, economic, and military interests of their respective nations. They were prime promoters of imperialism, and most of them remained as pro-consuls of provinces they charted and helped to appropriate.

Sheer love of adventure was a potent lure to imperialism. Africa in particular, by reason of the widespread advertising its marvels and dangers received at the beginning of the '70's, beckoned to bold and venturesome spirits in Europe, and some of the boldest became empire-builders in the grand style, in a few cases acquiring fabulous personal wealth, in all cases experiencing that sense of power which comes from great achievement. Stanley was patently an adventurer. He had no surplus goods to sell, no surplus capital to invest. He was a self-made man, if ever there was one. A Welshman by birth, with the original name of Rowlands, he ran away from home and school at an early age to find work in Liverpool, first in a haberdasher's shop, then with a butcher. When this grew tedious he worked his way across the Atlantic to New Orleans and fell in with a merchant by the name of Stanley, who adopted him. At the outbreak of the American Civil War he enlisted in the Confederate army, only to be taken prisoner at the battle of Shiloh; then, "with ready versatility he joined the Union army to fight against his former comrades-in-arms. Toward the close of the war he discovered a latent talent for journalism, which, when peace returned, led him to Salt Lake City to describe the extraordinary customs of the Mormons, then to Asia Minor in search of thrilling adventure, then with General Hancock against the Indians, with the British against Abyssinia, and to Crete, and Spain."[23] He went to central Africa in 1871 because he was sent, but he remained to build a huge empire for another and the queerest kind of adventurer—a man who was not self-made and who never set foot in Africa, but who was as hypnotized by African dreams as by female realities—Leopold of the Belgians, Leopold of the Congo Free State.

But the adventurer-imperialist *par excellence* was Cecil Rhodes, and his extraordinary career began by accident. A sickly youth, son of an Anglican clergyman and intended for the church, he was bundled off in 1870, for purposes of health, to an elder brother's farm in southern Africa. He arrived just when diamonds were discovered in the near-by Kimberley fields. He joined other diggers, dug more industriously and successfully, and within a year found himself wealthy and healthy. He returned to England for study at Oxford, but the study was desultory and he was soon back permanently in South Africa, adding gold mines to diamond mines, running Cape politics, projecting British sway the entire length of the Continent up to Cairo, and doing much to realize it.

The star German adventurer was Carl Peters. Son of a Lutheran clergyman and graduate of the University of Berlin, he contracted imperialist fever on a visit to England and set out in 1884 in disguise and under an alias—he was still in his twenties—to build an empire in East Africa. His method was simple, and the results startling, even to Bismarck. By a judicious distribution of toys plus injudicious application of grog, he got twelve big black chieftains, within ten days, to make their X's on documents conveying to Germany a total of 60,000 square miles. But that was only a start. Peters kept right on enlarging German East Africa until an Anglo-German convention of 1890 set bounds to his activity.

Explorers and adventurers gave rise to a peculiar species of organizer and administrator, despotic and ruthless and most devotedly imperialistic. Peters and Rhodes were transmuted by the African environment into this species, and so too were Cromer in Egypt

23 P. T. Moon, *Imperialism and World Politics* (New York, 1926), 65.

and Milner at the Cape. For the glory of themselves and their countries, such local potentates carried on without too much regard for merely economic considerations or for the international engagements of their distant home governments. They were on the spot and knew better than London or Berlin or any other capital what had to be done, and they usually did it in an expansive way.

The actual course of empire—the order in which distant areas were appropriated by European powers—was determined less by design than by chance. Murder of a missionary or trader and consequent forceful intervention might occur anywhere. In some instances, curiously frequent in Moslem countries, native rulers practically invited intervention by living far beyond their means and contracting debts which they were unable to repay. Such was the basis of European imperialism in Egypt, Tunis, Persia, and to a large extent in Turkey. For example, the Khedive Ismail of Egypt, a squat, red-bearded gentleman with a passion for ostentation and the externals of European culture, spent half a billion dollars in the twelve years after his accession in 1863, running up the Egyptian public debt from 16 million to 342 million and continuing to borrow money from European bankers at ever more onerous rates. In 1875 he could only get a quarter of the face value of short-term bonds bearing 20 per cent interest. In 1876 he sold his shares of Suez Canal Company stock to England, and consented to joint supervision of his finances by representatives of England, France, Italy, and Austria. Soon this control was narrowed to England and France, and in 1882 to England alone. No doubt bankers and investors egged on both the khedive to spend and the English government to collect, but a less prodigal khedive, and one more intelligently concerned with the welfare of his subjects, might have staved off foreign rule. The contemporary Mikado of Japan did.

Especially active in directing the course of empire after 1870 were the European colonists already settled in Algeria, South Africa, and Australasia. These performed the same function in the latter part of the nineteenth century as their prototypes in the America of the eighteenth century. French settlers in Algeria were more eager than the government at Paris to make all adjacent African lands French. British and Dutch settlers in South Africa had almost a psychosis about others getting anywhere near them, and from the former, rather than from London, came the main drive for British expansion northward. Australians and New Zealanders were continually pressing the home government to forestall alien seizure of South Sea islands.

In many instances European flags were hoisted as a sport—a competitive sport—with about the same indifference to economic motives as characterized the later planting of American and other flags on cakes of ice around the North or South Pole. As one reads of successive French flag raisings in oases of the Sahara and on coral reefs of the Pacific, one gets a lively impression that it was all *pour le sport*.

Some capitalists undoubtedly promoted imperialism, and more profited by it. But in the last analysis it was the nationalistic masses who made it possible and who most vociferously applauded and most constantly backed it. Disraeli and Joseph Chamberlain were good politicians as well as patriots, and with a clairvoyance greater than Gladstone's, they perceived that in a country where the masses were patriotic, literate, and in possession of the ballot, a political party which frankly espoused imperialism would have magnetic attraction for them. So it proved. An unwonted popularity attended the Conservative parties of Britain and Germany during the '80's and '90's. The masses, of course, had no immediate economic interest in the matter, and it would have required an extraordinary act of faith on their part to believe the predictions of imperialistic intellectuals that somehow, sometime, everybody would be enriched from the Congo or the Niger or Tahiti. Rather, the masses were thrilled and stirred by front-page news in the popular press of far-off things and battles still to come. They devoured the yarns of a Rider Haggard—he had been secretary to the governor of Natal in the '70's and he *knew* his Africa. They learned by heart the vulgar verses of a Rudyard Kipling—he had lived in India and been a chum of doughty, swearing British soldiers. And the sporting impulse which drew crowds to prize fights and to football and cricket matches, evoked a whole nation's lusty cheers for its "team" in the mammoth competitive game of imperialism.

Into the imperial-mindedness of the masses, scarcely less than into that of Rhodes or Peters, Ferry or Chamberlain, fitted neatly the preaching of Darwinian sociology, that human progress depends upon struggle between races and nations and survival of the fittest. . Obviously most eligible for the "fittest" were the white peoples of Europe, who therefore owed it to science as well as to civilization (and religion) to establish their supremacy over inferior populations in all other continents. Which of them would ultimately be adjudged the absolutely fittest would depend on the outcome of conflict among themselves as well as with lesser breeds. This preaching justified competitive imperialism and cloaked attendant ruthlessness in the mantle of idealistic devotion to duty. It was summarized by Kipling at the close of the generation (1899) in his famous lines:

> Take up the White Man's Burden—
> Send forth the best ye breed—
> Go bind your sons to exile
> To serve your captives' need;
> To wait in heavy harness,
> On fluttered fold and wild—
> Your new-caught, sullen peoples,
> Half-devil and half-child.

v. *RES GESTAE* OF THE NEW IMPERIALISM

Positive achievements began in 1874 with the advent of Disraeli's Conservative ministry. Forthwith, a group of some two hundred Pacific islands, with the alluring name of Fiji, were ceremoniously added to the British Empire, and almost simultaneously a British protectorate was established over three native states in the Malay Peninsula north of Singapore. The next year, with twenty million dollars which he borrowed from the Rothschilds (at a profit to them of half a million), Disraeli made the sensational purchase for Great Britain of the khedive's controlling block of stock in the Suez Canal Company. Another sensation he caused by putting through parliament in 1876 a Royal Titles Bill which conferred upon Queen Victoria the pretentious title of Empress of India; if Germany now had an Emperor, why shouldn't Britain have an Empress? Incidentally, Disraeli authorized in the same year the

incorporation into British India of the large khanate of Baluchistan
on its northwest border. Then in 1877, under his auspices, the
Transvaal Republic in southern Africa was formally annexed, while
claims were asserted to several archipelagoes in the western Pacific.
In 1878, to "protect" Turkey against Russian aggression, the island
of Cyprus was occupied in the eastern Mediterranean. Thenceforth
events marched fast and wide. To thwart possible Russian designs
still farther east, British forces invaded Afghanistan and sought
by shootings to implant fear if not love in the soul of its Moslem
ameer. To consolidate gains and "restore order" in South Africa,
other British forces waged decimating war with Zulus (in which,
by a curious twist of fate, the son and heir of Napoleon III was
slain). To implement financial control of Egypt, Britain established
with France a "condominium" at Cairo.

Gladstone was returned to office by the parliamentary elections of
1880, but his anti-imperialist utterances during the famous Mid-
lothian campaign were not taken too seriously by colonial officials
and promoters, nor, for that matter, by the majority of Englishmen
at home. Indeed, the "Little Englander" himself adhered none too
rigidly to his pre-election promises. True, he halted hostilities in
Afghanistan, interrupted the Zulu War, and, after a revolt of the
Boers and their rout of a small British force at Majuba Hill (February 27, 1881), made peace with the Transvaal and recognized its
independence. Yet it was a British admiral, under Gladstone's
orders, who bombarded Alexandria in July 1882, and a British
general who quickly afterward imposed on the khedive and all
lower Egypt a virtual vassalage to Great Britain alone.[24] Moreover,
it was during Gladstone's ministry, if not with his approval, that
adventurers, traders, and armed forces established British posts in
Borneo and New Guinea (1881-84); that George Goldie's "United
African Company" bought off rival French claimants to Nigeria
(1884) and acquired title to large tracts of it by treaty with native
chieftains or by simple seizure; and that still other Britishers were
similarly active in southern Africa and in Somaliland. Gladstone

---

[24] A timid French cabinet of the day declined participation, and hence in Egypt
sole domination of Britain was substituted for the previous Franco-British "condominium." For Britain the Suez Canal was very important—strategically as the
main highway to India, and also commercially. The Canal was traversed in 1882 by over
3,000 ships, with a tonnage of seven million, of which 80 per cent was British.

entered office as an anti-imperialist. He left in 1885, a victim of popular resentment over the slaughter of a half-mad British general—"Chinese" Gordon—by Moslem dervishes at Khartum in the Egyptian Sudan.

A strong stimulant to British imperialism was the steady expansion of Russia through Turkestan toward India and through the Caucasus and Balkans toward the Mediterranean route to India, and incidentally her expansion in the Far East. In this last region, Russia had taken from China in 1860 the extensive Amur and Maritime provinces and constructed the ice-free Pacific port of Vladivostok; in 1875 she acquired from Japan the large offshore island of Sakhalin.[25] In Turkestan, Russian expeditionary forces subjugated the khanates of Samarkand and Zerafshan in 1868, imposed protectorates on Bokhara and Khiva in 1873, and appropriated the district of Ferghana in 1875. Then came the Turkish War of 1877-78 which temporarily shifted the efforts of Russia westward and enabled her, not only to gain Bessarabia and a presumable protectorate over Bulgaria, but to round out Transcaucasia with the province of Kars and to increase pressure against Persia. With these advantages secured, she turned anew to Turkestan, completing in 1881 the conquest of the territory southeast of the Caspian and pushing on through Merv in 1884 to the Afghan frontier.

In the meantime, France entered the lists. In 1874, while royalist Conservatives were still in office at home, an admiral in the Far East persuaded the Emperor of Annam to put his country under French "protection." This, however, was an isolated instance, until the Republican Jules Ferry became premier in 1880. He immediately annexed the island of Tahiti in the Pacific; and in 1881, acting upon assurances given France at the time of the Berlin Congress, he dispatched a "punitive expedition" of 35,000 French soldiers across the Algerian border into Tunis. Though a critical parliamentary majority deposed Ferry, in part for what Clemenceau termed his "coup de bourse," French troops stayed in Tunis, and in a year and a half Ferry was back in the premiership, more ener-

[25] It is to be recalled, however, that Russia had voluntarily parted with Alaska in 1867.

getically imperialist than before. He at once made Tunis a full-fledged French protectorate, and during the next two years waged warfare in the Far East, conquering Tonkin and compelling the Chinese Emperor to recognize its incorporation with Annam, Cochin China, and Cambodia in a veritable French empire of Indo-China. During the same years he warred on Madagascar and forced its native queen to accept a French protectorate. Nor did Ferry neglect any opportunity for French expansion anywhere in Africa. To fuel transports on their way to Tonkin and Madagascar, he established a naval base at Obock near the southern end of the Red Sea—the core of French Somaliland. To permeate West Africa with French influence he subsidized exploratory and military expeditions into the hinterland of the Ivory and Guinea coasts and up the Congo from Gabun. Ferry's second premiership ended in 1885, but not the French imperialism which he had done so much to inspire and direct.

In Italy, a wave of indignation at French occupation of Tunis brought to the premiership a nationalistic Liberal of the "Left," Depretis, who did not content himself with mere protests. While he forged the defensive Triple Alliance with Germany and Austria, he hoisted the Italian flag over the town of Assab on the Eritrean coast of the Red Sea in July 1882, and in February 1885 he seized Massawa on the same coast. An Italian East African empire was in the making.

The birthday of Germany's colonial empire was April 24, 1884. On that date, Bismarck finally issued a *Schutzbrief*, authorizing Dr. Lüderitz, explorer and commercial agent, to proclaim a German protectorate over Southwest Africa. In October of the same year he gave like authorization to Dr. Nachtigal in respect of the West African territories of Togoland and Kamerun, and in December he notified the other powers that Germany was extending imperial protection to trading posts on the Malaysian island of New Guinea. The following March he took official cognizance of Carl Peters' exploits in East Africa and accepted the extensive territorial fruits there as a "Kaiserliches Schutzgebiet."

Neither German nor French expansion in Africa was liked by British imperialists, and it was forwarded by an interesting co-operation between Bismarck and Ferry in the "Congo question." King Leopold II of Belgium had long been interested in African discoveries and enamored by the prospect of opening up the "Dark Continent" to European enterprise, and as early as 1876 he had formed an "International African Association" to realize his objects. Under the Association's auspices, and in its behalf, Henry Stanley prosecuted exploration of the Congo basin from 1879 to 1884, concluding hundreds of treaties with native chieftains and founding twenty-odd stations. Then in February 1884, in order to strangle Leopold's project, Great Britain recognized Portugal's dubious claim to sovereignty over the mouth of the Congo and arranged for an Anglo-Portuguese commission to control navigation on the whole course of the river. Leopold promptly turned to France and Germany for help. Ferry, anxious to extend French sway along the north bank of the river, agreed to respect the Association's territory to the south on the single condition that France should have first option to buy it if it should ever be sold. Bismarck, anxious to block Britain and to deter her from interfering with Germany's expansion, joined France, and with Ferry convoked an International Conference at Berlin to deal with the Congo question.

The Conference, representing fourteen powers, sat from November 1884 to February 1885 and adopted a program which had been agreed to in advance by its German and French sponsors. Leopold's International Association was accorded sovereign rights over the bulk of the Congo basin and its outlet on the Atlantic, under international guarantees of neutrality and free trade. Slavery was formally prohibited. The Niger as well as the Congo was opened to the commerce of all nations on equal terms. And a simple rule was laid down that any power might acquire African lands by effectively occupying them and notifying the other powers. Incidentally this Berlin treaty of 1885 was the first to employ the phrase "sphere of influence."

The Berlin Conference gave marked impetus to European imperialism. It widely publicized the movement, just at the time when protective tariffs and other policies of economic nationalism were nourishing a favorable popular mood and eliciting both economic and patriotic arguments for it. From 1885 dated the almost continuous rule of imperialistic Conservative governments in Great Britain, the definitive juncture in Germany of National Liberals with Conservatives, and the practical disappearance of anti-imperialist dissent in France and Italy.

Within an incredibly brief time, Africa was almost completely partitioned among European powers. The "International Association" transformed itself, in July 1885, into the Congo Free State with Leopold as its despotic sovereign and with boundaries so determined by adroit negotiation with other powers as to embrace a vast domain of 900,000 square miles rich in rubber and ivory.[26] Britain, pushing up from the Cape, appropriated Bechuanaland in September 1885, Rhodesia in 1889, Nyasaland in 1893. Pressing inland from the Indian Ocean, she founded British East Africa in 1885 and secured Uganda in 1894. Chartering the Royal Niger Company in 1886 and backing its operations inland from the Atlantic, she acquired by 1900 the whole territory of Nigeria. Incidentally, she conquered in 1896 the Negro kingdom of Ashanti.

France invaded the Negro kingdom of Dahomey in 1889, subjugated it after a four-year struggle, and gradually linked it with the hinterlands of Senegal, the Ivory Coast, Guinea, and even Algeria to constitute French West Africa, a huge empire of 1,400,000 square miles and twelve million subjects. Timbuktu was occupied in 1893; and from the French Congo, Lake Chad was reached in 1900. In eastern Africa, France founded in 1888, on the Somali coast, the town of Djibouti and began in 1897 the construction of a railway thence into Abyssinia. In 1896, after two years of armed native resistance, she finally subjugated all Madagascar.

Italy, under Depretis' successor, Crispi, added Asmara to Eritrea in 1889, and in the same year took the southern (and largest) part of Somaliland and asserted a protectorate over adjacent Abyssinia. This last, however, could not be effected: the rout of Italian expeditionary forces at Adowa in March 1896 by a native army trained and equipped by French officers, led to Crispi's downfall and Italy's recognition of Abyssinian independence.

---

[26] Sir Harry Johnston has estimated that Leopold's "humanitarian enterprise" netted him personal profits of twenty million dollars. His system of monopolies and concessions and enforced Negro labor virtually nullified the free-trade and anti-slavery stipulations of the Berlin Treaty of 1885.

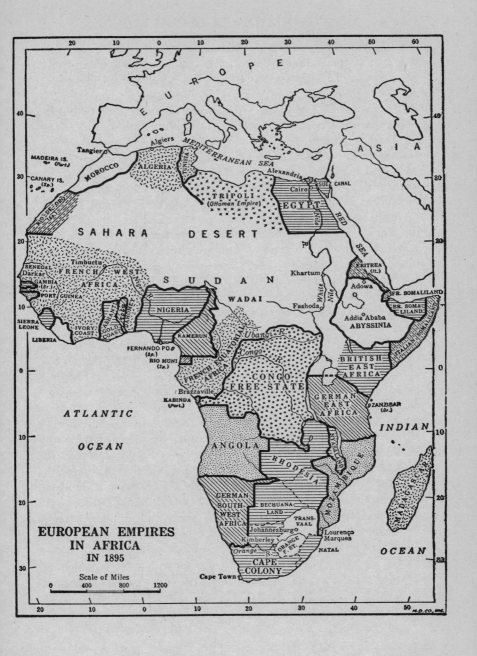

EUROPEAN EMPIRES
IN AFRICA
IN 1895

Scale of Miles

0   400   800   1200

Meanwhile Germany enlarged each of her four African protectorates and transformed them into outright colonies, while Portugal carried inland what had originally been the merely coastal
colonies of Angola (on the west) and Mozambique (on the east).
The whole process was crowned between 1890 and 1894 by a series
of agreements among the powers concerned, defining and delimit-
ing their respective claims.[27]

Prior to 1875 not one-tenth of Africa, the second largest continent, had been appropriated by European nations. By 1895 all but
a tenth of it was appropriated; and among the fragments constituting this tenth the Egyptian Sudan and the Boer Republics would
be swallowed before the turn of the century. The story of the fate—
the British fate—which befell them is reserved for a later chapter.

Africa was a main scene of European imperialism; so were the
innumerable archipelagoes of the broad Pacific, especially after
1884. New Guinea was partitioned in 1885, Holland retaining the
western half, Great Britain securing the southeastern quarter (now
styled "Papua"), and Germany the northeastern quarter (patriotically rechristened "Kaiser Wilhelmsland"). Simultaneously Germany obtained full proprietorship of near-by islands on which was
conferred the companion name of "Bismarck Archipelago," and
also the Marshall Islands to the northeast; and in 1899 she purchased from Spain job lots of islands—the Carolines and Mariannes
(or Ladrones)—and divided with the United States the Samoan
group. Great Britain established a protectorate over north Borneo
(Sarawak) in 1888, and between 1893 and 1900 annexed the South
Solomon, Gilbert, and Tonga Islands, while France occupied the
Society Islands, the Marquesas, and the Tuamotu Archipelago.

On the Asiatic mainland British India was rapidly consolidated
and considerably extended after 1884. Lands of native princes were
progressively incorporated into the empire and brought directly
under its administration: 15,000 square miles of them in the '70's;
90,000 in the '80's; 133,000 in the '90's. Moreover, French expansive
efforts from Indo-China westward invited a counter-expansion of

[27] Most notable among such arrangements were the Anglo-German Agreement of
July 1890; the Anglo-French Declaration of August 1890; the Anglo-Italian Protocols
of March-April 1891; the Anglo-Portuguese Treaty of June 1891; and the Franco-
German Convention of March 1894.

British India eastward, just as Russia's steady advance in the north-west fostered British fears and counter-schemings in that direction. In 1885 King Thebaw of Burma had the bad judgment to like the French and to concede them the right to build a railway from Tonkin to Mandalay, to open a bank in his capital, and to exploit his ruby mines. He was promptly handed a British ultimatum, ordering him to welcome a British envoy and in the future to follow British advice, and when, in good Oriental style, he hesitated to say either "yes" or "no," an army of 10,000 British and Indian troops crossed the border, mowed down Burmese resistance, and captured King Thebaw. On January 1, 1886, the kingdom of Burma was annexed to British India.

But while the British waged war, brief as it was, against Burma, Russia utilized the opportunity to seize Penjdeh on the Afghan frontier. Elated by this success, she dispatched military forces in 1891 into the mountainous Pamir country adjoining India itself; and, after another crisis and more threats of war, Russia managed by an agreement of 1895 with Britain to keep a good half of the disputed territory. On the other side, France seized in 1893 the country of Laos, lying between Annam and the Mekong River and connecting Cambodia with Tonkin. Thereby only a dwindling Siam was left as buffer between the British Empire of India and the French imperial domain of Indo-China. In the late '90's the whole "Far East" became the scene of a scramble by almost all the European great powers, and Japan and the United States also, for coaling stations and "spheres of influence," but this development can more appropriately be reviewed in a subsequent chapter.

Altogether, European imperialism during the three decades from 1871 to 1900 achieved immense conquests in Africa, the Pacific, and Asia. It added in these regions, during that comparatively brief period, some 4¼ million square miles and 66 million people to the British colonial empire, 3½ million square miles and 26 million people to the French, and a half million square miles and 6½ million people to the Russian, besides providing Germany with a new colonial empire of one million square miles and 13 million people, Italy with a minor one of 185,000 square miles and 750,000 people, and the King of the Belgians with a major one of 900,000 square miles and 8½ million people. And all these were without loss, but rather with gain, to the pre-existing colonial empires of Portuguese and Dutch. For the first time in history, the bulk of the entire world belonged to Europe.

Yet, however much the participating nations may have been moved to this new outburst of imperialism by economic considerations, however much they may have expected to reap from it in the way of financial gain, their expenditures on army, navy, and administration for it chronically exceeded their direct income from it; and one may well doubt whether most of the wealth which accrued to individual traders and investors, even to a Cecil Rhodes or a King Leopold, could not have been as readily amassed without the political dominion which was so costly and in the long run so provocative of international war. The new political imperialism, let us reiterate, was less economic than nationalist.

VI. THE NEW NAVALISM

"And finally a respectable navy." This had been last, but not least, among Friedrich List's desiderata for a patriotic and self-sufficing nation. Its general realization waited, nevertheless, upon the achievement of a large degree of economic nationalism and national imperialism. Great Britain had long possessed, of course, a premier navy, and France a respectable one. But until the Continental great powers supplemented their rivalry within Europe by imperialist rivalry in Africa, Asia, and Oceania, and until the economic arguments for external imperialism, as well as for internal tariff protection, sank deep into popular consciousness, armies were deemed far more important than navies and much more deserving objects of public expenditure.

Throughout the decade of the '70's, when size and cost of armies were rapidly mounting, expenditure on navies remained relatively modest and almost stationary. The British navy cost annually about 50 million dollars, the French 37½ million, the Russian 11¼ million, the German 8¾ million, the Italian 6¼ million. But as Russia found herself in humiliating collision with an all-powerful British fleet at Constantinople in 1878, and as possibility of other collisions developed on an ever-widening front—Persia, India, the

Far East—she quickened naval construction, built strong naval bases at Odessa and Vladivostok, and raised her naval expenditure in 1886 to 18¾ million dollars. France, too, unable with an inferior fleet to circumvent the British in Egypt or Burma, increased naval expenditures to 40 million in 1886, and two years later Italy was imposing extreme burdens on her people so as to spend 30 million dollars on her navy.

Alarm gripped Great Britain. It was not about Italy, whose fleet was obviously a "precautionary defense" against the Mediterranean neighbor that had "stolen" Tunis. It was rather about Russia and France. One or the other of these powers was now challenging British imperial hegemony almost everywhere, and their growing naval strength, combined as it was likely to be, might make their challenges widely effective. Even if the British battle fleet was still a match for the French and Russian on the high seas, it could hardly police all the British colonies and merchantmen and ward off raids by the swift cruisers in which Russia and France specialized. Now that England was largely industrialized and dependent upon seaborne commerce for her food supplies, indeed for her very existence, any serious interference with that commerce would spell disaster.

In 1888 a committee of three British admirals, appointed to report on the naval maneuvers of that year, gave it as their opinion that "no time should be lost in placing the British navy beyond comparison with that of any two powers." Lord George Hamilton, then first lord of the admiralty in the Conservative ministry of Lord Salisbury, immediately endorsed the proposed "two-power standard," and in 1889 put through parliament a Naval Defense Act, providing for addition to the navy, within four and a half years, of 70 vessels of 318,000 tons. In 1890 Britain's naval expenditure jumped to 86¼ million dollars.

This British action exerted far-reaching influence. France and Russia promptly increased their naval budgets by a million dollars each and presently entered into a defensive alliance. In 1890 Bismarck's successor, Count Caprivi, amid loud cheers of Emperor William II, obtained the Reichstag's sanction for building up the German navy and increasing the outlay on it to 22½ million dollars.

In the same year the United States naval board recommended to congress the formation of an American fleet of 100 vessels, of which twenty should be first-class battleships; and shortly afterward a corresponding program was evolved in Japan.

Soon, in all these countries, a definite doctrine of navalism was crystallized and industriously propagated; and before long the masses, no less than government officials, were imbued with it. Of many naval doctrinaires of the '90's, certainly the most influential was an American officer—Captain Alfred Mahan. His classic, *The Influence of Sea Power upon History,* first published in 1890, went through innumerable English editions and was translated into all the major languages of the Continent; and the doctrine it set forth, that no nation could maintain imperial sway and commercial greatness without possessing big battle fleets, was given vivid illustration in Mahan's succeeding books, *The Influence of Sea Power upon the French Revolution and Empire* (1892) and *Life of Nelson* (1897).

Roundly supplementing Mahan's writings were numerous expository volumes like Spenser Wilkinson's *Command of the Seas* (1894), a succession of exhilarating verse from Swinburne's *Armada* (1888) to Kipling's *Fleet in Being* (1898), and an epidemic of alarmist tales akin to William Le Queux's *Great War in England* (1894) which graphically described the consequences of British naval defeat—invasion of England by French and Russians, their capture of Manchester and Birmingham, their horrifying assault upon London. In 1894 a "Navy League" was formed in Great Britain to disseminate just such propaganda, and in Germany an imitative "Flottenverein" was launched in 1897 by none other than the newly appointed minister of marine, Alfred von Tirpitz, who confessed that he "devoured" Mahan. "Without sea-power," Tirpitz concluded, "Germany's position in the world resembled that of a mollusc without a shell."[28]

Various arguments were employed to convince different kinds of people that they should support a strengthened navy. It would be a form of "national insurance" for merchant marine and foreign commerce. It would "protect" traders and investors, tourists and missionaries. It would bring "order and security" to "backward"

[28] *My Memoirs* (New York, 1919), I, 77.

peoples and help to civilize them. It would heighten the "prestige" of a "progressive" people and assure it a commensurate "place in the sun." Without a powerful navy, no nation could be a "world power." Without imperial power, a European nation could not be a great power. And according to the clear dictates of "biological science," second-rate nations must decline and eventually die.

That navalism was extraordinarily popular toward the close of the 1890's is evidenced by two facts. First, naval expenditure steadily increased (except in semi-bankrupt and colonially unsuccessful Italy): in 1900 it reached the sum of 130 million dollars in England, 62½ million in France, 42½ million in Russia, 37½ million in Germany; it stood at 22½ million in Italy. Second, practically all political parties, except the Marxist, now voted unquestioningly for naval bills: these had become the concern, not merely of "conservatives," but of nations. Navalism was a natural product of the combination of economic nationalism with national imperialism.

Chapter Seven

SEED-TIME OF TOTALITARIAN NATIONALISM

I. PLANTERS AND CULTIVATORS

TREITSCHKE wrote in 1884 that the older generation whose catchword had been liberalism was giving way to a new generation of lusty singers of *Deutschland, Deutschland über Alles*.[1] He was quite right, and a shining example himself of this very transition. In his youth Treitschke had been a pronounced Liberal, and the nationalism which then enthralled him was the kind that appealed almost universally to liberal intellectuals—the kind which postulated an atomized Europe of self-conscious nationalities, each one, whether large or small, romantically prizing its distinctive language and historic traditions, peacefully attaining to political independence and constitutional government, and, of course, not denying to others the right of national self-determination it claimed for itself. Such liberal nationalism had been at least implicit in Prussian "regeneration" and Italian "risorgimento," in revolutionary movements of 1830 and 1848, in the patriotic activities not only of Stein and Mazzini, but of Palmerston and Gladstone in Britain, Guizot and Thiers in France, Daniel O'Connell among the Irish and Ján Kollár among the Slavs, František Palacký in Bohemia and Baron Eötvös in Hungary, Ljudevit Gaj, the apostle of Yugoslav unity and freedom, and Émile Laveleye, the Belgian sociologist; and it had been an ostensible object of Napoleon III's foreign policy.

But the fruitage of liberal nationalism proved to be war rather than peace; and the generation of intellectuals who grew up during the series of nationalist wars from 1859 to 1878 naturally associated the outcome with current material progress and also with the newly discovered and widely advertised "scientific" principle of "the struggle for existence and survival of the fittest." The result was at

[1] "Die ersten Versuche deutscher Kolonialpolitik," in *Zehn Jahre deutscher Kämpfe*, 3rd ed. (Berlin, 1896).

once an intensification of nationalism and a change in its character. Divested of romantic trappings of altruism and cosmopolitanism, it was rendered nakedly "realist" and unblushingly self-centered. No longer modest or pacific, it grew blatant and bellicose; and with pride of success substituted for mere aspiration, it took on an imperialistic complexion. For a nation which by force of arms had demonstrated its fitness to survive must be superior to others, and entitled, in so far as it could, to dominate them. This type of nationalism was obviously not liberal. It represented, indeed, a central feature of that complex of forces which by the 1880's was swinging Europe away from earlier liberal moorings.

The change was particularly marked in Germany, where the Prussian army and Bismarck's *Realpolitik* had recently achieved most gloriously what the speeches and resolutions of '48 had notoriously failed to achieve—national consolidation, and with it Germany's hegemony on the Continent. Treitschke registered and forwarded the change by his pamphlets during the Franco-Prussian War, by his lyrical *History*, by the lectures on politics he delivered at Berlin throughout the '80's and '90's. Only great and powerful states ought to exist, he reiterated; small states cannot protect their subjects against invasion and hence cannot engender among them any real patriotism or national pride. With great national states the worst sin and the most contemptible is feebleness; "it is the political sin against the Holy Ghost." In the new age the national state must be the "power state"; its "highest moral duty is to increase its power." It must extend its functions to the totality of human interests and activities. It must provide through universal education "a training in the active love of the Fatherland." It must nationalize all minorities under its sway by penetrating them with "the same speech and culture," and incidentally by treating Catholics as "deficient in true Germanism" and Jews as "an element of decomposition." The power state must be safeguarded against individualism, party strife, and parliamentary inefficiency.[2]

Treitschke professed to be a National Liberal, but his liberalism after 1870 was merely a vermiform appendix to his functioning

[2] See especially *Die Politik*, I, *passim; History* (Eng. trans., New York, 1915-1919), I, 6, 46, 329, and IV, 112, 117; and "Zum Gedächtnis des grossen Krieges" (1895) in *Ausgewählte Schriften* (Leipzig, 1915), 325, 335.

nationalism, and this was scarcely distinguishable from that of his Conservative colleague at the University of Berlin, Adolf Wagner, who punctuated constant campaigning in behalf of economic nationalism with forays against Jews, Catholics, Poles, Frenchmen, and any other group, domestic or foreign, that he deemed dangerous to Germany's unity and might. Nor should one overlook the complementary role of that other Wagner—Richard—who, looking back from the vantage point of 1871 upon his own youthful participation in the revolution of 1848, declared it "un-German" and went on to explain that there was no German word for democracy and that the thing itself was a "Franco-Judaic" invention. The musical genius republished in 1869, with sharpened barbs, his early diatribe against the Jews; and in 1876 he crowned Germany's new imperial nationalism with his *Ring der Nibelungen*, a new sort of aesthetic nationalism resoundingly resurrecting the demigods of pre-Christian Teutonic Valhalla.

Three other significant contributors to totalitarian nationalism were camp followers of the victorious German armies of 1870: an army chaplain, Adolf Stöcker (the name Adolf recurs through the later nationalist drama like a Greek chorus); an army surgeon, Ernst Hasse; and an ambulance driver, Friedrich Nietzsche. The first specialized in "national socialism," combating Jews and Marxians and comparing "the majesty of war" with "the majesty of God";[3] and the second, in national imperialism, becoming head of the Pan-German League in 1894. The third was not much of a nationalist himself, not even an anti-Semite, but his "philosophy of the will" and his "contempt of pity" provided an exhaustless arsenal for the younger generation of militant patriots and imperialists. "As the smaller surrenders himself to the greater," said Nietzsche, "so the greater must surrender himself to the will to power and stake life upon the issue. It is the mission of the greatest to run risk and danger—to cast dice with death."[4]

In Austria the talented Georg von Schönerer called upon his fellow Germans in the '80's to mobilize against Jews and other "alien" peoples of the Hapsburg Empire, and to prepare for their

---

[3] *Christlich-Soziale Reden und Aufsätze* (Bielefeld, 1885), p. 286.
[4] *Also sprach Zarathustra* (1883), 11.

own reception into a Greater Germany by cutting loose from the Roman Catholic Church and adopting a German—and heroic—"racial Christianity." It is not without interest that in the region of Austria most affected by Schönerer's "Los von Rom" movement, was born in 1889 a certain Adolf Hitler, who developed in boyhood a passionate fondness for Wagner's music and Stöcker's demagoguery and was punished at school for singing instead of the courtly *Kaiserlied* the provocative *Deutschland über Alles*.

Much the same nationalist fever which military victories brought on in Germany, was superinduced in France by the military defeat of 1870-1871. French patriots, whether of the "Right" or the "Left," would not accept the disastrous encounter of that "terrible year" as any conclusive denial of their country's right to survive as a great power with all its old-time prestige and "civilizing mission." The disaster had been fortuitous and must be repaired as quickly as possible. On the one hand, Taine, with aristocratic leanings, blamed it upon the individualism and democracy which eighteenth-century Enlightenment and Revolution, reinforced by a maddening romanticism, had foisted upon the nation; and in the brilliant volumes of his *Origines de la France contemporaine*, half history and half tract, which he put forth from 1871 to 1893, he mordantly diagnosed the ills and by implication prescribed the remedies—a return to monarchy, aristocracy, and the traditions of the old regime, and a "realistic" recognition of the "scientific" fact that the ordinary man is a primeval savage, a gorilla, who must be forcibly subdued.

On the other hand, Paul Déroulède, of Jacobin background, blamed the disaster of 1870 on the timidity of Napoleon III and the insufficiency of patriotic passion among the masses, and consecrated his life to the arousing of national spirit and the preaching of a war of revenge against Germany. He penned hundreds of stirring soldier songs. He inspired the formation in 1882 of a "League of Patriots"—including Gambetta, Victor Hugo, Henri Martin, Sadi Carnot, and Felix Faure—and long presided over it. He lectured up and down the land, distributed myriads of patriotic pamphlets, sponsored rifle clubs among the youth, organized annual national fêtes at Paris about the image of Jeanne d'Arc and the veiled statue of Strasbourg. Unable to persuade Gambetta or other

Republican politicians to go to war with Germany, Déroulède gradually reached the conclusion that the Third Republic was as cowardly as the Second Empire had been and that it should be supplanted by a military dictatorship. "I have found my man," he said in 1883; "his name is Boulanger."[5] But the Boulangist movement, to which he pinned his hopes and for which he zealously labored, collapsed in 1889. He then joined the anti-Semitic forces which the Dreyfus case arrayed, and when they were about to be routed he made a forlorn attempt in 1899 to execute a *coup d'état* himself against the Republic.

A young physician, Dr. Gustave Le Bon, had attended French troops in the war of 1870. After the war he turned to "scientific" research in chemistry, physiology, and anthropology, and presently blossomed forth in innumerable articles and tomes as an "authority" on "crowd psychology."[6] He was a credulous as well as an indefatigable fellow, but his solemn cocksureness, buttressed by constant obeisance to Darwinian biology, made his worst nonsense pass muster as sound science and assured him a wide circle of devout disciples. There were, it seemed, four distinct races of mankind in an ascending scale of cultural and intellectual talents: (1) "primitive" Fuegians and Australians; (2) "inferior" Negroes; (3) "average" Chinese, Japanese, and Semites; and (4) "superior" Indo-Europeans. The last, it appeared, were perpetually in danger of succumbing to "mob psychology," which was something dreadful, and the only way in which they could preserve their superiority was essentially the Tainesque way of opposing democracy and building up an elite of brains and military prowess.

A nationalist by-product of the Franco-Prussian War was Maurice Barrès. He was only eight years of age when German troops took possession of his native village in Lorraine, but what the precocious boy then saw left an indelible impression upon the man, as he

5 Jerôme and Jean Tharaud, *La vie et la mort de Déroulède* (Paris, 1914), 42.

6 His most publicized work was *Psychologie des foules* (Paris, 1895), which reached a 31st edition in 1925; its English version, entitled *The Crowd*, appeared in 1899. His "scientific" reputation was founded on an earlier work, crowned by the Academy of Science and the Anthropological Society: *Recherches anatomiques et mathématiques sur les variations de volume du crâne et sur les rélations avec l'intelligence*, 8 vols. (Paris, 1879). Among the host of Le Bon's other works are *L'Homme et les sociétés* (1881); *Les Premières civilisations* (1889); *La Psychologie du socialisme* (1898); *La Psychologie de l'éducation* (1907); *La Psychologie politique* (1910); *La Psychologie des révolutions* (1912).

recorded thirteen years later: "We who look back to the dark year in the vague mist of our childhood feel that the honor of *la Patrie* is embodied in the marching ranks of a regiment; all the military fanfares carry us back to the conquered soil; the waving of the flags seems to us a distant signal to the exiles; our fists clench; and we have only to make ourselves provocative agents."[7] Such an agent Barrès certainly made himself; and the tonic he dispensed was nicely compounded of ingredients furnished by Taine, Déroulède, Boulanger, the anti-Semitic Drumont, and Nietzsche, all flavored with Barrès's own "lyrical exaltation." The "national egotism" which he celebrated in his trilogy, *Le Roman de l'énergie nationale* (1897-1903), and in his collection of essays, *Scènes et doctrines du nationalisme* (1902), was not only an ultimate expression of the Generation of Materialism but also a fitting prelude to the succeeding generation of "Action Française" and World War, and an unwitting salutation to the Mussolinis and Hitlers still to come.

It must not be imagined that the sowers of totalitarian nationalism were all anti-Semites. Some Jews were effective planters—for example, Émile Durkheim, who started out to be a rabbi and ended up as a world-famous sociologist. He taught that the national state, the *patrie*, is a "psychic being," that of all "societies"—family, class, church, *etc.*—it is the most basic and by right the most powerful, and that, as its function is the supreme one of directing and giving harmony to the ideal "corporative society," so its members owe it supreme allegiance and the highest public worship.

In Russia the militantly racial and imperialistic nationalism known as Slavophilism received marked impetus from Danilevski, to whose *Russia and Europe* (1871) reference has already been made;[8] and in the heat of the Turkish War of 1877-1878 and especially after the accession of Alexander III in 1881 it was widely propagated by Russian intellectuals and exerted no little influence upon the Emperor's key administrators, Plehve and Pobêdonostsev. As outlined by the gifted Aksakov brothers and filled in by Michael Katkov, the ablest Russian journalist of the '80's, Slavophilism

7 *Les Taches d'encre,* Nov. 5, 1884, cited by Victor Giraud, *Maurice Barrès* (Paris, 1922), 33.
8 See above, p. 13.

posited the superiority of Slavs to other Europeans and the superiority of Russians to other Slavs. Russia was "holy Russia," blessed
with "orthodox" Christianity as over against Protestant and Catholic
heresies outside, and with a traditional political and social order—
Tsar, nobility, and village community, all predominantly agricultural in outlook and hence mutually respectful and quite stable—
which was incomparably better than the demagogic democracy and
industrial selfishness of western Europe. But Russia, the Slavophiles
said, should be altruistic and not keep her blessings to herself. She
should liberate the Slavs beyond her frontiers from every alien yoke
and guard them from debasement whether by Moslem Turks or by
heretical Germans; and if certain Slavs, for instance the Poles, were
already so contaminated by the West as to be renegades from true
Slavism and antagonistic to Holy Russia, then they must be brought
to their senses by forceful blows. Katkov was a strenuous opponent
of Polish national aspirations, and at the same time intensely anti-
German. He received Paul Déroulède with open arms at Moscow
in 1886 and strongly seconded his proposal of a Franco-Russian
military alliance against Germany.

All over Europe similar seeds were being sowed. In Norway
Björnson fell under the spell of Darwin and Spencer and turned
from romantic liberalism to "realism" and militant "activism." In
Bohemia Karel Kramář led a "Young Czech" revolt against "Old
Czech" moderation and compromise. Among the Poles Roman
Dmowski began to agitate for an imperial Poland, a *Polonia magna*,
which should properly subject to the "superior" Polish race its
"inferior" neighbors—Lithuanians and Letts, White Russians and
Ukrainians. In Hungary, Count Tisza signalized his long premiership from 1875 to 1890 by persistent preaching and practice of
nationalistic discrimination against the non-Magyars who comprised a half of the country's population.

In Italy, after her debut as a great power, Mazzini, with his
tilting at the injustice of one people's mastering another, must have
seemed like a Don Quixote to the "realistic" generation of Don
Sanchos who followed. Not that these Sanchos were cowardly. Some
were very bold, at least in utterance. One group, centering in the
faculty of philosophy at the University of Naples and including

Francesco de Sanctis and Bertrando Spaventa, became ardent apostles of the teaching of Hegel, particularly of his ideal of an omnipotent state, and inveighed against the cliques of liberal politicians and machinations of special interests that impaired national unity. The Italian state, said Spaventa, should be strengthened as the German state under Bismarck had been; more than that, it should be "adored." A second group comprised semi-pagan and ultra-patriotic poets and dramatists: Giosuè Carducci, who invoked the ancient spirit of the "great Roman race"; Enrico Corradini, who urged heroic deeds in emulation of Julius Caesar; and Gabriele d'Annunzio, who, like Barrès, dipped into the Nietzschean bath and came out dripping with "national egotism." A third group embraced the statesmen Depretis and Crispi and their parliamentary supporters, nominal "Liberals of the Left," actual proponents of economic nationalism and national imperialism.

In mid-Victorian Britain, Carlyle had been something of an anomaly, and it seemed charitable to ascribe to chronic dyspepsia his choleric ridicule of humanitarianism, denunciation of parliamentary government, advocacy of industrial regimentation along military lines, and apostrophe to "rule by the hero, the man of action who must not hesitate to use force." But the completion of his monumental eulogy of Frederick the Great on the eve of the creation of the Hohenzollern German Empire and his passionate espousal of the German side in the Franco-Prussian War were timely, to say the least; and in the subsequent drift of nationalism (and imperialism) Carlyle was invested with the halo of a major prophet. Froude was his intimate friend and Ruskin a devoted disciple, while other English intellectuals echoed his doctrines. Sir James Stephen returned in 1872 from civil service in India profoundly convinced that civilization could be maintained only by force, and in the next year he published *Liberty, Equality, Fraternity,* a frontal attack upon the whole liberal position of J. S. Mill. Sir Henry Maine, another veteran of Indian service, brought up supporting artillery in 1886 with his volume on *Popular Government*: civilization, he insisted, was a technical skill held in trust for the many by the few; it was a hardly won entity which force created, habit perpetuated, and patriotic statesmanship guarded. Then in 1896 William Lecky climaxed his career as an historian of ideas with a two-volume work, *Democracy and Liberty,* the moral of which was that real liberty is for supermen and antithetical to democracy.[9]

Moreover, the Hegelian idealization of the state was transplanted to England, particularly to its intellectual capital of Oxford, by a galaxy of dons—T. H. Green, Edward Caird, Francis H. Bradley. Green, for example, taught that the state is an organic society superior to its component individuals, that it is usually right in whatever it does because it draws on the whole inheritance of past wisdom, and that it should actively intervene to insure the possibility of a "good life" to all its members. The neo-Hegelians in Britain, like their contemporaries in Italy, wished to serve the cause of personal liberty, but practically the method they advocated was conducive less to the continuance of traditional liberalism—and liberal nationalism—than to its underpinning, in domestic and foreign affairs, with props of power politics.

In England, too, "left-wing" Liberals such as Joseph Chamberlain and Sir Charles Dilke were soon joining hands with Tory Democrats like Lord Randolph Churchill and with the old-line Conservative statesman Salisbury to back the racial and imperialistic nationalism so splendidly exemplified by men of action of the stamp of Cecil Rhodes, and so gloriously lauded by the psalmist of the new dispensation, Rudyard Kipling. How happy even Carlyle might have been, and perhaps quite freed from dyspepsia, had he lived into the '90's and witnessed the ousting of liberal "charlatans" by forceful "heroes."

II. FAVORABLE SOIL AND CLIMATE

Recorded history has usually ignored the myriad sowers of seed fallen by the wayside or on stony ground or among thorns, and remembered only those whose seed "fell on good ground and sprang up and yielded fruit a hundred-fold." Nationalistic seed was, of course, but one of many kinds of seed which intellectuals strewed broadcast during the thirty years from 1870 to 1900. That it proved remarkably fruitful must be attributed not so much to the particular planters whom we have just named as to the fact

9 See B. E. Lippincott, *Victorian Critics of Democracy* (Minneapolis, 1938).

that their particular seed, more than any other, fell on fertile soil in an auspicious climate, although one should not rob the planters of credit due them. They had a knack of choosing seed adaptable to the environment, and they carefully cultivated what they sowed.

Conditions were very favorable from the 1880's onward. By then, certain results of the series of nationalistic wars from 1859 to 1878 were manifest to ordinary Europeans as well as to intellectuals, and influential with them all. To a considerable extent the political map of Europe had been redrawn along lines of nationality. Germans and Italians had acquired national states ranking as great powers; Hungarians had obtained full sovereignty; and the scrambled peoples of southeastern Europe—Greeks, Serbs, Rumanians, Bulgarians—had been largely segregated in newly established or newly confirmed national states. Moreover, large-scale popular participation in the wars which produced this nationalizing of political geography had served to arouse a bellicose national spirit among the masses, not only of the victorious nations (including Russia), but also of the defeated peoples of France and Austria and vicariously of a country like Great Britain whose populace had merely sat on the side lines and watched. There was heightened popular pride in national military accomplishments; heightened popular veneration of national military heroes; heightened popular expectation that national arms would keep what had been gained or recover what had been lost.

Back in the '50's and early '60's there had been some chance that the principle of nationality and the practical establishment of national states might be harmonized with a federative polity guaranteeing a degree of unity and solidarity to Europe as a whole.[10] The chance was lost in the ensuing wars and attendant intensification of national feeling. The dream of a federated Europe dissolved into the reality of a nationally disparate Europe, and in the '80's political separatism of the various national units was buttressed by an economic separatism, involving the repudiation of international free trade and the adoption of tariff protection and other adjuncts of economic nationalism. Both political and economic separatism

10 This chance for a federative polity is the central theme of the late Professor Robert Binkley's companion volume in the present series, *Realism and Nationalism, 1852-1871* (New York, 1935).

were inspired, in the main, by nationalist sentiment, and this in turn was greatly quickened by political and economic rivalries in which the several national states consequently engaged.

It cannot be too strongly stressed that nationalism was now popular and commonplace. In earlier days it had been a special concern of particular groups of intellectuals, and its propagation by means of learned societies and heavy tomes and fugitive articles had been uphill work among a skeptical aristocracy and an indifferent peasantry. Now, however, classes and masses alike were readily responsive to nationalist propaganda, and marvelously effective instruments were available for it—the new national school systems, the new cheap popular journalism, the new democratic procedure and "pressure politics." Conditions favoring the formation and multiplication of chambers of commerce and trade-unions, co-operative societies and agrarian leagues, also favored the spawning of national organizations with ultra-patriotic objectives: army leagues and navy leagues, national defense societies, colonial societies, societies of war veterans and of sons and daughters of veterans, societies for the nationalizing of dissident minorities. In Great Britain the Primrose League (1883) soon counted its adherents by the hundreds of thousands. In France the League of Patriots (1882) secured a numerous following. In Germany the Colonial Society, starting with 200 members in 1882, had 25,000 in 1900; the Pan-German League, originating in 1890, numbered 22,000 fifteen years later; the anti-Polish "Society of the Eastern Marches" (1894) speedily enrolled 30,000 members; the Navy League (1898) enlisted half a million within two years.

Conservatives and "reactionaries," who in Metternichean times had been almost as chary of "nationalism" as of "revolution," were now in the van of every ultra-patriotic movement—economic nationalism, imperialism, etc.—and by the 1880's they had an unusually large and loyal clientele. Liberals (with the capital letter) might be dwindling a bit in number but not in patriotic fervor, and many of them—National Liberals in Germany, Liberal Unionists in Britain, the majority of Radicals in France and Italy—were approximating in this respect the attitude of contemporary Conservatives. Apparently they had to do so to retain popular support.

Some pacifistic intellectuals continued to distinguish between patriotism and nationalism and to criticize the latter's jingoist tendency, but the general public was now apt to regard them as incorrigible idealists, tiresome if not dangerous. The growing Marxian parties, to be sure, had the reputation of being anti-patriotic, and their "theoreticians" and parliamentarians certainly waged a wordy campaign against standing armies, protective tariffs, imperial enterprises, and other conspicuous features of the newer political and economic nationalism. Yet the bark of Marxian dogs was worse than their bite. The noise came from "leaders," the great majority of whom were not real "proletarians," but bourgeois intellectuals with a heritage of earlier liberal idealism and humanitarianism. The "followers" comprised such a small segment of any nation prior to the 1890's that they couldn't have inflicted very serious wounds if they had been minded to bite. Probably, if the expressed attitude of trade-unionists is any index, the Socialist rank and file were not minded to bite at all and not lacking in patriotism. At any rate, the Marxian parties made their most spectacular gains—though still remaining minority parties—just when "Reformist" leaders in the late '90's were eschewing talk of class warfare and criticism of nationalist policies. The Fabians, Shaw and Wells included, frankly defended British imperialism in South Africa "in the interest of civilization" and applauded the conquest of the Boer Republics.

Whatever Marxians might say or do, the large majority of ordinary people, rural and urban, voted in democratic elections of the '80's and '90's for political groups pledged to the pursuit of nationalist ends. It was naturally so, for the voting masses, like leading politicians and intellectuals, were profoundly affected by the climate—the *Zeitgeist*—of those decades, and the climate was extremely favorable to nationalism.

Functions of the state—now normally the national state—were being rapidly expanded to foster technological progress, to multiply public works and creature comforts, to cope with a wide latitude of economic and social problems issuing from the latest stage of industrialization, to elaborate and maintain vast systems of public education, to carry the advance of medical science into the big realm of public health. More and more, therefore, the national state was becoming, in the eyes of its citizens, a fairy godmother, the dispenser or expected dispenser of all good things. No wonder that Hegel's dithyrambic exaltation of the state assumed new and vital significance.

Furthermore, the extraordinary mobility and urbanization of population served to create during those decades an extraordinary number of *déracinés*, as Barrès called them, that is, persons uprooted from ancestral soil and local allegiance. Experiencing grave economic insecurity and psychological maladjustment, these were very susceptible to demagogic propaganda, socialist or nationalist or both; and in any event, with the exception of a few who turned anarchist, they proved a help rather than a hindrance to the growth of *étatisme*, the enlargement and centralization of state functions, which led more or less inevitably to the adoption of nationalistic policies.

To the same end operated the contemporaneous loosening of the hold of Christian faith and practice upon a sizable portion of Europe's population. Thereby a kind of religious and moral void was created for relatively large numbers, who promptly though unconsciously sought to fill it with a new faith, a new object of worship, a new cult. Some found the desired substitute in "science," others in Marxian socialism (which was as much a religion as a system of economics), still others—doubtless the majority—in nationalism. Almost all of them, however, put national state in place of church as the cement of human society and as the intermediary between man and his salvation. On the other hand, professed and practicing Christians, being now on the defensive in most European countries, felt obliged, if they were not to suffer still greater losses, to prove themselves invaluable to their national states and to outdo everybody else in protestations of national patriotism, especially when such pagans as Barrès and d'Annunzio pointed proudly and at times wistfully to the "beauty" of Christianity and claimed it as a traditional glory of the particular nationalism they inculcated. In this way, many sincere Christians, along with militant anti-Christians, were acclimatized to the ultra-patriotism of the Material-ist Generation.

Finally, let us emphasize, this same generation as a whole was acclimatized to certain "scientific" conceptions, or at least to certain "scientific" slogans, which were of inestimable utility not only in stimulating the intellectual sowers of totalitarian nationalism but also in enrooting it among the masses. One, borrowed from biology, was "the struggle for existence and survival of the fittest." Another, taken from physics, was "the supreme reality of matter and force." Others, derived from physiological psychology, were "man's animal mind" and "man's fighting instincts." Still others, stemming from sociology, were "herd instinct," "crowd psychology," "consciousness of kind," "social solidarity." It was the currency of such phrases and their implications which made the competitive national militarism, imperialism, and navalism of the period seem natural and scientific, and which expedited the association of all these phenomena with a "realistic" nationalism whose characteristic tone was forcefulness. In fact, any doctrine of forcefulness, by whomsoever preached or for whatsoever purpose, was likely sooner or later to be integrated with nationalism. This was true of Nietzsche's "forceful superman" and "will to power." Even Marx's forceful "proletariat" and "class conflict" had a common denominator with the "forceful nation" and "international conflict."

III. RACIALISM AND ANTI-SEMITISM

The newer nationalism was "forceful." Also it was characteristically "racial."

Of course, all sorts of earlier nationalists had talked much about "race," but their talk had usually been loose and "literary" and without pretense to scientific exactitude. Ever since Schlegel delivered the dictum that there were as many races as there were languages, reference to "German race," "French race," "Celtic race," "Slavic race," etc., had been à la mode in writing and conversation. All this, however, was a manner of speaking, a merely conventional use of "race" as a synonym for "nationality."

A change came with the vogue of social Darwinism after the national struggles of the '60's and '70's. Obviously the "fittest" nations "survived." But what made a nation "fittest"? Social scientists, becoming obsessed with the transcendent importance of heredity, jumped to the conclusion that it must be the one whose biological racial stock was best. The problem of finding out what the different human species were and which was best, seemed simple and soluble in either of two ways. You could classify races, superior and inferior, according to mental traits and then discover which one a man belonged to by observing his behavior and measuring his intelligence. Or you could classify them according to physical features. It appeared axiomatic that Germans, now being clearly a very fit people, must belong to a superior race. Hence anyone who displayed "German" qualities of boldness, energy, and bravery must belong to that race; and conversely, anyone who, like the prevalent physical type of German, was tall, blond, blue-eyed, and dolichocephalic, must possess superior qualities of courage and intellect.

The fitting of men into races according to their behavior was the special concern of a swarm of "social psychologists," of whom Gustave Le Bon was the most verbose and one of the most influential. On the other hand, hundreds of anatomists and anthropologists devoted themselves with scientific fervor to measuring physiological differences among men in respect of stature, shape of skull, color of hair, eyes, and complexion, and deducing therefrom different races (with correspondingly different qualities).[11] One of the most persistent and instructive of these, one who beguilingly styled himself an "anthropo-sociologist," was the Frenchman Vacher de Lapouge. He found three "racial species" of "homo sapiens" in Europe and tagged them, in appropriate zoological manner, with Latinized names: (1) *Homo Europaeus,* tall, blond, long-headed, blue-eyed, and also adventurous, energetic, domineering, idealistic, creative, distinctly superior, and Protestant; (2) *Homo Alpinus,* short, stocky, dark, round-headed, full-bearded, broad-nosed, and also cautious, slow, and agricultural; and (3) *Homo Mediterraneus,* short, slim, dark, long-headed, and also less creative and morally inferior, cowardly, shifty, fond of show and bright colors, sadistic, and Catholic. Lapouge likewise satisfied himself by a curious com-

---

11 As early as 1842 A. A. Retzius, a Swede, had put forth a system of classifying human types according to head form and facial angle and had formulated concepts of dolichocephaly and brachycephaly, of prognathism and orthognathism. Extensive application and development of his "system" occurred after 1871.

parative study of cephalic indices of Frenchmen he examined in the flesh and of Frenchmen he exhumed from their graves that each Germanic invasion of France had resulted in a measurable improvement of French stock. Unfortunately, according to him, there was in contemporary France a growing scarcity of tall dolichocephalic blonds, which betokened progressive national degeneration; the supermen were being submerged by democratic Alpines and Mediterraneans.[12]

It is hardly necessary to point out the inconsistencies, the highly dubious assumptions, and the faulty techniques in this sort of racial "science."[13] Most of its devotees during the '80's and '90's simply assumed, like Darwin, the inheritance of acquired characteristics; and so subjective were the methods they generally employed that no two of them reached the same conclusions as to what were the different races of mankind or what were their distinguishing marks. Yet if one contradicted another with a zeal and constancy befitting earnest searchers after truth, it only confirmed the conviction of all that there must be something fundamental in the whole business —that race can, even if it doesn't immediately, explain everything.

Scientific contributors to racialism were legion in the last decades of the nineteenth century.[14] Later on, of course, a goodly number of

12 See his articles in the *Révue d'Anthropologie* for 1887-1889, his *L'Aryen, son rôle social* (Paris, 1889), and his essay on "The Fundamental Principles of Anthropo-Sociology," *Journal of Political Economy* (Chicago, 1897-1898).

13 It has repeatedly been done, most devastatingly by F. H. Hankins, *Racial Basis of Civilization* (New York, 1926); Jacques Barzun, *Race, a Study in Modern Superstition* (New York, 1937); L. L. Snyder, *Race, a History of Modern Ethnic Theories* (New York, 1939); and Ruth Benedict, *Race* (New York, 1940).

14 Among authors of memorable treatises on the subject were: L. A. J. Quetelet, *Anthropométrie* (Brussels, 1871); P. P. Broca, *Instructions craniologiques et craniométriques* (Paris, 1875); Ludwik Gumplowicz, *Rasse und Staat* (Vienna, 1875) and *Der Rassenkampf* (Innsbruck, 1883); J. L. A. Quatrefages, *L'espèce humaine* (Paris, 1877; Eng. trans., New York, 1879); Paul Topinard, *Elements d'anthropologie générale* (Paris, 1885); John Beddoe, *The Races of Britain* (Bristol, 1885) and *Anthropological History of Europe* (Paisley, 1893); D. G. Brinton, *Races and Peoples* (New York, 1890); Otto Ammon, *Die natürliche Auslese beim Menschen* (Jena, 1893) and *Die Gesellschaftsordnung und ihre natürlichen Grundlagen* (Jena, 1895; 3rd ed. 1900); Rudolfo Livi, *Anthropometria militare*, 2 vols. (Rome, 1896-1905); Joseph Deniker, *Les races de l'Europe*, 2 vols. (Paris, 1899-1908) and *Les races et les peuples de la terre* (Paris, 1900; Eng. trans., London, 1900); Gustaf Retzius and C. M. Fürst, *Anthropologia suecica* (Stockholm, 1902); Ludwig Woltmann, *Politische Anthropologie* (Eisenach, 1903); C. H. Stratz, *Natürgeschichte der Menschen* (Stuttgart, 1904). Other names would include Carlier, Collignon, Durand de Gros, and Muffang in France; Brandt, Haeckel, Hansen, von Hölder, Schemann, Virchow, and Weissner in Germany; Schimmer and Weisbach in Austria; Steensby in Denmark; Anutchin in Russia; Chalumeau in Switzerland; Houzé in Belgium; Levasseur and Olóriz in Spain; Calori, Lombroso, Nicolucci, Reseri, Riccardi, and Sergi in Italy; Galton, Huxley, and A. R. Wallace in England; Ripley in the United States.

anthropologists and other social scientists, impressed by Weismann's argument against the inheritance of acquired characteristics and by new biological conceptions resulting from the application of Mendelian principles, evinced a healthy skepticism about the rather naïve racialism of the Generation of Materialism. But so far as pseudo-scientific publicists and popularizers were concerned (and their number was still more legion), the harm was already done. These had so effectively implanted racialism in the minds of multitudes and so fructified it with nationalist passion and prejudice that henceforth it had a life and popularity of its own quite unaffected by the doubts of scholars or the findings of scientific investigators. Ironically enough, a "realistic" generation prepared the way for the triumph of racial fancies over racial facts.

One of the most successfully propagated offshoots of racialism was the Aryan myth. For some time previously, philologists had used the word "Aryan" (or "Indo-European") to denote the group of related languages including Sanskrit, Greek, Latin, Celtic, Slavic, German; and students of history and comparative law had contended that institutions and customs common to nations speaking Aryan tongues must have originated with a single primitive "Aryan" people. But now appeared the racialists, identifying this linguistic and cultural people with the tall, blond, long-headed race. Inasmuch as Germans were credited with being wholly or predominantly of this type, and especially as they superlatively displayed in 1870-1871 the valor imputed to it, then Germans must be, so to speak, the standard Aryans physically and spiritually—the purest, noblest, strongest, most culture-bearing of all peoples of the world. Which was very flattering to German patriots and "scientifically" confirmatory of their own suspicions. Small wonder that they plumped *en masse* for the new racialism. As Adolf Stöcker exuberantly expressed it: "German blood flows in every German body, and the soul is in the blood. When one meets a German brother and not merely a brother from common humanity, there is a certain reaction that does not take place if the brother is not German. Peoples can be compared to birds; there are different species.[15]

[15] Dietrich von Oertzen, *Adolf Stöcker, Lebensbild und Zeitgeschichte* (Schwerin, 1912), pp. 260-61.

Into the service of German Aryanism was pressed a nice old French aristocrat, the Comte de Gobineau. His *Essay on the Inequality of the Human Races* had attracted little attention when it originally appeared in four erudite volumes in 1853-54, and it did not ascribe racial superiority to any nation as a whole, certainly not to the German. Rather, the Count had sought to explain a superiority he posited for himself and fellow French aristocrats over the mass of Frenchmen on the ground that the former represented pure Aryan stock while the latter were degenerate products of racial intermixture; and it was only after the decisive political defeat of patrician Royalists by plebeian Republicans in the '70's that disappointed French nationalists with aristocratic sympathies were properly disposed to find consolation in the pages of Gobineau. In 1884, when racialism was everywhere becoming fashionable, a new two-volume edition of his *Essay* was published at Paris. It sold much better than the original.

But while Gobineau had only a class following in France, he soon obtained a popular one in Germany. Here the whole nation was presumably Aryan, and endowed with all the fine and noble qualities he so liberally attributed to his own ancestors. Germans in general could applaud his pronouncements that European history began with the German migrations and that these produced the high civilization which is the outward manifestation of the superior innate tendencies of an Aryan. Richard Wagner acclaimed Gobineau as a master mind and great prophet. Presently a "Gobineau Museum" was opened at Strasbourg. In 1894 a "Gobineau Vereinigung" was founded at Freiburg. In 1899 a disciple, the self-Teutonized Houston Stewart Chamberlain, brought out the famed *Foundations of the Nineteenth Century*, surpassing the master in laudation of the Germanic, Teutonic, Nordic, Aryan *race* (it was all one now). By pursuing, too, what he termed "rational anthropology," a "new science" based on "intuition born of ceaseless observation," Chamberlain arrived at a position far in advance of Gobineau's. It was that anyone who has thought or acted like a German, equally with anyone who looks like one, must belong to that superior race, and that consequently such "Germans" as Columbus, Dante, and St. Paul are proof of German cultural supremacy. This was racial imperialism *in excelsis*. But it was popular. Chamberlain's book sold like hot cakes.

Meanwhile English (and American) publicists were recalling that "Anglo-Saxons" belonged to the superior Teutonic race. No less an authority than Gobineau had pointed to England, rather than to Germany, as the modern country where the "great race" survived with least adulteration. To be sure, Englishmen had not recently displayed in Europe the race's valor, as Germans had so sensationally done. But what about their adventurous spirit on the seas and throughout the huge British Empire overseas? Seeley in his *Expansion of England* proclaimed the Empire to be the very embodiment of Anglo-Saxon racial superiority, and in stirring prose called the English race to action to maintain its rich heritage. To him and likewise to the entire succeeding generation of British imperialists, the *motif* in all of England's greatness—political, commercial, industrial, and moral, no less than naval and colonial— was "the Anglo-Saxon race." And what easier explanation could be put forth of the rapidly growing strength and expansionist ambition of the United States? "If I read not amiss," declared a Congregationalist clergyman of New England in 1885, "this powerful race will move down upon Mexico, down upon Central and South America, out upon the islands on the sea, over upon Africa and beyond. And can anyone doubt that the result of this competition of races will be the 'survival of the fittest'?"[16] John Fiske, with more truth than he was aware of, gravely pronounced "the revolution in theory concerning the Aryans" to be as "remarkable as the revolution in chemical theory which some years ago introduced the New Chemistry."[17]

There were other nationalist offshoots of the new racialism. Patriotic publicists among Latins and Slavs resented the alleged superiority of Teutons and Anglo-Saxons, and either put in counterclaims for "Mediterranean" and "Alpine" races,[18] or magnified the Aryan element in their respective nations and urged its strengthening. In any case they could all pride themselves and their nations

[16] Josiah Strong, *Our Country, its Possible Future and its Present Crisis*, 2nd ed. (New York, 1891), 175.
[17] *The Discovery of America* (Boston, 1892), I, vii.
[18] The Italian anthropologist Giuseppe Sergi published a sympathetic account of the "Mediterranean" race in 1885.

on belonging to the "white" race, which was patently superior to the blacks of Africa, the yellows of Asia, the browns of Malaysia and Oceania, and duty-bound therefore to conquer and rule these inferior breeds in the interest of "the higher civilization." Racialism was a kind of vitamin in the national imperialism of the age.

It also, within Europe, gave new vigor and direction to anti-Jewish sentiment. Dislike of Jews was, of course, nothing new, and in some respects was understandable. They were everywhere a minority who, even after their "emancipation," preserved a good deal of clannishness and a good many traditions and customs different from the majority's. Christians disliked their religious recalcitrance; farmers, their urban-mindedness; Conservatives, their flocking with Liberals or Marxians. But all this dislike was more or less latent until the widespread Conservative and intensely nationalist reaction of the early '80's and the rise of racialism. Then it was crystallized and rationalized as "anti-Semitism." The Jews, it was averred, because ancient ones had spoken a Semitic language, must all belong to a Semitic race which couldn't help but transmit physical and mental traits different from the Aryan and irreconcilable with it. Hence there was no hope of changing Jewish habits and every reason for safeguarding Aryan nations against the degrading influence of Semitic minorities. As Adolf Stöcker said, "The Jews are a nation within the nation, a state within the state, a race in the midst of another race. All other immigrants are finally assimilated in the nation where they live, but not the Jews. Their unbroken Semitism and their rigid ritual system and enmity to Christianity stand in direct contrast to the Germanic spirit."[19]

Occasionally an anti-Semite, like the crotchety German biblical scholar Paul de Lagarde, made light of the racial argument and appealed to nationalistic exclusiveness and intolerance. Lagarde maintained that "Germany must be full of German men and German ways, as full of itself as an egg; then it will have no room for Palestine."[20] He would absorb Protestants and Catholics into a "national German Christianity," and Jews who resisted absorption

19 Dietrich von Oertzen, op. cit., p. 151.
20 Anna de Lagarde, Paul de Lagarde (Göttingen, 1894), p. 140. See also Lagarde's Deutsche Schriften, 4th ed. (Göttingen, 1903), and Juden und Indogermanen (1887).

he would expel altogether from the country. If they were suffered to remain, their "internationalism" and their "control of money and the press" would spell disaster for Germany.

Of all Jew-baiters of the era, the Frenchman Édouard Drumont was the most inveterate and vituperative. Beginning with his two-volume *La France juive* (1886) and continuing through a long series of similar books[21] and in the columns of the newspaper, *La Libre Parole,* which he founded in 1892, Drumont's constant cry was against the "Semites" and their mental and physical traits—he even charged them with emitting a peculiar and most objectionable "odor." According to him, they caused all the ills which afflicted contemporary France. Though a minority, their shrewdness and trickery and pushing qualities enabled them to get a strangle hold on the wealth, the press, and the government of France and thus to dominate the nation. Their greed and dishonesty were responsible for the impoverishment of peasants and workingmen; and their hatred of Christianity, for anti-clerical and irreligious legislation. Their cowardice made the Third Republic cowardly, and their internationalism and devotion to their kinsmen in Germany led them to honeycomb the French army with treason and unfit it for the task of recovering Alsace-Lorraine. The immediate remedy was forceful expulsion of Jews from France. Ultimately the European states might together deal the Jews "a big and simultaneous blow."[22]

However preposterous in themselves were such rantings as Drumont's, especially when directed at the whole Jewish population, they were accepted, in a time of intensifying nationalism and of much theorizing about race, as substantially true, not only by unbalanced agitators but by a surprising number of pseudo-intellectuals and by sizable groups among the masses. Stöcker, with the aid of Adolf Wagner, organized an expressly anti-Semitic party in Germany in 1887: it polled 47,500 votes in 1890, and 285,000 in 1898. In Austria the Nationalist party which Schönerer gathered

21 *La France juive devant l'opinion* (1886); *La Fin d'un monde, étude psychologique et sociale* (1888); *La dernière bataille* (1890); *Le Testament d'un Anti-Semite* (1891); *De l'or, de la boue, du sang* (1896); *Les Juifs contre la France, une Nouvelle Pologne* (1899); *Les Juifs et l'affaire Dreyfus* (1899).
22 *La France juive,* I, 184.

about him in the '80's was anti-Semitic, and in the '90's the Christian Socialist party under Karl Lueger's leadership became so.[23]

In France two events in the early '90's served to revive and extend the motley Nationalist coalition which had waxed and waned with the personal fortunes of General Boulanger and to give it a definitely anti-Semitic complexion. One was the exposure of large-scale bribery of Republican ministers and members of parliament (chiefly to cover up shady transactions of the Panama Canal Company) by unscrupulous Jews—the banker Baron Jacques de Reinach and the blackmailer Cornelius Herz. The other was the conviction by court-martial of a Jewish army officer, Captain Alfred Dreyfus, on a charge of selling military secrets to Germany and Italy. Here, apparently, was double substantiation of Drumont's allegations. All sorts of disaffected Frenchmen joined in the hue and cry: nationalists of the Radical stamp of Déroulède or of the traditionalist bent of Barrès; Royalists; Bonapartists; ultra-patriotic army officers, clergymen, and laymen; a not inconsiderable element among shopkeepers and workingmen. For several years anti-Semitism was the spearhead of a popular movement seriously threatening the replacement of the Third French Republic by some form of nationalist dictatorship.

Of the financial scandals associated with Reinach and Herz, no exculpation was possible. But they were pushed into the background by accumulating (and eventually substantiated) doubts about the guilt of Dreyfus and the integrity of the evidence on which he had been convicted. In 1898 the novelist Zola publicly accused anti-Semitic army officers of having forged the evidence and the anti-Semitic press of having prompted and exploited the injustice for political purposes; and the next year the "anti-Dreyfusards" found themselves confronted with an equally determined and numerically superior bloc of "Dreyfusard" Republicans and Socialists, which at once began the rehabilitation of the Jewish captain.

In general the anti-Semitic agitation of the '80's and '90's, though noisy, proved politically ineffectual. While widely fostering popular prejudice and social discrimination against Jews, it led to no legal restrictions upon them in France, Germany, Austria-Hungary,

23 Lueger repudiated "racial" anti-Semitism.

where in western and central Europe. Only in eastern Europe, specifically in Russia and Rumania, did it produce discriminatory legislation. In Rumania, where peasant antipathy to Jewish traders and moneylenders was deep-seated, and where national sentiment had recently been outraged by the provision in the Treaty of Berlin (1878) requiring the country, as a condition of its independence, to accord "equal rights" to Jews, the government practically nullified this treaty obligation and permitted only a very few of the quarter million Jewish residents to vote or hold office. In Russia the Tsar Alexander III, responding to earnest pleas of Slavophiles, to counsels of his chief advisers in church and state, and to public clamor, issued a series of ukases against Jews. In 1882 he forbade them to acquire landed property. Then, to keep them out of the learned professions, he restricted their admission to universities and secondary schools, at first fixing a "quota" of ten per cent, and later reducing it to three per cent. In 1890 he obliged those who resided in the interior of Russia to move to the western provinces—the so-called Jewish Pale—where they were forbidden to own or lease land and were subjected to close police surveillance. What was still worse, many government officials, taking their cue from the attitude of the Tsar, gave free rein to anti-Semitic incitements to mob violence and tolerated if they did not direct anti-Jewish pogroms, attended by plundering and burning and in some instances by massacre. From pogroms as well as from repressive legislation Russian and Polish Jews suffered grievously; and despite efforts of the Tsar's government to make them stay, some 300,000 left the Empire in the single year 1891. It was the start of the high tide of Jewish migration to the United States.

One should not overlook what was perhaps the most fateful of all the consequences of the era's anti-Semitism—the consequence for the Jews themselves. Suffering from imputations against their "racial" character, they became acutely race conscious and in a sense exemplars of racialism; at least they tended to sink religious and cultural differences in an assumed ethnic unity. Suffering, too, from nationalist taunts that they were "aliens" and could not be good citizens of countries where they lived, they tended, in defense or as compensation, to develop a Jewish nationalism. In 1896 an Hungarian Jew, Theodore Herzl, came forward with principles and a program for just such nationalism: Zionism, he called it. The Jews, he asserted, were really, after all, a distinctive nationality, with a language, a culture, and historical traditions peculiar to themselves, and as such they were entitled to an independent national state of their own, preferably in Palestine. The next year the first general congress of Zionists was held at Basel, and soon the movement enlisted an enthusiastic following among Jews in many lands. Zionism was a result of anti-Semitism. In turn it aggravated anti-Semitism and that totalitarian nationalism of which racialism was a conspicuous mark.

IV. THE NATIONALIZING OF MINORITIES

Jews were but one of many European minorities to experience in the generation after 1871 the tightening strictures of an exclusive and intolerant nationalism, and indeed they experienced them less universally and gallingly than did others. For while anti-Jewish agitation was practically nonexistent in Great Britain, the Low Countries, Scandinavia, Iberia, and Italy, and productive of no legal disabilities elsewhere in western or central Europe, nationalistic agitation against other minorities was rife all over Europe and legislatively fruitful in most countries.

These minorities, in some instances, were religious and Christian. Especially were Catholics accused of being a state within the state and qualifying their loyalty to the nation by undue deference to a foreign potentate; and wherever they were a feared or despised minority, as in the German and Russian Empires, they were visited with a Kulturkampf or outright repression. Moreover, the anti-clerical campaigns and enactments in traditionally Catholic countries, such as Italy and France, had nationalist as well as other motivation. And the vigorous profession of Catholicism by the Irish and Polish peoples evidenced to the nationalistic non-Catholic majority in Great Britain, no less than in Germany and Russia, that those peoples were inferior and must be held in tutelage.

Marxian socialism aroused the special ire of patriots, not only property-owning ones, but all those who saw in its internationalism and in its arraying of class against class a menace to national

THE NATIONALITIES OF EAST-CENTRAL EUROPE

KEY

- Scandinavians
- Germans
- Poles
- Letts and Lithuanians
- Great Russians
- White Russians
- Little Russians
- Czechs
- Slovaks
- Magyars
- Rumanians
- Italians
- Slovenes and Croats
- Serbs
- Bulgarians
- Turks
- Greeks

Scale of Miles
0   100   200

solidarity and a serious obstacle to the attainment of national ends. In Germany a drastic law against Socialist propaganda was spread upon the statute books in 1878, and there and elsewhere the civil administration and the police were ever on the alert to keep the Socialist minority in check.

Yet neither religious nor Marxian groups—not even professional pacifists—fell foul of intensifying nationalism so universally and so continuously as did ethnic minorities. Pacifists were scattered individuals, too few to be feared; they were usually credited with good intentions, and for their lack of realism they were pitied more than blamed. In most countries, too, anti-Catholic movements lost driving force with the decline of the sectarian Liberalism which had promoted them and with the consequent reaction in the '80's toward conservatism; and with the retirement of Bismarck in 1890 even the German anti-Socialist legislation was allowed to lapse. Not so, however, the efforts to mold subject nationalities to the image and likeness of dominant ones. These efforts, begun somewhat unwittingly by Liberals, were continued with conscious purpose by Conservatives; and in general they commanded wide popular support.

The period, it must be borne in mind, was one of transition and novel adjustment for the European state system in respect of nationalism. To the "national" states already existing in western Europe, there had just been a forceful addition of similar states in the central and southeastern portions of the Continent—Italy, Germany, Hungary, Rumania, Serbia, Bulgaria—which was an obvious sign, at least to Liberals, that real progress was being made toward the complete reshaping of Europe's political geography along frontiers of language and nationality. Nevertheless, none of the so-called national states was strictly national; that is, none embraced, or was confined to, a single nationality. Many German-speaking people were still outside the German Empire, and within it were Poles, Danes, and French-speaking Lorrainers. Italy lacked important "irredentas," and so too did every one of the Balkan states. Hungary included Magyars, but a larger total of non-Magyars. Belgium was bilingual, and Switzerland trilingual. Spain comprised Catalans and Basques as well as Castilians, and France, a variety of "submerged" and "forgotten" peoples; while England was part of the "United Kingdom of Great Britain and Ireland."

Moreover, while the principle of nationality was newly vital and effectual in Europe, it was conditioned almost everywhere by surviving habits and attitudes of the earlier age of dynastic empires; and in eastern and east-central Europe still flourished the extensive polyglot domains of Tsar, Sultan, and Hapsburg Emperor. The first of these approximated to a "national state" in that the majority of its total population was compactly Great Russian, but in the second the dominant Turks were a minority, and in the third, though Austrian and Sudeten Germans tried to maintain a traditional dominance, there was nationalist chaos.

This halting between a partially and an entirely nationalized Europe occurred just when "the state" was being lavishly exalted and its functions vastly expanded. It occurred likewise just when doctrines and examples of forcefulness, racialism, and colonial imperialism were convincing "successful" and dominant nationalities that they were "superior" and in duty bound to curb any agitation of "inferior" peoples for separate statehood and to keep these under the higher civilizing influence of the existing "national state." In other words, *raison d'état* compromised the working out of the principle of nationality; "national self-determination" gave way to a "determination by superior races"; and nationalism became imperialistic not only overseas but within Europe.

Though of varying intensity in different countries, the phenomenon was ubiquitous. In Scandinavia the Swedish regime merely declined to make any concessions to Norwegian separatism. In Spain, under the restored monarchy, both Conservative and Liberal statesmen combated autonomous movements of Catalans and Basques. The Third French Republic was adamant against any revival of "regionalism" or the public use of any "patois." The half of Belgium's population which spoke French strove to "gallicize" the half that spoke Flemish. In the Balkans, in a manner *sui generis*, bands of Bulgarian, Greek, and Serbian nationalists, frequently with the connivance of their respective governments, perpetrated rapine and murder upon Macedonian peasants who happened to espouse the wrong nationalist cause.

Englishmen who profusely sympathized with "oppressed" peoples on the Continent and warmly upheld their right of national self-determination could perceive slight justification for the exercise of any such right in Ireland. The Irish were an inferior "Celtic" race,[24] Catholic, volatile, improvident, quarrelsome, whose violent outbreaks, as in the Fenian outrages of the late '60's and the Phoenix Park murders of the early '80's, had to be repressed with a strong arm. They were obviously unfit to govern themselves, and what a blow it would be to the British Empire—and the future of civilization—if some foreign power should intervene in Ireland and establish there a naval and military base! Besides, Ireland had in Ulster a decent and "progressive" Protestant minority which was faithful to Britain and the empire and which must not be "betrayed" into the hands of a superstitious, backward, and disloyal peasant people. If England showed the Irish that she "meant business," they would come to respect her and, like the Scotch and Welsh, prefer the material advantages she could give them to the siren songs of nationalist agitators.

Gladstone, it is true, threw some agrarian and ecclesiastical sops to the Irish, but he repeatedly resorted to "coercion," and any idea of granting them even a modicum of "home rule" he flatly rejected until 1886, when, by a strange balancing of political forces in the British parliament, he found himself dependent on Parnell's Irish Nationalists. His conversion was unavailing, however. A large fraction of his own party, including such Radicals as John Bright and Joseph Chamberlain, deserted him and with the Conservatives and Imperialists threw out his Home Rule Bill. He tried again in 1893, and again failed. In turn, the Conservatives and Liberal Unionists threw sops to the Irish—some bigger sops, in the form of Land Purchase Acts and a Local Government Act, than the Grand Old Man of Liberalism had thrown—but, backed by unmistakable majority sentiment throughout Great Britain, they would not truckle to "Irish nationalism."

In the very same year in which Britain denied "home rule" to

24 Later, H. G. Wells was sure that a "hairy folk," a "short dark Iberian race," "pre-Celtic," "pre-Aryan," and "pre-Nordic" survived in Ireland and accounted in large part for its "backwardness" and "primitivism." *Outline of History*, new ed., 2 vols. in 1 (New York, 1927), pp. 266, 281, 1015.

the Irish (1886), German Conservatives and National Liberals put through the Prussian parliament a resolution calling upon the government to speed up the "Germanization" of the three million Poles in Posen and West Prussia (the later "Corridor"). In reply, Bismarck set forth a dual policy: Poles serving in the army or civil service "would be given an opportunity to avail themselves of the advantages of German civilization by being posted in German provinces far from their own homes"; and Polish land would be bought up and distributed among German farmers pledged "to remain German and, above all, to marry German wives." The parliament immediately appropriated a hundred million marks for land purchase, and the next year the government forbade further teaching of the Polish language in any part of Prussia. The retirement of Bismarck in 1890 halted anti-Polish legislation, though only temporarily. Agitation in behalf of it was soon stimulated and magnified by the efforts of three fiery German nationalists —Hansemann, Kennemann, and Tiedemann—and the "Society of the Eastern Marches" (or "HKT Society") which they founded in 1894. Bismarck's anti-Polish measures proved but a foretaste of those sponsored and applied by Bülow after 1900.

"Germanization" was also directed, in the '80's, against Danes in Schleswig and against French influence in Alsace-Lorraine. The latter provinces remained under practically military rule, and the conciliatory efforts of the German governor from 1879 to 1885, Field Marshal von Manteuffel, were exceptional. Under his successor, Prince Hohenlohe (later chancellor of the empire), French was finally and completely banished from the schools and all "autonomist" protests were silenced.

"Russification" was a kindred process. Its goal, as formulated and popularized by Slavophiles like Katkov and Aksakov, and actually pursued by ministers such as Dmitri Tolstoy, Plehve, and Pobêdonostsev, was "one law (the Russian Tsar's), one language (the Great Russian), and one religion (the Russian Orthodox)." It began, in an important way, as an aftermath of the crushing of the Polish insurrection of 1863, and reached an advanced stage under Alexander III in the '80's. Every semblance of an autonomous Poland was obliterated; and in what had once been their country Poles were excluded from public office, obliged to use Russian in schools and law courts, and forbidden to sell land to anyone except a Russian. In White Russia and Lithuania, the population, chiefly Catholic, was coerced into employing the services of the Orthodox Church to legitimize marriages and children. In the Ukraine, the Little Russian language was treated as a "dialect" and prohibited in printing, reciting, or singing. In the Baltic provinces, Russian was prescribed as the official tongue; the consent of Orthodox authorities was required for the construction of any Protestant church building; local law courts were suppressed; and German place names were changed to Russian. The harsh anti-Jewish ukases of the time were part of the same "Russification"; so, too, was the persecution of numerous sects of Dissenters from the Russian Orthodox Church; and so also were milder measures taken against Georgians, Armenians, and still other dissident peoples within the Russian Empire. Even the Finns, whose separate state and liberal constitution had long been solemnly guaranteed and usually respected by Russian Tsars, were not proof against the new Russification. A manifesto of 1890 incorporated their postal system with the Russian, and in 1899 the Tsar Nicholas II virtually annulled the Finnish constitution and made the Grand-Duchy a Russian satrapy.

In the Austrian half of the Hapsburg Empire, German Nationalists, abetted curiously enough by centralizing Liberals and by Jews (who felt more at ease with urban Germans than with rural Slavs), championed the maintenance of traditional German hegemony and the repression of subject nationalities. But both Christian Socialists and Marxian Social Democrats were critical of repressive policies, and the subject peoples were too numerous and well-organized to admit of the adoption or execution of such policies. In the trying circumstances, the imperial government at Vienna steered a middle course throughout the '80's and '90's between the Scylla of "home rule" for the various peoples and the Charybdis of "Germanization." The lodestar of the course was not the newer nationalism but the much older imperialism, and its attendant lights were the Emperor, the Church, the army, the still cosmopolitan bureaucracy and nobility—and the Austrian Poles.

For these last, by a stroke of irony, were very grateful to Vienna for the free hand given them to "Polonize" the Ruthenians (Ukrainians) in Galicia.

On the other side, the Hungarian half of the Hapsburg Empire, while almost as heterogeneous as the Austrian, was subjected by its historically ruling element to a drastic "Magyarization." This outcome had appeared unlikely for a brief time just after the settlement of 1867 between Hungary and Austria. In a moment of magnanimity in 1868, Deák and Baron Eötvös conceded "home rule" to Croatia, and put through parliament a "Nationality Act" guaranteeing to every ethnic group its own language, schools, ecclesiastical institutions, and "equal membership in the Hungarian nation." But Eötvös's death in 1871 and Deák's in 1876 brought to power a new generation of Magyar nationalists who forgot all about "equal rights" and devoted themselves to "assimilating" the other peoples to a Magyarized (and therefore presumably Greater) Hungary. Under the leadership of three or four noble families,[25] and with the backing of high finance, the Hungarian Jewry, and a vociferously demagogic press, they dominated the unreformed Hungarian parliament and monopolized the kingdom's administration and judiciary. Through these agencies they nullified the Nationality Act and steadily extended the compulsory use of the Magyar language to elementary schools (1879), secondary schools (1883), and kindergartens (1891), and to all public services. They likewise abridged the autonomy previously accorded to Croatia and imposed upon its unhappy population for twenty years after 1883 the despotic governorship of Count Khuen Hedervary with his ill-famed policy of "horsewhip and oats." Throughout the Hungarian state—among Serbs, Slovaks, Germans, and Rumanians—"Magyar cultural associations" were fostered, village and family names were Magyarized, and judicial persecution was visited upon opponents and critics of the process.

v. the "pan" movements

Among offspring of the romantic indiscretions of philology and anthropology when the nineteenth century was young, were certain

25 The Tiszas, Andrássys, Apponyis, and Károlyis.

"pan" movements which "realistic" nationalists of the century's closing decades adopted and fostered. The most notable, perhaps, was Pan-Slavism. Its first apostles had been scholars and poets, chiefly in the Hapsburg Empire,[26] who regarded the different Slavic tongues as dialects of one common language and the different Slavic peoples as tribes of a single nation, and who sang in verse or lyrical prose the past glories of Slavdom and its abiding mission. One of the foremost, the Slovak poet and Lutheran clergyman, Ján Kollár, in a series of passionate sonnets, *Daughter of Slava,* had apostrophized the colossal statue he would make of the various branches of Slavs—from Russia the head, from Poland the breast, from Bohemia the arms, from Serbia the legs—and before which he would have all Europe kneel down. For, whereas the Germanic and Latin peoples were declining and their day in world history was waning or gone, the Slavs in their uncorrupted innocence were the coming heroes of history, provided only that they felt and acted upon their essential unity.

They didn't so act. Instead, each of the Slavic peoples proceeded forthwith to develop its own particularistic nationalism, so that by the time the first Pan-Slavic Congress met at Prague in 1848 the expressed aim of the movement was not unity but mutual assistance, and by the time the second Congress assembled at Moscow in 1867 this "mutual assistance" was being exploited by Russian nationalists for imperialistic purposes. The Russian historian, Michael Pogodin; the Russian army officer, General Rostislav Fadeyev; the Russian scientist, Nicholas Danilevski: these were now the mentors of Pan-Slavism, and they infused it with racialism and the dogma of Russia's special "mission."[27] Inside Russia they joined with the mystical Slavophiles to promote the Russification of Poles, Ukrainians, and other subject nationalities, Slavic as well as non-Slavic, while outside they invoked the blood brotherhood of Russians with

26 Such as the Czechs Josef Dobrovský, Josef Jungmann, Karel Havlíček, and František Palacký, the Slovak Josef Šafařik, the Slovene František Prešeren, the Croatian Ljudevit Gaj. See F. B. Artz, *Reaction and Revolution, 1814-1832* (New York, 1934), pp. 241-5.

27 This Russian Pan-Slavism received classic formulation in Pogodin's *Historico-Critical Essays* [*Istoriko-Kriticheskie Otrivki*], 2 vols. (Moscow, 1846-1867); in Fadeyev's *Opinion on the Eastern Question* (1869), Eng. trans. by T. Mitchell, 2nd ed. (London, 1876); and in Danilevski's *Russland und Europa* (1871), Germ. trans. by K. Nötzel (Stuttgart, 1920).

Bulgarians and Serbs, or with Czechs and Croatians, as justification for Russian belligerence against the Ottoman Empire or for Russian machinations against the Hapsburg Empire. Although the Tsar's government was inclined to frown on Pan-Slavism as an incitement to revolutionary disturbance and a handicap to international *Realpolitik*, it was not above utilizing it whenever the opportunity seemed favorable; and it was the Pan-Slavist Russian ambassador at Constantinople, Count Ignatiev, who engineered the Russo-Turkish War of 1877-78 and the construction of what he hoped would be a Bulgarian state dependent upon the Russian Empire.

Polish nationalists, for good and sufficient reasons, did not take to Russian Pan-Slavism. On the contrary, many followed Roman Dmowski in cherishing a Pan-Polish ideal and claiming for the future resurrected Poland, with utter disregard of ethnographic factors and national sentiments, the imperial Poland of the historic Jagiello dynasty—a vast territory stretching from the Baltic to the Black Sea and including Lithuania, White Russia, and all of the Ukraine. Moreover, both Serb and Croatian nationalists were so antagonized by the favoritism the Tsar showed Bulgaria in 1878 that they long remained critical of Russian Pan-Slavism and devoted themselves to projecting some form of Pan-Yugoslavism. Even the Bulgarians ungratefully displayed less zeal for Pan-Slavism than for Bulgarian nationalism. Only the younger generation of Czech nationalists—Masaryk, Beneš, etc.—were warmly sympathetic with Russian dominance of Pan-Slavism, and only because they perceived in it the most hopeful agency for disintegrating the Hapsburg Empire and enabling them to establish an independent—and possibly imperial—Bohemia. They staged an impressive Pan-Slavic demonstration at Prague in 1898, the centenary of Palacký's birth and the fiftieth anniversary of the first Pan-Slavic Congress.

Yet, despite internal dissensions and radical differences of opinion about its political objectives, Pan-Slavism of the 1890's, in a cultural and sentimental way, was a widespread and fairly popular movement, begetting unions of Slavic journalists, congresses of Slavic students, federations of Slavic athletic clubs (sokols). Furthermore, non-Slavs were now acutely aware of it and of its being backed and fronted by Imperial Russia; and on neighboring Germans, Magyars, and Turks it had the effect of a first-class bogey: they exaggerated its coherence and strength and readily supported counter-offensives, such as Pan-Germanism, Magyarization, or eventually a terribly entitled "Turkification."

A fine rejoinder to Pan-Slavism should have been "Pan-Teutonism," uniting all peoples with Teutonic languages (and presumably of Teutonic race)—Germans, Englishmen, Americans, Netherlanders, Scandinavians. It was actually bruited now and then by individual scholars and publicists, and such expansive statesmen as Cecil Rhodes, Joseph Chamberlain, and Theodore Roosevelt occasionally talked, as did certain German pundits, about blood being thicker than water and Teutons having a common (and of course superior) "mission." Rhodes was, indeed, so faithful a Pan-Teutonist that the scholarships he munificently endowed at Oxford were to be open alike to Germans, Americans, and British Colonials. Yet "Pan-Teutonism" never really grew up. It was smothered in its youth by the lusty nationalism of the several Teutonic great powers, and its assets were divided, somewhat unevenly, between Pan-Germanism and Pan-Anglo-Saxonism.

Pan-Germanism was to Pan-Teutonism what *Klein Deutsch* had once been to *Gross Deutsch*—something less extensive but something more practical and compact. It simply ruled out Britain, Scandinavia, and the United States and concentrated on the unity and high mission—linguistic, cultural, racial, and (it was hoped) political—of *German*-speaking people, whether they lived in Germany or Austria-Hungary, Switzerland or the Baltic regions, or overseas. To be sure, Netherlandish being but a German "dialect," Pan-Germanism might properly encompass Holland and most of Belgium. The movement, a very real one, centered in the Pan-German League[28] which Carl Peters founded in 1890 "for the promotion of overseas German national interests" and which was reorganized in 1891 with these broadened objects: "to arouse patriotic self-consciousness at home and to oppose vigorously any devel-

---

28 The original name was "Allgemeiner deutscher Verband." The more popular "Alldeutscher Verband" was officially adopted in 1894.

opment of the German people along unpatriotic lines; to support and aid German endeavors in all lands where members of the German people must struggle to retain their individuality, and the union of all Germans on the earth for the furthering of these aims; to promote an energetic German policy of might in Europe and oversea; above all, to carry forward the German colonial movement to tangible results." From 1894, when Hasse assumed its presidency, the League throve. By 1900 it had 173 branches in Germany and 28 outside, some hundred salaried agents, a dozen spokesmen in the Reichstag, and a total membership, active and associate, of close to 100,000. It held congresses and demonstrations, published a journal and much other propagandist literature, and co-operated closely with a large number of more specialized nationalist organizations: a "General German School Association" (to maintain German schools in foreign countries); a "General German Language Association" (to purify the language of foreign words and phrases); Navy League; etc.

Pan-Germanism, like Pan-Slavism, was taken more seriously abroad than at home. The German government and the bulk of the German press usually belittled it and frequently chided its spokesmen and agents, although on occasion the government was glad to utilize whatever popular favor its clamors elicited for colonial measures and army and navy bills. Probably, too, the Pan-German League and its allies implanted the seed of intensive imperialistic "Germanism" more deeply and widely than was imagined at the time by German critics. There can be no doubt, however, that the agitation complicated German foreign relations after 1890 and aroused increasing resentment abroad.

Pan-Anglo-Saxonism was less definite and much less effectual. Except for a brief spell of mutual admiration between the United States and Great Britain at the end of the '90's, when the story spread that their fleets had squared off for possible joint action against Germany's in Manila Bay, the movement, if there was one at all, was confined to a few intellectuals and a slightly larger number of social snobs. Anglo-Saxonism was too intimate a part of English nationalism to be shared, and America had too many non-Anglo-Saxons.

A "Pan-Latinism" had been cultivated by Napoleon III, but at best it had been a tender plant, and after the French *débâcle* at Sedan and Italy's seizure of Rome in 1870 it shriveled and died. French nationalists could only denounce the ingratitude of Latin sisters—Italy, Rumania, and Spain—who one by one gravitated toward Teutonic Germany, and seek comfort for France in the arms of Slavic Russia. Pan-Slavism might be a bugbear to everybody else, but by Rambaud and Leroy-Beaulieu, Déroulède and Hanotaux, it was hymned as a fit companion goddess to pure Gallic Latinity.

"Pan" was easily fastened to a bewildering variety of real or imaginary movements of the period. The effort of the United States to draw Latin American countries closer to it commercially and politically, was dubbed Pan-Americanism. A few philological scholars, finding some affinities among the Finnish, Magyar, and Turkish languages, manufactured a corresponding Pan-Turanian-ism. And a generation that got into the habit of being alarmed—without too serious consequences—felt thrills of alarm when they were told in the late '90's that Pan-Islam threatened Europe and that Pan-Mongolians (the "yellow race") were about to threaten it.

Yet however unreal and insignificant most of these pan-movements were, they indicated a startling new trend in popular thinking. At least in the case of Pan-Germanism and Pan-Slavism, the coupling of nationalism with linguistics and race on a large scale helped immeasurably to render nationalism imperialistic and to feed the forceful ambitiousness of great powers.

VI. AGITATION AMONG SUBMERGED NATIONALITIES

"In regions where half-animal men are living, let us establish schools, let us construct a railway, and tolerate a printing-press. Twenty years later national feeling will be born. After two generations it will explode if you try to suppress it. In this manner the national question is born out of the very nature of civilization."[29]

When the sympathetic Laveleye made this analysis and prediction, nationalist agitation had been going on in Europe for well-

29 Émile de Laveleye, cited by Oscar Jászi, *The Dissolution of the Habsburg Empire* (Chicago, 1929), p. 251.

nigh a century, not only among major peoples (French, British, German, Italian, Russian), for whom it served to create or consolidate first-class "national states," but also among lesser peoples who still remained in political and social subjection to others, and who, being preponderantly agricultural and hence "backward," were apt to be described by a progressive Liberal sociologist as "half-animal men." Since at least the 1820's and 1830's there had been hardly one of these latter peoples anywhere in Europe that had not had in its midst a galaxy of romantic intellectuals, resurrecting its folk speech, folk ballads, folk customs and costumes, celebrating in epic verse or ponderous tome its more or less mythical past, and founding little societies and schools, theaters and publishing houses, to spread its cult among the "masses." Railway construction (and wood-pulp paper) merely expedited the popular propaganda already under way.

Nationalist agitation among "subject" or "submerged" peoples had almost invariably been directed, in first instance, toward cultural, rather than political, ends; and unless and until it turned to politics, disturbing public "order" and evoking legislative action in an existent state, little or no attention was paid to it by Europe at large. Among Bulgarians, for example, nationalist agitation had been rife for some time before 1870, but few persons in western Europe knew anything about it—or who the Bulgarians were—until the heralded disorders and massacres of 1875 and the resulting Russo-Turkish War. Likewise, Europe enriched its previous scanty knowledge of Catalans and Basques and their autonomist demands during the Spanish commotions of the early '70's.

The haziest notions endured still longer about a people variously referred to as Little Russian or Ukrainian or Ruthenian. In the middle '80's one learned from the public press that the Tsar was "Russifying" the Ukraine; and later, in 1908, one was startled to read of the assassination of the Polish governor of Galicia, Count Potocki, by a "Ruthenian" student. One recognized that nationalism was at work among "Ukrainians" and "Ruthenians," though one was not sure yet whether they were a single people, or two— or maybe three.

In fact, developing nationalist activity thrust quite a variety of

hitherto neglected peoples into the European limelight during the
three decades after 1871. Russifying decrees of the Tsar's government publicized (and accentuated) the nationalism of Lithuanians
and Finns, and more vaguely that of other Baltic peoples as well
as of Little Russians and White Russians. Within the Grand Duchy
of Finland, political pressure of the Finnish-speaking peasants
induced the Swedish-speaking governmental class to concede statu-
tory equality of Finnish with Swedish in the law courts (1883),
in the administration (1886), and in the university (1894). In Norway, also, a particularistic nationalism came to the fore with the
increasing influence of the peasantry on the local parliament. For
the Norwegian peasants, resentful of Swedish "aristocracy," backed
those politicians who were most insistent on Norway's "rights"
under the political Union with Sweden, just as they backed patriotic professors who were trying to break cultural ties with Denmark
by substituting, as the country's literary language, an artificial
synthesis of indigenous rural dialects (the *landsmaal*) for the
Danish speech of the cities (the *riksmaal*). The Norwegian parliament recognized the "equality" of *landsmaal* with *riksmaal* in
1885, and successively admitted the former to teacher-training institutions (1890), elementary schools (1892), secondary schools (1896),
and university (1899). By this time a loudly vocal element of
Norwegian nationalists was punctuating denunciation of the Swedish Union with demands on Denmark for the "return" of the Faroe
Islands, Iceland, and Greenland, and even with protests against
Britain's retention of the Hebrides and Orkneys.

A Provençal nationalism of a purely literary and cultural sort
had been inaugurated by Frédéric Mistral and six fellow poets
with their founding of the Félibrige Society back in 1854. In 1876,
the society, now much enlarged, elaborated its organization and
propaganda for a "Provençal revival" throughout the French
regions of Provence, Languedoc, and Aquitaine and the Spanish
province of Catalonia. Then in 1892 a group of its members, headed
by Frédéric Amouretti and Charles Maurras, formally put forth
a demand for Provençal autonomy within a federalized France,
with which demand immediately concurred representatives of other
recently born "regionalisms"—Breton, Corsican, and Basque. The

persons involved were not numerous and their prime loyalty was unquestionably to France, but inasmuch as they were mainly Royalist in politics and Catholic in religion, they were denounced by centralizing and anti-clerical Republicans as an insidious element of "reaction."

In Belgium Flemish nationalism passed in the '70's from intellectuals to the compact masses of the northern and western districts; and, entering politics in the '80's, it helped to discomfit the Liberals, whose chief strength was among the French-speaking Walloons, and to put the Catholic party in power. In 1889 an act of parliament prescribed the use of Flemish in legal cases involving a defendant of that nationality; and another act, in 1898, made Flemish, equally with French, an official language of Belgium. Beginning in 1887 there were monster Flemish demonstrations every July 11, the anniversary of French defeat, in the medieval "Battle of the Golden Spurs"; and in 1895 the writer August Vermeylen, a disciple of Hegel and Max Stirner, initiated a left-wing "Activist" movement by his attack on "Belgian tyranny." "All young and fighting forces," he wrote, "wrench themselves free from oppression, disregard law in so far as possible, and turn their backs on parliaments and democracies."[30] Two years later a Flemish teacher at Ypres, in collaboration with a group of Dutch intellectuals, founded a Pan-Netherlandish League[31] to emphasize and safeguard "the essential oneness of Netherlandish language and race" in Flanders, the Dutch Netherlands, French Artois, and South Africa.

One striking feature of the period's nationalist agitation, obviously, was that it affected and widely publicized a number of European peoples that had not previously been supposed to have national self-consciousness or political aspirations. Another of its features, even more startling, was its quickened *tempo* and fiercer manifestation among subject peoples already generally known to be nationalist (at least culturally)—Poles, Czechs, Irish, etc. Nationalism of these peoples was magnified by their desire to emulate

[30] *Kritiek der vlaamsche Beweging,* 2nd ed. (Bussum, 1905), p. 48. Vermeylen later disclaimed these doctrines. See the preface to this second edition.
[31] This "Algemeen Nederlandsch Verbond" enrolled, among others, the distinguished Dutch historian, J. P. Blok, and the Transvaal President, "Oom" Paul Kruger.

the recent successes of Germans, Italians, Magyars, and Balkan peoples, and then quickly aggravated and embittered by their being treated as inferiors and made the object of Germanization, Russification, or other repressive measures. Besides, they could now utilize the new popular journalism and in most countries the new democratic franchise (and constitutional guarantees of freedom of press, speech, and association) to give their grievances unprecedented airing and to create extraordinary difficulties for their "oppressors." From the '80's it was clear that nationalism among these peoples was not an affair of intellectuals or a class but that it represented a real mass movement.

Irish nationalism entered a new phase at this time. In 1879 the magnetic Charles Stewart Parnell, Anglo-Irish Protestant whose almost fanatical hatred of England he seems to have imbibed from his American mother, was drawing the Catholic Irish electorate into his newly formed "Nationalist Party" and collecting funds for it from Irish settlers and sympathizers in the United States, with the result that four-fifths of all the Irish members of the British parliament soon constituted a solid Nationalist phalanx in support of his demand for a separate Irish parliament. Also in 1879, Michael Davitt, ex-peasant, ex-Fenian, and professional agitator, launched a "Land League," which speedily enlisted the bulk of Irish peasants in the cause of national agrarian reform. Neither Land League nor Nationalist parliamentarians employed conventional methods of the kid-glove kind. While the one incited to acts of physical violence against objectionable landlords or treated their land agents as it treated unobliging Captain Boycott, the other raised fracases at Westminster by heckling speakers, obstructing parliamentary business, and hurling inkstands. Gladstone, having failed to quiet the agitation by the sedative of a Land Act, resorted anew to coercion, putting Ireland under martial law and jailing Parnell, Davitt, and several of their lieutenants. But coercion was a failure, too; it brought so many reprisals that only the stationing of the whole British army in Ireland could have coped with them. Finally, in 1886, Gladstone accepted Parnell's terms and agreed to sponsor Irish "home rule." Sponsor it he actually did that very year, and again in 1893; but both of his bills the British parliament threw out.

In the '90's Irish nationalism was in a transitional stage. The Nationalist Party was weakened by the failure of the home rule bills, and still more by internal dissensions following Parnell's disgrace and death; and the Irish Land Purchase Acts which the Conservatives enacted stole much of the thunder of the Land League. In the same decade, however, developments below the surface were shaping new and more radical ends for Irish nationalism. In 1893 Douglas Hyde inaugurated the "Gaelic League" for the preservation and extension of the native Irish language. In 1894 Sir Horace Plunkett founded the "Agricultural Organization Society" to promote co-operative enterprise and material well-being among the Irish farmers. In 1899, most momentous of all, there returned from the diamond mines in South Africa an obscure young man, Arthur Griffith by name, with an idea that Ireland, like Hungary, should not beg home rule or anything else of a "foreign" parliament, but rely on herself and her own powers of passive resistance to achieve full statehood. It was the conception of Sinn Fein.

Czech nationalism ran a course similar to Irish. Though Bohemia had the form of local self-government in a surviving semi-feudal diet, this body possessed few powers, and it had long been dominated by the province's German minority (the so-called Sudetens), who collaborated most zealously after 1867 with fellow German nationalists in the Reichsrat at Vienna to maintain German ascendancy throughout the Austrian dominions. Opposition of the Czech majority in Bohemia (and Moravia) was intensified thereby; and as a mark of special resentment against the withholding from them of the national autonomy accorded to Hungary, their elected deputies absented themselves from the Reichsrat during the period of centralizing Liberal ministries from 1867 to 1879. With the succession of Count Taaffe's more sympathetic Conservative ministry in the latter year, the Czech deputies took their seats at Vienna. They comprised two nationalist groups: the "Old Czechs," led by Palacký's aging and conciliatory son-in-law, von Rieger; and the "Young Czechs," followers of the more youthful and radical Dr. Karel Kramář. Between them, they obtained some favors. Alongside the German university at Prague was established in 1882 a new Czech university. In 1883 the Czechs were enabled to secure a majority in the Bohemian diet, and in 1886 local officials were obliged to use the Czech as well as the German language in the transaction of business.

Nevertheless, what the Czechs most desired—the restoration of a fully autonomous Bohemia—they were denied. The result was the electoral defeat of the moderate "Old Czechs" and the adoption by the reinforced "Young Czechs" of the disorderly methods of contemporary Irish Nationalists. Indeed, the Austrian Reichsrat fared worse than the British parliament, for Czech obstructionists were ably seconded by deputies of numerous other disgruntled nationalities—Slovenes, Italians, Croats, Ruthenians, Rumanians.[32] The Austrian government retaliated in 1893 by placing Prague under martial law and suspending jury trial and freedom of the press in Czech territories. For two years this forceful repression continued, followed then by an ominous lull in Bohemia and new but unavailing protestations of friendliness at Vienna. Kramář was already advising the Czechs to expect deliverance by Russia, and Professor Masaryk was preaching a still more radical "realist" nationalism which should overspread Slovaks as well as Czechs and build, by war if necessary, a free and united Czechoslovakia.

The subject nationalities of Hungary were less in the limelight during the period, mainly because the Hungarian electoral laws prevented them from using the parliament at Budapest, as the Czechs used the parliament at Vienna, to advertise their grievances and demands. This is not to say, however, that they acquiesced in the Magyarization which was inflicted upon them and which was far more repressive than anything felt by the Czechs. On the contrary the masses of Croatian, Serb, Slovak, and Rumanian peasantry were now more determined than ever to hold to their respective national traditions and "rights" and more ready to accept the leader-

---

[32] In the Reichsrat elected in 1897, for example, were 63 Czechs, 16 Slovenes, 19 Italians, 13 Croatians, 11 Ruthenians, and 6 Rumanians—a total of 128 "dissident nationalists," as over against 126 German Liberals, 89 German Conservatives, 68 Poles, and 14 Social Democrats. The franchise in Austria, it should be recalled, was still not democratic. When it became so, after 1900, it greatly enlarged the dissident representation and thereby rendered parliamentary government practically impossible.

ship of extremists. Incidentally it may be remarked that their intensifying nationalism had a sharp note of anti-Semitism in it, a reaction against the support which Hungarian Jewry gave to Magyarization.

Poles, distributed among three powerful states, were in a peculiarly difficult position. None of them was without the dream of a gloriously resurrected and reunited Polish state, but they differed as to how it might be realized. One group—rapidly diminishing— looked to Russia or Pan-Slavism to perform the miracle; another, to the Germanic Central Powers; while a third, skeptical about the early appearance of any messiah, urged self-reliance, a stimulated solidarity among Russian, Prussian, and Austrian Poles, and a vigorous campaign looking to the defense of common national culture and the securing of provincial autonomy.

From practical necessity, Polish nationalism actually developed along the lines of this last program. In Prussian Posen it concentrated on opposing and countering, alike in parliament and in the countryside, the "Germanizing" efforts and enactments of the time. In "Congress Poland" it reacted bitterly—about all it could do against the severer "Russification." In Austria, the Poles were happier. Here, where the imperial government wanted their help as a counterpoise to the hostility of other minorities, they escaped all cultural repression and virtually dominated the entire province of Galicia. Here, too, Polish nationalists from Posen or Warsaw were free to congregate with those of Cracow or Lemberg, and by speech and press to stimulate ever more militant Polish nationalism across the borders.

Laveleye proved a good prophet with his prediction about the nationalism of submerged peoples, that "after two generations it will explode if you try to suppress it." It did explode just about forty years after the start of Russification, Magyarization, Germanization, and other large-scale attempts at repression and coercion. As one looks back upon the nationalist agitation of subject peoples in the 1870's and 1880's, one is likely to be struck by the modesty of its demands and the patience with which, even under increasing provocation, it awaited their fulfillment. The "home rule" for which the Irish Nationalists asked in 1879 was such a slight boon, and they asked for nothing else for so long! The Czechs of that time had no wish to smash the Hapsburg Empire; they and the Croatians, and even more the Serbs, Slovenes, Slovaks, and Rumanians, thought in terms of a federalized empire under which they would cherish their particular cultures and practice national "home rule"; and, with an optimism perhaps infectious in the Danube basin, they long clung to that thought in the face of Austrian rebuffs and Magyar assaults. Even the Poles were long-suffering, and might eventually have been content with mere dreaming if they had been interfered with as little by Russia and Prussia as by Austria.

But this is idle speculation. Nationalism of great, "successful" peoples was too strong and proud, too saturated with racialism and imperialism and a sense of "historic mission," to remain tolerant of lesser, submerged peoples. And these, taking their cue from their "betters," presently gave indications that they might become equally intolerant if they ever got the chance. Only tiny Switzerland, perched high above the rest of Europe, offered practical demonstration of how, through sane federalism and real liberty, diverse nationalities could live together in amity and evince a common patriotism. Although no great power paid serious attention to the Swiss demonstration, Switzerland remained at peace when later the world was at war, and Switzerland outlasted the empires of Hapsburg, Hohenzollern, and Tsar.

Chapter Eight

THE EUROPEAN STATE SYSTEM IN THE CENTURY'S LAST DECADE

I. DROPPING THE PILOT

IN 1890 Prince Bismarck was seventy-five years of age. For almost thirty years he had occupied in European public life a position comparable with Napoleon's or Metternich's earlier in the century. Indeed, the three decades from 1860 to 1890 might appropriately be labeled the Age of Bismarck.

It was not merely that his astute statesmanship had been instrumental in constructing the Hohenzollern Empire and maintaining it as the mightiest power on the Continent. It was also that Bismarck symbolized, and, through his curious suppleness of mind along with remarkable strength of character, actually gave guidance to, much of Europe's internal evolution during his generation. He, more than anyone else, had dissolved the dream of a federative Europe in the reality of "blood and iron" and the heat of intensified nationalism. A country gentleman by heritage and an ultra-reactionary by youthful conviction, he had learned to sympathize with, and to foster, the developing industrialization, and during the late 1860's and the decade of the '70's to patronize the moderate constitutionalism, the qualified political democracy, and the economic liberalism then fashionable with the middle classes. Moreover, his original ardent Prussianism he had transformed into an equally ardent but more comprehensive Germanism; and he had been the first statesman in Europe to recognize the force of the popular nationalist reaction which set in at the end of the '70's against economic liberalism, and the first to utilize it for state adoption of those policies of tariff protection and social legislation which characterized the '80's. Likewise, for patriotic as well as economic motives, he had overcome his early scruples against colonial enterprise and had steered Germany into the overseas imperialism of that decade. The growing nationalistic intolerance he had also nicely exemplified and forwarded. Only to anti-Semitism had he given no official countenance: he was too reliant on Jewish banking friends. He had led the Kulturkampf against the Catholic Church in the '70's, and only gradually had he retreated in the face of gathering counter-attacks and then because he needed Catholic support for his economic policies. From studied efforts to Germanize the Poles in Prussia, however, he had never desisted, nor from campaigning against the Social Democrats. The Anti-Socialist Law which he put through the Reichstag in 1878 he had had repeatedly re-enacted up to 1890. And by reason of the enormous prestige which Germany enjoyed under Bismarck, whatever was done there was bound to be viewed as the norm for Europe.

Bismarck liked power, and he had grown accustomed to exercising it with little interference, or even supervision, by the much older and very grateful Hohenzollern King William I whom he had made German Emperor and who showered him with words of praise and material tokens of esteem.[1] Parliament had frequently irked him, but almost invariably since 1867 he had contrived to command some sort of majority in it for his pet legislative projects. Only twice—in 1878 and again in 1887—had such a majority failed him, and on those occasions he had dissolved the Reichstag, appealed to the country, and come off triumphant. With advancing age and steadily lengthening record of success in both domestic and foreign policy, he seemed to himself—and to a multitude of Germans—a quite indispensable "mayor of the palace" for a *"roi fainéant."* And being a good family man as well as a great statesman, he groomed his elder son, Herbert, to succeed him when death should at last supervene.[2]

1 How the tokens had accumulated! Order of the Black Eagle in 1864; title of Count in 1865; the Hohenzollern Order in 1866; gift of $300,000 in 1867; two honorary army appointments in 1868; Iron Cross and Victory Medal in 1870; title of Prince and gift of a million dollars in 1871; some captured French cannon and a marble bust of William I in 1872; insignia in brilliants of the Order of the Black Eagle in 1873; grand cross of the Order of the Red Eagle in 1878; Ordre pour le Mérite in 1884; gift of $300,000 in 1885.

2 Herbert von Bismarck (1849-1904) was private secretary to his father, 1871-81; counselor of the embassy at London, 1881-84, and at St. Petersburg, 1884-85; undersecretary of foreign affairs, 1885-86; and imperial minister of foreign affairs, 1886-90.

William I died in March 1888, at the over-ripe age of ninety-one; his son and heir, Frederick III, already an elderly and very sick man, died ninety-nine days later; and the next Hohenzollern in line, the grandson and namesake of William I, gave every indication for a year and a half that he would follow dutifully in grandfather's footsteps, which meant in Bismarck's. William II wired the old chancellor on January 1, 1890: "I pray God He may vouchsafe me, in my heavy responsibilities of reigning, your trusty and experienced advice these many years to come."

Nevertheless, while Bismarck soberly and confidently neared the age of seventy-five, William II was barely thirty-one and amazingly youthful in volatility and volubility; and their contrasting ages and temperaments augured ill for continuing harmony between them. As William expressed it, before the year was out, "it was a question whether the Hohenzollern dynasty or the Bismarck dynasty should rule."

Bismarck did not lack critics and outright opponents. William II's mother, a daughter of Queen Victoria, distrusted him and intrigued constantly against him, and so, to some extent, did the Emperor's uncle, the Grand Duke Frederick of Baden. Many officials, including men of his own nomination, were resentful of the old man's growing arbitrariness and secretiveness and jealous of his son's rapid promotion. A particularly scheming and influential dignitary in the foreign office, Friedrich von Holstein, opposed the Bismarckian policy of maintaining simultaneous (and, in his opinion, conflicting) alliances with Russia and Austria-Hungary; and in insinuating his dislike of Russia and depreciation of Bismarck into the impressionable mind of the youthful Emperor, he was stealthily aided by a cabal of military courtiers, chief among whom was General von Waldersee, a favorite of William's. In the country at large, Adolf Stöcker and the anti-Semitic party complained that the chancellor was too friendly with Jews and Liberals and that his appointment of the liberal theologian Harnack to a chair at Berlin in 1888 was an affront to conservative German Protestantism. On the other hand, neither Social Democrats nor Catholic Centrists, to say nothing of Poles or Alsatians, had reason to love Bismarck, and the doctrinaire Liberals (the *Freisinnige*) were habitual and very vocal critics of his repudiation of free trade and his flouting of full parliamentary government.

The Reichstag majority on which Bismarck relied from the election of 1887 to that of 1890 consisted of a *cartel* of Conservatives and National Liberals. It loyally voted the army bill and the tariff and old-age insurance measures he requested, but late in 1889 a cleavage developed over the question of the Anti-Socialist Law, which, unless re-enacted in the meantime, would automatically expire in June 1890. Bismarck, with the Conservatives, wanted it re-enacted this time, not for a specified term of years, but in perpetuity, while the National Liberals held out for another temporary re-enactment and with the Centrists, Freisinnige, and Social Democrats, who opposed it altogether, rejected the chancellor's proposal. Bismarck stuck to his guns, however. He was reverting in old age to something of the uncompromising conservatism of his youth, and he felt sure that the regular parliamentary elections, due in February 1890, would so strengthen the Conservative forces in the Reichstag as to open the eyes of the National Liberals to the need of preserving the *cartel* and renewing the Anti-Socialist Law just as he proposed.

The elections proved most upsetting. The Conservatives lost twenty-four seats, and the National Liberals fifty-seven, and the majority which the *cartel* had possessed in the previous Reichstag passed in the new one to the strange loose coalition of parties which were traditionally anti-Bismarckian and specifically inimical to any re-enactment of the Anti-Socialist Law. The Centrists (with Polish, Guelph, and Alsatian allies) gained thirteen seats, the Social Democrats twenty-four, and the Freisinnige forty-four.

Still Bismarck did not despair. He was not responsible to the Reichstag but only to the Emperor, and he speedily mapped a course of firm action. He would lay the anti-Socialist bill before the new Reichstag; if it refused assent (as he expected it would) he would have the Bundesrat dissolve it and call for new elections on a clear issue of national patriotism; and if, peradventure, these too turned out unfavorably, he would have the Emperor proclaim martial law and cow the country into acceptance of constitutional amendments abridging the democratic franchise and the rights of parliament. This, at any rate, appears to have been the program which he put before William II and which in an interview on February 25 he was given to understand the Emperor agreed to. But the more William II thought it over, and the more he took counsel of officials jealous of the chancellor, the more convinced he became of the truth of the Grand Duke Frederick's suspicion that "it was nothing but a trick of old Bismarck, who wanted to pit Emperor and People against one another in order to make himself indispensable." It would mean civil war in Germany, William vividly imagined, a setback to social amelioration, and probably his own disgrace and deposition! It would be infinitely better to kill socialism with kindness than to try to suppress it with bullets.

Within a few days William II was completely hostile to Bismarck's program, and henceforth he applied to the elderly statesman a quick succession of sharp "pin-pricks" calculated to bring about his resignation and retirement. He peremptorily demanded the abrogation of a Prussian ordinance which made the prime minister the intermediary between the other ministers and the crown and which to Bismarck seemed essential to the orderly and consistent operation of government. He insisted upon seeing Bismarck on routine business in early morning hours without respect for his age, and disconcertingly neglected to answer important written communications from him. He got very excited about news that Bismarck, in an effort to construct a working majority in the new Reichstag, had had a "secret" conference with the Centrist leader, Windthorst, and irritably rebuked him for "scheming behind my back." He got still more excited about gossip that Russian military maneuvers then in progress were designed "to precipitate war"; he angrily accused Bismarck of withholding knowledge from him and from Austria of "this terrible threatening danger" and blocked the chancellor's plan of negotiating a renewal of the "reinsurance treaty" with Russia.

Stubbornly and irascibly Bismarck held on, until on March 17, 1890, William II sent him an emissary to demand his instant resignation. The next day the veteran statesman complied in a confidential and bitter twenty-page "request for retirement." This epistle William II did not make public. Instead, he gave out to the

press the letter he himself addressed to Bismarck on March 20.
". . . The reasons advanced for your decision convince me that
further efforts to induce you to withdraw your request would be
fruitless. I therefore comply with your wishes and grant you the
requested discharge from your offices of Imperial Chancellor, President of the Cabinet, and Minister of Foreign Affairs, under pleasant
circumstances and in the firm assurance that your advice and energy,
your loyalty and devotion will not fail me and the fatherland in
the future. . . . As a sign of my regard I bestow upon you the
dignity of Duke of Lauenburg. I will also send you a life-size
portrait of myself."

Two days later the young Emperor telegraphed the Grand Duke
of Weimar: "I am as miserable as if I had again lost my grandfather.
But by God's help it must be borne, even if I have to break down.
The office of watch on the ship of state has fallen to me. The course
remains as of old. Full steam ahead!"

On March 26 Bismarck was received in chilly farewell audience
by the Emperor and Empress. On the 28th he went out to Char-
lottenburg and laid three roses on the grave of William I. On the
29th, amid a great popular demonstration, he drove with his wife
and his sons (the Bismarck "dynasty") to the railway station in
Berlin and departed for private life on his ancestral estates. The
old experienced pilot was dropped, and Germany and all Europe
experienced a queer sense of loss and bewilderment.

II. REFORMATION OF ALLIANCES

Bismarck's retirement synchronized with a change in international alignments. His cardinal policy of isolating France and thus
restraining her from a "war of revenge" for the recovery of Alsace-
Lorraine, he had successfully maintained for nineteen years by
means of an increasingly complex web of alliances and under-
standings among the other great powers. Especially intricate had
been his diplomacy in 1887, when he negotiated a five-year renewal
of the Triple Alliance of Germany, Austria-Hungary, and Italy
and a three-year "reinsurance treaty" between Germany and Russia, and sponsored a special Mediterranean agreement among

Austria-Hungary, Italy, and Great Britain.[3] Still not content, however, he had proposed to Lord Salisbury in January 1889 the conclusion of a direct defensive alliance between Great Britain and Germany. The British premier had personally favored it in the face of fast-developing imperialist rivalry between England and France, and also between England and Russia; but he had had to acknowledge that, in view of existent colonial controversies between England and Germany, it would encounter embarrassing opposition in parliament and should therefore be "deferred." Bismarck had then urged at least an Anglo-German entente. In August he sent his Emperor on a loudly acclaimed visit to England, and William II returned with the much-prized honor and showy habiliments of "Admiral" of the British navy. Developments at London were promising.

It doubtless required a Bismarck's diplomatic experience, agility, and prestige to yoke all the great powers (save one) to Germany, and to reconcile their mutual jealousies and divergent interests sufficiently to keep them yoked. Even Bismarck had occasionally slipped, and during his last years in office he unwittingly helped to loosen those Russo-German ties which he had always deemed essential to the continuing isolation and impotence of France. At the very time when he arranged the "reinsurance treaty," pledging Russia or Germany, as the case might be, to observe benevolent neutrality if the other should be attacked by a third power, he had put through the Reichstag, at the behest of his Conservative supporters, a steep scaling up of the German tariff on agricultural imports, which adversely affected Russian landlords and made them especially responsive to anti-German propaganda of the Slavophiles. At the same time, to protect German investors who were particularly numerous among his National Liberal friends, he had forbidden the Reichsbank to accept Russian securities as collateral for loans, which practically estopped Russia from borrowing at Berlin the requisite foreign funds for domestic industrialization and drove her to seek them at Paris. In December 1888 a Russian loan of five hundred million francs was obtained in France, and some of the

3 For these intricate arrangements, see above, pp. 44-45.

proceeds were spent on the building of strategic military railways near the German and Austrian frontiers.

Yet neither these provocations nor the growing strain in Austro-Russian relations, nor his own current flirtations with an England traditionally antagonistic to Russia, prevented Bismarck from hoping and planning for a renewal of the Russo-German "reinsurance treaty" when it should expire on June 18, 1890. Nor was there serious thought of not renewing the treaty on the part of the Tsar Alexander III and his pro-German foreign minister, Giers: they feared that without it Russia would be dangerously isolated, and the alternative of an alliance with flighty Republican France was still very distasteful to them. Indeed, they commissioned the Russian ambassador to Germany, Count Shuvalov, to negotiate a renewal of the treaty for a further term of six years, and he arrived at Berlin, for the purpose, on March 17, 1890—at the height of the crisis between Bismarck and William II. The next day Bismarck resigned, and three days later William II assured the somewhat troubled Shuvalov that no change of policy was contemplated and that the treaty would be renewed.

But the new German chancellor, General von Caprivi, and the new foreign secretary, Baron Marschall von Bieberstein, lacked experience and distrusted their ability to maintain the extraordinarily complicated system of alliances and agreements which they had taken over from Bismarck. In their perplexity they sought counsel of Baron von Holstein, who had no trouble in convincing them, and through them the Emperor, that the "reinsurance treaty" should not be renewed. If it were continued, they reasoned, it might operate against Austrian interests and impair the more fundamental Austro-German alliance, and, besides, it might embroil Germany in quarrels between Russia and Great Britain and militate against a desirable entente with the latter. There had been too much double-dealing by Bismarck. The need now was for a simpler and more open foreign policy, and for one which would command popular favor. Surely, almost all the parties in the Reichstag would greatly prefer alliances with Austria and Britain, to one with Russia.

So William II reversed himself, and advised Shuvalov and the

Tsar that, while he intended to remain on the friendliest terms with Russia, he would not renew the secret treaty. And so, in June 1890, ended the last of the special engagements which had long tied Russia to Germany. It was the first fruit of Bismarck's dismissal.

While William II and Caprivi thus abandoned the Russian alliance, they persevered with Bismarck's project for an entente, perhaps eventually an alliance, with England. They accordingly welcomed a suggestion from Lord Salisbury in May 1890 that, in return for colonial compensation in Africa, England might consent to the cession of her North Sea island of Heligoland; and in June the suggestion was carried into effect by a definitive Anglo-German agreement. Germany got Heligoland and a narrow corridor ("Caprivi's Finger," it was facetiously styled) connecting Southwest Africa with the Zambesi River; England got Zanzibar and the extensive territory of Uganda in East Africa. Carl Peters and other German imperialists protested bitterly against the agreement, but it was hailed by the governments concerned as removing sources of friction and inaugurating a real Anglo-German entente.

In May 1891 Germany renewed the Triple Alliance with Austria-Hungary and Italy for a term of twelve years, and the gala visit of a British squadron to Fiume and Venice in June 1891 advertised England's solidarity with Germany's allies. Rudini, the Italian premier of the day, labored hard to draw England formally into the Triple Alliance, and it was believed in Germany—and widely throughout Europe—that the Triple would very shortly become a Quadruple Alliance. Quite likely it would have become so if the British elections of 1892 had not turned Salisbury out of office and brought in again—if only briefly—the octogenarian Gladstone, who still cherished the memories of a "Little Englander."

To Russia the lapse of the "reinsurance treaty" had been annoying and disconcerting, but to that insult was added the seemingly permanent injury of an Anglo-German entente, perhaps even, it was imagined, of a secret and most formidable Quadruple Alliance. The injury was to Russia, and also to France. It was not simply that England's co-operation with Germany, Austria, and Italy would effectually isolate Russia as well as France and interpose insurmountable obstacles to the former's hegemony in the

Balkans no less than to the latter's recovery of Alsace-Lorraine. It was also that England and Germany together would be able to dominate the big imperialistic contest, which had got off to such a good start in the '80's, and to nose out Russia in Asia and France in Africa and Oceania. The obvious thing for Russia and France to do was to combine.

To such a combination there was some repugnance in France on the part of dyed-in-the-wool Jacobins, who regarded the Tsar as a kind of Satanic Majesty, and more in Russia on the part of the governing class, who habitually thought of Republican France as revolutionary, mercurial, and undependable. On the other hand, the French government, which in the early '90's was directed by moderate and conservative politicians, worked steadily and energetically, with the backing of a multitude of nationalistic patriots, to forge a Franco-Russian alliance; and to the same end contributed the propaganda of Russian Slavophiles and Pan-Slavists. By 1891 the French government was putting the screws on the Tsar and his harassed finance minister in the form of a veto on further loans from Paris until the receipt of political favors from St. Petersburg; and the visit of the British squadron to Fiume in June of that year clinched the matter with the Tsar and even with his foreign minister, Giers. The very next month they extravagantly welcomed the visit of a French squadron to Cronstadt, and while Alexander III bared his head to the playing of the *Marseillaise*, Giers talked politics with the admiral. An entente was arranged in August between the two governments, pledging each to "consult" with the other over any threat to peace. The French, not yet content, pressed for an outright military alliance, but its conclusion was delayed by the unsavory and engrossing Panama scandals of 1892 and not agreed to until after England had threatened France with war over Siam, and Germany had again increased her army.[4] In October 1893 the Russian fleet at last paid a return visit to Toulon, and at

4 This army increase was provided for in a "quinquennate" (instead of the usual "septennate") which Caprivi put through the Reichstag by a vote of 201 to 185 in July 1893, after he had dissolved the Reichstag elected in 1890 with its hostile majority of Centrists, Social Democrats, and Freisinnige, and obtained, through patriotic appeals, a more amenable one with a larger representation of Conservatives and National Liberals. Caprivi was not such a bad disciple of his predecessor as the retired Bismarck in his chronic bitter revilings tried to make out.

the end of December Giers finally authorized the signing of a secret military convention. By its terms Russia promised France to employ all her forces against Germany if France should be attacked by Germany, or by Italy supported by Germany, and France promised to combat Germany if Russia should be assailed by Germany, or by Austria-Hungary supported by Germany. It was to last as long as the Triple Alliance.

Thus was consummated, as the second fruit of Bismarck's dismissal, what he had most feared: an end to French isolation; a Franco-Russian alliance. It marked, in subsequent popular opinion, the passing of the German hegemony associated with Bismarck's chancellorship, and the substitution, under Caprivi and his successors, of a balance of power between Dual Alliance and Triple Alliance.

The new alignment was not really as significant as it seemed. It did not materially change affairs. The Dual Alliance, no less than the Triple, was expressly "defensive," and though France derived from it a new sense of security and self-importance, it practically served to ease tension over Alsace-Lorraine. In actual military strength and efficiency the Dual Alliance was hardly a match, anyway, for the Triple Alliance, and what brought Russia and France together was not so much a common hostility to Germany as common imperialist rivalry with Great Britain. Russia, in particular, viewed the alliance as merely precautionary in respect of Germany; she certainly had no intention of risking war with Germany just to enable France to regain Alsace-Lorraine. It was against British hegemony outside Europe, rather than against German hegemony inside, that Russia wanted to direct the alliance, and in this she was largely successful during the '90's. France became a junior partner in the combination and for ten years subordinated anti-German feeling and policy to anti-British.

In truth, no sooner was the Franco-Russian Alliance arranged than Russia and Germany were negotiating a reciprocity treaty to lower the trade barriers which Bismarck's tariff of 1887 had reared between them; and despite vehement opposition from Prussian agrarians it was ratified by the Reichstag in March 1894 for a term of ten years. Russia was newly tied, though in a different way, to Germany.

If England had actually joined the Triple Alliance, or if the expected Anglo-German entente of 1890 had really materialized, Germany as well as Britain would doubtless have been the object of Russian hostility, and cleavage between Triple and Dual Alliance would have been deeper. As it was, however, the Gladstone ministry, which took office in August 1892, was averse to entangling alliances or commitments on the Continent, and its foreign minister, Lord Rosebery,[5] a good imperialist withal, was convinced that the manifold world-wide interests of Britain could be served better by a free than by a fettered hand. Wherefore Rosebery remained deaf to the importunate pleas of the Italian premier, Rudini, in 1893; and in the spring of 1894 he rejected a similar plea from the Austrian foreign minister, Kalnóky, for British adherence to the Triple Alliance. The German chancellor was sorely disappointed with this repeated refusal to bring the Anglo-German entente of 1890 to what he thought was its natural fruition; and in the summer of 1894 he dealt a body blow to the entente itself by having Germany second France in vigorous and efficacious protest against an African deal between England and the Congo Free State.[6]

Henceforth, for several years, there was greater co-operation between Germany and the Dual Alliance than between either of them and England. In the spring of 1895 Germany united with Russia and France to compel Japan to revise her peace settlement with China, and by concerted action afterwards they severally acquired bases in China—to the obvious discomfiture of Britain. In

[5] On the final retirement of Gladstone in March 1894, Rosebery became prime minister and so remained until supplanted by the Conservatives under Salisbury in June 1895. Rosebery's ardent imperialism was in strange contrast with the surviving "Little Englandism" of his old Liberal chieftain, but both contributed to a policy of "splendid isolation" for Great Britain—a policy which Salisbury continued and boasted of after 1895.

[6] This deal, made by treaty in May 1894, awarded to King Leopold, as head of the Congo Free State, the "lease" of a huge tract of the Egyptian Sudan, which England did not then hold and on which France had designs, comprising the whole left side of the Nile from Lake Albert to Fashoda; and it awarded to England a "lease" of a corridor within the Congo Free State, connecting British Rhodesia with British East Africa and hemming in German East Africa. France and Germany between them exerted such pressure on Leopold that by August he repudiated the deal. England was thus deprived of a continuous land connection between the Cape and Cairo, and France was free to advance in the Sudan toward Fashoda and the upper Nile.

the autumn of 1895 Germany and Austria-Hungary made common cause with Russia and France against a plan which Lord Salisbury put forward for a virtual partition of the Ottoman Empire.[7] Then, at the turn of the year, when Dr. Jameson, with the connivance of Cecil Rhodes and Joseph Chamberlain, made his famous filibustering expedition into the Transvaal Republic—only to be taken prisoner by the Boers—the impetuous German Emperor, to the delight of the whole Continent and the chagrin of Great Britain, put the finishing touches on any Anglo-German entente by his equally famous telegram to the Boer President: "I express to you my sincere congratulations that you and your people, without appealing to the help of friendly Powers, have succeeded, by your own energetic action against the armed bands which invaded your country as disturbers of the peace, in restoring peace and in maintaining the independence of the country against attacks from without."

III. STABILITY AND FLUX IN THE STATE SYSTEM

The stability and peace of Europe, and some "system" in its interstate relations, had long been sought in three ways: through a concert of powers; through an hegemony of one power; or through a balancing of one set of allied powers by another. Just as the concert of Metternich's devising or Napoleon III's dreaming had been succeeded in the 1870's by the hegemony of Germany under Bismarck, so in the '90's, after his retirement, the "system" of Europe became ostensibly a balance of power between Triple and Dual Alliances. This balance, however, was precarious, in part because Great Britain could theoretically tip it one way or the other, and in part because neither of the counterweights was really solid or substantial. In other words, the European system of alliances in the '90's was not a system—except on ceremonial occasions

7 Salisbury's plan, put forth in the midst of sorry Armenian and Macedonian massacres of 1895, must have made Disraeli turn over in his grave: it contemplated the surrender of Constantinople and the Straits to Russia, of the western Balkans to Austria, of Syria to France, of Tripoli to Italy, and of Egypt and Mesopotamia to England. It was now the turn of Russia, backed by Germany, to pose as the protector of the Sultan and of the "integrity" of his Empire. What actuated the general opposition was, of course, the thought of each power that it stood to gain more from a dying than from a dead Ottoman Empire. France was particularly solicitous about her big financial loans to the Sultan, and Germany was already entertaining the hope of becoming his trusty and well-paid counselor.

and for gullible persons. When the Emperors of Germany and Austria, the King of Italy, and their respective foreign ministers held periodic conferences with fanfare of trumpets and effulgence of gold braid, or when French and Russian generals and admirals banqueted together amid an incessant popping of champagne corks, the public which liked to read about such things, was easily tempted to overestimate their significance and to believe the chit-chat of journalists that a sinister move of the Dual Alliance was being checkmated by the Triple Alliance, or *vice versa*. Most readers simply overlooked or ignored the quiet commonplace negotiations and "deals" between members of different alliance groups—between Germany and Russia, Austria and Russia, Germany and France, Italy and France. Nor did they, as a rule, give much heed to the bickerings and divergencies between members of the same alliance group—between France and Russia, or Austria and Italy.

In reality, the solidarity of alliances, and certainly of Europe as a whole, was now quite incidental to the pursuit of particular national interests. This gained steadily in vigor, thanks both to intensifying nationalism within Europe and to ramifying imperialist competition without. The more nationalistic a state was and the more ambitious for colonial dominion (and of course the heavier its armaments), the greater was its claim to international prestige and to the rank of great power. Any alliance or entente it now might make with another was chiefly to advertise its greatness and enhance its prestige. That was precisely what France, for example, got from the Dual Alliance, or Italy from the Triple Alliance; and Germany's failure to get it from the abortive English entente sent her in quest of compensatory prestige through bewildering co-operation with her "sworn" foes, Russia and France.

Yet, however unstable and unsubstantial was the "system" of alliances in the '90's, most of the individual states, at least in western and central Europe, now possessed a seemingly superlative internal stability. With the exception of the Paris Commune of 1871 and a series of disorders at about the same time in "backward" Spain, there had been no revolutionary outbreaks in almost half a century. Each state was busily promoting the health and national well-being of its citizens, affording them all a free schooling, admitting them to democratic participation in government, and in a hundred ways strengthening their loyalty. Moreover, for the security of its citizens against foreign invasion, each state now had a larger armed force than ever before, and a much more efficient police for the repression of violence and the preservation of order at home. All its multiplying functions the state was enabled to discharge by reason of contemporary progress of technology and the industrial arts; industrialization made vastly more wealth, and this provided the state with vastly more revenue. And the more things the state did, the better it seemed to do them, for, in last analysis, what contributed most to the political stability of Europe in the '90's was the high average of efficiency attained by the administrative bureaucracy and civil service of the several states. This, now pretty well developed, was an army in itself, with a good deal of "red tape," to be sure, but also with extraordinary *esprit de corps*, devotion to duty, and technical expertness; and while titular sovereigns and parliamentary leaders, chancellors and ministers, might come and go, the bureaucracy went on forever. It cemented and solidified the state, amid the flux of international alliances and the deliquescence of the Concert of Europe.

What did impair the orderly and consistent functioning of the state system of Europe in the '90's, especially in respect of international relations, was a remarkable dearth of first-rate statesmen and a growing tendency on the part of such statesmen as there were to bow before every fresh gust of "public opinion." It was a decade characterized, as we have elsewhere explained, by the "emergence of the masses," when newly literate multitudes took to devouring the new type of popular journalism, joining the new kinds of patriotic societies, engaging in "pressure politics," and otherwise forming and expressing opinion on public questions; and the preponderant part of this "public opinion" was likely to be more nationalist, more imperialistic, more jingoistic, than the informed judgment of responsible statesmen. Bismarck had skillfully guided and exploited "public opinion" for his own ends; he had been its master rather than its servant. William II, on the contrary, was very sensitive to popular favor or disfavor, and the successive chancellors whom he appointed to Bismarck's place were barometers, so to speak, that recorded changes in the climate of public opinion and hence of the Emperor's mind.

Caprivi, a good military man but a totally inexperienced statesman, was made chancellor in 1890 to conciliate popular elements critical of certain Bismarckian policies, and then dismissed in 1894 because his own policy of tariff reciprocity, especially regarding Russia, aroused the hostility of landlords and the agricultural masses. The next chancellor, Prince Hohenlohe, was a fine gentleman with much administrative experience, but he was seventy-five years of age when appointed to the office, and from 1894 to his retirement in 1900 he was little more than an ornamental figurehead for such imperial favorites as the theatrical chief of the general staff, General von Waldersee, and the easygoing and easily adaptable foreign minister, Count von Bülow. It was natural, in the circumstances, not only that no titan of Bismarckian stature appeared on the German political scene in the '90's, but that German public policy, domestic and foreign, was notably opportunist and flighty.

It was much the same in other countries. An inordinate number of elderly men headed ministries and clung tenaciously to the trappings of power, which was apt to be actually exercised by younger lieutenants in closer touch with the popular electorate and consequently of different outlook. Gladstone was eighty-three when he resumed the British premiership in 1892, with a cabinet confusingly compounded of "little Englanders" like himself and ardent imperialists like his foreign minister, Lord Rosebery. Lord Salisbury was already sixty-five when he succeeded in 1895 to a seven-year premiership, and the natural caution of his years and temperament hardly counterbalanced the impetuosity of his colonial secretary, Joseph Chamberlain. Crispi was seventy-seven when the Italian offensive which he directed against Abyssinia broke down in 1896 and he was forced into retirement. Freycinet, French premier in the early stages of the Franco-Russian Alliance, was seventy when, after being implicated in the Panama Canal scandal, he returned to the war ministry in 1898. Giers, the Russian foreign minister, was seventy-five when he died in 1895.

It seemed as though every government was subject, in unusual degree, to "pressure politics," *pro* or *contra*, about whatever development, as interpreted by the new sensational journalism, was absorbing for the moment the interest of the populace. In Germany it was pretty constant agrarian agitation, interspersed with spectacular imperialist forays in Africa, the Far East, the Near East. In Great Britain it was Irish home-rule bills and Queen's Jubilees, equally recurrent, and the "interests" and "honor" of the Empire, now steadfast and supreme. In France it was a series of *causes célèbres*—Panama scandal, Dreyfus affair, Déroulède's attempted *coup*—punctuated by almost annual cabinet crises and colonial expeditions. In Italy it was personal fortunes and financial peculations of politicians, spasmodic riots in Sicily and at Milan, and in 1896 an acute fluctuation of imperialist fervor as ten thousand Italian troops marched up the Abyssinian hills and then marched down again.

Nevertheless, despite dearth of first-rate leadership and fitfulness of policy, the states of western and central Europe gave every appearance in the '90's of a continuing and even increasing stability. It was somewhat different, however, with the empires of eastern Europe. For a variety of reasons these states were regarded as in a condition of flux. While the Hapsburg Empire still put up a showy front and was accounted a great power, and while everyone expected it to last as long as its venerated Emperor Francis Joseph, doubts were frequently expressed as to whether it could survive him. He was sixty in 1890, and in the previous year his only son Rudolf had killed his mistress and himself. During the ensuing decade, the conflict of nationalities within the empire grew ever more bitter and disturbing, and none of the numerous Austrian ministries which rose and fell seemed able or willing to effect a satisfactory compromise.

The Russian Empire was better off in that its dissident nationalities were minor and less troublesome. But while no one imagined that it would break up, or cease to be a great power, most outside observers felt that the railway construction and the industrialization which had been going forward within it by leaps and bounds during the reign of the Tsar Alexander III must perforce be followed by a radical recasting of its political and social institutions along liberal and democratic lines, a recasting which would involve most serious strains and crises and which, if eventually consummated, would require almost superhuman strength and purpose on the part of its sovereign.

Alexander III was certainly a "strong man," but he employed his strength to shore up the reactionary autocracy and to beat down its assailants and critics. His son, who succeeded him in 1894, had not even the quality of strength. Indeed, Nicholas II was a peculiarly weak man, with a streak of petty obstinacy characteristic of weak men, and also with a cringing deference to his wife, a neurotic, hysterical woman, who, though a granddaughter of Queen Victoria and quite English in upbringing, displayed in Russia an almost insane devotion to autocracy and orthodoxy. Nicholas had neither the mind nor the will to reform anything; and in the absence of firm guidance from him, a sharp cleavage soon appeared among the ministers whom he inherited from his father and was presently reflected in the spread of partisanship and popular unrest throughout the empire. On the one hand, he kept as his finance minister Count Serge Witte,[8] whose vigorous patronage of public works, a stable gold currency, and a high protective tariff for domestic manufacturers helped immensely to speed up the large-scale industrialization and at the same time to arouse the jealousy and opposition of agricultural interests. On the other hand, the Tsar retained the "old-guard" minister of the interior, Plehve, and the procurator of the Holy Synod, Pobêdonostsev, both of whom were resolutely Slavophile, particularly sympathetic with reactionary landlords, and adept at detecting and penalizing any variation from the traditional norm. The more Witte fostered manufacturing and trade, the larger grew the cities at the expense of the countryside, and the more numerous were the bourgeois liberals and proletarian revolutionaries for his colleagues to become alarmed about and to prosecute. By the end of the '90's the conservative rural *zemstvos* were finding fault with the Tsar because he let Witte "sacrifice" agriculture, while the middle classes were giving ready ear to the protests of "westernizing" intellectuals against the tyranny and

[8] A native of the Caucasus and long identified with railway promotion in southern Russia, Witte had been made head of the department of railways in the imperial ministry of finance by Alexander III in 1888, and appointed minister of communications in 1892 and minister of finance in 1893. In this last post Witte succeeded Vishnegradski, who in turn had succeeded Bunge in 1887.

repression of the Tsardom. From opposite sides, the ground was being prepared for the advent of a Liberal party, demanding political reform, and perhaps, if necessary, political revolution. Besides, in 1898 a Social Democratic party was formed to convert the urban masses to Marxian Socialism, and in 1900 a Socialist Revolutionary party, to persuade the peasant masses to possess themselves of the land they tilled.

For the moment, the internal *malaise* of the Russian Empire was disguised to the outer world by the pomp of the imperial court and the seeming military might and diplomatic prestige of the Tsarist regime. Europe would not know how serious the disease was until a disastrous war should puncture the disguise, and that did not befall until 1905.

There was no disguising the illness of the Ottoman Empire in the '90's. The Sultan Abdul-Hamid II had been adroit in playing off one foreign power against another, and one subject nationality against another; but while he thus prolonged the empire upon its sick-bed, he could not raise it and make it stand alone. Its finances (including its debts) were regulated and administered by an international council representing foreign bondholders in France, England, Germany, Austria, and Italy.[9] Its army was "inspected" and "instructed" by a German general,[10] and its guns and ammunition were supplied by French, German, and English firms. Most of its public works were owned and operated by foreign *concessionnaires*; German bankers, for example, had obtained in 1889 the concession for the profitable railway line from Constantinople to Ankara, and at the end of the '90's they were negotiating, through their government, for an extension of the line to Bagdad and Basra.

The Sultan, if frequently pestered by one or another of the European powers, was continually plagued by the dissident nationalities within his empire, and in the '90's these set in motion a new wave of disorder and revolt comparable with that in the 1870's

9 This "Council for the Administration of the Public Debt" had been established in December 1881, shortly after the War of 1877-1878. It directly administered all Turkish revenues from tobacco, salt, wine and spirits, commercial stamps, fisheries, and silk, and collected an average of ten million dollars every year for foreign bondholders, the largest number of whom were French.

10 Baron Colmar von der Goltz, a veteran of the Franco-Prussian War, began the reorganization of the Turkish army in 1883 and remained in charge of it until 1896, when he returned to Germany with the Turkish titles of Pasha and Field Marshal.

which had brought on the Russo-Turkish War. Roving bands of Bulgarians, Serbs, and Greeks terrorized Macedonia. Arab tribesmen flouted Turkish authority throughout Arabia. And in the autumn of 1894 Armenian nationalists, irked by the Sultan's failure to carry out "reforms" he had promised in 1878, provoked an uprising in the mountainous province of Bitlis. The uprising was quickly suppressed by the Sultan's faithful and fanatically Moslem Kurds, who wreaked vengeance upon the Christian Armenians by massacring from ten to twenty thousand of them.

This "Armenian massacre" raised a greater popular commotion in Europe, especially in England, than had the earlier "Bulgarian massacres," and this time the British government (rather than the Russian) took the lead in expostulating with the Sultan and threatening him with punitive action. Following an "investigation" by a special commission, Russia and France joined Britain in presenting to the Sultan in May 1895 an elaborate program of "reforms" to be applied to the Armenian districts. But knowing that with Russia and France the program was a mere gesture and that neither would back it with forceful intervention,[11] as Britain desired to do, the Sultan dilatorily withheld formal acceptance of it until October, and then postponed its publication. Meanwhile he tolerated and almost certainly incited further and worse massacres of Armenians at Constantinople, Trebizond, and elsewhere, so that in 1895-1896 the number of the victims mounted above forty thousand. In vain Great Britain proposed a partition of the Ottoman Empire. The powers of the Triple and Dual Alliances alike spurned the proposal, and the "Armenian massacres" stopped only when the attention of the Sultan—and of Europe—was diverted to another revolt, that of the Greeks on the island of Crete.

Here there had been recurrent rebellions. A new one broke out in 1896, sympathized with and abetted by the independent Greek kingdom on the mainland. In spite of repeated pleas of all six great powers to Greece to keep out of the conflict and let them arrange with the Sultan for appropriate "reforms" for Crete, the

11 The Russian government, which had Armenian subjects of its own whom it was trying to "Russify," was wary of helping Ottoman Armenians to possible independence or autonomy; and France, in the interest of her many holders of Turkish bonds, seconded her "ally."

Greek government, responding to jingoistic public opinion, went to war with the Ottoman Empire in April 1897. The war was astonishingly brief. The German-trained Turkish army put the Greek forces to almost instant rout and quite inglorious flight, and within a month Greece sued for an armistice. The peace treaty, signed in December 1897, obligated Greece to pay the empire an indemnity of twenty million dollars and to rectify her northern frontier to the empire's advantage.

Yet though Greece was not permitted to annex Crete, the Ottoman Empire practically lost it. Russia was interested in the Greeks as she was not in the Armenians, and she therefore, together with France and Italy, joined Great Britain in compelling the Sultan to grant full autonomy to Crete and to withdraw Turkish troops from it. In November 1898, on the nomination of the four "Protecting Powers," Prince George of Greece was appointed governor. It proved that while the Ottoman Empire might still win a war, it could not win a peace.

IV. IMPACT OF JAPAN AND THE UNITED STATES ON EUROPE

International relations and rivalries of the European great powers (with the exception of Austria-Hungary) had to do in the '90's less and less with strictly European affairs and more and more with the world politics of national imperialism. The "Near Eastern Question" no longer centered in the fate of the Sultan's European provinces, but concerned the whole Ottoman Empire in Asia and Africa; and the Graeco-Turkish War of 1897 over Crete was quite incidental to Franco-British quarreling over Egypt and the Upper Nile, to Russo-British disputings over Armenia and the Persian Gulf, or to Italian ambitions in Tripoli and German in Anatolia. Even in these larger aspects the "Near Eastern Question" was now dwarfed by other and more sensational questions of world power arising from mighty new imperialistic thrusts along the extensive north-and-south axis of Africa and in that vast and populous area of the Earth's surface known as the "Far East."

The "Far Eastern Question," involving the fate of the huge Chinese Empire, was brought to the fore rather dramatically in the '90's, not so much by any European power as by Japan. Hitherto

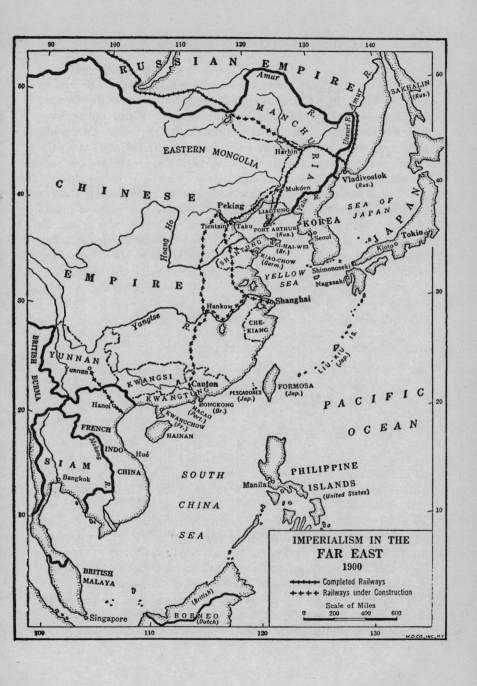

IMPERIALISM IN THE
FAR EAST
1900

++++ Completed Railways
++++ Railways under Construction

Scale of Miles
0   200   400   600

the relations of Europe with the Chinese Empire had been mainly commercial and missionary; and, although Great Britain had fairly early appropriated Hongkong, and Russia and France at different times had deprived China of nominal suzerainty respectively over the northern Maritime Province and over Annam in the far south, the empire as a whole had remained territorially intact. It was four times as large as the Ottoman Empire and twelve to fifteen times as populous, and its natural resources were incomparably greater.

How Japan from the '60's to the '90's underwent internal transformation, adopting the industrial, material, and military features of contemporary European civilization and becoming intensely nationalistic, constitutes one of the most extraordinary and fascinating chapters in human annals, but one which lies outside the purview of the present book, just as does the simultaneous and almost equally phenomenal development of the United States. Suffice it here to remark the bald fact that an Asiatic nation, and likewise an American nation, products themselves of "Europeanization," were sufficiently strong and assertive by the '90's to enter the characteristically European game of national imperialism and to take rank as great powers alongside the six in Europe.

Japan made her formal debut in a war against China in 1894-1895. For ten years previous China had been trying to re-establish suzerainty over the virtually independent kingdom of Korea, with such success that in 1894 the Korean government, confronted by domestic insurrection, was persuaded to invoke Chinese military assistance. And, though the insurrection was actually put down without their help, some three thousand Chinese soldiers established themselves in Korea. But already fully 90 per cent of Korea's foreign trade was with Japan, and Japanese companies operated most of Korea's banks and business enterprises, so that, simultaneously with the entrance of Chinese troops into the country, Japan, "to protect her interests," despatched thither an army of eight or ten thousand men. Matters reached a crisis on July 20, when Japan presented an ultimatum to the Korean monarch, demanding that he immediately repudiate Chinese suzerainty. Three days later a Japanese force seized the royal palace at Seoul and dictated to the hapless monarch a change of ministers and policy. On August 1 Japan, "in concert with Korea," declared war against China.

It was generally believed at the time that, while Japan might score a few initial successes in Korea, China in the long run would triumph by means of a superior navy, an impregnable base at Port Arthur, and immensely greater resources of men and supplies. All the more staggering to Europe as well as to China, therefore, was Japan's uninterrupted succession of victories. The Chinese navy failed to prevent Japan from quickly and heavily reinforcing her troops on the mainland, and in mid-September, while these were winning the battle of Pingyang and clearing the Chinese out of Korea, the Japanese navy inflicted heavy losses upon the main Chinese fleet and drove the remnants to shelter at Port Arthur and Weihaiwei. Next month Japanese armies overcame Chinese resistance at the Yalu River on the Korean border and carried the war into Manchuria and also into the Liaotung peninsula to the south. In November, through co-operation of land and sea forces, the Japanese captured Port Arthur, and early in the new year they took Weihaiwei and destroyed the Chinese warships there. The way was open for an advance upon Peking, and the Chinese, apparently helpless and hopeless, sued for peace.

The resulting peace treaty of Shimonoseki, in April 1895, was dictated by Japan. It obligated China to renounce all claims to Korea; to cede to Japan Formosa, the Pescadores Islands, and the whole of the Liaotung Peninsula, including Port Arthur; to pay an indemnity of $150,000,000; to grant Japan most-favored-nation treatment; and to open seven new ports to international commerce. These were big profits from an enterprise which had cost Japan the lives of only about 4,000 men, of whom more had been victims of Manchurian winter weather than of Chinese guns.

The European great powers no longer had illusions of Chinese strength and Japanese weakness. The Russian government, particularly its finance minister and promoter of public works, Count Witte, was now very fearful lest victorious Japan might cut off a greatly desired warm-water outlet, through Manchuria, for the Trans-Siberian Railway, which was under construction. The French government was ready to back its Russian ally; and the German

Emperor, obsessed with forebodings about a "Yellow Peril" incar-
nate in Japan, was eager to support Russia in the Far East, since
such support might serve to distract the Tsar from affairs nearer
home and show him that Germany no less than France could be
Russia's collaborator. All three powers accordingly stepped forward
as China's "friends"; and on the morrow of the signing of the
Treaty of Shimonoseki, they united in demanding of Japan the
retrocession of the Liaotung Peninsula to China. Japan hesitated.
Conceivably she might get aid from Great Britain, for just as
Britain had been pro-Chinese so long as China seemed to be the
strongest bulwark in the Far East against Russia, so now, when
Japan was proved stronger, Britain was becoming pro-Japanese. But
Great Britain was unwilling to risk war, and in May 1895 Japan
finally acceded to the demands of Russia, Germany, and France,
and, in return for additional indemnity, surrendered the Liaotung
Peninsula, including Port Arthur.

Japan clearly demonstrated by the war of 1894-1895 not only her
military prowess and her right to be reckoned a great power, but
also the impotence of the Chinese Empire to withstand invasion
and dismemberment. Thus was invited a scramble of imperialistic
powers for Chinese spoils, and the response was peculiarly hearty
and voracious from the European powers which as China's "friends"
had just restricted Japan's gains. In June 1895 France obtained a
favorable "rectification" of her Tonkin frontier and a "sphere of
influence" in three adjoining Chinese provinces. In June 1896
Russia secured the chartering of a Russo-Chinese bank and of a
"Chinese Eastern Railway" as a short cut for the Trans-Siberian
across Manchuria and into the Liaotung Peninsula. Meanwhile the
German government was debating what port and "sphere of influence" it should demand for the "services" it had rendered China,
and in the summer of 1896 Admiral von Tirpitz, in command of a
German squadron, visited Kiaochow and recommended its acquisition. This was finally decided upon at Berlin in the summer of
1897, and a splendid opportunity to realize it was presented in the
following November by the murder of two Catholic misisonaries
of German nationality by some provincial gangsters in Shantung.
German marines were immediately landed at Kiaochow, and from

Germany was sent out a supporting naval and military expedition amid frenzied huzzas and grandiloquent exchange of toasts between its commander, Prince Henry, and his brother, the Emperor William II. Said the Emperor: "May it be clear out there to the German merchant, and above all to the foreigner whose soil we may be on and with whom we shall have to deal, that the German Michael has planted his shield, adorned with the eagle of the Empire, firmly on that soil, in order once for all to afford protection to those who apply to him for it. . . . Should anyone attempt to affront us or to infringe our good rights, then strike out with mailed fist. . . ." Prince Henry, in reply, expressed a single purpose: "to proclaim and preach abroad to all who will hear, as well as to those who will not, the gospel of Your Majesty's anointed person."

China heard German guns, if not the gospel of anointment, and consented in March 1898, in compliance with an ultimatum, to lease the port of Kiaochow to Germany for a term of ninety-nine years and to reserve the province of Shantung as a German "sphere of influence." But the sound of German guns was the signal for China's other "friends" to make similar demands in March and April 1898. Russia got a lease of Port Arthur; France, of Kwangchow. And Great Britain, not professing any special solicitude for China and yet not willing to be outdone by Continental rivals, got a lease of Weihaiwei "for as long a period as Port Arthur shall remain in the possession of Russia," and, in addition, a ninety-nine-year lease of the Kowloon Peninsula opposite Hongkong and a "sphere of influence" in the rich Yangtze valley. The only power whose demand for territory the Chinese Empire ventured to deny was Italy, which had recently been routed out of Abyssinia and which in March 1899 put in a belated request for the lease of a port on the Chinese coast of Chekiang. A successful rebuff to Italy, however, was slight compensation for the grave loss of land and prestige which China had suffered since Japan pounced upon her in 1894. There was now, indeed, a Far Eastern Question of vast dimensions and import.

If Japan exerted novel influence on the international relations of Europe in the '90's, so did the United States. The latter's debut as a great power was not so sudden or surprising as Japan's, for ever since the close of the American Civil War in 1865 Europe had been aware of the steady material development and increasing potential might of the United States. Not, however, until the end of the '80's did the American Republic show signs of overstepping her "Continental" frontiers and engaging in overseas imperialism. Then, in 1889, she thrust out into the Pacific by assuming a joint protectorate, with Germany and Great Britain, over the Samoan Islands. In the same year she convened at Washington the first of the Pan-American Conferences, not only as an instrumentality for the settlement of disputes between the numerous republics of the New World, but also as a means of warding off European imperialism from the Western Hemisphere and furthering her own imperial hegemony in it. In 1893 an attempt was made by American residents and naval forces in Hawaii to secure the annexation of that Pacific archipelago to the United States; and though it was then disavowed and thwarted by President Cleveland, it was eventually crowned with success under his more imperially minded successor, McKinley, who signed a congressional resolution formally annexing Hawaii in July 1898. Even Cleveland did not hesitate to put the Monroe Doctrine to a crucial test by threatening Great Britain with war in 1895-1896 unless the latter immediately submitted to international adjudication a long-standing boundary dispute between Venezuela and British Guiana. Great Britain, astonished and somewhat chagrined, more or less graciously acquiesced. The United States was obviously a great power, with interests and ambitions beyond her own North American shores.

Soon Great Britain was co-operating with the United States for much the same reason as with Japan: to offset the co-operation of her imperialist rivals on the European Continent—Germany, Russia, and France. In 1897 Lord Salisbury rejected a German proposal for vigorous joint protest against the impending American annexation of Hawaii, and at the beginning of 1898 his colonial secretary, Joseph Chamberlain, advocated formal alliances of Great Britain with both the United States and Japan and also a renewed effort to detach Germany from Russia and France and to tie her to Britain. Overtures to this latter end were actually made by the Salisbury government, but they collapsed with the outbreak of the Spanish-American War.

Since 1895 Spain had been endeavoring to crush a revolt in Cuba; and her inability to do so, together with the harshness of the measures she took, had aroused a kind of crusading zeal in the United States for the "deliverance" of Cuba. This was touched off by the blowing up of the American battleship *Maine* in Havana harbor on February 16, 1898. Rightly or wrongly, Spain was blamed for the disaster, and without waiting for the conclusion of peaceful negotiations between the two governments, President McKinley on April 20 approved a congressional resolution demanding the withdrawal of Spain from Cuba. The Spanish government at Madrid responded by handing the American minister his passports, and on April 25 the United States declared war.

This war proved as one-sided as the Chinese-Japanese War. Naval superiority was with the United States, and it was decisive. On May 1 an American squadron under Admiral Dewey easily overpowered Spanish warships in Manila Bay, and on July 3, off the Cuban port of Santiago, the principal American fleet engaged and destroyed what effective naval force remained to Spain. Meanwhile American armies were being safely transported to Cuba, Puerto Rico, and the distant Philippines, and everywhere they were winning successes. Almost simultaneously with the fall of Manila on August 14, Spain sued for peace; and the war was formally terminated by the Treaty of Paris, signed on December 10, 1898.

On the European continent both popular and governmental sympathy during 1898 was pretty constantly pro-Spanish and anti-American. Most publicists, whether in Moscow, Berlin, or Paris, represented the United States as an upstart and bully, while the German government in particular posed as a "friend" of Spain in the hope of getting some such reward from her as had just been obtained from China. A strong German fleet, ostentatiously stationed in Manila Bay at the beginning of the war, was bothersome to Admiral Dewey and a source of apprehension to the American public, and only late in the war, after the United States had amply demonstrated its might, did Germany adopt a more discreet and conciliatory attitude.

On the other hand, Great Britain sympathized with the United States, as with Japan, perceiving in the victories of each a realization of Canning's old hope about a New World's redressing the balance of the Old, and a promise of decisive support for herself against any combination of European great powers. In the end Britain urged the United States to demand not merely the Spanish West Indies but also the big archipelago of the Philippines in the Far East. President McKinley hardly needed British prompting. He assured a delegation of Methodist clergymen who waited upon him that he had knelt in prayer about the Philippines and had been directed by God to take them. So, from the war of 1898 the United States obtained Puerto Rico, a protectorate over Cuba, and outright ownership of the Philippines and, as a naval base on the way thither from Hawaii, the island of Guam. And the toll paid by the victor was even less in this war than in the Chinese-Japanese War. Only eighteen American sailors had been killed, and only 469 American soldiers.

Germany again received some reward from the vanquished. As a result of secret arrangements in September 1898, she publicly purchased in the new year the job lot of Spanish possessions in the Pacific which the United States had overlooked—the Caroline, Pelew, and Marianne islands (except Guam). Thereby the historic Spanish Empire, save for a few insignificant stations in Africa, disappeared entirely from the map of the world. Germany, however, was but a residuary legatee. The principal heir was the United States, whose role henceforth was unmistakably that of an imperial great power in the Far East as well as in the Western Hemisphere. Germany recognized the fact by amicably agreeing in 1899 to a partition of the Samoan Islands between herself and the United States. And despite protest and rebellion of ungrateful natives in the Philippines, a thumping majority of the American people in the presidential election of 1900 joyously accepted the "manifest destiny" of the United States.

V. THE APOTHEOSIS OF THE BRITISH EMPIRE—AND ENGLAND'S ISOLATION

In the summer of 1897—two years after the Chinese-Japanese War and less than a year before the Spanish-American War—London staged a superlative pageant in celebration of Queen Victoria's diamond jubilee and of Britain's imperial predominance in a crowning age of imperialism. A procession, such as the world had not previously beheld, passed from Buckingham Palace up Constitution Hill, through Piccadilly, Trafalgar Square, the Strand and Fleet Street, to solemn service of Thanksgiving in St. Paul's. First went detachments of armed forces from beyond the seas: Dyak police from North Borneo, Maoris from New Zealand, Hausas from West Africa, twenty-six cavalrymen from Cape Colony, forty-two helmeted soldiers from Hongkong, black fighters in the employ of the Royal Niger Company, mounted Zaptiehs from Cyprus, a contingent of Rhodesian horse, men of Australia clad in brown, and Canadians in variant uniforms of thirty military organizations. Followed Dominion premiers in sober black and scores of colonial governors with swords and gold lace; next, representatives of all ranks of the royal navy; then, for the army of the United Kingdom, scarlet coats, Highland kilts, Coldstream Guards, Welsh Guards, Irish Guards, the Queen's own Hussars, Inniskilling Dragoons, generals and field marshals. After which went carriages with ministers and ambassadors accredited to the Court of St. James's, foreign princes, kings, and emperors, and the Queen's family—she had nine children, forty grandchildren, and thirty great-grandchildren. Finally passed Victoria, Queen and Empress, in coach of gold and crimson drawn by eight cream-colored horses and surrounded by a bodyguard of Indian soldiery.[12]

Victoria, obviously, had been properly named. She personified the victories of her generation, and indeed of her century; and she seemed immortal. For sixty years she had been Queen, and for twenty, Empress. Only Gladstone and Bismarck, of all the European statesmen she had known in the 1860's, were still alive. Both, however, were in enfeebled retirement, the former still penning ineffectual pleas for Armenians, and the latter querulously criticizing a government which had no further use for him. Gladstone died in May 1898, at the age of eighty-eight, and Bismarck in July of the same year at the age of eighty-three. Of reigning

12 For this reference to the procession I am indebted to the impressive account of Professor Walter P. Hall in his *Empire to Commonwealth* (New York, 1928).

sovereigns of comparable age, there remained, besides Victoria, only Francis Joseph and Leo XIII. These, like her, would survive the turn of the century; but the Austrian Emperor was eleven years her junior, and Leo (nine years her senior) had not become Pope until she had been Queen some forty years.

And what, to the vast concourse of loyal Britishers who saw that procession on a summer's day of 1897, were the victories of Victoria's long reign? Victories of material progress, of industrial invention and production, yes; of emergence of the masses into literacy and political life, yes; of physical health and national wealth, yes. But above all, to sovereign and subjects alike, they were victories of world empire and of that sea power upon which such empire ultimately rested. Britain had been, of course, a relatively important colonial and naval power when Victoria came to the throne in 1837. Yet since then, and especially during the two decades of intensified European imperialism from 1877 to 1897, Britain had newly acquired more territory and population overseas than had all her Continental rivals lumped together, while in the later race of naval armaments she had outdistanced the combined efforts of any two of her competitors. By now, moreover, both navalism and imperialism were prime articles of faith and supreme objects of devotion in Britain. Of both, Queen Victoria was the popular embodiment, as Kipling was the popular laureate and the ministry of Salisbury and Chamberlain the popular official agency.

Nor was there any thought of Queen, ministry, or masses that the British Empire had reached its maximum in 1897. With stakes in every part of the world and with superabundant sea power, it simply must keep on expanding. It had only to set bounds to the imperialism of others—particularly Russia, France, and Germany. Current circumstances were propitious. Japan's success in 1895 against China, while revealing the latter's weakness and opening up the whole Far East to imperialistic enterprise, had made Japan a natural ally of Britain in opposing Russian ambitions in that quarter. In this very year of 1897 the Graeco-Turkish War promised Britain a stellar role, once more, in the chronic Near Eastern Question. Presently the Spanish-American War of 1898 would discomfit Britain's Continental rivals and bring the United States into Oceania and the Far East as a counterweight there to Germany and France as well as to Russia. Britain got the lion's share of leases and concessions from the Chinese Empire in April 1898, just a few days before an American admiral won the battle of Manila Bay in the presence of a disapproving and disappointed German fleet.

But Britain's eyes in 1897-1898 were chiefly on Africa, particularly on the lengthy north-and-south axis from Egypt to the Cape of Good Hope. This axis had two glaring gaps. One, north of Cape Colony, comprised the practically independent Boer republics of Transvaal and Orange Free State. The other, immediately south of Egypt, embraced the huge Sudanese basin of the Upper Nile, which, since its conquest by the mad Mahdi and his fanatical Dervishes and the slaughter of General Gordon and a British garrison at Khartum in 1885, had been, for Europeans, a "no man's land."

In view of the pestilential climate and difficult terrain of the Sudan, and of the fierce fighting reputation of its wild Mahdi, Britain had been in no hurry to attempt its conquest. For some time she had been content to "reserve" it against appropriation by anyone else. In the '90's, however, France evinced what to the British government seemed an unholy and highly dangerous interest in the Sudan. Ever since Britain went into Egypt without France in 1882, the French government had been pressing the British to evacuate it, and now the government at Paris conceived the brilliant idea that if the French controlled the sources of the Nile, they could cut off the water supply of lower Egypt and compel British withdrawal. Besides, many French officials and publicists thought, in the grandiose imperialistic manner of the decade, how nice it would be to construct an all-French east-and-west axis from Somaliland on the Red Sea, right across the Sudan, to Senegal on the Atlantic.

At first, France resorted to diplomatic intrigues, in which she was seconded consistently by Russia and on occasion by Germany. When Great Britain "leased" a part of the Sudan to Leopold II of Belgium for his Congo Free State in 1894, France with German backing persuaded him to repudiate the "lease" and to seek eventual larger gains by opposing Britain. Then when Menelek of Abyssinia asserted claims in the Sudan and Britain tried to nullify them by encouraging Italy to undertake the subjugation of Abyssinia,

France with Russian approval supplied Menelek with the arms and munitions with which he routed the Italians at Adowa in March 1896.

On the eve of Adowa, the French government decided upon direct intervention in the Sudan, and selected an army captain, J. B. Marchand, to lead a military expedition thither. As Marchand was leaving Paris in May 1896 the foreign minister Hanotaux told him that "France is going to fire her pistol."[13] The plan, as evolved by Hanotaux, was for Marchand, with a small select body of Senegalese soldiers and French officers, to make the long journey eastward from Brazzaville in French Congo to Fashoda in the Sudan, where he would be reinforced by Abyssinian troops and a co-operating French expedition from Djibouti on the Red Sea.

After some delay occasioned by a native revolt, Marchand finally set out from Brazzaville with his little expedition in March 1897 on one of the most arduous and exciting adventures in human annals. He took along, up the Congo River, a small steamboat, the *Faidherbe*, which, with almost superhuman effort, was carried and dragged over the hilly watershed between the Congo and Nile basins. Eventually launching the boat on a tributary of the Upper Nile and aided by the spring rains of 1898, Marchand then coursed down to Fashoda. Here he arrived on July 10 and immediately hoisted a French flag on the ruins of an old Egyptian fort. In vain, however, he awaited the arrival of supporting columns from Djibouti and Abyssinia. These had been badly mismanaged, and by the time they could come to his assistance the British had moved in force and victoriously.

For the British government had been fully aware of the French plan and had already determined upon a counter-offensive. In October 1897 Field Marshal Lord Wolseley, the commander in chief of the British army and the man who had directed the original "occupation" of Egypt in 1882, ordered General Kitchener, the commander in Egypt, to make ready an Anglo-Egyptian force adequate for speedy "recovery" of Khartum and conquest of the entire Sudan; and in December the British ambassador at Paris warned Hanotaux

13 General Mangin, "Lettres de la Mission Marchand," *Revue des Deux Mondes,* Sept. 15, 1931, pp. 241-283.

that "no other European Power than Great Britain has any claim to occupy any part of the valley of the Nile." With all despatch, Kitchener assembled an Anglo-Egyptian army of some 25,000 men and pushed a vigorous advance from Cairo up the Nile into the Sudan. In April 1898 he swept aside native resistance at Atbara, and on September 2, on the plain outside Omdurman, he decisively defeated 40,000 Dervishes. Ten thousand of the latter were killed and five thousand wounded, as against fifty killed and two hundred wounded in Kitchener's army. The British had Maxim rifles and the Dervishes hadn't.

The Khalifa, successor of the Mahdi, escaped the rout and slaughter of his followers, but his power was utterly broken. Kitchener occupied Khartum and proclaimed the Sudan an Anglo-Egyptian protectorate. It remained only to deal with the little French expedition at Fashoda. Continuing up the Nile, therefore, Kitchener arrived here and met Marchand on September 19. The Britisher and the Frenchman, with soldiers' mutual respect, had a whisky and soda together and amiably agreed that their respective flags should fly over different parts of the town pending final settlement between London and Paris.

The ensuing excitement in France and Britain over Fashoda eclipsed that over the Spanish-American War and the Far Eastern Question. Many persons in both countries shouted for war, and for a time neither government appeared at all conciliatory. France, however, was in no position to wage successful war. Russia would pledge her no military or naval assistance, and her own sea power was shockingly inferior to Britain's. Moreover, she was harassed internally by bitter partisan strife over the Dreyfus affair, while Britain was superbly united and resolute. In the circumstances Delcassé, Hanotaux's successor in the foreign office, reluctantly agreed to order French withdrawal from Fashoda, and on December 11, 1898, the French flag was hauled down and the valiant Marchand departed. An Anglo-French convention in the following March formally ended the dispute. France was allowed to retain Wadai (east of Lake Chad) but she had to renounce all claims to the Egyptian Sudan and recognize it as a British protectorate. Britain thus closed in the spring of 1899 one of the great gaps in her imperial sway from Cairo to the Cape. She now had 2,600 miles of continuous territory southward from Alexandria on the Mediterranean to Mombasa on the Indian Ocean.

There was still the annoying Boer gap in the 2,000 miles from Cape Town northward to the Congo Free State. In British opinion, it too must be filled; and provocations for a British-Boer clash were plentiful in 1899. On the British side, both Sir Alfred Milner, the high commissioner for South Africa, and Joseph Chamberlain, the colonial secretary at London, saw eye to eye with the ultra-imperialist Cecil Rhodes; and these men, by fostering and airing the "grievances" of the British *Uitlanders* in the Transvaal—chiefly workers in the gold mines—and demanding their enfranchisement by the Boer government, aroused popular sympathy in England, as well as in Cape Colony, for a militantly aggressive policy toward the Boer Republic. On the Boer side, the attempted "Jameson raid" of December 1895 and the leniency shown its leader by the British courts had created a bitterness and an intransigence which found expression in the re-election of the veteran anti-*Uitlander* Paul Kruger to the presidency of the Transvaal in 1898 for another term of five years, and in the military alliance which he forthwith concluded with the Orange Free State. While British-Boer negotiations dragged on about enfranchising the *Uitlanders*, both sides prepared for war. The British imagined they could easily overwhelm the Boers if no third power made trouble; and Germany, as most likely to create difficulties, was bought off in August 1898 by a secret agreement concerning Portugal's empire. In case Portugal should be induced to surrender her colonies, Angola would be divided into three zones, the north and south going to Germany and the middle to Great Britain; the northern half of Mozambique would pass to Germany and the southern to Britain; and Germany would get Timor in the East Indies.[14]

By September 1899, negotiations between Boers and British reached an impasse. Kruger had offered, with some restrictions, to enfranchise *Uitlanders* after five years of residence in the Transvaal.

[14] But Britain later turned about and by a secret declaration of October 14, 1899, guaranteed to Portugal the territorial integrity of her empire in return for a pledge from Portugal that she would allow British warships to coal freely at her African port of Lorenzo Marquez and would not allow the shipment of arms thence to the Boers.

Chamberlain had demanded the five-year franchise without restrictions. Kruger had refused and Chamberlain had insisted. The only way out was war, and on October 9 it was precipitated by a Transvaal ultimatum which barely heaued off a similar ultimatum from Britain. The Orange Free State immediately joined the Transvaal.

The British had no such easy contest with the Boers as they had just had with the Dervishes. General Buller, the commander of the British army, instead of concentrating it for an attack in superior force upon a single objective, split it into three separate expeditions which the more mobile Boers defeated piecemeal in December 1899. Whereupon the hapless Buller was recalled and Field Marshal Lord Roberts sent out as commander, with Kitchener as his chief of staff. Under this new leadership and with heavy reinforcements drawn from the whole British Empire, the tide of battle slowly changed. Boer besiegers of Kimberley and Ladysmith were driven off late in February 1900, and in September of this year the first and regular phase of the war closed with decisive Boer defeat in the open field, flight of Kruger, and proclamation of Britain's annexation of the Transvaal and Orange Free State. There followed, nevertheless, almost two years more of desultory guerrilla warfare before resistance of the hardy valorous Boers was finally overcome. During the struggle the British lost almost 6,000 killed and 23,000 wounded, while the number of Boers killed was 4,000. But two South African republics had lost their independence and been added to the ever-expanding British Empire.

Yet the Boer War cost the British government many anxious moments. The protracted and long uncertain fighting was bad enough in itself. Even worse was its effect upon Britain's international position. Her European rivals were elated by her military setbacks and by the evidence these afforded that she was not invulnerable. There were recurrent rumors and signs of diplomatic maneuvers at Berlin, St. Petersburg, and Paris looking toward joint intervention by Germany, Russia, and France. And in the United States, whose friendship Britain had sedulously cultivated in 1897-1898 and counted upon to offset the enmity of Europe, public opinion after the outbreak of the South African War was conspicuously pro-Boer and anti-British.

England was clearly isolated, and it was hardly the "splendid isolation" of which Salisbury was wont to boast. True, the British navy was still intact and supreme, and in assuring the uninterrupted transport of troops and supplies to South Africa and thus enabling the British at last to vanquish the Boers, it had signally performed the service which Mahan and other navalists ascribed to paramount sea power. But this lesson was taken to heart no less by Britain than by her rivals. There was a new spurt of naval construction in Russia and France, and likewise in the United States and Japan, while the German navy, already being strengthened in accordance with action of the Reichstag in 1898 in the midst of the Spanish-American War, would be strengthened immensely more by additional enactment of 1900 in the midst of the Boer War. England's isolation was becoming really perilous. As the century ended the British government began a new and serious search for friends.

VI. THE INTERNATIONAL PEACE CONFERENCE OF 1899

When the nineteenth century closed, there had been, for well-nigh thirty years previously, no war between European great powers. Yet there had been recurrent war scares and rumors of war, and some actual hostilities in the "backward" Balkans: between Russia and Turkey in 1877, between Serbia and Bulgaria in 1885, between Greece and Turkey in 1897. Latterly, too, there had been a veritable epidemic of imperialistic forcefulness overseas: in 1894-1895 the Chinese-Japanese War; in 1896 the Italian-Abyssinian War; in 1898 the aggressions of Germany, France, Russia, and Britain against China, the Spanish-American War, the British conquest of the Egyptian Sudan and dislodgement of France from Fashoda, and preparations for the Boer War of the next year. And the peace which still obtained among the great powers was more than ever an "armed peace."

On August 24 of the eventful year of 1898 the Tsar's foreign minister, Count Muraviev, communicated to the diplomatic corps at St. Petersburg an "imperial rescript" declaring that "the preservation of peace has become an object of international policy" and inviting their respective governments to participate in a conference on "possible reduction of the excessive armaments which weigh upon all nations." The move was sensational, and doubly so by reason of its being made by Russia.

The Tsar Nicholas II had not been generally regarded as either a liberal or a pacifist, and yet he was now giving point and crystallization to latent aspirations for international peace on the part of a considerable body of liberals and humanitarians. Especially within England and the United States, where "militarism" was assumed to be non-existent and "navalism" to be purely "defensive," various peace societies were spreading among church and labor groups the conviction that, if only armies could be reduced in size and international disputes referred to arbitration, something like a millennium would ensue. The multiplying profits from industrialization could then be devoted more fully to popular education and enlightenment, and this would ensure the permanence of a peaceful order among the great as well as the lesser powers of Europe and confine whatever unfortunate struggles might be temporarily necessary to minor ones for the civilizing of barbarous peoples in out-of-the-way places of the world.

On the European Continent, where large armies were more usual than large navies, specifically pacifist propaganda was less in evidence, though the growing Marxian parties uniformly included in their electoral pronouncements attacks on "warmongering" and demands for limitation of armaments, and "bourgeois" parties paid at least lip service to the ideal of international peace. The Interparliamentary Union, which had been formed at Paris in 1889 by members of different European legislatures for periodic discussion of matters of common interest, had advocated from the outset an extension of international arbitration, and the first Pan-American Conference, held at Washington, also in 1889, had affirmed that "arbitration constitutes the public law of the American nations."

In the latter part of the '90's, moreover, several influential individuals, combining grave alarm over existent armaments with sublime faith in the ability of progressive nations, through concerted effort, to find better insurance against war, became earnest apostles of pacifism. There was, for example, the Norwegian dynamite manufacturer, Alfred Nobel; the Scottish-American steel magnate, Andrew Carnegie; the Russian-Jewish author of a six-volume diatribe against war, Ivan Bloch; the brilliant French descendant of Benjamin Constant, the Baron D'Estournelles de Constant. These were all elated by the Tsar's apparent conversion; and in the autumn of 1898 a distinguished British publicist, William T. Stead, editor of the important *Review of Reviews* and erstwhile doughty champion of British navalism, toured the Continent to enlist all European states in the Tsar's "peace crusade."

Neither the Tsar nor his foreign minister quite merited the reputation for idealistic pacifism which their "rescript" gained them. They had been pushed into sponsoring it by the Russian finance minister, Count Witte, and he was actuated by very realistic considerations. Russia was a comparatively "backward" and hence a poor country, and what with maintaining an army and navy comparable with its vast size and population and building extensive railways and other essential, yet terribly costly, public works, its finances were strained to the utmost. Witte had been helped out by heavy borrowings from France, but the larger these were, the more interest he had to pay every year to Paris; and foreign loans might not always be obtainable. In 1898 he was almost beside himself. France had recently adopted the famous 75-millimeter artillery for her army, and now Germany was introducing a new rapid-firing field gun which could discharge six shells per minute, as against the single shell per minute fired by Russian guns. Obviously Russia must have artillery as good as Germany's, but to procure it would necessitate an immediate special outlay of fifty million dollars, which Germany or France (or Britain) could afford, but hardly Russia. Besides, there was increasing friction over Chinese railway concessions with both Japan and Great Britain, and Russia must not let them get ahead of her in the armaments race. So Witte conjured up the bright idea of coaxing Russia's rivals to suspend further additions to their armaments for a term of years— a "holiday" of ten years, he suggested. The idea appealed to the Tsar and to Muraviev, who appreciated that Austria-Hungary and Italy, being almost as hard-pressed financially as Russia, would most likely agree to it, and who hoped that perhaps Germany, France, and Britain could be cajolled into concurring.

The governments to which the Tsar made his proposal were as

realistic about it, in their several ways, as was Witte, and they were backed, in most instances, by a preponderance of public opinion which viewed Russia with suspicion and pacifism with horror. The French government, which had not been consulted in advance, was shocked by what seemed at first thought a deliberate attempt on the part of its ally to weaken French preparedness and to banish indefinitely any prospect of recovering Alsace-Lorraine, but on second thought, not wishing to offend the Tsar and satisfied that no harm would result, it promised, with customary politeness, to send a delegation to the projected conference. So did the twenty-four other powers invited—comprising all in Europe, Japan and China in the Far East, and the United States and Mexico in the New World— though behind the scenes few statesmen said anything good about the plan or its sponsor. At London Lord Salisbury thought it should not be taken "too seriously," and at Berlin William II termed it "utopian." Nevertheless, only the Italian government attached a condition to taking part in the conference: it would stay out if the Pope were invited. Russia obligingly accepted the condition, and Leo XIII had to deliver his own homily on peace within the walls of the Vatican.

At length on May 18, 1899, the Tsar's birthday, his much heralded Peace Conference opened at The Hague under the honorary presidency of Queen Wilhemina of the Netherlands, and remained in session until the end of July. Of all the delegates attending, only a few were sincerely attached to the cause of international peace, such as D'Estournelles among the French; Sir Julian Pauncefote, negotiator of an Anglo-American arbitration treaty, among the British; M. de Martens, distinguished authority on international law, among the Russian; and Andrew D. White among the American. Most of the delegates were wordy or simply ornamental old men, or else determined defenders of army and navy interests. These latter included a blunt-spoken German military expert, Colonel Schwarzhoff; a fire-eating British admiral, Sir John Fisher; and the world-famous author of *The Influence of Sea Power*, Captain Mahan of the United States Navy. Their labors in the Conference were more assiduous—and fruitful—than anyone else's.

The primary object of the Conference was dealt a mortal blow, almost at the beginning, by Colonel Schwarzhoff. He could not understand why Germany should be expected to stint her own military might because other nations lacked the resources to equal it, nor why, with her new overseas responsibilities, she should be deterred from expanding her fleet. Indeed, so evidently difficult did he make the problem of limiting armaments or declaring a "holiday," that by common consent it was immediately dismissed as insoluble.

The Conference did do something. Thanks to some of its specialists in international law, it adopted a number of minor amendments and additions to the rules of war. The state and conditions of belligerency were defined; better treatment of war prisoners and of sick and wounded soldiers was prescribed; the Red Cross convention was extended to naval warfare; gas attacks and dumdum bullets were banned; the throwing of projectiles from balloons was prohibited for five years. But what finally aroused major interest and debate was the question of a permanent court of arbitration. There was general agreement that any such court should have no jurisdiction over cases which were "non-justiciable" or which involved any nation's "vital interest" or "honor." Over other cases, however, there was heated debate whether jurisdiction should be compulsory or voluntary. The German delegation for a time opposed the establishment of any court at all, and in the end agreed to it only after the other powers had accepted the voluntary principle. Even then the unbending Baron von Holstein resigned the key position he had long held in the German foreign office, as a solemn protest against what he deemed a sinister specter of international arbitration and a most dangerous flirtation with peace.

Altogether, the concrete results of the Hague Peace Conference of 1899 were not impressive. Count Witte got no relief for Russian finances, and no statesman elsewhere got any respite from piling up armaments. There was now, to be sure, a legally constituted list of jurists from which nations might select judges to adjudicate disputes between them, but recourse to arbitration was still entirely voluntary, and so too was acceptance of any arbitral decision.

Nonetheless the Hague Conference talked about peace, and undoubtedly set in motion among the general public in Europe and

America a pacifistic agitation of a character and intensity without previous parallel. By the time another Peace Conference met at The Hague in 1907, and still more by the time the League of Nations was inaugurated at Geneva in 1920, the Conference of 1899 was looked back upon as the first—and therefore highly significant—step in the devising of practical machinery for world peace. For the era from 1871 to 1900, let us remember, was an era both of developing machinery and of continuing humanitarian impulse.

Chapter Nine

THE CLIMAX OF THE ENLIGHTENMENT

I. THE CULT OF PROGRESS

IN THE correspondence columns of popular journals, a desultory, though occasionally heated, debate was carried on in 1899 as to whether this year or the next would bring the nineteenth century to a close. Ecclesiastical authority at Rome, appealed to by an enterprising American daily, confirmed the seemingly odd judgment of historians and mathematicians that the year 1900 belonged to the 1800's and that not until January 1, 1901, would a new century dawn.

The passing of the nineteenth century, its posterity can now see, had significance beyond the merely arbitrary timekeeping of calendars and almanacs. Whether its actual demise be dated from 1899 or 1900 doesn't matter, but it does matter that about this time the generation which had come into the European limelight in the days of the Franco-Prussian War of 1870 was fast disappearing. The generation had been preponderantly materialist. That is, it had been especially devoted to, and proud of, material achievements, and it had been imbued, in so far as it had a philosophy, with simply material and mechanical conceptions and a frankly this-worldly pragmatism.

The materialism of this generation must not obscure, however, its intimate relationship to, and its apostolic succession from, those eighteenth-century generations which gave birth and mission to the most distinctive intellectual movement of modern times—the so-called Enlightenment. The Enlightenment did not end, as one might gather from textbooks, with Voltaire, Gibbon, or Beccaria, with Hume, Adam Smith, or the French Encyclopedists. It extended to a climax in the final decades of the nineteenth century. The Generation of Materialism was the supreme one of Enlightenment.

Of abiding features of the Enlightenment, probably the most characteristic and most cherished was the belief in progress, and in a progress which proceeded not along a jagged line of ups and downs, with the ups only slightly exceeding the downs, but rather along a straight line steeply ascending. Such progress had originally been posited for science, education, and reform; and after two centuries it was most strikingly evident in precisely these three domains.

There had certainly been steady and glorious progress in science. Crowning the pioneer labors of Galileo and Newton were such ultimate physicists as Helmholtz and James Thomson and Röntgen; and the fruitful method of the physical sciences was now being applied with ever greater fruitfulness to the chemical and biological sciences, to the social sciences, to psychology and sociology. All phenomena, it seemed, were explicable in terms of matter and force; all were governed by mathematical and mechanical laws; and matter was so simple and so real. Science, moreover, was so practical and beneficent. Its continually multiplying applications were enabling men to converse with one another wherever they might be, to escape physical pain, to lengthen their span of life, and to possess knowledge and enjoy creature comforts beyond the experience of any philosopher or prince of previous ages.

Progress in education was quite as clear. The generation of materialism was finally realizing the hopes of eighteenth-century *philosophes* and the *projets* of French Revolutionaries; it was putting the youth of entire nations into school and teaching them to read and write and to aspire to fuller knowledge. Thereby, with increasing leisure for self-improvement and greater opportunities for higher technical education, the masses no less than the classes bade fair to assure the continuity of progress.

There was palpable progress in the reforming of government and society. Throughout central as well as western Europe, both constitutional government and personal liberty, which had once been deemed wildly revolutionary, were now usually regarded as respectably evolutionary and quite normal. Not merely Jacobins and Liberals accepted them, but likewise most Conservatives and most Marxians. Indeed, reforms were now being wrought, not violently or dictatorially in the perverse manner of a Robespierre or a Bonaparte, but intelligently by a process of enlightened free consent. Liberty was being supplemented by democracy, and the abuses of economic liberalism by a socializing state solicitude for the health and material well-being of the whole citizenry.

Progress in these and all other respects depended, the eighteenth-century champions of Enlightenment had believed, on man's proper use of his own reasoning powers, which were then assumed to be very real and very great. To the later materialistic generation of the Enlightenment, however, such confidence in rationalism might have seemed a bit naïve. In the light of the newer evolutionary conceptions of Darwinian biology and physiological psychology, one could well question whether man's "animal mind" was capable of independent direction or truly rational functioning. Yet perhaps because the men of the 1880's and 1890's were more inclined to the practical than to the theoretical, few pushed the lessons of biology and psychology to upsetting conclusions. Most of them talked and acted as if they shared the full rational faith of the men of the 1770's. But if peradventure one seriously doubted the efficacy of "pure reason" in a being akin to cave men and gorillas, and ultimately maybe to carbon compounds, one could now repose a new and livelier faith in the efficacy of the evolutionary process itself. To this, Herbert Spencer pointed the way, and Francis Galton landmarked it with eugenics, and Nietzsche with supermen. Individual men might not be so reasonable as had been imagined in the eighteenth century, but the race was evolving upward and could be assisted by science or "will" to evolve faster. In fine, evolution bolstered the generation's optimism by rendering progress automatic.

The Enlightenment from its inception had been associated not only with humanitarianism, which found progressive expression in social reform, in emancipation of slaves and serfs, in ameliorative penal and labor and health legislation. It had been associated also with the humanism of still earlier modern times—the neo-paganism of a Boccaccio, for example; the delighting in man as man, and in man's body as well as in his mind. There had been, of course, an interregnum in the sway of this humanism in the nineteenth century, especially in "mid-Victorian" England. But prudery and smug respectability proved transitory. By the 1890's a complete restoration of humanism impended. The English word "sport" passed into every other European language. Outdoor games and athletic contests multiplied and spread. Women everywhere took to bicycling. Circumlocution gave place to startling paradox, and this in turn to stark frankness. And while such literary artists as Anatole France, George Moore, and Samuel Butler inveighed against hypocrisy, the nude became once more a favorite subject of pictorial art. Here, too, one detected vitalizing progress.

To be sure, the climax of the Enlightenment was attended, as had been its initial stages, by some curious anomalies which smacked of credulity and even superstition. Just as Voltaire and Hume had had to divide popularity back in the 1770's with Mesmer and Cagliostro, so in the 1880's and 1890's multitudes of Europeans (and Americans) were not sufficiently scientific to be deterred from patronizing astrologers, palmists, or phrenologists, who still plied their lucrative professions in every sizeable town. Besides, since the astonishing exploits of the Fox sisters in America in the late 1840's, there had been a constant crescendo of spiritist séances, with mysterious mediums and strange rappings and tumultuous table-turnings. Even scientists as distinguished as Alfred Russel Wallace and Sir Oliver Lodge insisted that there must be something in all this spiritism, and in 1882 was founded at London a *Society for Psychical Research*, which over succeeding years and in voluminous reports recorded its testing of various hypotheses—"telepathy," "suggestion," "psychical radiation," "disembodied spirits." It was queer business for a generation of materialism, but in justice to the generation it should be said that the chief concern was with material manifestations (and explanations) of the "spirits."

Another and allied curiosity of the era was hypnotism. It was eighteenth-century mesmerism with Mesmer's "animal magnetism" expurgated. One no longer stroked the patient with magnets. One merely fixed him with a look. Yet there was a progressive popularity about it. It provided entertainment alike for the masses and for persons of fashion; and by many contemporary medical men and psychologists it was regarded as a phenomenon of the highest importance. One of the most popular stories of the 1890's was George Du Maurier's about Svengali's hypnotic power over Trilby.

Curious also was the attraction of would-be intellectuals to semi-esoteric cults imported into Europe from the Orient or from America. Some found a kind of escape from materialism in the gospel of Mary Baker G. Eddy and dismissed physicians to call in Christian Science "readers." Others discovered in a Syrian mystic, Abdul Baha, an up-to-date prophet, a new incarnation of the divine. Still others, following the lead of that much-traveled Russian lady, Helena Blavatsky, joined the *Theosophical Society* which she founded at New York in 1875 to propagate "the occult wisdom of the East," and which ushered in a vogue of quaintly garbed mahatmas and yogis. Despite numerous "exposures" of Madame Blavatsky and her cult,[1] the professed Theosophists in Europe numbered over 100,000 at the time of her death in 1891. Apparently there were many different ways of being enlightened and progressive.

II. GREAT EXPECTATIONS

The Enlightenment, since its beginnings in the seventeenth and eighteenth centuries, had been essentially an intellectual movement, and for long its progress had been measured chiefly by the advance of experimental science, of education and literacy, and of individual liberties and constitutional government. In the latter part of the nineteenth century, however, a new and more material measuring rod was applied—that of the machine production of goods. The Generation of Materialism saw industrial machinery on all sides, doing all sorts of work and doing it ever faster and more efficiently. Machinery was indeed dynamic, not static. By a kind of parthenogenesis, it multiplied itself; so that everybody was now minded to talk, in the manner of the enlightened Englishman described by Chesterton, "as if clocks produced clocks, or guns had families of

[1] To Blavatsky's own exposition of her doctrines, *Isis Unveiled* (New York, 1875), a major counterblast was Edmund Garrett's *Isis Very Much Unveiled* (London, 1895). One of Blavatsky's most celebrated converts, the English feminist and socialist Annie Besant, succeeded her as head of the Theosophical Society.

little pistols, or a penknife littered like a pig."[2] And the resulting output of manufactured commodities must continue to grow, it seemed fair to expect, as by a geometric progression approaching infinity.

Increase of mechanical production was tangible and statistically measurable proof of progress—and of progress in which everyone could share and from which were derivable the greatest expectations for the future. By the aid of machinery, the time should soon come, it was reasoned, when nobody need fear famine or inclement weather, when more food would be provided than could be consumed, more clothing made than could be worn, more houses built than could be inhabited. Not just the bare necessities of life would be available, but an abundance and range of luxuries, and withal a leisure and a physical health, beyond the ken of any lord of previous ages. Europe, once reputed a poor and sparse continent, was already rich and populous. The prediction did not seem too sanguine that by the turn of another century at least eight hundred million persons would be living quite comfortably and happily in Europe.

At the turn of the nineteenth century there appeared to be no serious problem about the production of wealth. Machinery was solving it. There were, admittedly, some new-found paradoxes about capitalism and some stubborn problems about the distribution of wealth. But these, too, it was confidently believed, would in time be solved. The Enlightenment had led to machinery and physical health and material wealth, and these things must inevitably lead to still greater and more diffused enlightenment, through which some sort of utopia was sure to be achieved for everybody. Not Marxians alone expected it, but the general run of intellectuals and also industrialists and statesmen. One had only to follow the latest trends of corporate enterprise and social legislation.

Material progress was spatial, as well as temporal. As it had already spread from England to the Continent, so now from Europe it was spreading fanlike to the whole world. This was, after all, the role of the newest imperialism, to Europeanize all the other continents in the sense of superimposing on their several traditional cultures the material civilization of Europe—the same science and technology, the same mechanical modes of production, the same ways of working, traveling, and living. And with common civilization over the entire globe, where could barbarians come from to destroy, or even threaten, the civilization of Europe?

An interesting index to the advancing international character of material civilization was furnished by the series of industrial expositions which had begun with the one in the Crystal Palace at Hyde Park, London, in 1851. None of those held down to and including the Vienna Exposition of 1873 was really "universal" or attended by any extraordinary number of visitors. But then, with the expansion of industry and education and the greater facilities for transport and travel brought about by the extension of railways and steamship lines, a change occurred. At the Philadelphia Exposition of 1876 the display of machinery was the largest and finest yet seen, and the visitors numbered close to ten million.

The Paris Exposition of 1878 covered sixty-six acres of the Champ de Mars, with an Avenue des Nations devoted to specimens of domestic architecture and products of almost every country in Europe (except Germany) and of several in Asia, Africa, and America, and with capstone, on the right bank of the Seine, in the bizarre Palace of the Trocadero. The visitors totaled thirteen million. Still more impressive was the Paris Exposition of 1889. This, covering seventy-two acres, drew its thirty-two million visitors to the latest miracle of steel construction, the Eiffel Tower, a thousand feet high, and especially diverted them with a faithful reproduction of a street in Cairo. Industrial America was host to the next great universal exposition, that of Chicago in 1893, with most countries represented and with plethora of side shows along a "Midway Plaisance."

Then came the Paris Exposition of 1900. It was the climax of one cycle and harbinger of another. It brought to the French capital mountains of marvelous exhibits and multitudes of awe-struck tourists from practically every country of the world, this time including Germany. It was high-lighted with magnificent electrical displays, and graced with two exquisite palaces of the fine arts and a beautiful new bridge named in honor of the Tsar Alexander III. The grounds embraced five hundred and fifty acres, and the attendance reached the amazing figure of thirty-nine million.

As civilization was becoming worldwide, why shouldn't the world have a common language? And if everything else could be manufactured, why not language? Very progressive people were as expectant of synthetic philology as of synthetic rubber, and inventors of either were not lacking. A German priest, Johann Schleyer, invented the odd-looking language of "Volapük" in 1879-1880. A first congress of its devotees was held on Lake Constance in 1884, a second at Munich in 1887, a third at the Paris Exposition of 1889. By this date there were 316 textbooks in the new language.

But in the 1890's Volapük was largely supplanted by a still newer language, the invention of a Polish Jew, Louis Lazarus Zamenhof. He published in 1887 a pamphlet entitled "La Lingvo Internacia de la Doktoro Esperanto," meaning, of course, to English-speaking people, "The International Language of Dr. Hopeful"; and Esperanto was created. It was subsequently improved and perfected, like any industrial product, and in 1898 it began to be advertised by a French Society for the Propagation of Esperanto. It was the subject of a paper read before the French Academy in 1889; and at the Paris Exposition of 1900 it was, so to speak, placed upon the world market. Great expectations were attached to the future of Esperanto.

At least to many optimists in the year 1900, a made-to-order world language was but the natural accompaniment of a trend toward a new world order which would be not only mechanically productive but spiritually pacific. One felt pretty sure of this trend as one looked back from 1900 over the preceding quarter-century. One beheld so many ripening fruits of international co-operation —the Universal Postal Union of 1875, the convention of 1883 for the standardization of patent laws and that of 1887 for uniform copyright laws, the succession of world's fairs from the Viennese of 1873 to the Parisian of 1900. What was still more reassuring, one failed to descry latterly within Europe any bloody revolution or deadly civil war or any large-scale international war. Armed conflict was now confined to "backward" areas, principally outside Europe, and was incidental to the imperialism which was Europeanizing and civilizing the world. It appeared reasonable to expect that the trend would continue, that just as the duel and the blood feud had disappeared, just as interurban and internecine warfare had ceased, so in another generation even imperialistic wars would not have to be waged. At any rate, the great civilized powers must already be too intelligent and too humane to resort to war among themselves; and besides, in the face of constantly expanding industrialization, any struggle between huge national armies equipped with the latest mechanical implements of destruction must be quite too costly and too risky. It seemed not inappropriate that the nineteenth century—and the Generation of Materialism—should culminate in the Hague Conference which discussed the limitation of armaments and established the Permanent Court of International Justice.

III. THE LURKING NEMESIS

Yet from the standpoint of a later and much more disillusioned generation, it is easy to perceive that logically, as well as chronologically, the materialistic age which opened with the Franco-Prussian War of 1870-1871 did not really close with the Hague Conference of 1899, but rather with far-flung military exploits of 1900—British battling Boers, Americans fighting Filipinos, Europe combating Chinese Boxers. The war in South Africa was no slight affair. It dragged on during the entire year of 1900, and beyond; and it required the major combined resources of Great Britain and the British Empire to beat down the Boers. To be sure, the danger of joint intervention by Germany, France, and Russia, which had alarmed London in 1899, and which, if actually realized, might have precipitated a catastrophic world war, was practically removed in 1900. Britain's rivals found a more inviting field for forceful action in China.

Nor was the subjugation of the Philippine Islands precisely a picnic for the United States. It had been comparatively easy to expel Spain in 1898; but if the American Republic was to maintain its newly won position as an imperialistic (and civilizing) World Power, it must suppress rebellious natives, who resolutely asserted the right of national self-determination and impartially damned Americans along with Spaniards. Throughout 1900 the United States waged war against the Filipinos, and not until two years later were they fully subdued.

In China, trouble had been brewing since the Japanese War of 1894-1895, and especially since the enforced lease of ports to European great powers in 1897-1898. Toward the end of 1898 the Chinese government, sharing its people's hatred of "foreign devils," ordered the strengthening and drilling of local militia companies as defense ostensibly against bandits, though actually against Europeans. These companies bore traditionally the quaint Chinese title of "Righteous and Harmonious Bands," but, by reason of the gymnastic exercises in which they indulged, they acquired the nickname of "Boxers." With official connivance, the Boxers inaugurated in the autumn of 1899 attacks upon European missionaries and Chinese converts in the province of Shantung, Germany's "sphere of influence"; and the next spring they extended their assaults and depredations along the Hankow-Peking and Tientsin-Peking railways. In vain the European powers protested. On June 10, 1900, a British admiral, with a small force of men picked from various European gunboats in the port of Taku, tried to go to the aid of foreigners in Tientsin; he met with stout Boxer opposition and was turned back. A few days later, Boxers occupied Peking, killed the German minister, and laid siege to the British legation, where other foreign ministers and residents had taken refuge. Concurrently, Boxers incited outbreaks in Manchuria, particularly along the railway which Russia was building there.

The Russian war minister, General Kuropatkin, on learning of the Boxer uprising, said: "I am very glad. This will give us an excuse for seizing Manchuria."[3] Although other members of the Tsar's government, notably Count Witte, tried to restrain the general, both the British and the Japanese governments were fearful of Russia's intentions and reluctant to have her intervene in China. Nevertheless, the British had their hands so full in South Africa

3 *The Memoirs of Count Witte* (New York, 1921), 107.

that they could not themselves undertake intervention in China on any large scale or really prevent Russia from undertaking it. And both France and Germany backed Russia's proposal that an international expedition be despatched from Europe to put down what was euphemistically styled "the Boxer insurrection," the German Emperor attaching the condition that the commander in chief should be his own favorite, the head of the German general staff, Field Marshal von Waldersee.

On July 27, 1900, William II rather outdid himself in addressing the German expeditionary contingent which was being assembled. He boldly exposed the "yellow peril," fearlessly demanded that "no quarter" be given the Chinese, and perorated with a startling metaphor: "Just as the Huns a thousand years ago, under the leadership of Attila, gained a reputation by virtue of which they still live in history, so may the German name become known in such a manner in China that no Chinese will ever again dare to look askance at a German." On August 22, amid showers of similarly electrical messages from the Kaiser, Waldersee in dazzling gold braid finally embarked for the Far East. The Field Marshal was hardly gone, however, when William II must have suffered indescribable disappointment. News reached him that Peking had already been delivered from the Boxers by a special relief column in which a Russian general took the leading part and from which German soldiers were wholly absent.

This relief column had been gotten together, as an emergency measure and without too much consultation with faraway European capitals, from among foreign marines and guards in or near China. Japan contributed most, and Russia next; Great Britain and the United States furnished petty detachments; altogether the column numbered 18,000. After relieving Tientsin, it set out thence for Peking on August 4; and ten days later, after overcoming some resistance *en route,* it fought its way into the Chinese capital and found the British legation and its valiant defenders still intact. That was the virtual end of the Boxers, although Russia carried on military operations in Manchuria through the remainder of the year, and a final peace settlement with China was not arrived at until September 1901.

The outcome of the "Boxer affair" of 1900 was hailed at the time as a triumph of international co-operation. Within four years, nevertheless, it was followed by the first war to be fought between great powers since the Franco-Prussian War of 1870-1871. This was the Russo-Japanese War of 1904-1905.

Hindsight is notoriously superior to contemporary judgment. Looking backward from 1914, or better from 1939, one can readily perceive a nemesis lurking in the era after 1871 such as was hardly perceptible at all at the fag end of that era in 1900. The nemesis had two aspects. On the one hand, the mechanistic and materialistic conception of physical science, which then seemed quite obvious and sure, and which lay at the base of most of the thinking and much of the action of the era, was proved shortly afterwards to be erroneous. Thanks to the "quantum" theory which Planck set forth in 1901, to ensuing atomic investigations, and to the work of Einstein (who was twenty-one years of age at the turn of the century), the certitudes of physical "law" eventually gave way to principles of "probability" and "relativity," and to skepticism about "mechanics," "matter," and even "causation." Apparently there were processes in nature which did not operate mechanically or according to mechanical laws. Apparently, too, matter could no longer be conceived of, in the time-honored way, as something extended in space and persistent in time, but merely as a mysterious sequence of events indistinguishable from energy and behavior. And the extraordinary discovery that the behavior of an electron was unpredictable, dealt a blow at the previously accepted doctrine of determinism. A veritable intellectual revolution would be the consequence.

On the other hand, while the ultimate scientific basis of the materialism of the generation from 1871 to 1900 was thus destined to disappear, only physicists and a few other individuals would be quick to recognize the fact or to deem it significant. Most people remained so fascinated by the passing generation's positive achievements that they continued to accept them unquestioningly as a whole and as a permanent legacy of the race.

Occasionally a doubt might be expressed, as in Kipling's line of

1897, "Lo, all our pomp of yesterday is one with Nineveh and Tyre," but certainly it required a much deeper disillusionment than any contemporary was capable of to question whether men of the era, with all its mechanical inventions and material gains, were actually any wiser or happier or clearer-eyed or more virtuous than men of pre-machine ages. For almost a full generation after 1900 the Enlightenment was all but universally assumed to be continuing. There remained the same optimism, the same reliance on machinery, the same supreme faith in material progress.

There remained, also, the popular vogue of "social Darwinism" —the incessant application of Darwin's evolutionary formula to social phenomena and human affairs, to law and religion, to classes, nations, and races. Few laymen paid serious attention to the drastic amendments which biology was making to the Darwinian formula itself, or to the strictures which isolated scholars were imposing on its general applicability, any more than they remarked the impending revolution in physical science. With the populace at large, as well as with most "social scientists," publicists, and statesmen, the errors no less than the truths of Darwinism enjoyed by 1900 a seemingly indestructible repute. For example, Karl Pearson, a popular English writer on science, declared in that year: "You may hope for a time when the sword shall be turned into the ploughshare . . . but, believe me, when that day comes mankind will no longer progress; . . . the relentless law of heredity will be controlled and guided by natural selection." Prince Bülow, who in the same year became German chancellor, wrote in like vein: "We must realize that there is no such thing as permanent peace, and must remember Moltke's words: 'Permanent peace is a dream, and not even a beautiful one, but war is an essential element of God's scheme of the world.' "

Did not nemesis decree the fulfillment of these precepts of 1900? At any rate, it was boys schooled by the Generation of Materialism who would grow up to fight the World War, and it was some of their sons who would follow supermen into the totalitarian state and into totalitarian war. This would mark the eclipse alike of liberalism and of conservatism as these had been known and fruitfully cherished during the three decades from 1871 to 1900.

BIBLIOGRAPHICAL ESSAY

(Revised as of January, 1963)

FOR the period from 1871 to 1900, national histories, rather than general histories, constitute the outstanding feature of historiography and the scattered stuff from which any synthesis has to be constructed. This is as true of economic or cultural as of political developments. They are usually set forth as British or French or German or Russian, and only incidentally as European. Within each national category there is an amazing number of highly specialized monographs—a tribute to the technological advance of printing and likewise to the mass production of scholars whose enthusiasm for "fact-finding" has been fed by the positivist heritage of the Generation of Materialism. Besides, the national state itself has latterly gone into the business of research and publication on a large scale, with the result that for the period here under discussion we have a wealth of official documents and statistics relating to almost every human activity within the framework of a particular nation. No historian or anyone else can possibly read, let alone master and appraise, all such material, both official and monographic.

The following bibliography is, therefore, a very select one. It aims merely at citing those works which have provided some data for the account of European (rather than national) history attempted in the preceding pages, or which, in the author's judgment, may throw additional light upon it.

First are listed the few general works—chiefly co-operative—which come nearest to surveying Europe as a whole during the period. Next are presented the titles of the most significant national histories. Thereafter, in order roughly corresponding to the succession of chapters in the present book, are noted the most pertinent works, both general and special, on diplomacy, constitutional government, industry, science, religion, art, etc., etc.

General Works

Vol. XI of the *New Cambridge Modern History, Material Progress and World-Wide Problems, 1870-1898,* ed. by F. H. Hinsley (Cambridge, 1962), is a fairly broad topical treatment of the period by a group of scholars, chiefly British. Other important co-operative treatments of the period include: Robert Schnerb, *Le XIXe siècle: l'apogée de l'Expansion européenne, 1815-1914,* vol. VI of *Histoire générale des civilisations* (Paris, 1955), social, economic, and intellectual; J. R. Salis, *Die historischen Grundlagen des 20. Jahrhunderts, 1871-1904,* vol. I of *Weltgeschichte der neuesten Zeit* (Zurich, 1955); Paul Schmitthenner, *Geschichte der Zeit seit 1871,* vol. V of the *Weltgeschichte* newly ed. by Wilhelm Schaefer, Arnold Reimann, and Schmitthenner (Leipzig, 1933); and vols. VIII-X of *Propyläen-Weltgeschichte,* ed. by Walter Goetz (Berlin, 1933). An elaborate *Oxford History of Modern Europe* is projected in 16 vols. under the editorship of Alan Bullock and F. W. Deakin, of which the first to appear is A. J. P. Taylor, *The Struggle for Mastery in Europe, 1848-1918* (Oxford, 1954). Another series, *University of Michigan History of the Modern World,* ed. by Allan Nevins and H. M. Ehrmann (Ann Arbor, 1958—), is projected in 15 vols., each treating of a leading nation or region with emphasis on the last two centuries. A thoughtful brief survey is J. W. Swain, *Beginning the Twentieth Century, a History of the Generation that made the War* (New York, 1933).

Much historical data, and some excellent historical articles, covering a wide range, are furnished by the great standard encyclopedias. For the period from 1871 to 1900, the 11th ed. of the *Encyclopædia Britannica,* 28 vols. (1910-1911), is vastly superior to the later editions.

Many useful articles by competent authorities, and with helpful bibliographies, are to be found in the *Encyclopedia of the Social Sciences,* 15 vols. (New York, 1930-1935), in *The Columbia Encyclopedia,* 2nd ed. (New York, 1950), in *An Encyclopedia of World History,* ed. by W. L. Langer, rev. ed. (Boston, 1952), and in the *Handwörterbuch der Staatswischenschaften,* 4th ed., 8 vols. (Jena, 1921-1929). The annual *Statistisches Jahrbuch für das deutsche Reich* (Berlin, 1880—) includes a wealth of comparative statistics of other countries. Certain well-known annuals furnish convenient and fairly detailed summaries of current events in Europe at large, as well as in the particular countries where they are published: The *Annual Register* (London, 1761—); *Europäischer Geschichtskalender* (Munich, 1861—); and *L'Année politique* (Paris, 1875—).

The well-known bibliographical *Guide to Historical Literature,* ed. by G. M. Dutcher and others for the American Historical Association (New

York, 1931), is still useful though largely superseded by the new version, ed. by G. F. Howe and others (New York, 1961). Among other aids are: L. J. Ragatz, *A Bibliography for the Study of European History, 1815-1939* (Ann Arbor, 1942, and later supplements); Alan Bullock and A. J. P. Taylor, *A Select List of Books on European History, 1815-1914* (Oxford, 1957); H. L. Roberts, ed., *Foreign Affairs Bibliography* (New York, 1955); and the *International Bibliography of Historical Sciences* (Paris, 1930—).

National Histories, Political and Economic

German. The masterly guide to German historiography, and model for all others, is, of course, Dahlmann-Waitz, *Quellenkunde der deutschen Geschichte,* 9th ed., 2 vols. (Leipzig, 1931-1932); a 10th ed. is in preparation. The best surveys in English are: K. S. Pinson, *Modern Germany, Its History and Civilization* (New York, 1954); Ralph Flenley, *Modern German History* (London, 1953); and Veit Valentin, *The German People, Their History and Civilization from the Holy Roman Empire to the Third Reich,* Eng. trans. by Olga Marx (New York, 1946). Of histories devoted more specifically to the Hohenzollern Empire, the best or most typical are: Johannes Ziekursch, *Politische Geschichte des neuen deutschen Kaiserreiches,* 3 vols. (Frankfurt, 1925-1930), republican in tone, but judicious and well documented; Adalbert Wahl, *Deutsche Geschichte von der Reichsgründung bis zum Ausbruch des Weltkriegs,* 4 vols. (Stuttgart, 1926-1936), comprehensive and scholarly; K. G. Lamprecht, *Deutsche Geschichte der jüngsten Vergangenheit und Gegenwart,* 2 vols. (Berlin, 1912-1913), treating, in the author's peculiar sociological and often suspect manner, of industrial and social developments and of inner and outer politics; Arthur Rosenberg, *The Birth of the German Republic, 1871-1918,* Eng. trans. by I. F. D. Morrow (New York, 1931), a condemnatory interpretation of Bismarck and especially of William II; W. H. Dawson, *The German Empire, 1867-1914,* 2 vols. (London, 1919), an excellent account by a liberally minded and sympathetic Englishman, whose *Evolution of Modern Germany* (London, 1908) is also illuminating on a variety of special topics; and Erich Eyck, *Das persönliche Regiment Wilhelms II, politische Geschichte des deutschen Kaiserreiches von 1890 bis 1914* (Zurich, 1948).

Bismarckian literature is very copious. The beginning of a bibliography of it has been made by Arthur Singer, *Bismarck in der Literatur* (Würzburg, 1909). Here, mention can be made of only a few of the most important titles: Bismarck's own memoirs, *Gedanken und Erinnerungen,* 2 vols. (Stuttgart, 1899), with the originally suppressed third volume (Stuttgart, 1921); the diaries, *Tagebuchblätter,* of his indefatigable attendant and secretary, Moritz Busch, 3 vols. (Leipzig, 1899); the articles written or inspired by Bismarck after his dismissal and collected in Hermann Hofmann, *Fürst Bismarck, 1890-1898,* 11th ed. (Stuttgart, 1922); Friedrich Thimme, ed., *Die gesammelten Werke von Fürst Otto von Bismarck,* 15 vols. to date (Berlin, 1929—); Heinrich von Poschinger, *Fürst Bismarck und die Parlamentarier,* 3 vols. (Breslau, 1894-1896), *und der Bundesrat, 1876-1890,* 5 vols. (Stuttgart, 1896-1901), *und die Diplomaten, 1852-1890* (Hamburg, 1900); Horst Kohl, ed., *Die politischen Reden,* 14 vols. (Stuttgart, 1892-1904); the patriotic biography by Gottlob Egelhaaf, 3rd ed. (Stuttgart, 1922); the scholarly and new standard biography by Erich Eyck, *Bismarck, Leben und Werk,* 3 vols. (Zurich, 1941-1944), with an abridged one-volume Eng. trans., *Bismarck and the German Empire* (London, 1950); and the critical revaluation by Wilhelm Mommsen, *Politische Geschichte von Bismarck bis zur Gegenwart, 1850-1933* (Frankfurt, 1935). A remarkably informing monograph on Bismarck's readiness to execute a *coup d'état* in 1890 is Egmont Zechlin, *Staatsstreichpläne Bismarcks und Wilhelms II, 1890-1894* (Stuttgart, 1929).

Biographies or memoirs of other German statesmen are frequently illuminating, for example: Hermann Oncken, *Rudolf von Bennigsen,* 2 vols. (Stuttgart, 1910), the leader of the National Liberals; Siegfried von Kardorff, *Wilhelm von Kardorff* (Berlin, 1936), the leader of the Free Conservatives; Ludwig von Pastor, *August Reichensperger,* 2 vols. (Freiburg, 1899), a founder of the Center party; Prince Chlodwig zu Hohenlohe-Schillingsfürst, *Denkwürdigkeiten der Reichskanzlerzeit,* ed. by K. A. von Müller (Stuttgart, 1931); Graf Alfred von Waldersee, *Denkwürdigkeiten,* 3 vols. (Stuttgart, 1923), diaries of the military favorite of William II in the 1890's; Philipp Fürst zu Eulenburg-Hertefeld, *Aus fünfzig Jahren* (Berlin, 1923), memoirs of William II's closest confidant; Johannes Haller, *Philip Eulenburg, the Kaiser's Friend,* Eng. trans., 2 vols. (New York, 1930); Richard Berkeley, *The Empress Frederick, Daughter of Queen Victoria* (New York, 1957), and Sir Frederick Ponsonby, ed., *Letters of the Empress Frederick* (New York, 1928), the mother of William II. There is also an invaluable dictionary of German national biography, with articles mainly by scholars of the first rank: *Allgemeine deutsche Biographie,* ed. by Rochus, Freiherr von Liliencron, etc., 56 vols. (Leipzig, 1875-1912).

German economic developments of the period are depicted in: Gustav Stolper, *German Economy, 1870-1940* (New York, 1940) and W. F. Bruck, *Social and Economic History of Germany from William II to Hitler, 1888-1938* (London, 1938), both emphasizing the continuity of state ascendancy over the economic life of the nation; Georg Steinhausen, *Deutsche Geistes- und Kulturgeschichte von 1870 bis zur Gegenwart* (Halle, 1931), maintaining that the internal economic and technical revolution from 1875 to 1900, rather than external imperialism, was responsible for Germany's break with her previous idealist tradition; A. Zimmermann, *Die Handelspolitik des deutschen Reiches, 1871-1900* (Berlin, 1901), classic treatment of German trade policy; T. von der Goltz, *Geschichte der deutschen Landwirthschaft,* 2 vols. (Stuttgart, 1902-1903); Sarah R. Tirrell, *German Agrarian Politics after Bismarck's Fall* (New York, 1951); R. H. Bowen, *German Theories of the Corporative State, with special reference to the period 1870-1919* (New York, 1949); Thorstein Veblen, *Imperial Germany and the Industrial Revolution,* new ed. by J. Dorfman (New York, 1939); W. O. Henderson, *The Zollverein* (Cambridge, 1939), an admirable monograph bringing the story of the customs union down into the period of the Hohenzollern Empire.

Austro-Hungarian. The guide to writings on the history of the Habsburg Empire is Richard Charmatz, *Wegweiser durch die Literatur der österreichischen Geschichte* (Stuttgart, 1912). The same author has also produced a pretentious political history of the empire during our period: *Österreichs innere Geschichte, 1848-1895,* 3rd ed., 2 vols. (Leipzig, 1918), and *Österreichs äussere und innere Politik von 1895 bis 1917* (Leipzig, 1918). Useful and more recent accounts are provided by A. J. May, *The Hapsburg Monarchy, 1867-1914* (Cambridge, Mass., 1951); A. J. P. Taylor, *The Hapsburg Monarchy, 1809-1918,* 2nd ed. (London, 1948); and Hugo Hantsch, *Die Geschichte Österreichs,* vol. II, *1648-1918,* 2nd ed. (Graz, 1955); Albert Fuchs, *Geistige Strömungen in Österreich, 1867-1918* (Vienna, 1949). The most thorough and judicious treatment of the nationalities problem is R. A. Kann, *The Multinational Empire: Nationalism and National Reform in the Habsburg Monarchy, 1848-1918,* 2 vols. (New York, 1950). The standard treatment of the constitutional relationship between Austria and Hungary is Louis Eisenmann, *Le compromis austro-hongrois de 1867, étude sur le dualisme* (Paris, 1904), and a standard text on subsequent Austrian public law is Alfons Huber, *Oesterreichische Reichsgeschichte: Geschichte der Staatsbildung und des öffentlichen Rechts,* 2nd rev. ed. by A. Dopsch (Vienna, 1901). Noteworthy biographies are: Joseph Redlich, *Emperor Francis Joseph of Austria,* Eng. trans. (New York, 1929); Otto Ernest, *Franz Joseph as Revealed by his Letters,* Eng. trans. (London, 1927); and a variety of others in Anton Bettelheim, ed., *Neue österreichische Biographie, 1815-1918,* 3 vols. (Vienna, 1923-1925).

On Hungary note may be made of the strongly nationalist ten-volume co-operative *History of the Magyar Nation* [in Hungarian], ed. by Sandor Szilágyi (Budapest, 1895-1898); the almost as nationalist two-volume *Political Evolution of the Hungarian Nation* by C. M. Knatchbull-Hugesson, Baron Brabourne (London, 1908); Count Paul Teleki, *The Evolution of Hungary* (New York, 1923), with an important bibliographical appendix by Charles Feleky; D. G. Kosáry, *A History of Hungary* (Cleveland, N. Y., 1941); Louis Eisenmann, *La Hongrie contemporaine, 1867-1918* (Paris, 1921), excellent on the political side; and Sandor Jasznigi, *Das geistige Ungarn, biographisches Lexikon,* 2 vols. (Vienna, 1918), a biographical dictionary for Hungary. For the country's economic position, useful data are supplied by A. von Matlekovits, *Das Königreich Ungarn volkswirtschaftlich und statistisch dargestellt,* 2 vols. (Leipzig, 1900).

On the nationalities problem in Austria-Hungary, see also the bibliography under Chapter VII, below.

English. The national history of England from 1871 to 1900 is recounted, in whole or in part, in almost a superfluity of volumes: R. C. K. Ensor, *England, 1870-1914,* in the "Oxford History" (Oxford, 1936), comprehensive treatment of political, economic, social, and cultural factors; David Thomson, *England in the 19th Century,* being vol. VIII of the Pelican History of England (Harmondsworth, 1955), brief but interesting; G. M. Trevelyan, *British History in the 19th Century and After,* 2nd ed. (London, 1937), G. M. Trevelyan, *British History in the Nineteenth Century* (London, 1922), well-written, chiefly political; Sir J. Marriott, *England since Waterloo* and *Modern England, 1885-1932, a History of My Own Times,* vols. VII and VIII in the series ed. by Charles Oman (London, 1912, 1934); G. M. Young, *Victorian England, Portrait of an Age* (New York, 1954), an "Anchor" book; H. W. Paul, *A History of Modern England,* 5 vols. (London, 1904-1906), covering years from 1846 to 1895, lively style with some shrewd judgments; Justin McCarthy, *A History of Our Own Times,* 7 vols. (London, 1880-1909), contemporaneous narrative by a liberal parliamentarian; Sir Spencer Walpole, *The History of Twenty-Five Years, 1856-1880,* 4 vols. (London, 1904-1908), urbane and optimistic; Esmé Wingfield-Stratford, *The Victorian Sunset* (London, 1932), "debunking"; Elie Halévy, *Histoire du peuple anglais au XIXe siècle: Epilogue,* vol. I, *Les Impérialistes au pouvoir, 1895-1905* (Paris, 1926), a lucid synthesis; Sir Ernest Barker, *Political Thought in England from 1848 to 1914,* 2nd ed. (London, 1950). Somewhat more specialized are: Helen M. Lynd, *England in the 1880's* (New York, 1945), on the socializing drift; E. P. Cheyney, *Modern English Reform, from Individualism to Socialism* (Philadelphia, 1931); and E. Guyot, *Le socialisme et l'évolution de l'Angleterre contemporaine, 1880-1911* (Paris, 1913).

Biographies of all Englishmen of note of the period are included in the monumental *Dictionary of National Biography,* ed. by Leslie Stephen and Sir Sidney Lee, 63 vols. (London, 1885-1900), with numerous supplements: 3 vols. (1901), 22 vols. (1908-1909), 5 vols. (to 1940), etc. Among innumerable separate biographies and memoirs, the following are particularly pertinent and valuable: G. E. Buckle, ed., *Letters of Queen Victoria,* 2nd series, 1862-1885, 3 vols. (London, 1926-1928), and 3rd series, 1886-1901, 3 vols. (London, 1930-1932); E. F. Benson, *Queen Victoria* (London, 1935), respectful; Lytton Strachey, *Queen Victoria* (New York, 1921), quite disrespectful; W. F. Monypenny and G. E. Buckle, *Life of Benjamin Disraeli, Earl of Beaconsfield,* 6 vols. (London, 1910-1920); Hesketh Pearson, *Dizzy, Life and Nature of Benjamin Disraeli* (London, 1951), amusing; John Viscount Morley, *The Life of William Ewart Gladstone,* 3 vols. (London, 1903); W. P. Hall, *Mr. Gladstone* (New York, 1931); Sir Philip Magnus, *Gladstone* (London, 1954), now the best biography of the Liberal leader; Philip Guedalla, *The Queen and Mr. Gladstone* (Garden City, 1934); F. W. Hirst, *Gladstone as a Financier and an Economist* (London, 1931); Paul Knaplund, *Gladstone and Britain's Foreign Policy* (New York, 1927); T. P. O'Connor, *Memoirs of an Old Parliamentarian,* 2 vols. (London, 1929); G. M. Trevelyan, *The Life of John Bright* (London, 1913); Lady Gwendolen Cecil, *Life of Robert, Marquis of Salisbury,* 4 vols. to 1892 (London, 1921-1932); J. L. Garvin and Julian Amery, *Life of Joseph Chamberlain,* 4 vols. to 1903 (London, 1932-1951); Stephen Gwynn and Gertrude Tuckwell, *Life of the Right Honorable Sir Charles W. Dilke,* 2 vols. (London, 1917); W. S. Churchill, *Lord Randolph Churchill,* 2 vols. (London, 1906); A. G. Gardiner, *Life of Sir William Harcourt,* 2 vols. (London, 1923).

For the economic history of England: G. R. Porter, *The Progress of the Nation, in its various social and economical relations, from the beginning of the nineteenth century,* rev. ed. brought up to date by F. W. Hirst (London, 1912), invaluable handbook of statistical information regarding population, pauperism, emigration, education, trade, manufacturing, currency, banking, taxation, etc.; A. L. Bowley, *Wages and Income in the United Kingdom since 1860* (Cambridge, 1937), a standard and indispensable work; J. H. Clapham, *An Economic History of Modern Britain,* vol. II, *Free Trade and Steel,* 1850-1886, and vol. III, *Machines and National Rivalries,* 1887-1914 (Cambridge, 1932-1938), a masterpiece of research and writing; L. C. A. Knowles, *The Industrial and Commercial Revolutions in Great Britain during the Nineteenth Century,* 4th rev. ed. (London, 1926), well-balanced discussion; Pauline Gregg, *A Social and*

Economic History of Britain, 1760-1955, rev. ed. (London, 1956); F. C. Dietz, *Economic History of England* (New York, 1942); R. E. Prothero, Baron Ernle, *English Farming Past and Present,* 5th ed. by Sir A. D. Hall (London, 1936).

On British imperialism and on the Irish question, see the bibliographies, below, under Chapters VI and VII respectively.

French. Bibliographical aids are furnished by Pierre Caron, *Bibliographie des travaux publiés de 1866 à 1897 sur l'histoire de la France depuis 1789,* and its various continuations (Paris, 1907-1912). Louis Halphen, *L'Histoire en France depuis cent ans* (Paris, 1914), is a clear survey of nineteenth-century French historiography. The standard descriptive and statistical work is P. B. Joanne, ed., *Dictionnaire géographique et administratif de la France,* 7 vols. (Paris, 1890-1905).

Of general histories of the Third French Republic, the quantity exceeds the quality. In one way or another the following are notable: Charles Seignobos, *Le Déclin de l'empire et l'établissement de la troisième république, 1859-1875,* and *L'Evolution de la troisième république, 1875-1914,* vols. VII and VIII of Lavisse, *Histoire de France contemporaine,* the best and most detailed, though with obvious republican bias and some inaccuracies; D. W. Brogan, *France under the Republic* (New York, 1940), both sane and brilliant, though pretty strictly political; R. W. Hale, Jr., *Democratic France, the Third Republic from Sedan to Vichy* (New York, 1941), a reasonably objective survey; J. P. T. Bury, *France, 1814-1914,* 3rd rev. ed. (London, 1949), a readable sketch; Edgar Zévort, *L'Histoire de la troisième république,* 4 vols. (Paris, 1898-1901), concerned only with administrative and parliamentary details and ending with the presidency of Carnot; Gabriel Hanotaux, ed., *Histoire de la nation française,* 15 vols. (Paris, 1920-1929), each vol. devoted to a single topic—art, science, etc.—vol. V. by the editor, treating of *Histoire politique de 1804 à 1920,* Gambettist in outlook and more literary than factual; J. Labusquière, *Histoire socialiste, 1871-1900,* vol. XII in the series ed. by Jean Jaurès (Paris, 1909), largely partisan polemic; J. Héritier, ed., *Histoire illustrée de la troisième république,* 2 vols. (Paris, 1933), very uneven co-operative work, with good discussion of social developments in vol. II and with some refreshing viewpoints; Jean Galtier-Boissière, *Histoire de la troisième république,* 3 vols. (Paris, 1935), a Leftist recounting of various scandals, in muckraking fashion; Jacques Bainville, *La troisième république* (Paris, 1935) and Léon Daudet, *Panorama de la troisième république* (Paris, 1936), royalist tirades against the Republic; R. David, *La troisième république* (Paris, 1934), the view of a conservative republican who deplores almost everything which happened after 1870; J. E. C. Bodley, *France,* new ed. (London, 1907), interesting commentary rather than history, critical of republican politicians; Robert Burnand, *La vie quotidienne en France de 1870 à 1900* (Paris, 1847).

More specialized works include: Marcel Sibert, *La constitution de la France, 1870-1944* (Paris, 1946); Léon Cahen and Albert Mathiez, *Les lois françaises de 1815 à 1914,* 3rd ed. (Paris, 1927), a useful collection of principal legislation; A. Pilenko, *Les moeurs du suffrage universel en France, 1848-1928* (Paris, 1930), indispensable for study of French electoral procedure; Léon Jacques, *Les partis politiques sous la troisième république* (Paris, 1913), useful for party programs and organization; Maurice Deslandres, *Histoire constitutionnelle de la France,* vol. III, *L'Avènement de la troisième république* (Paris, 1937); E. S. Mason, *The Paris Commune* (New York, 1930) and F. Jellinek, *The Paris Commune of 1871* (New York, 1937), both excellent on a celebrated episode; J. T. Joughin, *The Paris Commune in French Politics, 1871-1880: the History of the Amnesty of 1880,* 2 vols. (Baltimore, 1955), also a valuable study; F. H. Brabant, *The Beginning of the Third Republic in France* (London, 1940), a distinguished monograph on the early days of the National Assembly in 1871; Jacques Goualt, *Comment la France est devenue républicaine, 1870-1875* (Paris, 1954); Gabriel Hanotaux, *Histoire de la fondation de la troisième république,* 4 vols. (Paris, 1925-1926), definitive treatment of the crucial years 1871-1876, if supplemented by Robert Dreyfus, *La république de Monsieur Thiers* (Paris, 1930), by Maurice Réclus, *L'Avènement de la troisième république* (Paris, 1930), and by D. Halévy, *La Fin des notables* (Paris, 1930) and *La république des ducs* (Paris, 1937); Émile Simond, *Histoire de la troisième république,* 4 vols. (Paris, 1913-1922), a Rightist study of the years 1887-1906, which should be checked by the series of monographs by Adrien Dansette, *Les affaires de Panama* (Paris, 1934), *L'affaire Wilson et la chute du président Grévy* (Paris, 1936), and *Le Boulangisme, 1886-1890* (Paris, 1938), and by G. Charensol, *L'affaire Dreyfus et la troisième république* (Paris, 1930), Armand Charpentier, *Histoire de l'affaire Dreyfus* (Paris, 1933), D. C. McKay, ed., *The Dreyfus Case by the Man Alfred Dreyfus and His Son Pierre Dreyfus* (New Haven, 1937), and Guy Chapman, *The Dreyfus Case: a Reassessment* (New York, 1955). Other valuable monographs include: Evelyn Acomb, *French Laic Laws, 1879-1889* (New York, 1941); T. F. Power, Jr., *Jules Ferry and the Renaissance of French Imperialism* (New York, 1944); Mildred J. Headings, *French Freemasonry under the Third French Republic;* Charlotte T. Muret, *French Royalist Doctrines since the Revolution* (New York, 1933); Albert Milhaud, *Histoire du radicalisme* (Paris, 1951).

Among numerous biographies and memoirs relating to the period, the following merit mention: Adrien Dansette, *Histoire des Présidents de la République* (Paris, 1956); H. Malo, *Thiers, 1797-1877* (Paris, 1932); J. M. S. Allison, *Monsieur Thiers* (New York, 1932); Maurice Réclus, *Jules Favre, 1809-1880* (Paris, 1912); Paul Deschanel, *Gambetta,* Eng. trans. (London, 1920); P. G. Gheusi, *La vie et la mort singulière de Gambetta* (Paris, 1932); Gabriel Hanotaux, *Mon Temps,* especially vol. II, *Gambetta et Jules Ferry* (Paris, 1938); P. de Luz, *Henri V* (Paris, 1931); *Mémoires du Duc de Broglie,* vol. I (Paris, 1938); Charles de Freycinet, *Souvenirs, 1878-1893,* 8th ed. (Paris, 1913); Geoffrey Bruun, *Clemenceau* (Cambridge, Mass., 1943); G. Michon, *Clemenceau* (Paris, 1931); Jerôme and Jean Tharaud, *La vie et la mort de Déroulède,* 2nd ed. (Paris, 1925); Georges Suarez, *Briand,* vol. I (Paris, 1938).

The best survey of French economic developments is S. B. Clough, *France, a History of National Economics, 1789-1939* (New York, 1939). Other significant general works in this field are: Gaston Jèze, *Cours de science des finances et de législation financière française,* 6th ed. (Paris, 1922); Léon Say, *Les finances de la France sous la troisième république,* 4 vols. (Paris, 1898-1901); Gaëtan Pirou, *Les doctrines économiques en France depuis 1870* (Paris, 1925); F. A. Haight, *A History of French Commercial Policies* (New York, 1941); E. O. Golub, *The Meline Tariff: French Agricultural and Nationalist Economic Policy* (New York, 1944); Émile Levasseur, *Histoire du commerce de la France,* vol. II (Paris, 1912), and by the same author, *Questions ouvrières èt industrielles en France sous la troisième république* (Paris, 1907); Georges Weill, *Histoire du mouvement social en France, 1852-1910,* 2nd ed. (Paris, 1911); Augé Laribe, *L'Évolution de la France agricole* (Paris, 1912).

Italian. A suggestive history and criticism of Italian historiography is Benedetto Croce, *Storia della storiografia italiana nel secolo decimo nono,* 2nd ed., 2 vols. (Bari, 1930). *Cinquanta anni di storia italiana,* 3 vols. (Milan, 1911) comprises valuable monographs on various aspects of Italian life from 1861 to 1911—population, army and navy, industry, commerce, finance, emigration, etc. Valuable surveys in English for the period are René Albrecht-Carrié, *Italy from Napoleon to Mussolini* (New York, 1950); Janet P. Trevelyan, *A Short History of the Italian People,* 4th rev. ed. (London, 1956); D. M. Smith, *Italy, a Modern History* (Ann Arbor, 1959), political, from 1861; Luigi Salvatorelli, *A Concise History of Italy,* Eng. trans. by Bernard Miall (New York, 1940); and C. M. S. Sprigge, *The Development of Modern Italy* (New Haven, 1944). Among major Italian works are Alfredo Comandini,

L'Italia nei cento anni del secolo XIX, vol. V, *1871-1900* (Milan, 1939); Antonio Monti, *Il Risorgimento, 1814-1914,* 2 vols. (Milan, 1948) in the series *Storia politica d'Italia delle origini ai giorni nostri;* Gioacchino Volpa, *Italia moderna,* vol. I *1815-1898,* vol. II 1898-1910 (Florence, 1943, 1952); Carlo Morandi, *I partiti politici nella storia d'Italia* (Florence, 1945). Benedetto Croce, *A History of Italy, 1871-1915,* Eng. trans. (Oxford, 1929) is a characteristic interpretation rather than a history. The *Memoirs* of Francesco Crispi, Eng. trans., 3 vols. (London, 1912-1914), are important, but partisan and not always trustworthy, and those of Giovanni Giolitti, Eng. trans. (London, 1923), are less significant for the period before 1900 than for that after. Other significant works: Robert Michels, *Italien von heute, politische und wirtschaftliche Kulturgeschichte von 1860 bis 1930,* vol. V in the series *Der Aufbau der modernen Staaten* (Zurich, 1930); Bolton King and Thomas Okey, *Italy Today,* rev. ed. (London, 1909); Epicarmo Corbino, *Annali dell' economia italiana, 1861-1900,* 4 vols. (Perugia, 1931-1934); Ernest Lémonon, *L'Italie économique et sociale, 1861-1912* (Paris, 1913); Roberto Tremelloni, *Storia recente dell' industria italiana* (Milan, 1956), since 1860.

Spanish and Portuguese. For our period, much less study has been made of the Iberian peninsula than of any other part of Europe. Among the few apposite studies of Spain are: Antonio Ballesteros y Beretta, *Historia de España y de su influencia en la historia universal,* vols. VII-VIII, 2nd ed. (Barcelona, 1943-1950); Rafael Altamira, *Historia de España y de la civilización española,* vols. V-VI (Barcelona, 1930); C. E. Chapman, *A History of Spain,* new ed. (New York, 1948), a survey based on Altamira; P. Aguado Bleye, *Manual de historia de España,* 6th ed., vol. III (Madrid, 1956), since eighteenth century; F. Soldevila Zubiburu, *Historia de España,* vol. VIII, *1873-1898* (Barcelona, 1960), Catalan; E. H. Strobel, *The Spanish Revolution, 1868-1875* (Boston, 1898), terse and too favorable to Castelar; J. A. Brandt, *Toward the New Spain* (Chicago, 1933), much better than the preceding on the revolutionary years, 1868-1874; J. B. Trend, *The Origins of Modern Spain* (Cambridge, 1934), emphasizing the enduring legacy of German-inspired Spanish liberals of the 1850's and 1860's; Charles Benoist, *Canovas del Castillo, la restauration rénovatrice* (Paris, 1930), a sympathetic biography. Helpful aids are Germán Bleiberg, ed., *Diccionario de historia de España desde sus origines hasta el fin del reinado de Alfonso XIII,* 2 vols. (Madrid, 1952, 1956), and Vicens Vives, ed., *Bibliografía histórica de España y Hispanoamérica* (Barcelona, 1953—).

H. V. Livermore, *A History of Portugal* (Cambridge, 1947), has largely superseded H. M. Stephens, *Portugal,* 4th ed. with continuation by M. A. S. Hume (London, 1908). Richard Pattee, *Portugal and the*

Portuguese World (Milwaukee, 1957) contains still later bibliographies.
Belgian. Henri Pirenne, *Bibliographie de l'histoire de Belgique,* 3rd ed.
(Brussels, 1931), and, by the same author, *Histoire de la Belgique con-
temporaine,* vol. I (Brussels, 1928); Léon van der Essen and others, *Atlas
de géographie historique de la Belgique,* 13 vols. to date (Brussels, 1919
—); J. A. Goris, ed., *Belgium* (Berkeley, 1945); Jean Deharveng, ed.,
Histoire de la Belgique contemporaine, 1830-1914, 3 vols. (1928-1930),
contributions by specialists; Louis Bertrand, *Histoire de la démocratie et
du socialisme en Belgique depuis 1830* (Brussels, 1906); Comte Louis de
Lichtervelde, *Léopold of the Belgians,* Eng. trans. (New York, 1929).
On Luxembourg: Arthur Herchen, *Manuel d'histoire nationale,* 5th ed.
(Luxembourg, 1947).
Dutch. P. J. Blok, *Geschiedenis van het nederlandsche Volk,* vol. VIII
(Groningen, 1908), of which the Eng. trans., *History of the People of
the Netherlands* (New York, 1912) omits most of the social and cultural
sections; Jan A. van Houtte, ed., *Algemene Geschiedenis der Neder-
landen,* vol. X, *1840-1885,* vol. XI, *1885-1914* (Utrecht, 1949-1956); B.
H. M. Vlekke, *Evolution of the Dutch Nation* (New York, 1945).
Swiss. Wilhelm Oechsli, *Geschichte der Schweiz im neunzehnten
Jahrhundert,* vol. II (Leipzig, 1913); Hans Schneider, *Geschichte des
schweizerischen Bundestaates, 1848-1918* (Stuttgart, 1931); E. Fueter,
Die Schweiz seit 1848 (Leipzig, 1928), stressing social forces; *Dictionnaire historique et biographique de la Suisse,* ed. by Marcel Godet and
others, 7 vols. (Neuchâtel, 1921-1936); André Siegfried, *Switzerland, a
Democratic Way of Life,* Eng. trans. (New York, 1950).
Scandinavian. B. A. Arneson, *The Democratic Monarchies of Scandi-
navia* (New York, 1939); Povl Drachmann and Harold Westergaard,
*Industrial Development and Commercial Policies of the Three Scandi-
navian Countries* (Oxford, 1915); Aage Friis and others, *Det danske
folks Historie,* vol. VII (Copenhagen, 1928); Knut Gjerset, *History of
Iceland* (New York, 1924); Emil Hildebrand, ed., *Sveriges historia,* new
ed., vol. XIII (Stockholm, 1945); Ingvar Andersson, *A History of Sweden,*
Eng. trans. by Carolyn Hannay (New York, 1956); A. A. Stromberg, *A
History of Sweden* (New York, 1931); Karen Larsen, *A History of
Norway* (Princeton, 1948); Knut Gjerset, *History of the Norwegian
People,* 2nd ed. (New York, 1932); J. E. W. Sars, *Norges politiske His-
torie, 1814-1884,* vol. VI in the series ed. by Alexander Bugge (Chris-
tiania, 1909-1917); Björn Collinder, *The Lapps* (Princeton, 1949).
Russian. Important general histories: Karl Stählin, *Geschichte Rus-
slands,* vol. IV (Berlin, 1939), a monumental account of the reigns of
Alexander II, Alexander III, and Nicholas II, not so much concerned
with details as with major ideas and personalities, chiefly political, social,

and cultural, short on economic and nationalist developments; A. G. Mazour, *Russian Historiography*, 2nd ed. (Princeton, 1958), from eighteenth century to 1917; Alexander Kornilov, *Modern Russian History*, Eng. trans., new ed. (New York, 195 :); J. D. Clarkson, *A History of Russia* (New York, 1961), excellent; M. T. Florinsky, *Russia, a History and an Interpretation*, 2 vols. (New York, 1953); Hugh Seton-Watson, *The Decline of Imperial Russia, 1855-1914* (London, 1952); George Vernadsky, *A History of Russia*, 4th rev. ed. (New Haven, 1954); B. H. Sumner, *A Short History of Russia*, rev. ed. (New York, 1949).

More specialized works: M. M. Kovalevsky, *Russian Political Institutions* (Chicago, 1902); Anatole Leroy-Beaulieu, *The Empire of the Tsars and the Russians*, Eng. trans. from Fr., 3 vols. (London, 1902-1903), descriptive of the population, institutions, and religion; P. N. Miliukov, *Outlines of Russian Culture*, ed. by Michael Karpovich, Eng. trans., 3 vols. (Philadelphia, 1942); T. G. Masaryk, *The Spirit of Russia, Studies in History, Literature, and Philosophy*, Eng. trans. from Ger., 2 vols., rev. ed. (New York, 1955); D. S. Mirsky, *Russia, a Social History*, ed. by C. G. Seligman (London, 1931); J. F. Hecker, *Russian Sociology* (New York, 1915), containing an intelligent discussion of Slavophiles and Westernizers; George Fischer, *Russian Liberalism: from Gentry to Intelligentsia* (Cambridge, Mass., 1957); A. Yarmolinsky, *Road to Revolution, a Century of Russian Radicalism* (London, 1957); D. W. Treadgold, *The Great Siberian Migration* (Princeton, 1957); George Kennan, *Siberia and the Exile System*, abridged from original ed. of 1891, with introd. by G. F. Kennan, 2nd ed. (Chicago, 1958); J. F. Baddeley, *Russia in the Eighties* (London, 1921), interesting and instructive memoirs: V. I. Kovalevsky, ed., *La Russie à la fin du 19ᵐᵉ siècle* (Paris, 1900); K. P. Pobêdonostsev, *Reflections of a Russian Statesman*, Eng. trans. (London, 1898); Friedrich Steinmann and Elias Hurwicz, *K. P. Pobjedonoszew, der Staatsmann der Reaktion unter Alexander III* (Königsberg, 1933); *The Memoirs of Count Witte*, ed. by A. Yarmolinsky (New York, 1921), incomplete and not wholly reliable; W. von Korostowetz, *Graf Witte* (Berlin, 1929); V. I. Gurko, *Features and Figures of the Past*, Eng. trans. (London, 1939), illuminating memoirs of an important official, very anti-Witte; Richard Hare, *Pioneers of Russian Social Thought* (London, 1951).

On economic conditions and developments in the Russian Empire during our period, the following are useful: M. M. Kovalevsky, *Le Régime économique de la Russie* (Paris, 1898); Valentin Wittschewsky, *Russlands Handels-, Zoll-, und Industrie-Politik* (Berlin, 1905); M. I. Tugan-Baranovsky, *Geschichte der russischen Fabrik*, Germ. trans. from Rus. (Berlin, 1900); G. T. Robinson, *Rural Russia under the Old Régime*

(New York, 1932); James Mavor, *An Economic History of Russia*, 2nd ed., 2 vols. (London, 1925).

Ottoman and Balkan. Convenient surveys are provided by L. S. Stavrianos, *The Balkans since 1453* (New York, 1958); J. N. Dudescu, *L'Évolution économique contemporaine des pays balkaniques* (Paris, 1915), with abundant statistical data; J. S. Rouček, *Politics in the Balkans* (New York, 1939); and William Miller, *The Ottoman Empire*, 3rd rev. ed. (Cambridge, 1927), which narrates the political story not only of the empire, but of Rumania, Bulgaria, Serbia, and Montenegro.

Specifically on the Ottoman Empire there are two important general works: Nicholas Jorga, *Geschichte des osmanischen Reiches*, vol. V, 1774-1912 (Gotha, 1913), and A. Vicomte de La Jonquière, *Histoire de l'empire ottoman*, vol. II, *1862-1913* (Paris, 1914). There are also some special studies of value: J. H. A. Ubicini and J. B. Pavet de Courteille, *État présent de l'empire ottoman* (Paris, 1876), survey of imperial organization in 1875; Sir Charles N. E. Eliot, *Turkey in Europe*, 2nd ed. (London, 1908); A. Heidborn, *Manuel de droit public et administratif de l'empire ottoman*, 2 vols. (Vienna, 1908-1912); G. Pélissié du Rausas, *Le Régime des capitulations dans l'empire ottoman*, 2nd ed., 2 vols. (Paris, 1910-1911); A. O. Sarkissian, *History of the Armenian Question, 1869-1885* (Urbana, 1938); E. E. Ramsauer, *The Young Turks, Prelude to the Revolution of 1908* (Princeton, 1957); D. C. Blaisdell, *European Financial Control in the Ottoman Empire* (New York, 1929).

On Greece: E. S. Forster, *A Short History of Modern Greece, 1821-1956*, 3rd ed. (London, 1958); William Miller, *A History of the Greek People, 1821-1921* (London, 1922); Nicholas Kaltchas, *Introduction to the Constitutional History of Modern Greece* (New York, 1940); J. A. Levandis, *The Greek Foreign Debt and the Great Powers, 1821-1898* (New York, 1944).

On Rumania: Nicholas Jorga, *Geschichte des rumänischen Volkes im Rahmen seiner Staatsbildungen*, vol. II (Gotha, 1905); Frédéric Damé, *Histoire de la Roumanie contemporaine, 1822-1900* (Paris, 1900); J. S. Rouček, *Contemporary Roumania and Her Problems* (Stanford Univ., 1932), with helpful bibliography; R. W. Seton-Watson, *History of the Rumanian People* (London, 1930); H. L. Roberts, *Rumania, Political Problems of an Agrarian State* (New Haven, 1951); *Aus dem Leben König Karls von Rumänien*, 4 vols. (Stuttgart, 1894-1900); Constantin Xeni, *Take Ionescu* (Bucharest, 1932).

On Serbia: Stanoje Stanojević, *Istorija srpskoga naroda* [History of the Serb Nation], 2nd rev. ed. (Belgrade, 1910), documented political history by native scholar; Vasic Čubrilović and Vladimir Čorović, *Srbija od 1858 do 1903 godine* (Belgrade, 1938), a volume in a co-operative national history; H. W. V. Temperley, *History of Serbia* (London, 1917), very pro-Serb; R. J. Kerner, ed., *Yugoslavia* (Berkeley, 1949).

On Bulgaria: Nikola Stanev, *Histoire de Bulgarie, 1878-1912* (Paris, 1924), valuable account by native scholar; Constantin Jiraček, *Das Fürstentum Bulgarien* (Vienna, 1891); C. E. Black, *The Establishment of Constitutional Government in Bulgaria* (Princeton, 1943); H. R. Madol, *Ferdinand of Bulgaria,* Eng. trans. from Ger. (London, 1933).

Chapter I

The militarism—and armed peace—which characterized Europe after the Franco-Prussian War is illuminated by these volumes: E. A. Pratt, *The Rise of Rail-Power in War and Conquest, 1833-1914* (London, 1915); Colmar Freiherr von der Goltz, *Nation in Arms,* Eng. trans., 2nd ed. (London, 1907); Johannes Kundler, *Das deutsche Heeresetat* (Leipzig, 1930); G. A. Craig, *The Politics of the Prussian Army, 1640-1945* (New York, 1955); R. D. Challener, *The French Theory of the Nation in Arms, 1866-1939* (New York, 1955); E. M. Earle, ed., *Makers of Modern Strategy* (Princeton, 1943); Alfred Vagts, *History of Militarism* (New York, 1937), and *Defense and Diplomacy, the Soldier and the Conduct of Foreign Relations* (New York, 1956); A. J. Marder, *The Anatomy of British Sea Power, 1880-1905* (New York, 1940); Bertrand de Jouvenel, *On Power, Its Nature and the History of Its Growth,* Eng. trans. (New York, 1949).

Of all aspects of European history from 1871 to 1900, the diplomatic is the one whose source material is now most readily available and the one, therefore, which has been most thoroughly explored and debated. It would almost seem as if every historian of the period has produced at least an article on diplomatic history.

The public debate about responsibility for the World War of 1914 led first the German government, and presently the British and the French, to publish a vast deal of the diplomatic correspondence of their several foreign offices for the preceding period, and the resulting collections constitute an unusually rich store of raw material for the mills of diplomatic historians. The major collections now are *Die grosse Politik der europäischen Kabinette, 1871-1914,* ed. by Johannes Lepsius, A. Mendelssohn Bartholdy, and Friedrich Thimme, 40 vols. (Berlin, 1922-1926), of which the first sixteen cover the period to 1900; *British Documents on the Origins of War, 1898-1914,* ed. by G. P. Gooch and Harold Temperley, 11 vols. (London, 1926-1938), of which the first two are here pertinent; *Documents diplomatiques français, 1871-1914,* published by the French foreign ministry, First Series, 1871-1900, 12 vols. to 1896 (Paris, 1929—). In addition, disclosures at Vienna have been embodied in A. F. Pribram, *The Secret Treaties of Austria-Hungary, 1879-1914,* 2 vols. (Cambridge, Mass., 1920-1921), with texts; Federico Chabot is now editing a series of Italian diplomatic documents covering the years from 1861 to 1943; and various political treaties of the period (to 1891) are available in the well-known Hertslet, *Map of Europe by Treaty,* vols. III and IV (London, 1875-1891).

The most exhaustive—and "definitive"—narrative history of all this international diplomacy is W. L. Langer, *European Alliances and Alignments, 1871-1890,* 2nd ed. (New York, 1950), and *The Diplomacy of Imperialism, 1890-1902,* 2 vols. (New York, 1935). Briefer but satisfactory surveys in English are R. J. Sontag, *European Diplomatic History, 1871-1932* (New York, 1933); René Albrecht-Carrié, *A Diplomatic History of Europe since the Congress of Vienna* (New York, 1958), Part II, *The Era of Stability, 1871-1914;* and A. J. P. Taylor, *The Struggle for Mastery in Europe, 1848-1918* (Oxford, 1954). There are numerous parallel narratives by European scholars, each colored by the national predilections of its author. One of the best is Pierre Renouvin, *Histoire des relations internationales,* vol. VI, *De 1871 à 1914: l'apogée de l'Europe* (Paris, 1955).

Among a multitude of more specialized studies of diplomatic relations, the following may here be cited: *Cambridge History of British Foreign Policy,* ed. by Sir Adolphus W. Ward and G. P. Gooch, vol. III, *1866-1919* (Cambridge, 1923); G. P. Gooch, *Franco-German Relations, 1871-1914* (London, 1923); A. C. Coolidge, *The Origins of the Triple Alliance,* rev. ed. (New York, 1926); Charles Bloch, *Les relations entre la France et la Grand-Bretagne, 1871-1878* (Paris, 1955); P. B. Mitchell, *The Bismarckian Policy of Conciliation with France, 1875-1885* (Philadelphia, 1935); J. V. Fuller, *Bismarck's Diplomacy at its Zenith* (Cambridge, Mass., 1922); Federico Chabod, *Storia della politica estera italiana del 1870 al 1896,* vol. I, *Le promesse* (Rome, 1951); A. F. Pribram, *England and the International Policy of the European Great Powers, 1871-1914* (Oxford, 1931). Certain other monographs, relating to the decade of the 1890's, are listed under Chapter VIII, below.

In particular, international relations concerning the Balkans, before and after the Russo-Turkish War, have latterly been re-explored with great thoroughness: J. A. R. Marriott, *The Eastern Question, an Historical Study in European Diplomacy,* 4th ed. (Oxford, 1940); B. H. Sumner, *Russia and the Balkans, 1870-1880* (Oxford, 1937); David Harris, *A Diplomatic History of the Balkan Crisis of 1875-1878, the First Year* (Stanford Univ., 1936), and, by the same author, *Britain and the Bulgarian Horrors of 1876* (Chicago, 1939); R. W. Seton-Watson, *Disraeli, Gladstone, and the Eastern Question* (London, 1935); M. D. Stojanović, *The Great Powers and the Balkans, 1875-1878* (Cambridge, 1939); W. N. Medlicott, *The Congress of Berlin and After,* and, as a supplement, *Bismarck, Gladstone, and the Concert of Europe* (London, 1956); Hajo Holborn, *Deutschland und die Türkei, 1878-1890* (Berlin, 1926); C. L. Smith, *The Embassy of Sir William White at Constantinople, 1886-1891* (London, 1957); Edouard Driault and Michel Lhéritier, *Histoire diplomatique de la Grèce,* vol. IV, *1878-1908* (Paris, 1926).

Supplementing the strictly diplomatic histories, some enlightening histories of "public opinion" have appeared: E. M. Carroll, *French Public Opinion and Foreign Affairs, 1870-1914* (New York, 1931), and, by the same author, *Germany and the Great Powers, 1866-1914* (New York, 1938); W. G. Wirthwein, *Britain and the Balkan Crisis, 1875-1878* (New York, 1935); R. J. Sontag, *Germany and England, Background of Conflict, 1848-1894* (New York, 1938); O. J. Hale, *Publicity and Diplomacy, with special reference to England and Germany, 1890-1914* (New York, 1940); Pauline R. Anderson, *The Background of Anti-English Feeling in Germany, 1890-1901* (Washington, 1939).

Additional memoirs and biographies of special interest: Ferdinand Graf von Beust, *Memoirs,* Eng. trans., 2 vols. (London, 1887); Eduard Wertheimer, *Graf Julius Andrássy,* 3 vols. (Stuttgart, 1910-1913); Winifred Taffs, *Ambassador to Bismarck, Lord Odo Russell* (London, 1938); Sir Edwin Pears, *Forty Years in Constantinople, 1873-1915* (London, 1916); Sir Thomas Barclay, *Thirty Years, Anglo-French Reminiscences* (Boston, 1914); Baron Roman Rosen, *Forty Years of Diplomacy,* 2 vols. (New York, 1922); Prince Bernhard von Bülow, *Memoirs,* Eng. trans., vol. I, 1897-1903 (Boston, 1931); Gaetano Salvemini, *La Politica estera di Francesco Crispi* (Rome, 1919), antidote to Crispi's *Memoirs;* C. W. Porter, *The Career of Théophile Delcassé* (Philadelphia, 1936).

Chapter II

There is no adequate history of liberalism, whether "general" or "sectarian." Guido de Ruggiero, *The History of European Liberalism,* Eng. trans. (London, 1927) is too partial to the radical intellectual variety; and H. J. Laski, *The Rise of Liberalism, the Philosophy of a Business Civilization* (New York, 1936) is too fragmentary and too partial to a Marxian interpretation. Luis Diez del Corral, *El Liberalismo Doctrinario* (Madrid, 1945) is an elaborate and highly critical Spanish work. The best available brief introductions to the general subject are J. S. Schapiro, *Liberalism, Its Meaning and History* (Princeton, 1958), an "Anvil" booklet, and T. M. Greene, *Liberalism, Its Theory and Practice* (Austin, 1957). Among peripheral studies may be cited: Alan Bullock and Maurice Shock, eds., *The Liberal Tradition from Fox to Keynes* (London, 1956), English source material; Roscoe Pound, *The Development of Constitutional Guarantees of Liberty* (Oxford, 1957); J. Heyderhoff and Paul Wentzcke, eds., *Deutscher Liberalismus im Zeitalter Bismarcks,* 2 vols. (Bonn, 1926); Karl Eder, *Der Liberalismus in Altösterreich: Geisteshaltung, Politik und Kultur* (Vienna, 1955).

Liberal "thought" of the period is expounded, usually with much else, in a variety of works: G. H. Sabine, *A History of Political Theory,* new ed. (New York, 1950); Yves Simon, *Philosophy of Democratic Government* (Chicago, 1951); Crane Brinton, *English Political Thought in the Nineteenth Century,* new ed. (Cambridge, Mass., 1949); R. H. Soltau, *French Political Thought in the Nineteenth Century* (New Haven, 1931); C. T. Muret, *French Royalist Doctrines since the Revolution* (New York, 1933); H. A. L. Fisher, *The Republican Tradition in Europe* (London, 1911). How "liberal" was the "conservatism" of the era, at least in England, may be gathered from F. J. C. Hearnshaw, *Conservatism in England, an analytical, historical, and political survey,* (London, 1932).

On the political aspect of liberalism—that of constitutional government—the historical output has been large and weighty. The constitutions of the era are conveniently assembled in W. F. Dodd, *Modern Constitutions, a Collection of the Fundamental Laws of Twenty-Two of the most important Countries,* 2 vols. (Chicago, 1909). The first edition of F. A. Ogg, *The Governments of Europe* (New York, 1913) provides a better synopsis of the constitutions in force in 1900 than does any later edition of the same work. On the parliamentary governments and parties of the various nations, the following are valuable: A. L. Lowell, *The Government of England,* new ed., 2 vols. (London, 1916), and *Governments and Parties in Continental Europe,* 5th ed., 2 vols. (Boston, 1900); A. V. Dicey, *Introduction to the Study of the Law of the Constitution,* 9th ed. by E. C. S. Wade (London, 1939), a famous Whig commentary on the English constitution as it was in the later Victorian years, and, by the same author, the suggestive *Lectures on the Relation between Law and Public Opinion in England during the Nineteenth Century,* 2nd ed. (London, 1914); J. A. Thomas, *The House of Commons, 1832-1901, a Study of Its Economic and Functional Character* (Cardiff, 1939), containing tabulations of economic interests of British

M. P.'s; W. R. Sharp, *The Government of the French Republic* (New York, 1938); Joseph Barthélemy, *Le gouvernement de la France*, 3rd rev. ed. (Paris, 1939), by leading French authority; Léon Duguit, *Traité de droit constitutionnel*, 2nd ed., 4 vols. (Paris, 1921-1925), the most elaborate discussion of French theory and practice; P. Laband, *Staatsrecht des deutschen Reiches*, 5th ed., 4 vols. (Tübingen, 1911-1914), standard for the Hohenzollern Empire; R. C. Brooks, *Government and Politics of Switzerland* (Yonkers, 1918); D. V. Verney, *Parliamentary Reform in Sweden, 1866-1921* (Oxford, 1957); H. F. Gosnell, *Why Europe Votes* (Chicago, 1930); R. H. Soltau, *French Parties and Politics, 1871-1921* (London, 1922); Friedrich Meinecke, *Deutscher Staat und deutsche Parteien* (Munich, 1922); Felix Salomon, ed., *Die deutschen Parteiprogramme*, 3rd ed., 3 vols. (Leipzig, 1920).

Chapter III

The best surveys of industrial development during our period are: S. B. Clough and C. W. Cole, *Economic History of Europe*, 3rd ed. (Boston, 1952); Herbert Heaton, *Economic History of Europe*, rev. ed. (New York, 1948); E. L. Bogart, *Economic History of Europe, 1760-1939* (London, 1942); Witt Bowden, Michael Karpovich, and A. P. Usher, *An Economic History of Europe Since 1750* (New York, 1937). A fuller account is presented in L. C. A. Knowles, *Economic Development in the Nineteenth Century: France, Germany, Russia, and the Uinted States* (London, 1932), and, for two important countries, in J. H. Clapham, *The Economic Development of France and Germany, 1815-1914*, 4th ed. (London, 1936). For individual countries, see titles of economic works listed under *National Histories*, above.

For the progress of technology in general, see A. P. Usher, *A History of Mechanical Inventions*, 2nd ed. (Cambridge, Mass., 1954); René Dugas, *A History of Mechanics* (New York, 1957); J. U. Nef, *War and Human Progress, an Essay on the Rise of Industrial Civilization* (Cambridge, Mass., 1950).

On transportation: C. E. R. Sherrington, *A Hundred Years of Inland Transportation, 1830-1933* (London, 1934), an authoritative study; L. G. McPherson, *Transportation in Europe* (New York, 1910); W. T. Jackman, *The Development of Transportation in Modern England*, 2 vols. (Cambridge, 1916); J. G. H. Warren, *A Century of Locomotive Building by Robert Stephenson & Co., 1823-1923* (Newcastle, 1923); E. Kech, *Geschichte der deutschen Eisenbahnpolitik* (Leipzig, 1911); Lord Monkswell, *French Railways* (London, 1911); Great Britain, Board of Trade, *Merchant Shipping, 1901, Table Showing the Progress of Merchant Ship-*

ping in the United Kingdom and the Principal Maritime Countries,
House of Commons Reports and Papers, 329 (London, 1902); J. D.
Whelpley, *The Trade of the World* (New York, 1913); A. W. Kirkaldy,
British Shipping, Its History, Organization, and Importance (London,
1914); D. B. Tyler, *Steam Conquers the Atlantic* (New York, 1939);
Rollo Appleyard, *Charles Parsons, His Life and Work* (London, 1933);
André Siegfried, *Suez and Panama,* Eng. trans. (New York, 1940); St.
John C. Nixon, *The Antique Automobile* (London, 1956); C. L. M.
Brown, *The Conquest of the Air* (London, 1927); Hugo Eckner, *Graf
Zeppelin, sein Leben* (Stuttgart, 1938).

On textile and other industries: M. S. Woolman and E. B. McGown,
Textiles, a Handbook for the Student and the Consumer (New York,
1916); G. von Schulze-Gävernitz, *Cotton Trade in England and on the
Continent* (London, 1895); R. M. R. Dehn, *The German Cotton Industry* (Manchester, 1913); R. B. Forrester, *The Cotton Industry in
France* (Manchester, 1921); J. H. Clapham, *The Woollen and Worsted
Industries* (London, 1907); D. L. Burn, *The Economic History of Steel-
making, 1867-1939* (Cambridge, 1940); G. I. H. Lloyd, *The Cutlery
Trades* (London, 1913); B. Lepsius, *Deutschlands chemische Industrie,
1888-1913* (Berlin, 1914); A. D. Spicer, *The Paper Trade* (London,
1907); C. F. Marsh, *Reinforced Concrete* (New York, 1904).

The outstanding historical treatment of industrial capitalism is Werner
Sombart, *Der moderne Kapitalismus,* 4th ed., 3 vols. in 6 parts (Munich,
1921-1928), supplemented by the same author's *Wirtschaftsleben im
Zeitalter des Hochkapitalismus,* 2 vols. (Tübingen, 1928). The former
of these works has been cleverly and faithfully condensed in an English
version: F. A. Nussbaum, *A History of the Economic Institutions of
Modern Europe* (New York, 1933). Other comparable works on the
same subject are Henri Sée, *Modern Capitalism,* Eng. trans. (New York,
1928), and J. A. Hobson, *The Evolution of Modern Capitalism,* new
rev. ed. (London, 1926). Different aspects of capitalistic development
are treated in: G. W. Edwards, *The Evolution of Finance Capitalism*
(New York, 1939); F. W. Hirst, *The Stock Exchange* (London, 1911);
A. Andréadès, *History of the Bank of England,* Eng. trans., 3rd ed.
(London, 1935); Karl Helfferich, *Georg von Siemens,* 3 vols. (Berlin,
1923), detailed biography of a prominent German banker; L. H. Jenks,
Migration of British Capital, to 1875, 2nd ed. (New York, 1938);
Herbert Feis, *Europe, the World's Banker, 1870-1914, an Account of
European Foreign Investment and the Connection of World Finance with
Diplomacy before the War* (New Haven, 1930); H. D. White, *The
French International Accounts, 1880-1913* (Cambridge, Mass., 1933).

The era's trend toward industrial combination is described in: J. W. Jenks, *Industrial Combinations in Europe*, vol. XVIII of U. S. Industrial Commission (Washington, 1901); A. Plummer, *International Combines in Modern Industry*, 2nd ed. (New York, 1938); R. Liefmann, *Kartelle, Konzerne, und Trusts*, Eng. trans. (New York, 1932); A. H. Stockder, *Regulating an Industry, the Rhenish-Westphalian Coal Syndicate, 1893-1929* (New York, 1932). Prosperity and depression are discussed in Joseph Schumpeter, *Business Cycles, a Theoretical, Historical, and Statistical Analysis of the Capitalist Process*, Eng. trans., 2 vols. (New York, 1939); Wesley Mitchell, *Business Cycles, the Problem and Its Setting* (New York, 1927); Sir William Beveridge, *Unemployment, a Problem of Industry*, 4th ed. (London, 1930). On the question of the gold standard: J. H. Curle, *The Goldmines of the World*, 3rd rev. ed. (London, 1905); L. Darwin, *Bimetallism* (London, 1897), most balanced contemporaneous discussion; N. G. Pierson, *Principles of Economics*, Eng. trans., vol. I (London, 1907), containing best short account of the monetary history of the later nineteenth century, by a Dutch scholar.

On urban growth and life and on emigration: A. F. Weber, *The Growth of Cities in the Nineteenth Century* (New York, 1899); Charles Booth and others, *Life and Labour of the People in London*, 18 vols. (London, 1903), a monument of sociological inquest; Émile Levasseur, *La Population française*, 3 vols. (Paris, 1889-1892), including full analysis of nineteenth-century French vital statistics; R. Gonnard, *L'Émigration européenne au XIXe siècle* (Paris, 1906); J. D. Whelpley, *The Problem of the Immigrant* (London, 1905); H. P. Fairchild, *Immigration, a World Movement and its American Significance*, rev. ed. (New York, 1933); F. Foerster, *The Italian Emigration of Our Times* (Cambridge, 1919); W. F. Adams, *Ireland and Irish Emigration to the New World* (New Haven, 1932); S. Joseph, *Jewish Immigration to the United States from 1881 to 1910* (New York, 1914); P. Berne, *L'Immigration européenne en Argentine* (Paris, 1915).

An excellent encyclopedia on science and scientists of the era is Eugen Korschelt and others, *Handwörterbuch der Naturwissenschaften*, 2nd ed., 10 vols. (Jena, 1931-1935). See also F. S. Taylor, *The Century of Science* (London, 1941). The development of medical science is traced in Charles J. Singer, *A Short History of Medicine* (Oxford, 1928); R. H. Shryock, *The Development of Modern Medicine, an Interpretation of the Social and Scientific Factors Involved*, new ed. (Philadelphia, 1947); C. D. Haagensen and W. E. B. Lloyd, *A Hundred Years of Medicine*, rev. ed. (New York, 1943); B. J. Stern, *Social Factors in Medical Progress* (New York, 1927); M. E. M. Walker, *Pioneers of*

Public Health (London, 1930). In addition, there are several noteworthy biographies of leading contributors to medical science: R. J. Dubos, *Louis Pasteur, Free Lance of Science* (London, 1951); W. W. Cheyne, *Lister and His Achievement* (London, 1925); C. Posner, *Rudolf Virchow*, 2nd ed. (Vienna, 1921); Karl Wezel, *Robert Koch* (Leipzig, 1912).

The chief manual for the general history of physical and biological science is W. T. Sedgwick and H. W. Tyler, *A Short History of Science*, rev. ed. (New York, 1939), and the most illuminating account is Sir William C. Dampier, *A History of Science in its Relations with Philosophy and Religion*, 4th ed. (Cambridge, 1948). Specifically on physical science, the standard text is F. Cajori, *History of Physics*, rev. ed. (New York, 1929), and on chemistry, Eduard Farber, *The Evolution of Chemistry* (New York, 1955) and F. S. Taylor, *A History of Industrial Chemistry* (London, 1957).

On biology and Darwinian evolution: Charles J. Singer, *A History of Biology*, rev. ed. (New York, 1950); G. G. Simpson, *The Meaning of Evolution* (New Haven, 1949); Geoffrey West, *Charles Darwin, a Portrait* (New Haven, 1938), one of the best of innumerable lives of the evolutionist; Sir P. C. Mitchell, *Thomas Henry Huxley* (New York, 1900); W. Bölsche, *Ernst Haeckel*, Eng. trans. (London, 1906); August Weismann, *The Evolution Theory*, Eng. trans. (London, 1904); Karl Pearson, *National Life from the Standpoint of Science* (London, 1901), which means, in this case, from the standpoint of racial and social Darwinism; Hugo Iltis, *Life of Mendel* (New York, 1932).

On physiological psychology: E. G. Boring, *A History of Experimental Psychology*, 2nd ed. (New York, 1950); H. G. Kurella, *Cesare Lombroso, a Modern Man of Science*, Eng. trans. (London, 1911).

The materialism and mechanism of the era are explicit or implicit, in a rather eulogistic manner, in the well-written classic, J. T. Merz, *A History of European Thought in the Nineteenth Century*, 2nd ed., 4 vols. (Edinburgh, 1912-1928). More questioning works on the subject are F. A. Lange, *The History of Materialism and Criticism of its Present Importance*, Eng. trans., 3rd ed. (New York, 1950); Karl Löwith, *Von Hegel bis Nietzsche* (Zurich, 1941); Ernst Mach, *Die Mechanik in ihrer Entwicklung historisch-kritisch dargestellt*, 9th ed. (Leipzig, 1933), with abridged Eng. trans. as *The Science of Mechanics* by T. J. McCormack, 5th ed. (La Salle, 1942); and with particular brilliance, Jacques Barzun, *Darwin, Marx, Wagner, the Fatal Legacy of "Progress,"* 2nd ed. (New York, 1954).

Strangely enough, little specific study has been devoted to the history of positivism and its manifold influence in our era. There is a monograph on English positivism as a religion: J. E. McGee, *A Crusade for Humanity, the History of Organized Positivism in England* (London, 1931); and there is a bibliography in Italian by F. Valsecchi (Milan, 1957). Positivist influence on the social sciences can be gathered from such notable works as Charles Gide and Charles Rist, *History of Economic Doctrines,* Eng. trans., 2nd ed. (Boston, 1948); G. P. Gooch, *History and Historians in the Nineteenth Century,* new ed. (New York, 1952); Pieter Geyl, *From Ranke to Toynbee* (Northampton, Mass., 1952); Antoine Guilland, *Modern Germany and Her Historians,* Eng. trans. (London, 1915); Rudolph Metz, *A Hundred Years of British Philosophy,* Eng. trans. (Cambridge, 1938); Crane Brinton, *Ideas and Men: the Story of Western Thought* (New York, 1950).

Chapter IV

The principal reference books on religion are *The Catholic Encyclopedia,* ed. by C. G. Herbermann and others, 15 vols. (New York, 1907-1912), now being drastically revised and supplemented; *Realencyklopädie für protestanische Theologie und Kirche,* ed. by J. K. Herzog and Albert Hauck, 3rd ed., 24 vols. (Leipzig, 1896-1913); *Encyclopædia of Religion and Ethics,* ed. by James Hastings and others, 13 vols. (Edinburgh, 1908-1927); V. T. A. Ferm, *A Protestant Dictionary* (New York, 1951); *Encyclopædia Judaica,* 10 vols. through letter L (Berlin, 1928-1934); H. A. R. Gibb and J. H. Kramers, *Shorter Encyclopædia of Islam* (Ithaca, 1957); *Die Religion in Geschichte und Gegenwart,* ed. by H. Gunkel and L. Zscharnack, 2nd ed., 6 vols. (Leipzig, 1927-1932); Christopher Dawson, *Religion and Culture* (London, 1947).

K. S. Latourette, *Christianity in a Revolutionary Age, a History of Christianity in the Nineteenth and Twentieth Centuries,* of which three vols. of the total five are here pertinent, *The 19th Century in Europe: Background and the Roman Catholic Phase* (New York, 1958), *The Protestant and Eastern Churches* (1959), *The 19th Century outside Europe, 1815-1914* (1961), a notably comprehensive work by a distinguished Protestant scholar; Fernand Mourret, *History of the Catholic Church,* Eng. trans. by Newton Thompson, vol. V (St. Louis, 1955), a standard Catholic work; J. H. Nichols, *History of Christianity, 1650-1950: Secularization of the West* (New York, 1956), part III, *1870-1914,* a brief Protestant survey; Philip Hughes, *A Popular History of the Catholic Church,* 3rd rev. ed. (London, 1947), a brief Catholic survey.

Illuminating on the "warfare" between science and theology: A. D. White, *Autobiography*, 2 vols. (New York, 1905); Sir Edmund Gosse, *Father and Son*, 10th ed. (London, 1930); Basil Willey, *More Nineteenth-Century Studies: a Group of Honest Doubters* (New York, 1956); Ferdinand Buisson, *La Foi laïque, 1878-1911* (Paris, 1913); Crane Brinton, *Nietzsche* (Cambridge, Mass., 1941); H. de Dorlodot, *Darwinism and Catholic Thought*, Eng. trans. (London, 1914); Arnold Lunn and J. B. S. Haldane, *Science and the Supernatural* (New York, 1935).

On "Church and State": J. N. Figgis, *Churches in the Modern State*, 2nd ed. (London, 1914); S. W. Baron, *Modern Nationalism and Religion* (New York, 1947); Georg Franz, *Kulturkampf: Staat und Katholische Kirche in Mitteleuropa* (Munich, 1956); Georges Goyau, *Bismarck et l'église, le Culturkampf, 1870-1887*, 4 vols. (Paris, 1911-1913); Karl Bachem, *Vorgeschichte, Geschichte, und Politik der deutschen Zentrumspartei*, vols. III-VI, *1870-1906* (Cologne, 1927-1930); E. Hüsgen, *Ludwig Windthorst*, 2nd ed. (Cologne, 1911); Adrien Dansette, *Histoire religieuse de la France sous la IIIᵉ République*, rev. ed., 2 vols. (Paris, 1948-1951); S. W. Halperin, *Italy and the Vatican at War, a Study of their Relations from the Outbreak of the Franco-Prussian War to the Death of Pius IX* (Chicago, 1939), and, by the same author, *The Separation of Church and State in Italian Thought from Cavour to Mussolini* (Chicago, 1937); A. C. Jemolo, *Chiesa e stato in Italia dal Risorgimento ad Oggi* (Turin, 1955); Lillian P. Wallace, *The Papacy and European Diplomacy, 1869-1878* (Chapel Hill, 1948); R. Aubert, *Le pontificat de Pius IX, 1846-1878* (Paris, 1952).

On the Catholic Church and Pope Leo XIII: Count Eduardo Soderini, *Il pontificato di Leone XIII*, 3 vols. (Milan, 1932-1933), utilizing Vatican archives, with an abridged Eng. trans. by Barbara Carter, *Leo XIII* (London, 1935); Josef Schmidlin, *Papstgeschichte der neuesten Zeit*, vol. II, *Pius IX und Leo XIII, 1846-1903* (Munich, 1934), a monumental work, also utilizing Vatican archives; Charles Pichon, *The Vatican and Its Role in World Affairs, 1878-1946*, Eng. trans. (New York, 1950); E. Perrier, *The Revival of Scholastic Philosophy in the Nineteenth Century* (New York, 1909).

On "social Christianity": E. Troeltsch, *Die Soziallehren der christlichen Kirchen und Gruppen* (Tübingen, 1912); J. N. Moody, ed., *Church and Society: Catholic Social and Political Thought and Movements, 1789-1950* (New York, 1953); A. M. P. Fogarty, *Christian Democracy in Western Europe, 1820-1953* (South Bend, 1957); P. T. Moon, *The Labour Movement and the Social Catholic Movement in France* (New

York, 1921); Georgiana P. McEntee, *The Social Catholic Movement in Great Britain* (New York, 1927); D. O. Wagner, *The Church of England and Social Reform since 1854* (New York, 1930); Gabriele de Rosa, *L'Azione Cattolica: storia politica dal 1874 al 1919,* 2 vols. (Bari, 1953-1954); W. O. Shanahan, *German Protestants Face the Social Question,* 2 vols. (South Bend, 1956, 1963).

On the Anglican Church and newer religious movements in England: F. W. Cornish, *History of the English Church in the Nineteenth Century,* vols. VIII and IX of series ed. by W. R. Stephens and W. Hunt (London, 1899-1933); Harold Begbie, *Life of William Booth, the Founder of the Salvation Army* (London, 1920).

On the Eastern Orthodox Church: Adrian Fortescue, *The Orthodox Eastern Church,* 2nd ed. (London, 1908); R. L. James, *A Dictionary of the Eastern Orthodox Church* (London, 1923); F. C. Conybeare, *Russian Dissenters* (Cambridge, Mass., 1921).

On Judaism: S. W. Baron, *The Social and Religious History of the Jews,* 8 vols. (New York, 1951-1958), of which vol. VII covers the period 1870-1900, best and most comprehensive treatment; S. M. Dubnow, *Weltgeschichte des jüdischen Volkes,* Ger. trans. from Rus., vols. IX and X (Berlin, 1929). On the Moslems: W. C. Smith, *Islam in Modern History* (Princeton, 1957); *The Shorter Encyclopedia of Islam,* ed. by H. A. R. Gibb and J. H. Kramers (Ithaca, 1957).

Much information on Christian missionary enterprise during the period may be gleaned from the Catholic biennial, published at Rome, *Missiones Catholicae cura S. Congregationis de Propagande Fide descriptae,* and from the Protestant *Encyclopædia of Missions,* ed. by H. O. Dwight and others, 3rd rev. ed. (New York, 1910). K. S. Latourette, *A History of the Expansion of Christianity,* 7 vols. (New York, 1937-1945), vol. IV on *The Great Century 1800-1914,* is the best general treatment. Specially pertinent is the same author's *History of Christian Missions in China* (New York, 1929); and likewise W. A. Young *Christianity and Civilization in the South Pacific,* (London, 1922), and G. D. Kittler, *The White Fathers* (New York, 1957) on Cardinal Lavigerie and his missioners in Africa.

The best general history of art during the period is vol. VIII of the co-operative French work ed. by André Michel, *Histoire de l'art* (Paris, 1929). See also B. S. Myers, *Art and Civilization* (New York, 1957). Scholarly articles on artists are available in Ulrich Thieme and Felix Becker, *Allgemeines Lexikon der bildenden Künstler,* 33 vols. (Leipzig, 1907-1935). E. Waldemann, *Die Künst des Realismus und des Impressionismus im XIX Jahrhundert* (Berlin, 1927), deals fairly with the major "schools" of the period. Among numerous surveys of the several arts, the following are typical: B. and B. F. Fletcher, *History of Architecture on the Comparative Method,* 7th rev. ed. (London, 1924); Richard Muther, *The History of Modern Painting,* Eng. trans., rev. ed., 4 vols. (New York, 1907); W. H. Wright, *Modern Painting* (New York, 1930); Alfred Leroy, *Histoire de la peinture française, son évolution et ses maîtres, 1800-1933* (Paris, 1934); G. G. Dehio, *Geschichte der deutschen Kunst,* 2nd ed., vol. IV (Berlin, 1934); G. H. Chase and C. R. Post, *A History of Sculpture* (New York, 1924); Louis Reau, *L'art russe de Pierre le Grand à nos jours* (Paris, 1922); P. H. Láng, *Music in Western Civilization* (New York, 1941), chaps. xvi-xix; Sir George Grove, *Dictionary of Music and Musicians,* ed. by H. C. Colles, 5th ed., 9 vols. (New York, 1955); Ernest Newman, *The Life of Richard Wagner,* 4 vols. (New York, 1933-1946), an exhaustive work, which, however, might be checked with Jacques Barzun, *Darwin, Marx, Wagner, the Fatal Legacy of "Progress"* (Boston, 1941).

Histories of literature all follow a national pattern, and few of them relate literature to contemporaneous social or intellectual developments. Among the better ones are: *Cambridge History of English Literature,* ed. by Sir A. W. Ward and A. R. Waller, vols. XII-XIV, *The Nineteenth Century* (Cambridge, 1925-1931); J. W. Cunliffe, *English Literature during the Last Half Century* (New York, 1919); G. K. Chesterton, *Victorian Age in Literature* (London, 1913), brief, but brilliant and very well related to contemporaneous intellectual currents; R. Lalou, *Histoire de la littérature française contemporaine, 1870 à nos jours,* rev. ed. (Paris, 1931); Kuno Francke, *History of German Literature as Determined by Social Forces,* 4th rev. ed. (New York, 1901); E. J. Simmons, *Outline of Modern Russian Literature* (New York, 1943); Roman Dyboski, *Modern Polish Literature* (London, 1924); Frigyes Riedl, *A History of Hungarian Literature* (New York, 1906); James Fitzmaurice-Kelly, *New History of Spanish Literature* (London, 1925). Two significant biographies: Aylmer Maude, *The Life of Tolstoy,* rev. ed., 2 vols. (Oxford, 1930); and Halvdan Koht, *Life of Ibsen,* Eng. trans., 2 vols. (New York, 1931).

Chapter V

The masses, their life, labor, and emergence, are treated, in general, in these informative or suggestive works: H. B. Lees-Smith, ed., *Encyclopaedia of the Labour Movement,* 3 vols. (London, 1927); Walter Galenson, ed., *Comparative Labor Movements* (New York, 1952); H. W.

Laidler, *Social-Economic Movements: an Historical and Comparative Survey of Socialism, Communism, Co-operation, Utopianism, and Other Systems of Reform and Reconstruction* (New York, 1944); Selig Perlman, *A Theory of the Labor Movement*, new ed. (New York, 1948); C. R. Fay, *Life and Labour in the Nineteenth Century* (London, 1920); Evelyn Anderson, *Hammer or Anvil, the Story of the German Working-Class Movement* (London, 1945); V. R. Lorwin, *The French Labor Movement* (Cambridge, Mass., 1954); W. J. Ashley, *The Progress of the German Working Class in the Last Quarter of a Century* (London, 1904); José Ortega y Gasset, *The Revolt of the Masses*, Eng. trans. (New York, 1932); G. A. Briefs, *The Proletariat, a Challenge to Western Civilization* (New York, 1937).

On trade-unionism: Sidney (Baron Passfield) and Beatrice Webb, *The History of Trade Unionism*, rev. ed. (London, 1920), authoritative for England; Henry Pelling, *The Origins of the Labour Party, 1880-1900* (London, 1954), on political activities of British trade-unionists; Emrys Hughes, *Keir Hardie* (London, 1957); W. S. Sanders, *Trade Unionism in Germany* (London, 1916); Paul Louis, *Histoire du mouvement syndical en France*, 3rd rev. ed. (Paris, 1921); Charles Cestre, *Confédération générale du travail* (Paris, 1925).

On the co-operative movement: J. F. Wilkinson, *Friendly Society Movement* (London, 1886); C. R. Fay, *Coöperation at Home and Abroad, a Description and an Analysis*, 4th ed., vol. I (London, 1939); G. J. Holyoake, *History of Coöperation in England*, 2nd ed., vol. II, 1845-1878 (London, 1906), and, by the same author, a pioneer in the movement, *Sixty Years of an Agitator's Life*, 2nd ed. (London, 1906); J. Gaumont, *Histoire générale de la coöperation en France*, 2 vols. (Paris, 1924); H. W. Wolff, *People's Banks, a Record of Social and Economic Success*, 4th rev. ed. (London, 1919); M. T. Herrick and R. Ingalls, *Rural Credits, Land and Coöperative* (London, 1914).

Works on mass education are legion, but relatively few have historical value. Paul Monroe, *A Textbook in the History of Education*, new ed. (New York, 1932), with bibliography, is the best brief introduction, along with *A Cyclopedia of Education*, ed. by him, 5 vols. in 3 (New York, 1926-1928). E. Levasseur, *L'Enseignement primaire dans les pays civilisés*, 2 vols. (Paris, 1897-1903) is a useful contemporaneous survey. E. H. Reisner, *Nationalism and Education since 1789* (New York, 1923) deals with an important constituent of popular education in France, Germany, England, and the United States. Evelyn Acomb, *Laic Legislation in France, 1878-1887* (New York, 1941) is a valuable monograph on the motivating forces, as well as on the actual laws, which reared the popular state school system of France. L. Dubreuil, *Paul Bert* (Paris, 1936) is a sympathetic study of one of the chief protagonists of that system.

On the rise of popular journalism the following shed some light: C. F. Carr and F. E. Stevens, *Modern Journalism* (London, 1931); W. G. Bleyer, *Main Currents in the History of American Journalism* (Boston, 1927); Karl Bömer, *Bibliographisches Handbuch der Zeitungswissen-schaft* (Leipzig, 1929); *The History of "The Times,"* vols. II, *1841-1884,* and III, *1884-1912* (London, 1935, 1939); Silas Bent, *Ballyhoo, the Voice of the Press* (New York, 1927); Lucy M. Salmon, *The Newspaper and Authority* (New York, 1923); R. D. Altick, *The English Common Reader, a Social History of the Mass Reading Public, 1800-1900* (Chicago, 1957).

Socialism, especially Marxism, has acquired a much greater bibliography than its actual role from 1871 to 1900 would seem to require. The best brief introduction is Thomas Kirkup, *History of Socialism,* 5th ed. rev. by E. R. Pease (London, 1920). Of the better biographies of Marx, H. J. Laski's (London, 1922) is very laudatory, and Isaiah Berlin's, 2nd ed. (London, 1948) rather critical; the commentary on Marx in Jacques Barzun, *Darwin, Marx, Wagner* (New York, 1941) is devastating. Marxism as a system of thought is appreciatively set forth by Karl Kautsky, *Economic Doctrine of Karl Marx,* Eng. trans. (London, 1925). Karl Federn, *The Materialistic Conception of History* (London, 1939) is an incisive critique of the procrustean methods employed by Marxians to force history into their "laws." A major work is G. D. H. Cole, *A History of Socialist Thought,* vols. II, *Marxism and Anarchism, 1850-1890,* and III, *The Second International, 1889-1914* (London, 1954, 1956). Another significant study is R. N. Carew Hunt, *Marxism, Past and Present* (London, 1954). Solomon Bloom, *Marx and the Society of Nations* (New York, 1941) presents Marx's varying views of nationalism and internationalism.

There is a useful monograph on Marx's ill-fated organization: G. M. Stekloff, *History of The First International,* Eng. trans. (London, 1928); and another, besides G. D. H. Cole's, on the *Second International* by James Joll (New York, 1956). Of the histories of the several national Marxian parties, some of which have been written by adherents with more or less propagandist fervor, the following should be mentioned: Franz Mehring, *Geschichte der deutschen Sozialdemokratie,* 12th ed., 4 vols. (Stuttgart, 1922); David Footman, *The Primrose Path, a Life of*

Ferdinand Lassalle (London, 1946); August Bebel, *My Life,* Eng. trans. (London, 1912); Samuel Bernstein, *The Beginnings of Marxian Socialism in France* (New York, 1933); Aaron Noland, *The Founding of the French Socialist Party, 1893-1905* (Cambridge, Mass., 1956); Paul Louis, *Histoire du socialisme en France de la Révolution à nos jours,* 5th ed. (Paris, 1950); H. R. Weinstein, *Jean Jaurès, a Study of Patriotism in the French Socialist Movement* (New York, 1936); Roberto Michels, *Storia critica del movimento socialista italiano dagli inizi fino al 1911* (Florence, 1926); Max Beer, *A History of British Socialism,* new ed. (London, 1940).

For variations or offshoots from Marxism, see E. R. Pease, *The History of the Fabian Society,* 2nd ed. (London, 1925); Eduard Bernstein, *Evolutionary Socialism, a Criticism and Affirmation,* Eng. trans., 2nd ed. (London, 1912); Peter Gay, *The Dilemma of Democratic Socialism: Eduard Bernstein's Challenge to Marx* (New York, 1952); R. D. Humphrey, *George Sorel, Prophet without Honor* (Cambridge, Mass., 1951); C. A. Barker, *Henry George* (New York, 1955).

On anarchism: E. H. Carr, *Michael Bakunin* (London, 1937); Aleksander Herzen, *Aus den Memoiren eines Russen,* 2 vols. (New York, 1924-1925); Prince Kropotkin, *Memoirs of a Revolutionist* (Boston, 1899); M. Nettlau, *Elisée Reclus, Anarchist und Gelehrter, 1830-1905* (Berlin, 1928).

The feminist movement has inspired an extensive literature, of which the following titles are typical: W. L. Blease, *The Emancipation of English Women,* rev. ed. (London, 1913); Rachel C. Strachey, *"The Cause,"* a Short History of the Women's Movement in Great Britain* (London, 1928); S. Grimberg, *Histoire du mouvement suffragiste depuis 1848* (Paris, 1926); F. W. Tickner, *Women in English Economic History* (London, 1923); Katharine Anthony, *Feminism in Germany and Scandinavia* (New York, 1915).

Chapter VI

The general socializing trend of the '80's and '90's (and afterwards) is sympathetically indicated by Werner Sombart in two works: *Socialism and the Social Movement,* Eng. trans. by M. Epstein (London, 1909), and *A New Social Philosophy,* Eng. trans. by K. F. Geiser (Princeton, 1937). In the latter, the veteran scholar devotes special attention to Adolf Wagner and the historical, nationalist school of economists. For further details on this "school" and its members, consult the *Encyclopædia of the Soical Sciences.* Insight into another factor—the intensification of international trade rivalry—is afforded by an excellent monograph, R. J. S. Hoffman, *Great Britain and the German Trade Rivalry, 1875-1914*

(Philadelphia, 1933), with a wealth of statistical data. And the influence of Conservative parties is well illustrated by a German dissertation: E. Stock, *Wirtschafts- und sozialpolitische Bestrebungen der deutchkon-servativen Partei unter Bismarck* (Breslau, 1928). On changing economic doctrines: Erich Roll, *A History of Economic Thought* (New York, 1942); Eduard Heimann, *History of Economic Doctrines, an Introduction to Economic Theory* (London, 1945).

On the return of tariff protection: Josef Grunzel, *System der Handelspolitik,* 3rd ed. (Vienna, 1928); F. W. Taussig, *Free Trade, the Tariff, and Reciprocity* (New York, 1920); Percy Ashley, *Modern Tariff History, Germany, United States, France,* 3rd ed. (London, 1920); W. H. Dawson, *Protection in Germany* (London, 1904); E. O. Golub, *The Méline Tariff: French Agricultural and Nationalist Economic Policy* (New York, 1944); L. Lang, *Hundert Jahre Zollpolitik, 1805-1905* (Vienna, 1906), for the Habsburg Empire.

Of social insurance systems and other social legislation in European countries, numerous *Bulletins* of the U. S. Bureau of Labor Statistics (Washington, 1912 ff.) furnish full and reliable details. More general and systematic treatments of first-rate importance are: W. H. Dawson, *Social Insurance in Germany, 1883-1911* (London, 1912); G. Zacher, ed., *Die Arbeiter-versicherung im Auslande,* 5 vols. (Berlin, 1900-1908); L. K. Frankel and M. M. Dawson, *Workingmen's Insurance in Europe* (New York, 1910); Georges Scelle, *Le Droit ouvrier, tableau de la législation française actuelle,* 3rd ed. (Paris, 1929); G. Prato, *Le protectionisme ouvrier,* Fr. trans. from Ital. (Paris, 1912). Particularly for Great Britain: S. J. Chapman, *Work and Wages,* 3 vols. (London, 1904-1914); E. L. Hutchins and Amy Harrison, *History of Factory Legislation,* 3rd ed. (London, 1926); George Dangerfield, *The Strange Death of Liberal England* (New York, 1935). On municipal socialism: F. C. Howe, *Socialized Germany* (New York, 1915); W. H. Laneson, *Municipal Life and Government in Germany,* 2nd ed. (London, 1916); W. G. Towler, *Socialism in Local Government* (London, 1908); Sir Gwilym Gibbon and R. W. Bell, *History of the London County Council, 1889-1939* (London, 1939).

The extensive and intensive imperialism of the era has been the subject of countless general and specialized historical works. The best and sanest summary for the period is still P. T. Moon, *Imperialism and World Politics* (New York, 1926). Other good surveys: Mary E. Townsend, *European Colonial Expansion since 1871* (Philadelphia, 1941); G. W. F. Hallgarten, *Imperialismus vor 1914,* 2 vols. (Munich, 1951), on England and France. Of interpretations of the process, the economic received first and classic expression in J. A. Hobson, *Imperialism, a*

Study, 3rd rev. ed. (London, 1938); the Marxian has been most elaborately advanced by Fritz Sternberg, *Der Imperialismus* (Berlin, 1926); and the anti-Marxian and nationalistic, by Walter Sulzbach, *Nationales Gemeinschaftsfühl und wirtschaftliches Interesse* (Leipzig, 1929), and Arthur Salz, *Das Wesen des Imperialismus, Umrisse einer Theorie* (Leipzig, 1931), both of which are admirable. See also L. J. Ragatz, *The Literature of European Imperialism*, 3rd rev. ed. (Washington, 1947); Ralph Linton, ed., *Most of the World: the Peoples of Africa, Latin America, and the East* (New York, 1949); E. M. Winslow, *Pattern of Imperialism, a Study in the Theories of Power* (New York, 1948); Grover Clark, *The Balance Sheet of Imperialism: Facts and Figures on Colonies* (New York, 1936).

Many of the most substantial histories of imperialism deal with the subject along national lines. The best on British imperialism are: *The Cambridge History of the British Empire* (Cambridge, 1929-1952), vol. III *from 1870*, vols. V-VIII on India, Canada, Australia and New Zealand, and South Africa, respectively; Sir Charles P. Lucas, ed., *Historical Geography of the British Colonies*, 2nd ed. by H. E. Egerton and others, 8 vols. (Oxford, 1905-1925); C. W. Domville-Fife, *Encyclopædia of the British Empire*, 3 vols. (Bristol, 1924); L. C. A. Knowles, *Economic Development of the British Overseas Empire*, 2 vols. (London, 1924-1936); C. A. Bodelsen, *Studies in Mid-Victorian Imperialism* (London, 1924); Edmond Carton de Wiart, *Les grandes compagnies coloniales anglaises du XIXᵉ siècle* (Paris, 1899); J. E. Tyler, *The Struggle for Imperial Unity, 1868-1895* (New York, 1938).

On Russian imperialism: F. H. Skrine, *The Expansion of Russia, 1815-1900*, 3rd ed. (Cambridge, 1915); B. H. Sumner, *Tsardom and Imperialism in the Far East and Middle East, 1880-1914* (London, 1942); G. F. Wright, *Asiatic Russia*, 2 vols. (New York, 1902); W. E. D. Allen and Paul Muratoff, *Caucasian Battlefields, a History of the Wars on the Turco-Caucasian Border, 1828-1921* (Cambridge, 1953); D. J. Dallin, *Rise of Russia in Asia* (New Haven, 1949). On French imperialism: Émile Levasseur, *La France et ses colonies, géographie et statistique*, 3 vols. (Paris, 1890-1893); H. I. Priestley, *France Overseas, a Study of Modern Imperialism* (New York, 1938); T. F. Power, Jr., *Jules Ferry and the Renaissance of French Imperialism* (New York, 1944); S. H. Roberts, *History of French Colonial Policy, 1870-1925*, 2 vols. (London, 1929). On German imperialism: Heinrich Schnee, ed., *Deutsches Kolonial-Lexikon*, 3 vols. (Leipzig, 1920); Mary E. Townsend, *The Rise and Fall of Germany's Colonial Empire, 1884-1918* (New York, 1930); Alfred Zimmermann, *Geschichte der deutschen Kolonial-*

politik (Berlin, 1914); R. Hermann, *Die Handelsbeziehungen Deutschlands zu seinen Schutzgebieten* (Munich, 1899). On other national imperialism: Alberto Botarelli, *Compendio di storia coloniale italiana* (Rome, 1914); Angel Marvaud, *Le Portugal et ses colonies, étude politique et économique* (Paris, 1912).

A large number of historical treatises and monographs on imperialism deal with particular extra-European areas. On British India and French Indo-China: D. G. E. Hall, *A History of Southeast Asia* (London, 1955); *Cambridge History of India,* vol. VI, ed. by H. H. Dodwell, *1858-1918* (Cambridge, 1932); W. H. Moreland and A. Chandra Chatterjee, *A Short History of India* (New York, 1957); H. L. Hoskins, *British Routes to India* (Philadelphia, 1928); J. F. Cady, *The Roots of French Imperialism in Asia* (Ithaca, 1954); Virginia Thompson, *French Indo-China* (New York, 1937); B. H. M. Vlekke, *Nurantara, a History of the East Indian Archipelago* (Cambridge, Mass., 1943); *Encyclopaedie van Nederlandsch-Indië,* 2nd ed. by J. Paulus and others, 8 vols. ('s Gravenhage, 1917-1939); Rupert Emerson, *Malaysia, a Study in Direct and Indirect Rule* (New York, 1937); Clive Day, *The Policy and Administration of the Dutch in Java* (New York, 1904). On the Middle East: Valentine Chirol, *The Middle Eastern Question* (London, 1903); Sir Arnold T. Wilson, *The Persian Gulf* (Oxford, 1928); P. K. Hitti, *History of the Arabs,* 6th ed. (London, 1956). On the Pacific and Oceania: G. H. Scholefield, *The Pacific, its Past and Future, and the Policy of the Great Powers from the Eighteenth Century* (London, 1919); K. L. P. Martin, *Missionaries and Annexation in the Pacific* (London, 1924); S. Baring-Gould and C. A. Bampfylde, *History of Sarawak under its Two White Rajahs, 1839-1908* (London, 1909); *Annuaire des établissements français de l'Océanie* (Papeete, 1894 ff.). On the Far East—Japan and China—and on the United States in the Pacific, see bibliography under Chapter VIII, below.

On the partition of Africa: Sir Edward Hertslet, *Map of Africa by Treaty,* 3rd rev. ed. by R. W. Brant and H. L. Sherwood, 3 vols. (London, 1908), storehouse of documents, with numerous maps; Roland Oliver, *Sir Harry Johnston and the Scramble for Africa* (London, 1957); Sir Harry H. Johnston, *History of the Colonization of Africa by Alien Races,* rev. ed. (Cambridge, 1930), standard work; Sir Charles P. Lucas, *Partition and Colonization of Africa* (Oxford, 1922), good survey by a competent authority; Leonard Woolf, *Empire and Commerce in Africa, a Study in Economic Imperialism* (London, 1920), severely critical; George Seaver, *David Livingstone, His Life and Letters* (New York, 1957); Sybil E. Crowe, *The Berlin West African Conference, 1884-*

1885 (London, 1942); Dorothy Stanley, ed., *Autobiography of Sir Henry Morton Stanley* (Boston, 1911). Specifically on the Congo: Sir Henry M. Stanley, *The Congo and the Founding of its Free State, a Story of Work and Exploration* (London, 1885); A. J. Wauters, *Histoire politique du Congo belge* (Brussels, 1911). On British West and East Africa: A. F. Mockler-Ferryman, *British West Africa* (London, 1898); C. W. J. Orr, *The Making of Northern Nigeria* (London, 1911); Sir Harry H. Johnston, *British Central Africa*, 2nd ed. (London, 1897), and, by the same author, *Uganda Protectorate*, 2 vols. (London, 1902); Zoë Marsh and G. W. Kingsnorth, *An Introduction to the History of East Africa* (Cambridge, 1957); Margery Perham, *Lugard, the Years of Adventure, 1858-1898* (London, 1956); R. Coupland, *The Exploitation of East Africa, 1856-1890, the Slave Trade and the Scramble* (London, 1939); A. J. Hanna, *The Beginnings of Nyasaland and North-eastern Rhodesia, 1859-1895* (Oxford, 1956); Lois A. C. Raphael, *The Cape-to-Cairo Dream* (New York, 1936). On German Africa: W. O. Aydelotte, *Bismarck and British Colonial Policy* (Philadelphia, 1937), a monograph relating to Southwest Africa, 1883-1885; H. R. Rudin, *Germans in the Cameroons, 1884-1914* (New Haven, 1938), an admirable study; Carl Peters, *Die Gründung von Deutsch-Ostafrika* (Berlin, 1906), autobiographical. On French Africa: Victor Piquet, *La colonisation française dans l'Afrique du Nord: Algérie, Tunisie, Maroc*, 2nd rev. ed. (Paris, 1914); André Demaison, *Faidherbe* (Paris, 1932); A. L. C. Gatelet, *Histoire de la conquête du Sudan français, 1878-1899* (Paris, 1901); Guillaume Grandidier, *Le Myre de Vilers, Duchesne, Galliéni, quarante années de l'histoire de Madagascar, 1880-1920* (Paris, 1923). On Italy in Africa: Luigi Chiala, *La spedizione di Massaua, narrazione documentata, 1869-1887* (Turin, 1888); Carlo Conte Rossini, *Italia ed Etiopia dal trattato d'Uccialli alla battaglia di Adua* (Rome, 1935).

On Egypt and the Egyptian Sudan: Lord Cromer, *Modern Egypt*, new ed. (London, 1916), classic apology for British occupation and rule; W. S. Blunt, *Secret History of the English Occupation of Egypt* (London, 1907), antidote to Cromer, but should be used with caution; Sir Francis R. Wingate, *Mahdiism and the Egyptian Sudan* (London, 1891), detailed account of the rise of the Mahdi and his conquest of the Sudan, 1884-1885; B. M. Allen, *Gordon and the Sudan* (London, 1931); Winston Churchill, *The River War, an Historical Account of the Re-conquest of the Sudan*, 2 vols. (London, 1899); Sir George Arthur, *Life of Lord Kitchener*, 3 vols. (London, 1920), authorized biography; Gabriel Hanotaux, *Fachoda* (Paris, 1909).

On British South Africa and the Boer War: E. A. Walker, *A History of South Africa,* new rev. ed. (New York, 1957); C. W. de Kiewiet, *A History of South Africa, Social and Economic* (Oxford, 1941); R. I. Lovell, *The Struggle for South Africa, 1875-1899, a Study in Economic Imperialism* (New York, 1934); Basil Williams, *Cecil Rhodes* (London, 1921), sympathetic; Sarah G. Millin, *Cecil Rhodes* (New York, 1933); Ian Colvin, *The Life of Jameson,* 2 vols. (London, 1922); H. M. Hole, *The Jameson Raid* (London, 1930); W. B. Worsfold, *Lord Milner's Work in South Africa, 1897-1902* (London, 1906), a defense, with much documentary material; Cecil Headlam, ed., *The Milner Papers, South Africa, 1897-1899* (London, 1931-1933); Paul Kruger, *Memoirs,* Eng. trans., ed. by A. Schowalter (London, 1902); Sir John F. Maurice, ed., *History of the War in South Africa, 1899-1902,* 4 vols. and 4 vols. of maps (London, 1906-1910), official British military history; C. R. De-Wet, *Three Years' War* (New York, 1902), account by a prominent Boer general.

The navalism which developed greatly in the '80's and '90's has been the subject of several important studies: A. J. Marder, *The Anatomy of British Sea Power, a History of British Naval Policy in the Pre-Dreadnought Era, 1880-1905* (New York, 1940), wholly admirable, although concerned with dynamics more than with anatomy; Archibald Hurd and Henry Castle, *German Sea-Power* (London, 1913); Eckart Kehr, *Schlachtflottenbau und Parteipolitik, 1894-1901* (Berlin, 1930), a brilliant study of the relationship of navalism to domestic politics and social movements within Germany; Vice-Admiral Henri Salaun, *La marine française* (Paris, 1934), on the naval policy and history of the Third French Republic; Serge Terestchenko and Nestor Monasterev, *Histoire de la marine russe,* Fr. trans. from Rus. (Paris, 1932); Harold and Margaret Sprout, *The Rise of American Naval Power* (Princeton, 1939), the first really detailed and well-documented study of navalism in the United States; E. B. Potter, ed., *The United States and World Sea Power* (Englewood, 1955), comprehensive.

Chapter VII

Of many scientific and pseudo-scientific attempts to distinguish and describe different "races" in Europe, one of the most judicious is C. S. Coon, *The Races of Europe,* new ed. (New York, 1950). Many of these made between 1871 and 1900 are shown to have been quite fallacious by Jacques Barzun, *Race, a Study in Modern Superstition* (New York, 1937). Other sane discussions of racialism are Ruth Benedict, *Race, Science and Politics* (New York, 1943); L. L. Snyder, *Race, a History of Modern Ethnic Theories* (New York, 1939); F. O. Hertz, *Race and*

Civilization, Eng. trans. (London, 1928); Otto Klineberg, *Race Differences* (New York, 1935). A racialist's nationalism is apparent in Arthur Keith, *Nationality and Race* (London, 1919).

Specifically of racial anti-Semitism, the most important work in support is Th. Fritsch, ed., *Das Handbuch der Judenfrage, eine Zusammenstellung des wichtigsten Materials zur Beurteilung des jüdischen Volkes,* 33rd ed. (Leipzig, 1933), and the most cogent in criticism is B. Lazare, *L'Antisemitisme, son histoire et ses causes,* new ed. by André Fontainas, 2 vols. (Paris, 1934). Other significant works on the subject: F. Bernstein, *Der Antisemitismus als Gruppenerscheinung, Versuch einer Soziologie des Judenhasses* (Berlin, 1926); S. Blitz, *Nationalism, a Cause of Anti-Semitism* (New York, 1928). On particular anti-Semitic leaders and movements: Erwin Mayer-Löwenschwerdt, *Schönerer, der Vorkämpfer, eine politische Biographie* (Vienna, 1938), the Austrian forerunner of Hitler; Walter Frank, *Hofprediger Adolf Stöcker,* 2nd ed. (Hamburg, 1935); Richard Breitling, *Paul de Lagarde und der grossdeutsche Gedanke* (Vienna, 1927); Ernst Seillière, *Houston Stewart Chamberlain, le plus récent philosophe du pangermanisme mystique* (Paris, 1917); J. Driault, *Drumont, La France juive et la Libre Parole* (Paris, 1935); L. Leblois, *L'Affaire Dreyfus, l'iniquité, la réparation* (Paris, 1929), Dreyfusard, with convenient collection of documents; Henri Dutrait-Crozon, *Précis de l'affaire Dreyfus,* new ed. (Paris, 1924), best of the anti-Dreyfusard accounts. On Jewish nationalism and Zionism: K. S. Pinson, ed., *Simon Dubnow, Essays on Old and New Judaism* (Philadelphia, 1958); Adolf Böhm, *Die zionistische Bewegung, eine kurze Darstellung ihrer Entwicklung,* 2 vols. (Berlin, 1920-1921), historical survey; Jacob de Haas, *Theodor Herzl,* 2 vols. (Chicago, 1927), documented biography of the founder of Zionism by his secretary.

The intensifying nationalism of the Generation of Materialism has attracted far more attention since the World War than it attracted contemporaneously. Since then there has been a wide range of historical study and writing about it. Basic studies include: C. J. H. Hayes, *Essays on Nationalism* (New York, 1926), *Historical Evolution of Modern Nationalism* (New York, 1931) and *Nationalism, a Religion* (New York, 1960); Hans Kohn, *Prophets and Peoples, Studies in Nineteenth-Century Nationalism* (New York, 1945); B. C. Shafer, *Nationalism, Myth and Reality* (New York, 1955); H. W. Chadwick, *The Nationalities of Europe and the Growth of National Ideologies* (Cambridge, 1945); Reinhard Wittram, *Das nationale als europäisches Problem: Beiträge zur Geschichte des Nationalitätsprinzips vornehmlich im 19. Jahrhundert* (Göttingen, 1954); H. L. Koppelmann, *Nation, Sprache und Nationalismus* (Leiden,

1956); K. S. Pinson, *A Bibliographical Introduction to Nationalism* (New York, 1936); K. W. Deutsch, *Interdisciplinary Bibliography on Nationalism, 1935-1953* (Cambridge, Mass., 1955).

The nationalism in countries already possessing national states and ranking as great powers is portrayed in Ernest Barker, *National Character and the Factors in its Formation* (New York, 1927), with special reference to England; Janet H. Robb, *The Primrose League, 1883-1906* (New York, 1942); C. F. Harrold, *Carlyle and German Thought* (New Haven, 1934); H. J. C. Grierson, *Carlyle and Hitler* (Cambridge, 1933); W. C. Buthman, *Rise of Integral Nationalism in France, with special reference to the Ideas and Activities of Charles Maurras* (New York, 1939); Walter Frank, *Nationalismus und Demokratie im Frankreich der dritten Republik, 1871 bis 1918* (Hamburg, 1933); E. R. Curtius, *Maurice Barrès und die geistigen Grundlagen des französischen Nationalismus* (Bonn, 1921); C. J. H. Hayes, *France, a Nation of Patriots* (New York, 1930); L. L. Snyder, *From Bismarck to Hitler, the Background of Modern German Nationalism* (Williamsport, 1935); Andreas Dorpalen, *Heinrich von Treitschke* (New Haven, 1957); Friedrich Meinecke, *Die Idee der Staatsräson,* 2nd ed. (Munich, 1925); R. W. Tims, *Germanizing the Prussian Poles, the H-K-T Society of the Eastern Marches, 1894-1914* (New York, 1941); Paul Molisch, *Geschichte der deutschnationalen Bewegung in Österreich* (Jena, 1926).

Pan-Germanism is treated in Mildred S. Wertheimer, *The Pan-German League, 1890-1914* (New York, 1924), and in Alfred Kruck, *Geschichte des alldeutschen Verbandes, 1890-1939* (Wiesbaden, 1954). Pan-Slavism is treated in Hans Kohn, *History of Pan-Slavism* (South Bend, 1955); Alfred Fischel, *Der Panslawismus bis zum Weltkrieg* (Stuttgart, 1919); and M. B. Petrovich, *The Emergence of Russian Pan-Slavism, 1856-1870* (New York, 1956).

The minorities problem in Austria-Hungary and the attempts to deal with it by Germanization or Magyarization are presented at length in R. A. Kann, *The Multinational Empire: Nationalism and National Reform in the Habsburg Monarchy, 1848-1918,* 2 vols. (New York, 1950); Bertrand Auerbach, *Les races et les nationalités en Autriche-Hongrie,* 2nd rev. ed. (Paris, 1917).

Irish nationalism is discussed historically in Sir James O'Connor, *History of Ireland, 1798-1924,* 2 vols. (London, 1925); Francis Hackett, *Ireland, a Study in Nationalism* (New York, 1918); Edmund Curtis, *A History of Ireland,* 6th ed. (London, 1950); J. C. Beckett, *A Short History of Ireland* (London, 1952); J. L. Hammond, *Gladstone and the Irish Nation* (London, 1938); J. D. Clarkson, *Labour and Nationalism in Ireland*

(New York, 1925), with special concern for urban labor; J. E. Pomfret, *The Struggle for Land in Ireland, 1800-1923* (Princeton, 1930); N. D. Palmer, *The Irish Land League Crisis* (New Haven, 1940), treating of the stirring events of 1879-1881; F. Sheehy-Skeffington, *Michael Davitt, Revolutionary, Agitator and Labour Leader* (London, 1908); C. C. O'Brien, *Parnell and His Party, 1880-1890* (Oxford, 1957); F. S. L. Lyons, *The Irish Parliamentary Party, 1890-1910* (London, 1951).

The rise of Czech nationalism is traced in: Elizabeth Wiskemann, *Czechs and Germans, a Study of the Struggle in the Historic Provinces of Bohemia and Moravia* (London, 1938), the best account in English; Alfred Fischel, *Das tschechische Volk,* 2 vols. (Breslau, 1928); Paul Molisch, *Vom Kampf der Tschechen um ihren Staat* (Vienna, 1929), a German-Austrian view.

On nationalistic unrest and agitation among the minorities in Hungary: R. W. Seton-Watson, *Racial Problems in Hungary* (London, 1908); Nicholas Jorga, *Histoire des roumains de Transylvanie et de Hongrie,* 2 vols. (Bucharest, 1915-1916); R. W. Seton-Watson, ed., *Slovakia Then and Now* (London, 1931); J. A. Freiherr von Helfert, *Geschichte der südungarischen Bewegung und Kämpfe gegen die Zumuthungen des Pan-Magyarismus* (Vienna, 1908); Hermann Wendel, *Aus dem südslawischen Risorgimento* (Gotha, 1921), on Jugoslav intellectual leaders; R. W. Seton-Watson, *The Southern Slav Question and the Habsburg Monarchy* (London, 1911).

On Polish nationalism: Oscar Halecki, *History of Poland,* 2nd ed. (New York, 1956); *Cambridge History of Poland,* ed. by W. F. Reddaway and others, vol. II, *From Augustus II to Pilsudski* (Cambridge, 1941); G. Brandes, *Poland, a Study of the Land, People, and Literature,* Eng. trans. (London, 1913); George Cleinow, *Die Zukunft Polens,* 2 vols. (Leipzig, 1908-1914), strong anti-Polish bias, but vol. II is fairly detailed on political history of Russian Poland, 1864-1883.

On the development of nationalism among other ethnic minorities in the Russian Empire: Reinhard Wittram, *Baltische Geschichte* (Munich, 1954), on Letts, Lithuanians, etc.; Stephan Rudnicki, *Ukraine, the Land and its People,* Eng. trans. (New York, 1918), with good bibliography; Alexander von Tobien, *Die livländische Ritterschaft in ihrem Verhältnis zum Zarismus und russischen Nationalismus,* 2 vols. (Riga and Berlin, 1925-1930), very detailed; J. H. Wuorinen, *Nationalism in Modern Finland* (New York, 1931); J. H. Jackson, *Finland* (London, 1938).

On rising nationalism among miscellaneous "submerged" peoples of Europe: O. J. Falnes, *National Romanticism in Norway* (New York, 1933); S. B. Clough, *History of the Flemish Movement in Belgium, a*

Study in Nationalism (New York, 1930); Sir Reginald Coupland, *Welsh and Scottish Nationalism, a Study* (London, 1954); Maurice Duhamel, *La Question bretonne dans son cadre européen* (Paris, 1929); Jaime Carrera Pujals, *Historia politica de Cataluña en el siglo XIX,* 4 vols. to date (Barcelona, 1957 ff.).

On nationalism in the Balkans: A. J. Toynbee, *The Western Question in Greece and Turkey,* 2nd ed. (Boston, 1923); R. W. Seton-Watson, *The Rise of Nationality in The Balkans* (London, 1907); Hans Kohn, *Nationalism and Imperialism in the Hither East* (New York, 1932).

Chapters VIII and IX

A goodly number of the general works cited in the bibliography of Chapter I, above, treat of international relations and diplomacy in the decade of the 1890's as well as in the two preceding decades; and similarly the major works on imperialism for the whole era from 1871 to 1900 are listed in the bibliography of Chapter VI, above.

Certain special studies of European diplomacy in the post-Bismarckian decade, which have not previously been referred to, are peculiarly pertinent here. Mention may be made, for example, of Erich Brandenburg, *From Bismarck to the World War, 1890-1914,* Eng. trans. (London, 1927); Theodore Bayer, *England und der neue Kurs, 1890-1895* (Tübingen, 1955); Helmuth Rogge, *Holstein und Hohenlohe* (Stuttgart, 1957); *The Holstein Papers,* 4 vols. (Cambridge, 1955 ff.), especially vol. II, *Diaries,* ed. by Norman Rich and M. H. Fisher (1957); W. L. Langer, *The Franco-Russian Alliance, 1890-1894* (Cambridge, Mass., 1929); E. M. Earle, *Turkey, the Great Powers, and the Bagdad Railway* (New York, 1923).

On the contemporaneous emergence of the United States as a world power and its impact on international relations: Dexter Perkins, *A History of the Monroe Doctrine,* rev. ed. (Boston, 1955); Wolfgang Mommsen, *Die letzte Phase des britischen Imperialismus auf den amerikanischen Kontinenten, 1880-1896* (Leipzig, 1933), an essay on the Venezuelan affair; C. S. Campbell, Jr., *Anglo-American Understanding, 1898-1903* (Baltimore, 1957); Walter Millis, *The Martial Spirit, a Study of Our War with Spain* (New York, 1931), popular and not concerned with diplomacy, but enlightening on the wave of imperialistic nationalism in the United States; J. W. Pratt, *Expansionists of 1898* (Baltimore, 1936), and *America's Colonial Experiment* (New York, 1950); H. K. Beale, *Theodore Roosevelt and the Rise of America to World Power* (Baltimore, 1956); T. A. Bailey, *A Diplomatic History of the American People,* 6th ed. (New York, 1958); S. F. Bemis, *A Diplomatic History of the United States,* 4th ed. (New York, 1955).

On the United States in the Pacific and the Far East: F. R. Dulles, *America in the Pacific, a Century of Expansion,* 2nd ed. (Boston, 1938); G. H. Ryden, *The Foreign Policy of the United States in Relation to Samoa* (New Haven, 1933); R. S. Kuykendall, *History of Hawaii,* with introductory chapters by H. E. Gregory, 2nd ed. (New York, 1938); J. A. LeRoy, *Americans in the Philippines, a History of the Conquest and First Years of Occupation, with an introductory account of Spanish Rule,* 2 vols. (Boston, 1914); L. H. Fernández, *The Philippine Republic* (New York, 1926), a study of native armed resistance to Spain and the United States; G. A. Grunder and W. E. Livezey, *The Philippines and the United States* (Norman, 1951); F. H. Harrington, *God, Mammon, and the Japanese: Korean-American Relations, 1884-1905* (Madison, 1944); Tyler Dennett, *John Hay* (New York, 1933), authoritative biography of the American Secretary of State who sponsored the "open door" for China.

Among good general histories of the Far East, treating of our period, are K. S. Latourette, *A Short History of the Far East,* 3rd ed. (New York, 1957); Sir John T. Pratt, *The Expansion of Europe into the Far East* (London, 1947); P. H. Clyde, *The Far East, a History of the Impact of the West on Eastern Asia,* 3rd ed. (New York, 1958); P. J. Treat, *The Far East, a Political and Diplomatic History,* rev. ed. (New York, 1935); H. M. Vinacke, *A History of the Far East in Modern Times,* 3rd rev. ed. (New York, 1950). Henry Norman, *The Peoples and Politics of the Far East* (London, 1895), is one of the best contemporaneous accounts, by a veteran traveler in the Far East.

Specifically on the rise of Japan as a "Europeanized" great power: A. C. Walworth, *Black Ships off Japan, the Story of Commodore Perry's Expedition* (New York, 1946); E. H. Norman, *Japan's Emergence as a Modern State, 1868-1904* (New York, 1940); K. S. Latourette, *History of Japan,* rev. ed. (New York, 1957); Hugh Borton, *Japan's Modern Century* (New York, 1956); Chitoshi Yanaga, *Japan Since Perry* (New York, 1949); T. C. Smith, *Political Change and Industrial Development of Japan, 1868-1880* (New York, 1955); W. W. Lockwood, *The Economic Development of Japan, 1868-1938* (Princeton, 1954); F. C. Jones, *Extraterritoriality in Japan, 1853-1899* (New Haven, 1931); Seiji G. Hishida, *Japan among the Great Powers, a Survey of her International Relations* (New York, 1940); Sir George Sansom, *The Western World and Japan, a Study of the Interaction of European and Asiatic Cultures* (New York, 1950).

On China, good brief introductions are L. Carrington Goodrich, *A*

Short History of the Chinese People (New York, 1951), and K. S. Latourette, *The Chinese, Their History and Culture,* 2 vols. (New York, 1934). The classic and most thoroughly documented history of Sino-European relations during our period is Henri Cordier, *Histoire des relations de la Chine avec les puissances occidentales, 1860-1902,* 3 vols. (Paris, 1901-1902). A standard collection of treaty texts is J. V. A. MacMurray, *Treaties and Agreements with and concerning China, 1894-1919,* 2 vols. (New York, 1921). Useful, too, for reference is A. W. Hummel, ed., *Eminent Chinese of the Ch'ing Period, 1644-1912,* 2 vols. (Washington, 1943-1944). Valuable studies of China as the crux of the Far Eastern problem in the 1890's: G. W. Keeton, *Development of Extraterritoriality in China,* 2 vols. (London, 1928); P. H. Kent, *Railway Enterprise in China* (London, 1908); J. O. P. Bland and E. Backhouse, *China under the Empress Dowager, being the History of the Life and Times of Tz'u Hsi,* new ed. (Peking, 1939); G. N. Steiger, *China and the Occident* (New Haven, 1927), and C. C. Tan, *The Boxer Catastrophe* (New York, 1955), both treating of the Boxer movement, the latter utilizing Chinese sources; A. H. Smith, *China in Convulsion,* 2 vols. (New York, 1901), notable eyewitness description, by a veteran American missionary.

The most systematic treatment of the Conference on the Limitation of Armaments at The Hague in 1899 is that by an American delegate: F. W. Holls, *The Peace Conference at The Hague* (New York, 1900). The documents are conveniently assembled in J. B. Scott, ed., *The Hague Peace Conferences of 1899 and 1907,* vol. II (Baltimore, 1909). Subsequent disillusionment is set forth by Merze Tate, *The Disarmament Illusion: the Movement for a Limitation of Armaments to 1907* (New York, 1942).

Aspects of the "internationalism" of the period are presented by: Devere Allen, *The Fight for Peace* (New York, 1930); Josephine Rich, *John Henri Dunant, Founder of the International Red Cross* (New York, 1956); Clara Barton, *The Red Cross, a History* (Washington, 1898); O. J. Falnes, *Norway and the Nobel Peace Prize* (New York, 1938); A. L. Guérard, *A Short History of the International Language Movement* (London, 1922).

For some of the more dubious developments of a Generation of Materialism, the following may be of interest: A. R. Wallace, *Miracles in Modern Spiritualism,* rev. ed. (London, 1901); C. R. Richet, *Thirty Years of Psychical Research,* Eng. trans. (New York, 1923); Gertrude M. Williams, *The Passionate Pilgrim, a Life of Annie Besant* (New York, 1931).

INDEX

hARPER ✦ ԵORCҺBOOKS

† The New American Nation Series, edited by Henry Steele Commager and Richard B. Morris.
‡ American Perspectives series, edited by Bernard Wishy and William E. Leuchtenburg.
a History of Europe series, edited by J. H. Plumb.
§ The Library of Religion and Culture, edited by Benjamin Nelson.
‖ Researches in the Social, Cultural, and Behavioral Sciences, edited by Benjamin Nelson.
Σ Harper Modern Science Series, edited by James A. Newman.
° Not for sale in Canada.
+ Documentary History of the United States series, edited by Richard B. Morris.
# Documentary History of Western Civilization series, edited by Eugene C. Black and Leonard W. Levy.
ʌ The Economic History of the United States series, edited by Henry David et al.
¶ European Perspectives series, edited by Eugene C. Black.
** Contemporary Essays series, edited by Leonard W. Levy.
* The Stratum Series, edited by John Hale.

RAY A. BILLINGTON: The Far Western Frontier: 1830-1860. † *Illus.*　　　　　TB/3012
STUART BRUCHEY: The Roots of American Economic Growth, 1607-1861: *An Essay in Social Causation. New Introduction by the Author.*　　　　　TB/1350
WHITNEY R. CROSS: The Burned-Over District: *The Social and Intellectual History of Enthusiastic Religion in Western New York, 1800-1850*　　　　　TB/1242
NOBLE E. CUNNINGHAM, JR., Ed.: The Early Republic, 1789-1828 +　　　　　HR/1394
GEORGE DANGERFIELD: The Awakening of American Nationalism, 1815-1828. † *Illus.* TB/3061
CLEMENT EATON: The Freedom-of-Thought Struggle in the Old South. *Revised and Enlarged. Illus.*　　　　　TB/1150
CLEMENT EATON: The Growth of Southern Civilization, 1790-1860. † *Illus.* TB/3040
ROBERT H. FERRELL, Ed.: Foundations of American Diplomacy, 1775-1872 + HR/1393
LOUIS FILLER: The Crusade against Slavery: 1830-1860. † *Illus.*　　　　　TB/3029
DAVID H. FISCHER: The Revolution of American Conservatism: *The Federalist Party in the Era of Jeffersonian Democracy* TB/1449
WILLIM W. FREEHLING: Prelude to Civil War: *The Nullification Controversy in South Carolina, 1816-1836*　　　　　TB/1359
PAUL W. GATES: The Farmer's Age: *Agriculture, 1815-1860* Δ　　　　　TB/1398
THOMAS JEFFERSON: Notes on the State of Virginia. ‡ *Edited by Thomas P. Abernethy*　　　　　TB/3052
FORREST MCDONALD, Ed.: Confederation and Constitution, 1781-1789 + HR/1396
BERNARD MAYO: Myths and Men: *Patrick Henry, George Washington, Thomas Jefferson*　　　　　TB/1108
JOHN C. MILLER: Alexander Hamilton and the Growth of the New Nation TB/3057
JOHN C. MILLER: The Federalist Era: 1789-1801. † *Illus.*　　　　　TB/3027
RICHARD B. MORRIS, Ed.: Alexander Hamilton and the Founding of the Nation. *New Introduction by the Editor* TB/1448
RICHARD B. MORRIS: The American Revolution Reconsidered　　　　　TB/1363
CURTIS P. NETTELS: The Emergence of a National Economy, 1775-1815 Δ TB/1438
DOUGLASS C. NORTH & ROBERT PAUL THOMAS, Eds.: *The Growth of the American Economy to 1860* +　　　　　HR/1352
R. B. NYE: The Cultural Life of the New Nation: 1776-1830. † *Illus.* TB/3026
GILBERT OSOFSKY, Ed.: Puttin' On Ole Massa: *The Slave Narratives of Henry Bibb, William Wells Brown, and Solomon Northup* ‡　　　　　TB/1432
JAMES PARTON: The Presidency of Andrew Jackson. *From Volume III of the* Life of Andrew Jackson. *Ed. with Intro. by Robert V. Remini*　　　　　TB/3067
FRANCIS S. PHILBRICK: The Rise of the West, 1754-1830. † *Illus.* TB/3067
MARSHALL SMELSER: The Democratic Republic, 1801-1815 †　　　　　TB/1406
JACK M. SOSIN, Ed.: The Opening of the West +　　　　　HR/1424
GEORGE ROGERS TAYLOR: The Transportation Revolution, 1815-1860 Δ TB/1347
A. F. TYLER: Freedom's Ferment: *Phases of American Social History from the Revolution to the Outbreak of the Civil War. Illus.*　　　　　TB/1074
GLYNDON G. VAN DEUSEN: The Jacksonian Era: 1828-1848. † *Illus.* TB/3028

LOUIS B. WRIGHT: Culture on the Moving Frontier　　　　　TB/1053

American Studies: The Civil War to 1900

W. R. BROCK: An American Crisis: *Congress and Reconstruction, 1865-67* ° TB/1283
T. C. COCHRAN & WILLIAM MILLER: The Age of Enterprise: *A Social History of Industrial America*　　　　　TB/1054
W. A. DUNNING: Reconstruction, Political and Economic: 1865-1877 TB/1073
HAROLD U. FAULKNER: Politics, Reform and Expansion: 1890-1900. † *Illus.* TB/3020
GEORGE M. FREDRICKSON: The Inner Civil War: *Northern Intellectuals and the Crisis of the Union*　　　　　TB/1358
JOHN A. GARRATY: The New Commonwealth, 1877-1890 †　　　　　TB/1410
JOHN A. GARRATY, Ed.: The Transformation of American Society, 1870-1890 + HR/1395
HELEN HUNT JACKSON: A Century of Dishonor: *The Early Crusade for Indian Reform.* † *Edited by Andrew F. Rolle* TB/3063
WILLIAM G. MCLOUGHLIN, Ed.: The American Evangelicals, 1800-1900: An Anthology ‡　　　　　TB/1382
ARNOLD M. PAUL: Conservative Crisis and the Rule of Law: *Attitudes of Bar and Bench, 1887-1895. New Introduction by Author*　　　　　TB/1415
JAMES S. PIKE: The Prostrate State: *South Carolina under Negro Government.* ‡ *Intro. by Robert F. Durden* TB/3085
WHITELAW REID: After the War: *A Tour of the Southern States, 1865-1866.* ‡ *Edited by C. Vann Woodward* TB/3066
FRED A. SHANNON: The Farmer's Last Frontier: *Agriculture, 1860-1897* TB/1348
VERNON LANE WHARTON: The Negro in Mississippi, 1865-1890 TB/1178

American Studies: The Twentieth Century

RICHARD M. ABRAMS, Ed.: The Issues of the Populist and Progressive Eras, 1892-1912 +　　　　　HR/1428
RAY STANNARD BAKER: Following the Color Line: *American Negro Citizenship in Progressive Era.* ‡ *Edited by Dewey W. Grantham, Jr. Illus.*　　　　　TB/3053
RANDOLPH S. BOURNE: War and the Intellectuals: *Collected Essays, 1915-1919.* ⊹ *Edited by Carl Resek*　　　　　TB/3043
A. RUSSELL BUCHANAN: The United States and World War II. † *Illus.*
　　　　　Vol. I TB/3044; Vol. II TB/3045
THOMAS C. COCHRAN: The American Business System: *A Historical Perspective, 1900-1955*　　　　　TB/1080
FOSTER RHEA DULLES: America's Rise to World Power: 1898-1954. † *Illus.* TB/3021
JEAN-BAPTISTE DUROSELLE: From Wilson to Roosevelt: *Foreign Policy of the United States, 1913-1945. Trans. by Nancy Lyman Roelker*　　　　　TB/1370
HAROLD U. FAULKNER: The Decline of Laissez Faire, 1897-1917 TB/1397
JOHN D. HICKS: Republican Ascendancy: 1921-1933. † *Illus.* TB/3041
WILLIAM E. LEUCHTENBURG: Franklin D. Roosevelt and the New Deal: 1932-1940. † *Illus.*　　　　　TB/3025
WILLIAM E. LEUCHTENBURG, Ed.: The New Deal: *A Documentary History* + HR/1354
ARTHUR S. LINK: Woodrow Wilson and the Progressive Era: 1910-1917. † *Illus.* TB/3023

2

BROADUS MITCHELL: Depression Decade: *From New Era through New Deal, 1929-1941* △ TB/1439

GEORGE E. MOWRY: The Era of Theodore Roosevelt and the Birth of Modern America: 1900-1912. † *Illus.* TB/3022

WILLIAM PRESTON, JR.: Aliens and Dissenters: *Federal Suppression of Radicals, 1903-1933* TB/1287

WALTER RAUSCHENBUSCH: Christianity and the Social Crisis. ‡ *Edited by Robert D. Cross* TB/3059

GEORGE SOULE: Prosperity Decade: *From War to Depression, 1917-1929* △ TB/1349

GEORGE B. TINDALL, Ed.: A Populist Reader: *Selections from the Works of American Populist Leaders* TB/3069

TWELVE SOUTHERNERS: I'll Take My Stand: *The South and the Agrarian Tradition. Intro. by Louis D. Rubin, Jr.; Biographical Essays by Virginia Rock* TB/1072

Art, Art History, Aesthetics

CREIGHTON GILBERT, Ed.: Renaissance Art ** *Illus.* TB/1465

EMILE MALE: The Gothic Image: *Religious Art in France of the Thirteenth Century.* § *190 illus.* TB/344

MILLARD MEISS: Painting in Florence and Siena After the Black Death: *The Arts, Religion and Society in the Mid-Fourteenth Century. 169 illus.* TB/1148

ERWIN PANOFSKY: Renaissance and Renascences in Western Art. *Illus.* TB/1447

ERWIN PANOFSKY: Studies in Iconology: *Humanistic Themes in the Art of the Renaissance. 180 illus.* TB/1077

OTTO VON SIMSON: The Gothic Cathedral: *Origins of Gothic Architecture and the Medieval Concept of Order. 58 illus.* TB/2018

HEINRICH ZIMMER: Myths and Symbols in Indian Art and Civilization. *70 illus.* TB/2005

Asian Studies

WOLFGANG FRANKE: China and the West: *The Cultural Encounter, 13th to 20th Centuries. Trans. by R. A. Wilson* TB/1326

L. CARRINGTON GOODRICH: A Short History of the Chinese People. *Illus.* TB/3015

DAN N. JACOBS, Ed.: The New Communist Manifesto and Related Documents. TB/1078

DAN N. JACOBS & HANS H. BAERWALD, Eds.: Chinese Communism: *Selected Documents* TB/3031

BENJAMIN I. SCHWARTZ: Chinese Communism and the Rise of Mao TB/1308

BENJAMIN I. SCHWARTZ: In Search of Wealth and Power: *Yen Fu and the West* TB/1422

Economics & Economic History

C. E. BLACK: The Dynamics of Modernization: *A Study in Comparative History* TB/1321

STUART BRUCHEY: The Roots of American Economic Growth, 1607-1861: *An Essay in Social Causation. New Introduction by the Author.* TB/1350

GILBERT BURCK & EDITORS OF *Fortune:* The Computer Age: *And its Potential for Management* TB/1179

SHEPARD B. CLOUGH, THOMAS MOODIE & CAROL MOODIE, Eds.: Economic History of Europe: *Twentieth Century* # HR/1388

THOMAS C. COCHRAN: The American Business System: *A Historical Perspective, 1900-1955* TB/1080

ROBERT A. DAHL & CHARLES E. LINDBLOM: Politics, Economics, and Welfare: *Planning and Politico-Economic Systems Resolved into Basic Social Processes* TB/3037

PETER F. DRUCKER: The New Society: *The Anatomy of Industrial Order* TB/1082

HAROLD U. FAULKNER: The Decline of Laissez Faire, 1897-1917 △ TB/1397

PAUL W. GATES: The Farmer's Age: *Agriculture, 1815-1860* △ TB/1398

WILLIAM GREENLEAF, Ed.: American Economic Development Since 1860 + HR/1353

ROBERT L. HEILBRONER: The Future as History: *The Historic Currents of Our Time and the Direction in Which They Are Taking America* TB/1386

ROBERT L. HEILBRONER: The Great Ascent: *The Struggle for Economic Development in Our Time* TB/3030

DAVID S. LANDES: Bankers and Pashas: *International Finance and Economic Imperialism in Egypt. New Preface by the Author* TB/1412

ROBERT LATOUCHE: The Birth of Western Economy: *Economic Aspects of the Dark Ages* TB/1290

W. ARTHUR LEWIS: The Principles of Economic Planning. *New Introduction by the Author°* TB/1436

WILLIAM MILLER, Ed.: Men in Business: *Essays on the Historical Role of the Entrepreneur* TB/1081

GUNNAR MYRDAL: An International Economy. *New Introduction by the Author* TB/1445

HERBERT A. SIMON: The Shape of Automation: *For Men and Management* TB/1245

RICHARD S. WECKSTEIN, Ed.: Expansion of World Trade and the Growth of National Economies ** TB/1373

Historiography and History of Ideas

J. BRONOWSKI & BRUCE MAZLISH: The Western Intellectual Tradition: *From Leonardo to Hegel* TB/3001

WILHELM DILTHEY: Pattern and Meaning in History: *Thoughts on History and Society.° Edited with an Intro. by H. P. Rickman* TB/1075

J. H. HEXTER: More's Utopia: *The Biography of an Idea. Epilogue by the Author* TB/1195

H. STUART HUGHES: History as Art and as Science: *Twin Vistas on the Past* TB/1207

ARTHUR O. LOVEJOY: The Great Chain of Being: *A Study of the History of an Idea* TB/1009

RICHARD H. POPKIN: The History of Scepticism from Erasmus to Descartes. *Revised Edition* TB/1391

MASSIMO SALVADORI, Ed.: Modern Socialism # HR/1374

BRUNO SNELL: The Discovery of the Mind: *The Greek Origins of European Thought* TB/1018

W. WARREN WAGER, ed.: European Intellectual History Since Darwin and Marx TB/1297

History: General

HANS KOHN: The Age of Nationalism: *The First Era of Global History* TB/1380

BERNARD LEWIS: The Arabs in History TB/1029

BERNARD LEWIS: The Middle East and the West ° TB/1274

History: Ancient

A. ANDREWS: The Greek Tyrants TB/1103

ERNST LUDWIG EHRLICH: A Concise History of Israel: *From the Earliest Times to the Destruction of the Temple in A.D. 70 °* TB/128
THEODOR H. GASTER: Thespis: *Ritual Myth and Drama in the Ancient Near East* TB/1281
MICHAEL GRANT: Ancient History ° TB/1190
A. H. M. JONES, Ed.: A History of Rome through the Fifth Century # *Vol. I: The Republic* HR/1364
Vol. II The Empire: HR/1460
NAPHTALI LEWIS & MEYER REINHOLD, Eds.: Roman Civilization *Vol. I: The Republic* TB/1231
Vol. II: The Empire TB/1232

History: Medieval

MARSHALL W. BALDWIN, Ed.: Christianity Through the 13th Century # HR/1468
MARC BLOCH: Land and Work in Medieval Europe. *Translated by J. E. Anderson* TB/1452
HELEN CAM: England Before Elizabeth TB/1026
NORMAN COHN: The Pursuit of the Millennium: *Revolutionary Messianism in Medieval and Reformation Europe* TB/1037
G. G. COULTON: Medieval Village, Manor, and Monastery HR/1022
HEINRICH FICHTENAU: The Carolingian Empire: *The Age of Charlemagne. Translated with an Introduction by Peter Munz* TB/1142
GALBERT OF BRUGES: The Murder of Charles the Good: *A Contemporary Record of Revolutionary Change in 12th Century Flanders. Translated with an Introduction by James Bruce Ross* TB/1311
F. L. GANSHOF: Feudalism TB/1058
F. L. GANSHOF: The Middle Ages: *A History of International Relations. Translated by Rémy Hall* TB/1411
DENYS HAY: The Medieval Centuries ° TB/1192
DAVID HERLIHY, Ed.: Medieval Culture and Society # HR/1340
J. M. HUSSEY: The Byzantine World TB/1057
ROBERT LATOUCHE: The Birth of Western Economy: *Economic Aspects of the Dark Ages °* TB/1290
HENRY CHARLES LEA: The Inquisition of the Middle Ages. || *Introduction by Walter Ullmann* TB/1456
FERDINAND LOT: The End of the Ancient World and the Beginnings of the Middle Ages. *Introduction by Glanville Downey* TB/1044
H. R. LOYN: The Norman Conquest TB/1457
ACHILLE LUCHAIRE: Social France at the time of Philip Augustus. *Intro. by John W. Baldwin* TB/1314
GUIBERT DE NOGENT: Self and Society in Medieval France: *The Memoirs of Guibert de Nogent. || Edited by John F. Benton* TB/1471
MARSILIUS OF PADUA: The Defender of Peace. *The Defensor Pacis. Translated with an Introduction by Alan Gewirth* TB/1310
CHARLES PETIT-DUTAILLIS: The Feudal Monarchy in France and England: *From the Tenth to the Thirteenth Century °* TB/1165
STEVEN RUNCIMAN: A History of the Crusades *Vol. I: The First Crusade and the Foundation of the Kingdom of Jerusalem. Illus.* TB/1143
Vol. II: The Kingdom of Jerusalem and the Frankish East 1100-1187. Illus. TB/1243
Vol. III: The Kingdom of Acre and the Later Crusades. Illus. TB/1298
J. M. WALLACE-HADRILL: The Barbarian West: *The Early Middle Ages, A.D. 400-1000* TB/1061

History: Renaissance & Reformation

JACOB BURCKHARDT: The Civilization of the Renaissance in Italy. *Introduction by Benjamin Nelson and Charles Trinkaus. Illus.* Vol. I TB/40; Vol. II TB/41
JOHN CALVIN & JACOPO SADOLETO: A Reformation Debate. *Edited by John C. Olin* TB/1239
FEDERICO CHABOD: Machiavelli and the Renaissance TB/1193
J. H. ELLIOTT: Europe Divided, 1559-1598 α ° TB/1414
G. R. ELTON: Reformation Europe, 1517-1559 ° α TB/1270
DESIDERIUS ERASMUS: Christian Humanism and the Reformation: *Selected Writings. Edited and Translated by John C. Olin* TB/1166
DESIDERIUS ERASMUS: Erasmus and His Age: *Selected Letters. Edited with an Introduction by Hans J. Hillerbrand. Translated by Marcus A. Haworth* TB/1461
WALLACE K. FERGUSON et al.: Facets of the Renaissance TB/1098
WALLACE K. FERGUSON et al.: The Renaissance: *Six Essays. Illus.* TB/1084
FRANCESCO GUICCIARDINI: History of Florence. *Translated with an Introduction and Notes by Mario Domandi* TB/1470
WERNER L. GUNDERSHEIMER, Ed.: French Humanism, 1470-1600. * *Illus.* TB/1473
MARIE BOAS HALL, Ed.: Nature and Nature's Laws: *Documents of the Scientific Revolution #* HR/1420
HANS J. HILLERBRAND, Ed., The Protestant Reformation # TB/1342
JOHAN HUIZINGA: Erasmus and the Age of Reformation. *Illus.* TB/19
JOEL HURSTFIELD: The Elizabethan Nation TB/1312
JOEL HURSTFIELD, Ed.: The Reformation Crisis TB/1267
PAUL OSKAR KRISTELLER: Renaissance Thought: *The Classic, Scholastic, and Humanist Strains* TB/1048
PAUL OSKAR KRISTELLER: Renaissance Thought II: *Papers on Humanism and the Arts* TB/1163
PAUL O. KRISTELLER & PHILIP P. WIENER, Eds.: Renaissance Essays TB/1392
DAVID LITTLE: Religion, Order and Law: *A Study in Pre-Revolutionary England. § Preface by R. Bellah* TB/1418
NICCOLO MACHIAVELLI: History of Florence and of the Affairs of Italy: *From the Earliest Times to the Death of Lorenzo the Magnificent. Introduction by Felix Gilbert* TB/1027
ALFRED VON MARTIN: Sociology of the Renaissance. ° *Introduction by W. K. Ferguson* TB/1099
GARRETT MATTINGLY et al.: Renaissance Profiles. *Edited by J. H. Plumb* TB/1162
J. H. PARRY: The Establishment of the European Hegemony: 1415-1715: *Trade and Exploration in the Age of the Renaissance* TB/1045
J. H. PARRY, Ed.: The European Reconnaissance: *Selected Documents #* HR/1345
J. H. PLUMB: The Italian Renaissance: *A Concise Survey of Its History and Culture* TB/1161
A. F. POLLARD: Henry VIII. *Introduction by A. G. Dickens. °* TB/1249
RICHARD H. POPKIN: The History of Scepticism from Erasmus to Descartes TB/1391
PAOLO ROSSI: Philosophy, Technology, and the Arts, in the Early Modern Era 1400-1700. || *Edited by Benjamin Nelson. Translated by Salvator Attanasio* TB/1458

4

Political Science & Government

Psychology

Religion: Ancient and Classical, Biblical and Judaic Traditions

MARTIN BUBER: Eclipse of God: *Studies in the Relation Between Religion and Philosophy* TB/12

MARTIN BUBER: Hasidism and Modern Man. *Edited and Translated by Maurice Friedman* TB/839

MARTIN BUBER: The Knowledge of Man. *Edited with an Introduction by Maurice Friedman. Translated by Maurice Friedman and Ronald Gregor Smith* TB/135

MARTIN BUBER: Moses. *The Revelation and the Covenant* TB/837

MARTIN BUBER: The Origin and Meaning of Hasidism. *Edited and Translated by Maurice Friedman* TB/835

MARTIN BUBER: The Prophetic Faith TB/73

MARTIN BUBER: Two Types of Faith: *Interpenetration of Judaism and Christianity* ° TB/75

MALCOLM L. DIAMOND: Martin Buber: *Jewish Existentialist* TB/840

M. S. ENSLIN: Christian Beginnings TB/5

M. S. ENSLIN: The Literature of the Christian Movement TB/6

HENRI FRANKFORT: Ancient Egyptian Religion: *An Interpretation* TB/77

MAURICE S. FRIEDMAN: Martin Buber: *The Life of Dialogue* TB/64

ABRAHAM HESCHEL: The Earth Is the Lord's & The Sabbath. *Two Essays* TB/828

ABRAHAM HESCHEL: God in Search of Man: *A Philosophy of Judaism* TB/807

ABRAHAM HESCHEL: Man Is not Alone: *A Philosophy of Religion* TB/838

ABRAHAM HESCHEL: The Prophets: *An Introduction* TB/1421

T. J. MEEK: Hebrew Origins TB/69

JAMES MUILENBURG: The Way of Israel: *Biblical Faith and Ethics* TB/133

H. H. ROWLEY: The Growth of the Old Testament TB/107

D. WINTON THOMAS, Ed.: Documents from Old Testament Times TB/85

Religion: Early Christianity Through Reformation

ANSELM OF CANTERBURY: Truth, Freedom, and Evil: *Three Philosophical Dialogues. Edited and Translated by Jasper Hopkins and Herbert Richardson* TB/317

MARSHALL W. BALDWIN, Ed.: Christianity through the 13th Century # HR/1468

ADOLF DEISSMAN: Paul: *A Study in Social and Religious History* TB/15

EDGAR J. GOODSPEED: A Life of Jesus TB/1

ROBERT M. GRANT: Gnosticism and Early Christianity TB/136

WILLIAM HALLER: The Rise of Puritanism TB/22

ARTHUR DARBY NOCK: St. Paul ° TR/104

GORDON RUPP: Luther's Progress to the Diet of Worms ° TB/120

Religion: The Protestant Tradition

KARL BARTH: Church Dogmatics: *A Selection. Intro. by H. Gollwitzer. Ed. by G. W. Bromiley* TB/95

KARL BARTH: Dogmatics in Outline TB/56

KARL BARTH: The Word of God and the Word of Man TB/13

WHITNEY R. CROSS: The Burned-Over District: *The Social and Intellectual History of Enthusiastic Religion in Western New York, 1800-1850* TB/1242

WILLIAM R. HUTCHISON, Ed.: American Protestant Thought: *The Liberal Era* ‡ TB/1385

SOREN KIERKEGAARD: The Journals of Kierkegaard. ° *Edited with an Intro. by Alexander Dru* TB/52

SOREN KIERKEGAARD: The Point of View for My Work as an Author: *A Report to History.* § *Preface by Benjamin Nelson* TB/88

SOREN KIERKEGAARD: The Present Age. § *Translated and edited by Alexander Dru. Introduction by Walter Kaufmann* TB/94

SOREN KIERKEGAARD: Purity of Heart. *Trans. by Douglas Steere* TB/4

SOREN KIERKEGAARD: Repetition: *An Essay in Experimental Psychology* § TB/117

SOREN KIERKEGAARD: Works of Love: *Some Christian Reflections in the Form of Discourses* TB/122

WOLFHART PANNENBERG, et al.: History and Hermeneutic. *Volume 4 of* Journal for Theology and the Church, *edited by Robert W. Funk and Gerhard Ebeling* TB/254

F. SCHLEIERMACHER: The Christian Faith. *Introduction by Richard R. Niebuhr.*
Vol. I TB/108; Vol. II TB/109

F. SCHLEIERMACHER: On Religion: *Speeches to Its Cultured Despisers. Intro. by Rudolf Otto* TB/36

PAUL TILLICH: Dynamics of Faith TB/42

PAUL TILLICH: Morality and Beyond TB/142

Religion: The Roman & Eastern Christian Traditions

A. ROBERT CAPONIGRI, Ed.: Modern Catholic Thinkers II: *The Church and the Political Order* TB/307

G. P. FEDOTOV: The Russian Religious Mind: *Kievan Christianity, the tenth to the thirteenth Centuries* TB/370

GABRIEL MARCEL: Being and Having: *An Existential Diary. Introduction by James Collins* TB/310

GABRIEL MARCEL: Homo Viator: *Introduction to a Metaphysic of Hope* TB/397

Religion: Oriental Religions

TOR ANDRAE: Mohammed: *The Man and His Faith* § TB/62

EDWARD CONZE: Buddhism: *Its Essence and Development.* ° *Foreword by Arthur Waley* TB/58

EDWARD CONZE: Buddhist Meditation TB/1442

EDWARD CONZE et al, Editors: Buddhist Texts through the Ages TB/113

ANANDA COOMARASWAMY: Buddha and the Gospel of Buddhism TB/119

H. G. CREEL: Confucius and the Chinese Way TB/63

FRANKLIN EDGERTON, Trans. & Ed.: The Bhagavad Gita TB/115

SWAMI NIKHILANANDA, Trans. & Ed.: The Upanishads TB/114

Religion: Philosophy, Culture, and Society

NICOLAS BERDYAEV: The Destiny of Man TB/61

RUDOLF BULTMANN: History and Eschatology: *The Presence of Eternity* ° TB/91

RUDOLF BULTMANN AND FIVE CRITICS: Kerygma and Myth: *A Theological Debate* TB/80

RUDOLF BULTMANN and KARL KUNDSIN: Form search. *Trans. by F. C. Grant* TB/96

LUDWIG FEUERBACH: The Essence of Christianity. § *Introduction by Karl Barth. Foreword by H. Richard Niebuhr* TB/11

KYLE HASELDEN: The Racial Problem in Christian Perspective TB/116

MARTIN HEIDEGGER: Discourse on Thinking. *Translated with a Preface by John M. Anderson and E. Hans Freund. Introduction by John M. Anderson* TB/1459

IMMANUEL KANT: Religion Within the Limits of Reason Alone. § *Introduction by Theodore M. Greene and John Silber* TB/FG

H. RICHARD NIEBUHR: Christ and Culture TB/3

H. RICHARD NIEBUHR: The Kingdom of God in America TB/49

JOHN H. RANDALL, JR.: The Meaning of Religion for Man. *Revised with New Intro. by the Author* TB/1379

Science and Mathematics

W. E. LE GROS CLARK: The Antecedents of Man: *An Introduction to the Evolution of the Primates.* ° *Illus.* TB/559

ROBERT E. COKER: Streams, Lakes, Ponds. *Illus.* TB/586

ROBERT E. COKER: This Great and Wide Sea: *An Introduction to Oceanography and Marine Biology. Illus.* TB/551

F. K. HARE: The Restless Atmosphere TB/560

WILLARD VAN ORMAN QUINE: Mathematical Logic TB/558

Science: Philosophy

J. M. BOCHENSKI: The Methods of Contemporary Thought. *Tr. by Peter Caws* TB/1377

J. BRONOWSKI: Science and Human Values. *Revised and Enlarged. Illus.* TB/505

WERNER HEISENBERG: Physics and Philosophy: *The Revolution in Modern Science. Introduction by F. S. C. Northrop* TB/549

KARL R. POPPER: Conjectures and Refutations: *The Growth of Scientific Knowledge* TB/1376

KARL R. POPPER: The Logic of Scientific Discovery TB/576

Sociology and Anthropology

REINHARD BENDIX: Work and Authority in Industry: *Ideologies of Management in the Course of Industrialization* TB/3035

BERNARD BERELSON, Ed., The Behavioral Sciences Today TB/1127

KENNETH B. CLARK: Dark Ghetto: *Dilemmas of Social Power. Foreword by Gunnar Myrdal* TB/1317

KENNETH CLARK & JEANNETTE HOPKINS: A Relevant War Against Poverty: *A Study of Community Action Programs and Observable Social Change* TB/1480

LEWIS COSER, Ed.: Political Sociology TB/1293

ROSE L. COSER, Ed.: Life Cycle and Achievement in America ** TB/1434

ALLISON DAVIS & JOHN DOLLARD: Children of Bondage: *The Personality Development of Negro Youth in the Urban South* || TB/3049

ST. CLAIR DRAKE & HORACE R. CAYTON: Black Metropolis: *A Study of Negro Life in a Northern City. Introduction by Everett C. Hughes. Tables, maps, charts, and graphs* Vol. I TB/1086; Vol. II TB/1087

PETER F. DRUCKER: The New Society: *The Anatomy of Industrial Order* TB/1082

LEON FESTINGER, HENRY W. RIECKEN, STANLEY SCHACHTER: When Prophecy Fails: *A Social and Psychological Study of a Modern Group that Predicted the Destruction of the World* || TB/1132

CHARLES Y. GLOCK & RODNEY STARK: Christian Beliefs and Anti-Semitism. *Introduction by the Authors* TB/1454

L. S. B. LEAKEY: Adam's Ancestors: *The Evolution of Man and His Culture. Illus.* TB/1019

KURT LEWIN: Field Theory in Social Science: *Selected Theoretical Papers.* || *Edited by Dorwin Cartwright* TB/1135

RITCHIE P. LOWRY: Who's Running This Town? *Community Leadership and Social Change* TB/1383

R. M. MACIVER: Social Causation TB/1153

GARY T. MARX: Protest and Prejudice: *A Study of Belief in the Black Community* TB/1435

ROBERT K. MERTON, LEONARD BROOM, LEONARD S. COTTRELL, JR., Editors: Sociology Today: *Problems and Prospects* || Vol. I TB/1173; Vol. II TB/1174

GILBERT OSOFSKY, Ed.: The Burden of Race: *A Documentary History of Negro-White Relations in America* TB/1405

GILBERT OSOFSKY: Harlem: The Making of a Ghetto: *Negro New York 1890-1930* TB/1381

TALCOTT PARSONS & EDWARD A. SHILS, Editors: Toward a General Theory of Action: *Theoretical Foundations for the Social Sciences* TB/1083

PHILIP RIEFF: The Triumph of the Therapeutic: *Uses of Faith After Freud* TB/1360

JOHN H. ROHRER & MUNRO S. EDMONSON, Eds.: The Eighth Generation Grows Up: *Cultures and Personalities of New Orleans Negroes* || TB/3050

ARNOLD ROSE: The Negro in America: *The Condensed Version of Gunnar Myrdal's* An American Dilemma. *Second Edition* TB/3048

GEORGE ROSEN: Madness in Society: *Chapters in the Historical Sociology of Mental Illness.* || *Preface by Benjamin Nelson* TB/1337

PHILIP SELZNICK: TVA and the Grass Roots: *A Study in the Sociology of Formal Organization* TB/1230

PITIRIM A. SOROKIN: Contemporary Sociological Theories: *Through the First Quarter of the Twentieth Century* TB/3046

MAURICE R. STEIN: The Eclipse of Community: *An Interpretation of American Studies* TB/1128

FERDINAND TONNIES: Community and Society: *Gemeinschaft und Gesellschaft. Translated and Edited by Charles P. Loomis* TB/1116

SAMUEL E. WALLACE: Skid Row as a Way of Life TB/1367

W. LLOYD WARNER and Associates: Democracy in Jonesville: *A Study in Quality and Inequality* || TB/1129

W. LLOYD WARNER: Social Class in America: *The Evaluation of Status* TB/1013

FLORIAN ZNANIECKI: The Social Role of the Man of Knowledge. *Introduction by Lewis A. Coser* TB/1372